P9-EER-777

DATE DUE

GAYLORD | | | PRINTED IN U.S.A.

CURRENT AMERICAN USAGE

BLAIRSVILLE SENIOR HIGH SCHOOL
BLAIRSVILLE, PENNA.

OTHER BOOKS BY MARGARET M. BRYANT

English in the Law Courts
Psychology of English (with Janet Rankin Aiken)
Essays Old and New (Ed.)
Prose Pieces (Ed., with R. H. Barker and C. T. Ernst)
A Functional English Grammar
Modern English and Its Heritage
Proverbs and How to Collect Them
English at Work (with M. L. Howe, P. R. Jenkins, and Helen Munn)

CURRENT AMERICAN USAGE

edited by Margaret M. Bryant

PROFESSOR OF ENGLISH,
BROOKLYN COLLEGE OF THE CITY UNIVERSITY
OF NEW YORK

FUNK & WAGNALLS COMPANY, INC.   NEW YORK

Copyright © 1962 by Funk & Wagnalls Company, Inc.
Library of Congress Catalog Card Number 62–9735
Manufactured in the United States of America
by H. Wolff, New York
Designed by Robin Fox

3

To Clara

Contents

Editor's foreword

The preparation of this book has been long and painstaking. It has grown out of the work by the Committee on Current English Usage appointed by the National Council of Teachers of English, the functions of which were to conduct the current usage department in the *English Journal* and *College English* and to disseminate in any other appropriate way knowledge about actual usage in America today. The planning began in 1950, and selection of points to be covered started in 1951; active collecting and editing of the necessary information continued from early 1952 into 1961. Not only the usage committee but dozens of others—specialists in the study of the English language and advanced students under their direction—participated.

Informal proposals for a work of this character had been made for decades in meetings of English teachers and scholars. During the convention of the Modern Language Association of America in 1950 the Committee on Current English Usage of the National Council of Teachers of English held an invitational conference of more than thirty experts in this field. The committee suggested a study of controversial points of usage in American English, dealing principally with usage in syntax and generally excluding matters of pronunciation and vocabulary, which are quite adequately treated in existing dictionaries. It further suggested that the study should be made to serve both teachers and the general public. The idea was favorably received by the experts both at this conference and at a similar one in 1951. The consensus of these two meetings was that there was great need for a work of this kind; and that the proposed publication should be both a compendium of existing scattered knowledge and a report of original investigations which would be undertaken to fill serious gaps in authoritative information. The committee decided to proceed at once.

Formal approval of the project came from the National Council of Teachers of English (with an appropriation of $2,500), the Modern Language Association of America, the Speech Association of America, and the American Dialect Society.

First, a tentative list of controversial points of usage was compiled, which after criticism and slight revision became the basic chart of the field to be covered. Professor James B. McMillan, of the University of Alabama, editor of the press at his university, undertook the editing of the material. Using the appropriation from the National Council of Teachers of English and a grant-in-aid from the University of Alabama Research Committee, he arranged with the university authorities the part-time release of Professor I. Willis Russell to serve as expert assistant. In correspondence with the other members of the Committee on Current English Usage, Professor McMillan planned and organized the collection of data, worked out the editing procedure, and assembled the bibliography. A survey of periodicals dealing with questions of usage made clearer just what investigations were still needed. Some members of the committee and other interested, competent persons agreed to read and listen in order to collect statistical evidence on individual items.

In 1956, with the editing much less than half complete, exhaustion of the available funds cut off Professor Russell's assistance and direct obligations to his university forced Professor McMillan to stop his work on this project. At this point the present editor took over and became the financial support of the study. As she completed the editing of the items, she sent them to her collaborators for criticism. In 1956 and 1957 she was able to confer in person with some members of the committee during conventions of the National Council of Teachers of English and the Modern

Language Association. By September, 1957, she had completed the editing of all the material in hand. At a meeting of the committee it was decided to seek additional new evidence for some of the items. Further studies were made, many of them by the students of the editor, and the new evidence was worked into the proper places. The revised manuscript was then submitted to all the committee members not at that time abroad and not completely occupied by prior commitments. Again the manuscript was revised with the collaborators' suggestions in hand, most of which were accepted.

Assistance by individuals is recorded in the Acknowledgments, but the editor wishes to thank here the organizations which encouraged the project at its beginning. To the National Council of Teachers of English the editor is especially grateful, both for the financial support which made possible the early work and now for the release of the manuscript for private publication in recognition of her large expenditure of time and money in its preparation.

Finally, the editor wishes to acknowledge the large contribution of the members of the Committee on Current English Usage not only in the planning and in the collection of material but also in the revisions of the manuscript. She also wishes it clearly understood that neither the National Council of Teachers of English nor her fellow committee members are responsible for any flaws in the editing.

Acknowledgments

In addition to the special thanks, explained in the Foreword, that go to the National Council of Teachers of English, the Modern Language Association of America, the Speech Association of America, and the American Dialect Society, the editor wishes to thank individually each member of the Current English Usage Committee of the National Council of Teachers of English who gave his time to the reading of the manuscript and to giving his expert advice on many points and on many occasions. Harold B. Allen, University of Minnesota, in the absence of the chairman, then out of the country, led the initial invitational conference on the project at the Modern Language Association in 1950, read the manuscript, and gave help in many ways. James B. McMillan, University of Alabama, organized the project and worked on it for several years. His colleague, I. Willis Russell, aided him and prepared the list of readings (current magazines, papers, novels, short stories, plays, etc.) to be used in gathering quantitative evidence on divided American usages. Russell Thomas, Northern Michigan College, furnished excellent citations of modern American usage, which he gathered from his studies and wide reading, faithfully read the manuscript, and helped in numerous capacities. John N. Winburne, Michigan State University, supplied many appropriate illustrations and types of usage from a particular body of material investigated, read the manuscript, and gave his expert advice as a lexicographer. W. Wilbur Hatfield, long-time editor of the *English Journal* and *College English,* helped to make the book readily usable by persons not specialists in linguistics. The other members of the Committee critically read the manuscript and made their contributions in various ways: W. Nelson Francis, Brown University; Archibald A. Hill, University of Texas; Kemp Malone, professor emeritus, Johns Hopkins University; Albert H. Marckwardt, University of Michigan. The late Adeline C. Bartlett, Hunter College, gave valuable aid at the beginning of the project.

In addition, the editor would like to express her gratitude to E. Bagby Atwood, University of Texas, for reading the manuscript and giving helpful suggestions and for contributing in other ways. In particular she would like to thank Raven I. McDavid, Jr., University of Chicago, for his critical reading of the manuscript and for his expert advice on many points.

She would also like to express her appreciation to Virginia G. McDavid of Chicago Teachers College and Jean Malmstrom of Western Michigan University for their contributions made in connection with their dissertations—studies in usage done at the University of Minnesota under Harold B. Allen, based on the Linguistic Atlas material.

Thanks likewise go to the well-known lexicographer Clarence L. Barnhart, whose files furnished extra evidence on many points of usage and who gave permission to use them; to Jessie Ryon Lucke, North Texas State College, and to Daniel Levy, Brooklyn College, for the bibliography of usage articles and items in *American Speech,* the *English Journal,* and *College English;* and to Malcolm S. Coxe, Brooklyn College, who recorded the radio broadcasts of most of the World Series in 1957 and then listened for various usage items employed. Professor Coxe was appointed by the Speech Association of America as a member of the Committee of Liaison between that organization and the National Council of Teachers of English in connection with this project.

The following should also be mentioned for securing aid from their students in making numerous studies: Harold B. Allen, University of Minnesota; E. Bagby Atwood, University of Texas; Muriel Bowden, Hunter College; Frederic G. Cassidy, University of Wisconsin; Gladys Haase, Brooklyn College; J. N. Hook, University of Illinois; Cecilia A. Hotchner, Hunter College; Jean S. Lindsay, Hunter College; Raven I. McDavid, Jr., University of Chicago; L. M. Myers, Arizona State University; Verna L. Newsome, University of Wisconsin, Milwaukee; Arthur M. Z. Norman, University of Chicago; Thomas Pyles, University of Florida; I. Willis Russell, University of Alabama. The editor also wishes to thank her students for the studies made under her supervision at Brooklyn College. Others who read entries, supplied evidence, or gave opinions from time to time are: Arnold Andersen and Robert Chapman, Funk & Wagnalls; Karl W. Dykema, Youngstown University; George P. Faust, University of Kentucky; Porter G. Perrin, University of Washington; Robert C. Pooley, University of Wisconsin; Alexander N. Sloan, *Newark Evening News,* New Jersey; Francis L. Utley, Ohio State University.

In particular I wish to thank Leo Hamalian, The City College of New York, for his editorial assistance in preparing the manuscript.

It is practically impossible to mention everyone who aided in this undertaking, for many participated. Individual studies, however, are mentioned in the text and the full name is given at the end of the volume with the list of contributions made.

Margaret M. Bryant

Brooklyn College,
The City University of New York

Introduction

This book attempts to bring together the most recent information about frequently debated points of usage in English speech and writing. It presents the dependable evidence available—not only that from the various scholarly dictionaries, from the treatises of linguists, and from articles in magazines featuring English usage, but also that from some 900 fresh investigations undertaken especially for use in this book. There are about 240 alphabetical entries discussing one or more points of usage; some points of usage are not discussed at their alphabetical entry but carry a cross-reference to another entry where they are treated.

HOW TO USE THIS BOOK

For ease of reference, the entries follow a set format. They are arranged alphabetically, as in a dictionary. An entry consisting of several words, such as "(in) back of, behind" or "each other, one another" is always entered under its first word and again under any key word in it. The entry itself is divided into three parts:

1. A conclusion, or "summary," of the total evidence; usually this conclusion is presented in a brief discussion, because this gives a more accurate impression than any mere single label such as "standard" or "nonstandard" could. However, these "summaries" are as unequivocal as the evidence permits them to be.

2. The body of the entry, under the heading of "data"; this section contains a discussion of the usage problem raised by the entry, the data, and the conclusions of investigators who studied the problem, and examples and illustrations taken from current writing and speech on various levels of usage. Hence, any readers with the necessary time, library facilities, and interest may check all the details for themselves. The full name and affiliation of the investigator, put in parenthesis in the entry itself, appears in Appendix E.

3. A final section under the heading of "other evidence"; this section contains specific references to the evidence in published books and articles relevant to the entry. A key to the title abbreviations appears in Appendix B and a full bibliography of all works cited.

The conclusions in this book do not depend upon personal impressions, which inevitably are based upon limited observation. The collective impressions of the contributors, even though they are more observant of usage than most people are, would still be an unsafe guide. Based upon evidence gathered in the field and from published writing, the conclusions are as objective as is practically possible in any study involving the behavior and habits of millions of human beings.

Nor does this book presume to prescribe how we *should* speak and write; it describes, rather, how Americans on all levels of education actually do speak and write, with clear distinctions among cultivated, less cultivated, and uneducated usage. In matters of form, whether language or table etiquette, the individual is usually wise to follow the customs of the majority of admired and influential people.

HOW THE EVIDENCE WAS GATHERED

The editor accepts the belief of modern linguists that the spoken language is basic to the written, and has therefore taken into account any reliable reports of usage in speech. But until recently speech was rarely recorded; even today only a small fraction of educated speech is caught on tapes or disks, and that which is recorded is usually formal discourse. Thus, most of the data in the files of dictionary makers and most of the statistical studies of usage are necessarily based upon printed matter. Writing, because it is usually addressed to a more general audience and because it is always more deliberate, tends to be more formal than speech and therefore more likely to retain older usages. Hence, most of the evidence presented here is from written English of the last twenty-five years, but the speech usage of educated persons which is *known* to differ materially from their writing usage is included in this book.

Likewise, on some points the regional differences in usage are reported. In most cases, these are items covered in the surveys for the *Linguistic Atlas of America and Canada* (see *Glossary of Terms* in Appendix C) because there is elsewhere little reliable, definite evidence of just what these regional differences are. Doubtlessly, regional differences exist for many of the other entries in this book, but the differences cited should be enough to alert the reader to such differences in his own region. How far any individual should follow regional custom when it differs from national usage he himself must decide with respect to his audience. Certainly teachers in elementary and secondary schools should be cautious in attempting to stamp out usages really dominant in any wide region.

LEVELS OF USAGE: THE PHILOSOPHY OF THIS BOOK

The reader who remembers the pronouncements about usage in the "composition" texts or usage handbooks of twenty years ago—even in many more recent ones—may be shocked by what seems to him the "laxity" of the judgments here. This is partly because language changes faster than textbooks, and partly because the textbooks were based upon quite limited information or even personal prejudice, and often did not reflect at all closely the actual usage.

In discussing language, one cannot altogether avoid technical terms, but in this book they are used as sparingly as possible. It uses the traditional terminology of grammar rather than that of the still new structural linguistics—not because the old terms are better, but because they are likely to be better understood by more readers. Other linguistic terms which may be unintelligible or unfamiliar to the reader are explained in one of three places: (1) in the paragraphs immediately following; (2) in the glossary of terms; (3) in parenthesis following the term itself in the entry.

Any expression is standard English if it is used by many cultivated people to communicate in speech or in writing. Standard English is the type of language employed by leaders of our society, those who command respect and esteem, such as important journalists, statesmen, political figures, scientists, and business and professional people. Since standard English is the language of the influential classes, its use is socially advantageous for the individual.

Nonstandard English is language rarely or never used by members of the influential classes: for example, double negatives, such as "We never got no money from him." Such expressions may put their users at a social and vocational disadvantage. It is not that these expressions do not communicate. They do, for they have many features in common with standard English. It is that they are disapproved of socially and the disapproval is likely to be attached to those who use them. Some nonstandard points of usage are noticed more universally and with stronger disapproval than others, but such gradation in objectionableness can hardly be marked here.

The division of standard from nonstandard English cannot be marked by a single sharply drawn line, like the boundary between France and Spain; there are no Pyrenees in usage. The separation is more like that of green and blue in the spectrum—a gradual transition. If nearly all educated influential people habitually say "He isn't" and do not under ordinary circumstances speak or write "He ain't," the first form is standard and the other one is nonstandard. But suppose that half of our cultivated, influential Americans habitually say "Two and two *are* four" and the other half say "Two and two *is* four." In this case we would have to say that usage is divided. Since both forms are used by many cultivated persons, both are standard spoken English. Neither form is nonstandard. The division is rarely so even as in our supposition, but the same principle applies where two-thirds of cultivated Americans use one form and only one-third use the other. Though no exact figure can be given, we may regard as standard spoken English any form or expression used by a considerable group of cultivated persons. In formal written English one must consider the writers and the publications, the type of publication and its circulation.

VARIETIES OF STANDARD ENGLISH

Standard and nonstandard indicate social levels of language. Within standard English there are varieties suitable to different kinds of situations. No one of these varieties is in itself superior to the others; it is merely more appropriate to one situation than to another. Students of the English language usually recognize three such varieties: formal, informal, and colloquial.

Formal English is used in serious writing—in dignified articles and books, where the grammar is conservative, the vocabulary learned, the mood subdued. In formal English there are no contractions and few ellipses. Most textbooks, reference works, scientific and scholarly treatises, philosophical and critical essays, literature (exclusive of dialogue), and magazines edited for a rather limited, highly educated audience are generally written in formal English. It is not much used in speech except for addresses on solemn or formal occasions.

Informal English is used in many books, magazines, and other writing intended for the general public. In it the words are more familiar, often lively and colorful; the sentences somewhat shorter with fewer clauses. Contractions, ellipses, and personal references appear in it. Columnists often employ informal English, using such contractions as *don't* and *didn't,* popular words such as *highbrow,* and expressions like *get ahead* or *get away with.*

Colloquial English is found in dialogue, and in writings that are conversational in nature, such as personal letters (the popular belief that words marked "colloq." in dictionaries are only semi-standard is erroneous). It is much used by sports writers and others who seek by employing idioms of conversation to create the effect of intimacy. It is the usual language within the family circle and among close friends. It is sometimes used by public speakers when the occasion is not formal and they feel sure of the sympathy of the audience.

TYPE LABELS IN SPOKEN ENGLISH

The discussions of many items mention speakers of Types I, II, and III. In general, Type I speakers or informants have had little formal education (not beyond the eighth grade of the common school), have done little reading, and have limited contacts outside of their own social milieu; those of Type II have better formal education (at least some secondary school work), and/or have read more widely; those of Type III have superior education (usually four years of college), have cultural backgrounds, and have read widely or have extensive social contacts. Usages prevalent among persons of Type III are unquestionably standard English; usages more common among persons of Type II than among those of Type III are questionable. Forms not employed by persons of Type III are not standard English. Universal use of a form by persons of Type I does not necessarily mark it either acceptable or undesirable.

CURRENT AMERICAN USAGE

ABOVE, adj., n.

Summary: above *is used as an adjective or as a noun in standard English sources.*

The statement that *above* should be used only as an adverb or as a preposition but not as an adjective or a noun is invalid. The *OED* and other standard dictionaries give full sanction to "the *above* explanation" and "the *above* will show." Employed by writers and scholars, these usages have a reputable history and appear with particular frequency in legal, business, and reference sources. In other types of writing, variants such as *preceding* and *foregoing* may be preferred, but as always, the requirements of style determine the choice of words.

Data: In a study of written English (Coles), *above* occurred as an adjective 25% of the time, *preceding* 25%, and *foregoing* 50%: "The *above* seaports of Wilmington and . . ." (*The New York Times Magazine,* Nov. 17, 1957, 7). It may, sometimes, according to another study (Sheridan), follow the noun it modifies instead of preceding it, as in: ". . . the chart *above* shows . . ." (*Fortune,* Dec., 1957, 52); and "In the picture *above* . . ." (*ibid.,* 206); and "Detail *above* shows . . ." (*Popular Mechanics,* Apr., 1953, 107).

Illustrations of *above* as a noun were found (Hotchner) in *The New York Times* (Arthur Krock, "News of the Week in Review,"

Dec. 15, 1957, Sec. 4, 3): ". . . in the President's absence, as the *above* suggests . . ."; in *Look* (Oct 1, 1957, 2): "The *above* are of course just rapid resumés. . . ." It may be the object of a preposition as well as the sentence subject, as in ". . . seen from *above* . . ." (*The New Yorker*, Nov. 16, 1957, 188), where *above* is the object of *from*.

According to the four studies made for this book (Coles, Hotchner, Mauchel, Sheridan), *above* occurs more frequently as an adjective (76.5% of the time) than as a noun (23.5%).

Other evidence: Bryant, *EJ*, XLV (Apr., 1956), 222; Hall, 31-32; Pooley, *TEU*, 128-30; Steinbach, *AS*, 4 (Feb., 1929), 165-68.

ABSOLUTE COMPARATIVE. See COMPARATIVE, ABSOLUTE.

ADVERBIAL GENITIVE

Summary: The adverbial genitive, in expressions like open evenings *and* work nights, *is well established in informal standard English speech and writing.*

In Old English, one of the functions of the genitive case was to indicate time relationships as in *dæg,* "day," *dæges,* "by day." This adverbial genitive survives in expressions such as *"Evenings* he would write letters" or the phrasal-genitive equivalent, *"Of an evening* he would write letters." The *Dictionary of American English* cites the use of *evenings* as an adverbial genitive. Such usage is no more objectionable than *always* or *nowadays,* which illustrate the same construction.

Data: A study of advertisements in New York newspapers (Samkoff) revealed that stores open in the evenings favored in a ratio of three to one the expression "open *evenings"* over the alternatives of "open *every evening"* or "open *in the evenings."* Both "Open *Evenings"* and "Open *Nights"* were found in *The New York Times.* Recently an English teacher, a Ph.D., wrote in a letter (Bryant): ". . . I am giving myself a kind of home extension course *evenings."*

A study of literature exclusive of advertising (Samkoff) showed that novelists and magazine writers use both the adverbial genitive and the equivalent prepositional phrase, but the preference is for the phrase ("at night" instead of "nights," "by day" instead of "days"). Nevertheless, Brooks Atkinson of *The New York Times* consistently used "evenings" and "nights," and William Worden was not adverse to employing two adverbial genitives in one sentence: "None of them realize that Mrs. Catter, working *days* and caring for two youngsters in the evenings, and Mrs. Conrad who works *evenings* as a waitress. . . ." (*Saturday Evening Post,* Nov. 20, 1954, 39).

While prepositional phrases are generally preferred in studied or formal writing, as another study (Joseph Schwartz) showed, it is nevertheless safe to say that the adverbial genitive will remain entrenched in informal writing.

Other evidence: Barnhart, Files; Bryant, *CE,* 22 (Feb., 1961), 358; Curme, *PSA,* 336-37; Marckwardt and Walcott, 38, 110.

AGENDA, n.

Summary: agenda *is used as a singular noun in standard English.*

Agenda was once a plural noun of Latin derivation, meaning "things to be done" and thus took a plural verb and plural modifiers, as in "There *were* few *agenda.*" However, *agenda* now commonly means "a list of things to be done or considered" and thus takes a singular verb and singular modifiers.

Data: The files of Barnhart provide the following illustrations: "An *agenda was* prepared . . ." (*The Atlantic Monthly,* Jan., 1955, 19); ". . . until *a firm agenda* can be agreed upon . . ." (*Newsweek,* Apr. 11, 1955, 29); and "ANTA's broadly impressive music, painting, dance, and theatre *agenda* for the 'Salute' *has* attracted attention . . ." [Abram Chasins speaking] (*Saturday Review,* May 14, 1955, 30).

Since the word occurs now in the singular, one also finds (R. Thomas) the plural *agendas,* as in ". . . we had covered extensive *agendas* each 'side' had prepared in advance" (William Benton, *Yale Review,* Summer, 1958, 553); and ". . . two different proposed summit *agendas* have been taking place" (*The New*

York Times, "News of the Week in Review," March 9, 1958, Sec. 4, E1). One study (Stone) found that *agenda* is generally singular in modern usage. Two other studies (Anderson, Schecter) supported the findings in this entry.

As an alternative, the word *docket* is heard in American speech: "What *is* on the *docket* (*agenda*) today?" *See* DATA.

Other evidence: Bartlett, *CE,* 15 (Apr., 1954), 417; Bryant, *CE,* 22 (Jan., 1961), 284; Pound, *AS,* 3 (Oct., 1927), 26-27.

AGREEMENT, COLLECTIVE NOUNS

Summary: When a noun refers to the group as a whole, the singular verb and singular pronoun reference is used, but when it refers to the individual members, the plural is used.

Ever since the Middle English period, the number of the verb with a collective noun subject has varied between singular and plural; expressions like *ten dollars, two-thirds, one hundred pounds, ham and eggs,* and *cake and ice cream* continue to be used very often with a singular verb, as in "Ham and eggs *is* a good dish" (but "Ham and eggs *are* not sold here"). However, modern standard usage consistently follows the above rule.

Data: Sixteen studies (Adams, Coxe, Hagopian, Hanson, Matia, Meyer, Morris, M. Richardson, Russell, Schwab, Starks, R. Thomas, J. Smith, Wanek, Weil, Word) undertaken for this book reveal that collective nouns were treated as singular in 65% of the examples, but one study (Frigand) found that when referring to firms or companies, the collective noun was treated as a singular in 35% of the cases and as a plural in 65%.

These studies show that most of the time the collective noun subject and its singular verb are in juxtaposition: "The *commission is* appointed" (*The New York Times Magazine,* Feb. 27, 1955, 64), but that one-fourth of the time plural words intervene: "A *group* of famous composers and conductors *has been invited* . . ." (*The New York Times,* Oct. 2, 1955, x9). In the examples with a plural verb or plural reference, the subject and the verb (or pronoun) are in juxtaposition or are without plural words intervening slightly more than half the time; plural words intervene slightly less than half the time. Illustrations of each are: "The *committee* extended *their* invitation directly to the lecturer . . ." (*The New Yorker*, Oct. 25, 1952, "Profiles"); "A splendid *group* of younger writers *are turning* out novels . . ." (*The New York Times Book Review*, Nov. 20, 1955, 53).

Collective nouns may also be followed by *who* as well as the impersonal *which* or *that*, or by a singular or plural pronoun of reference. As an illustration of the first usage, there is: "The *couple, who* first met a year ago when they appeared as Figaro and Rosina . . ." (*New York Daily News*, March 3, 1952) and as an illustration of the plural pronoun of reference, the citations from *The New Yorker* (*committee-their*) and the *New York Daily News* (*couple-they*).

Among the most commonly used collective nouns are *audience, committee, class, crowd, enemy, faculty, family, folk, group, herd, jury, lot, majority, minority, nation, number, party, people, team,* and *troop*. British usage employs a plural verb with *firm, government,* and *public:* "The public *were requested* to leave," whereas American usage favors the singular. *Couple* is a collective noun, sometimes singular and sometimes plural: "The *couple is standing* there" and "The *couple are traveling* to New Orleans and Mexico" (*Cleveland Plain Dealer*, March 2, 1952, Society Section).

Other evidence: Bartlett, *CE,* 15 (Apr., 1954), 417; Bryant, *CE,* 22 (Feb., 1961), 358-59; Fries, *AEG,* 48; Pooley, *AS,* 9 (Feb., 1934), 31-36; *TEU,* 85-86.

AGREEMENT, EITHER . . . OR. See AGREEMENT, NEITHER . . . NOR.

AGREEMENT, HERE IS (ARE), WAS (WERE). See AGREEMENT, THERE IS (ARE), WAS (WERE).

AGREEMENT, INDEFINITE PRONOUNS

Summary: When an indefinite pronoun is followed immediately by the verb or reference pronoun, both are almost always singular in standard written usage: when other words intervene, a plural verb or reference may occur. None may be either singular or plural, but occurs more often in the plural.

Data: Indefinite pronouns may be divided into four groups:

1. The first consists of a few indefinites, each of which is always singular or always plural. For example, *both* is always plural because it always occurs with a countable noun (*both of the boys are*); on the other hand, *much* is always singular because it always occurs with an uncountable or mass noun (*much of the news is bad*).

2. The second consists of those indefinites such as *all, any, half, more, most,* and *some,* which are singular when they occur with uncountable nouns and indicate all or a portion of a single mass, and plural when they occur with countable plural nouns. These examples from a recent study (Banker) illustrate the point: "*Some* of the requests [countable noun] . . . *have their* comical side" (*Saturday Evening Post,* Apr. 10, 1951, 30) and "*Some* of the domain [uncountable] *lies* in the Selway-Bitterroot area" (*ibid.,* 119). By the same token, one may say, "Of the box of paper, *half has* been used" and "Of the twenty students to be tested, *half are* late."

3. The third consists of only *none.* A unique feature of *none* is that even with a plural noun, it may be treated either as a singular or as a plural, as these illustrations from another study (Gentry) show: "*None* of Wright's principles *is* new" (*Harper's,* Jan., 1955, 98) and "*None* of these people would be doing what *they were doing* if they knew what was in store . . ." (*Saturday Review,* Apr. 9, 1955, 20). In modern usage, *none* is more often employed in the plural, according to the studies made. More than 69% of the examples were found to be in the plural.

4. The fourth consists of *anybody, anyone, each, either, everybody, everyone, neither, nobody, somebody,* and *someone.* When the verb or reference pronoun immediately follows the pronoun, the verb or reference is almost always singular in standard usage, but if other words intervene, a plural may occur, as in "*Each* of these people undoubtedly modified Latin in accordance with *their* own speech habits" (A. C. Baugh, *A History of the English Language,* 2nd ed., 1957, p. 32). Concerned primarily with number of quantity, these indefinites are similar to collectives: singular in form, often plural in meaning. For instance, "*Everyone* should go

to school" means that *all* should go. Since the indefinite is inclusive, a notional plural, one may find sentences like *"Everyone* of the students who were there *were* suspect," even though *everyone* is the subject of the second *were;* also "As *each* of us *go* through life, *we* are constantly meeting new situations." One study (R. Thomas) contains this example: "If *anyone* still believes the scandalous rumors about her . . . , this scholarly account of her life should undeceive *them"* (Joan Bennett, *Yale Review,* Mar., 1958, 448) and another (Sloan) this one: *"One* of the curious effects of the public violence *are* the implications left by some comment on the international consequences of these events" (Arthur Krock, *The New York Times,* Sept. 13, 1957, editorial page). Obviously the notional, if not the formal, subject is plural; hence a plural verb naturally follows. *In twenty-five studies on this question, it was found that indefinite pronouns were used with both singular and plural verbs, but that the singular verb occurred six times more often.*

A somewhat different situation arises from the lack of a common gender third person singular pronoun in English. When the gender reference of *anyone, each, everybody,* etc., is indeterminate or mixed, the pronouns *they, them, their* are used to avoid the cumbersome *he or she, him or her, his or her.* On this matter the handbooks call for simple *he/him/his,* but this rule is observed consistently only in formal usage. In standard English usage of all levels, studies show that both singular and plural reference pronouns are used but that the singular occurs more than twice as often.

Frequently, the whole concord of the sentence is singular, indicating that *they, their, them* are felt to be common-gender singulars, as in *"Everybody* in the room *is* scratching *their head"* (in contrast to the collective plural in *"Half* the people in the room *are* scratching *their heads"*). One study of *The New Yorker* for October 25 and December 20, 1952 (Weil) found these examples: ". . . *each one* producing *their* maximum . . ."; ". . . *each* received in *their* finally hopeless position. . . ." When the verb is in a tense without a distinctive third singular form, it is often impossible to tell whether singular or plural reference is intended, as for instance in *"Everybody* with so much money; selling *their* cotton for anything *they* chose to ask" (*O. Henry Prize Short Stories,* 1950, p. 208, cited by Gentry).

Thus, there are two points at issue: the singular or plural reference of the *anybody* group of indefinites and the use of *they/them/their* as a third person singular pronoun of common gender. On the first point, the common rule that these pronouns are singular is well grounded in usage; to say, for instance, *"Everybody* in the room *are* scratching *their* heads" is certainly substandard (if, indeed, it is ever said). On the second point, however, it seems clear that *they/them/their* is established as a common-gender singular form in all but the most formal usage, where *he/him/his* is preferred. The cumbersome *he or she,* etc. is unnecessary except in a very precise (e.g., legal) context, or where the antecedent also offers alternatives, as in "A *husband or wife* should assume *his or her* proper share of household duties." Many writers would avoid this last alternative by recasting in some such form as *"Both* husband and wife should assume *their* proper share. . . ."

In addition to the seven studies mentioned, twenty others (Adams, I. Altman, Augustine, Baus, Black, Broth, Bryant, Carter, Gay, Goldfarb, Goodman, Haase, Hanson, M. E. Krauss, Kravitz, Lakso, Martindale, Plevin, M. Richardson, Weiser) were made for this entry.

Other evidence: Bartlett, *CE,* 13 (Dec., 1951), 161-62; Bryant, *CE,* 17 (Feb., 1956), 313; Fries, *AEG,* 49-50, 56-59, 287; Hill, *CEA Critic* (Dec., 1954), 4; Rice, *EJ,* XXIII (Nov., 1934), 776-78; Roberts, *UG,* 86-88, 280-81; Thomas, *CE,* 1 (Oct., 1939), 38-45.

AGREEMENT, (N)EITHER . . . (N)OR

Summary: In formal written English, when a subject is compounded with neither . . . nor *or* either . . . or, *the verb is normally singular if the substantives joined are singular, and plural if they are plural. If, however, one substantive is singular and one plural, the verb agrees with the second or nearer subject. In informal and in spoken English, a plural verb is sometimes used when the substantives joined are singular.*

Data: The formal usage governing singular subjects is illustrated by this example from a study (E. Solomon): *"Neither* Iraq *nor* Iran *has* any adequate electronic warning system . . ." (Hanson W. Baldwin, *The New York Times,* Mar. 26, 1957, 4) and by *"Neither* Barnes *nor* Russell *deal* with the . . . doctrine of the resurrection" (Reinhold Niebuhr, *The New York Times Book Review,* Sept. 22, 1957, 6). In informal English, however, both the educated and the uneducated tend to employ a plural verb in this situation, especially in the negative, where "neither is" has the same meaning as "both are not," as in *"Neither* Cecil *nor* Coke *were* grateful" (Catherine Drinker Bowen, *The Lion and the Throne,* 1956, p. 248, cited by Sloan).

The study cited above (Solomon) shows that in formal English the plural subjects will take a plural verb, as in *"Neither* Federal mediators *nor* city officials *have been able* to find an acceptable peace formula" (*The New York Times,* Apr. 3, 1957, 30); and also that the verb will agree with the second or nearer substantive in number: "In spite of this, *neither* the committee's announced objectives *nor* the way in which the hearings have been run *suggests* [to agree with *way*] that the inquiry is anti-labor . . ." (*ibid.,* May 2, 1957, 30) and "Thus far *neither* American political pressure *nor* promises of economic aid *have been able* to dissuade Nasser . . ." (*ibid.,* Apr. 10, 1957, 32).

Two other studies (Conciglia, R. Thomas) were conducted for this entry.

Other evidence: Bryant, *EJ,* L (Mar., 1961), 215; Curme, *Syntax,* 56; *Princ. and Prac. of EG,* 118; Pooley, *TEU,* 83; Roberts, *UG,* 277-78.

AGREEMENT, *NEITHER* WITH MORE THAN TWO.
See *EITHER* (NEITHER) WITH MORE THAN TWO.

AGREEMENT, NUMBER OF VERB AFTER *ONE OF THOSE WHO (WHICH, THAT).*

Summary: In standard English sentences including the above construction, the verb in the dependent clause may agree in number with the plural antecedent of the relative pronoun (i.e., one of those who are) or it may agree in number with the singular one (one of those who is), with the prepositional phrase of those (and similar phrases) regarded as an intervening modifier.

It is true that about five out of every six writers would use the plural in sentences of the kind cited below, yet the construction with the singular verb form cannot be dismissed: it is found in educated writers from Old English times down to the present and occurs frequently in informal English, no doubt because the user regards *one* as the logical antecedent of *who* with the prepositional phrase as a subordinate intervening element. Similarly one may have the singular or plural after *which* and *that*.

Data: Several studies (Hotchner, Kovitz, Rannie, R. Thomas) support the above conclusion. One of them cites "Washington is *one of the few states that has* such a reforestation requirement on its statute books" (*The New York Times,* Nov. 13, 1949, editorial page); "The Copernican Revolution . . . was *one of the most staggering blows* at the dominant faith of the Western world *that has* ever been leveled against it" (Rufus Jones, "What the Modern Man Can Believe," *The Atlantic Monthly,* Nov., 1947, 88); ". . . *one of the best books* about the creative process *that has* been published in many years" (*Newsweek,* Feb. 2, 1948, 75); and "Herblock is *one of the few* around . . . *who understands* that *his* function is that of the watchdog" (*Saturday Review,* Aug. 30, 1958, 9) [note *understands* as well as the pronoun *his,* instead of *their*]. When the verb is not inflected for number, it is evident from the pronoun that the verb is considered singular, as in "She was *one of those women who,* by *her* carriage and the thrust of *her* head, could invest even a Mother Hubbard with style" (Louis Bromfield, *Pleasant Valley,* 1945, p. 86).

Typical examples of the plural verb come from another study (Bowden): *"One* of the shocking *facts that have* shown up . . ." (*Harper's,* Apr., 1957, 26) and "Then Eugene O'Neill made *one of those* remarks *that go* a long way . . ." (Stark Young, *Harper's,* June, 1957, 68).

Other evidence: Bryant, *CE,* 17 (Mar., 1956), 361; Kenyon, *AS,* 26 (Oct., 1951), 161-65; Thomas, *CE,* 13 (Oct., 1951), 43-44.

AGREEMENT, PRONOUN IN ONE OF THOSE (*THAT, WHICH*) CLAUSES. See AGREEMENT, NUMBER OF VERB AFTER ONE OF THOSE WHO (WHICH, THAT).

AGREEMENT, THERE IS (ARE), WAS (WERE)

Summary: Standard English sources favor there is *by an overwhelming proportion when there is a compound subject, the first member of which is singular.*

Data: From a study that supports the above conclusion (Geist), there is this example of the dominant usage: "On one side *there was* a pump and an outhouse and the foundations of the burned barn" (*Harper's,* Jan. 1953, 41); and an example of the less popular plural usage: "*There were* clothing and shoes for the Army assembled in Boston and no money anywhere for their transportation to the Hudson" (*The Atlantic Monthly,* Dec., 1952, 76).

Plural subjects following *there is* fall into certain patterns:

(*1*) two or more nouns with a modifier repeated before each, or with repetition implied, e.g., ". . . *there was* no rustle of falling leaves, no high pitched voices of Chinese, no dulled explosions . . ." (*Harper's,* Feb., 1953, 82)

(*2*) the subject may be repeated, e.g., "*There is* a time to be silent and a time to speak, a time for study and a time for resignation or action" (*Saturday Review of Literature,* July 20, 1946, 16)

(*3*) the subjects are often joined by correlative adjectives, such as *too much . . . not enough, more . . . less,* e.g., ". . . but here *there is* more grace and less carelessness" (*Journal of English and Germanic Philology,* 44: 329)

(*4*) the subjects often take the form of a listing or a series, as in the first sentence quoted in the first paragraph. *There's* instead of *there is* followed by an ordinary plural subject or by a compound subject occurs frequently in speech, but rarely in writing.

What is true of *there is* (*are*) or *there was* (*were*) also applies to *here is* (*are*) or *here was* (*were*), but the expression does not occur so frequently as *there is* in written English. One study (Geist) showed that the singular occurred eight times and the plural three with *here*. The singular was used with a plural subject nearly three times as often.

The Linguistic Atlas recorded the present tense form of *to be* showing number for New England and the Middle Atlantic, the South Atlantic, the North Central, and the Upper Midwest States in the expression "*Here are* your clothes." For the first three areas, it is also recorded in the context, "*There are* many people who think so."

In the first example, *here's* predominates strongly in the speech of Type II informants (those with at least some secondary school education), according to investigations by Allen and Malmstrom, and is used by a large percentage of Type III informants (usually with four years of college education) also: 50% in the New England and the South Atlantic States, 48% in the North Central States, 34% in the Middle Atlantic States, and 18% in the Upper Midwest States. This evidence shows that the usage is standard in speech.

In the other context, *there's* predominates only slightly less strongly in Type II speech, and in Type III the percentage of occurrence drops also, ranging from 34% to 25%. These figures cover only the Eastern areas, but the same kind of occurrence can reasonably be extrapolated westward. The decrease may be explained by the textbook prohibition (therefore, teachers as well) against *there's* before a plural noun.

Another study of spoken English, of the World Series of 1957 (Coxe), supported the findings in this entry.

Other evidence: Atwood, 29-30; Berkeley, *AS,* 28 (May, 1953), 92-96; Bryant, *CE,* 17 (Mar., 1956), 361-62; Fries, *AEG,* 56-57, 59; Geist, *CE,* 14 (Nov., 1952), 115-16; *CE,* 16 (Dec., 1954), 188-89; Kurath, *LANE,* Vol. II, Pt. 1, Map 357; Vol. III, Pt. 2, Map 678; Malmstrom, *SVTS,* 203-4; V.G. McDavid, 54-55.

AGREEMENT, WHAT—CLAUSES

Summary: The number of the verb, almost always the verb to be,. when the verb follows a what-clause *in the subject position and precedes a plural predicate noun, presents a clear case of divided usage: the plural occurs three times as often as the singular.*

Data: If *what* is plural, as indicated by structural signs (verb or complement) in the noun clause, the verb of the main clause is regularly plural, a five-year study reveals (Christensen): "What appear to be large windows in the second story *are* glass heat collectors" (*Scientific American,* Feb., 1951, 61); "Sometimes what appear to be disciplinary problems *are* easily *solved* by very elementary applied psychology" (Morton M. Hunt, *Harper's,* July,. 1953, 77).

If *what* is singular in the noun clause and the main verb is followed by a plural predicate noun, the main verb is usually plural: "What impresses them *are* planes and divisions and ships" (Harry S. Truman, radio address, June 26, 1953); "What interests and a little confuses me *are* the names he chose to call . . ." (Gilbert Seldes, *Saturday Review,* Nov. 8, 1952, 34); "What makes each division different *are* a few simple things—time, place, tradition, and leadership" (T. H. White, *The Reporter,* Aug. 4, 1953, 9).

If *what* is undetermined singular or plural (it is usually an object in the noun clause) and the main verb is followed by a plural predicate noun, usage favors the plural verb three to one, as in: "What they want *are* promises" (Edward R. Murrow, radio broadcast); "What we have in English poetry *are* several principles of rhythm . . ." (Victor M. Hamm, "Meter and Meaning," *PMLA,* Sept., 1954, 696). An example with the singular verb is: "What they hate and fear *is* their own neighbors who try to think" (Elmer Davis, *Harper's,* Aug., 1953, 29).

If the complement consists of two or more predicate nouns,. either singular or plural, the verb preceding is generally singular if the predicate nouns are singular, but generally plural if the predicate nouns are plural: "What is most striking about Johnson *is* the vigor of his ideas, the variety of his knowledge, the forcefulness of his conversation, and the dignity with which . . . he maintained his position" (J. C. Mendenhall, *English Literature, 1650-1800,*

1940); "What we want, both in government and everywhere else, *are* men and women who are morally aware and morally responsible . . ." (Paul Pickerel, *Harper's,* Jan., 1956, 89). An example, however, of the singular verb with a plural predicate noun is the following: ". . . what is smuggled *is* not guns but medicines and nylons" (Naomi Barker, *The New Republic,* July 7, 1953, 31).

Other evidence: Bryant, *CE,* 17 (Mar., 1956), 362; Christensen, *AS,* 30 (Feb., 1955), 30-37; *AS,* 33 (Oct., 1958), 226-29; Curme, *Syntax,* 50, 214-15; Jespersen, *MEG,* Pt. II, 58-59, 168; III, 41; Kruisinga, III, 307.

AIN'T, AM NOT, IS NOT, ARE NOT

Summary: In nonstandard speech, ain't *is the usual contraction of* am not, are not, is not, has not, *and* have not (*present tense in all three persons, singular and plural*), *but most standard speakers avoid it except in very informal situations, where* ain't *is homey or is written or uttered with tongue in cheek. Writers of fiction or drama commonly use it to mark a character as uneducated or self-made.*

Data: These conclusions are based upon seven studies (Flannery, Gabel, Louis, McMillan, Michalski, M. Richardson, Shafer) and Barnhart's Files, which contain the following illustrations: John Golden, speaking for the Actor's Fund of America, commented: "There ain't no theater until some one sits down with a pencil and a white paper and writes: 'Mary enters . . .' " (WJZ, Dec. 31, 1951). Syndicated columnist Robert Ruark, in his column of Jan. 16, 1952, wrote: "There *ain't* much to brag about. . . ." Writers of chatty columns sometimes use *ain't* to achieve a "plain folks" effect. One study (Shafer) based upon 5,974 pages of reading found 22 examples of *ain't,* used 55% of the time for *is not,* as in ". . . she *ain't* no good for nothing but trouble" (*Esquire,* Nov., 1959, 34); 18% for *are not,* as in "Honey, you *ain't* just a-woofin' " (*Reader's Digest,* Dec., 1959, 207), 9% of the time for *am not,* as in "I *ain't* got no one to leave it to" (Robert Molloy, *The Reunion,* 1950, p. 19), and 18% of the time for *have not,* as in "They *ain't* done it yet." (*Reader's Digest,* Oct., 1959, 16). All of these examples come from represented dialect speech.

According to one study of the Linguistic Atlas (Malmstrom),

in the context "I *am not* going to hurt him," *ain't* practically never occurs in the speech of Type III (usually with four years of college education) informants in the East; *I'm not* is the preferred form. In Type II (those with at least some secondary education) speech, however, *ain't* occurs often, from 25% of the time in the Upper Midwest to about 80% in North Carolina and Virginia. While this occurrence indicates that *ain't* in this context is used colloquially, it shows also that the usage is not expanding. *Ain't I,* as part of a question, is heard more frequently because the alternative expression, *am I not?* seems clumsy to many speakers.

Other evidence: Atwood, 30-31; Malmstrom, *SVTS,* 211-12; *CE,* 21 (Apr., 1960), 416-17; Marckwardt and Walcott, 54, 96; R.I. McDavid, *Lang.,* 17 (Jan.-Mar., 1941), 57-59; V.G. McDavid, 55-57, 202; R.I. and V.G. McDavid, *AS,* 35 (Feb., 1960), 17; Mencken, *Am. Lang.,* 202; *Supp. 1,* 404-6; Newsome, *AS,* 13 (Feb., 1938), 28; Stevens, *AS,* 29 (Oct., 1954), 196-201.

ALL (OF)

Summary: Though many writers object to of *in phrases like* "all of the stars" *on the grounds that it is uneconomical, the* of *is used with* all *before pronouns and with nouns indicating totality, as in* "all of them," "the total of her earnings."

Data: Four studies of current usage (McMillan, Spiegel, R. Thomas, Winburne) reveal these trends:

1. *All* is followed by *of* when it precedes *whom,* or a person's name used figuratively ("all of Shakespeare," "all of Beethoven"), *us, you, them, it, which,* as in "He would not remember, because he had seen too much—too many people, too many faces, *all of which* were merged in the trivialities of every day" (J. P. Marquand, *So Little Time,* 1943, p. 382); but *all us boys* and *all you people* may occur where *us* and *you* precede a noun.

2. *All* is much more frequent than *all of* where *of* is optional (before *this, that, these, those,* and definite nouns: *all (of) this paper; all (of) these books; all (of) the tables.*

3. When *of* precedes *all,* a following *of* is rare, as in *of all (of) these,* but when a word like *any* or *each* occurs in the construction,

all of is generally used: *any or all of the boats, each and all of the men.*

4. In a few common structures, *all of* is followed by the indefinite article: *all of a sudden, all of an instant,* both meaning "suddenly," as in ". . . and then *all of an instant* the universe became filled with a gigantic rattling . . ." (Ernie Pyle, *Brave Men,* 1944, p. 436). Another example is "According to nearly *all of the indices* . . . the economic growth of the South in recent years . . . exceeds . . ." (*Virginia Quarterly Review,* Summer, 1958, 325).

All of meaning "fully; as much as," is also used in informal English as in "It will cost him *all of* $1,000."

Other evidence: Bolinger, *CE,* 2 (Oct., 1940), 69-70.

ALL . . . NOT. See NOT, ILLOGICALLY PLACED.

ALL (adv.) PLUS *THE* (adv.) PLUS A COMPARATIVE

Summary: Locutions like "all the harder," "all the easier," "all the more remarkable" *occur in standard written English.*

This construction seems to have developed from such expressions as *the harder, the braver,* etc. found in Old English ("Courage must be the *harder,* heart the *braver," The Battle of Maldon,* l. 312). By Shakespeare's time, *all* followed by *the* and the comparative was established, as seen in *As You Like It,* where Celia says, *"All the better;* we shall be the more marketable" (I, ii, l. 102). This construction has continued until the present as has the one without *all,* which at times is paired with itself, as in *"The sooner, the better,"* or *"The farther* we go *the more tired* we shall be."

Data: One study (R. Thomas) in a representative selection of Modern Standard American English turned up sixteen examples of such expressions, represented by ". . . of a hush that seems *all the deeper* for the far-away mourning of the hounds . . ." (W. J. Cash, *The Mind of the South,* 1941, p. 46); ". . . for the boycott by the Congressional leaders should make it *all the easier* for the committee to work out a strategy . . ." (James MacGregor Burns, *The New York Times Magazine,* Jan. 27, 1957, 71).

Other examples contained the function word *more* instead of the inflection *-er,* as in "The Socialist task was made *all the more acute* when conservatives . . . patched together . . ." (Hyman Kublin, *Yale Review,* Summer, 1957, 575). In other examples, *all the more* was followed by a noun, as in "But that is *all the more* reason why we should not . . ." and "Now, twenty-three years after, the statement has *all the more* force."

Other evidence: OED; Thomas, *CE,* 20 (Jan., 1959), 190-91.

ALL THE FARTHER (FURTHER), AS FAR AS

Summary: Each of the expressions is standard spoken form in certain areas; in formal written English, as far as *is the preferred form.*

Data: One study (Malmstrom) shows that the majority of Type II (of some education) and III speakers (cultivated) in New England and the Middle Atlantic, the South Atlantic, the North Central, and Upper Midwest States prefer *as far as* (often pronounced "as fur as," or shortened to "far as" or "fur as") in a context such as "Two miles is *as far as* (*all the farther, all the further*) he can go." In the Midland, both *all the farther* and *all the further* are frequent, especially in Type I (uneducated) and Type II speech, with the latter strongly preferred, particularly in the Middle Atlantic States. In Southern speech, it occurs frequently, but *all the farther* is rare. In the North Central States, Type III usage of *all the further* is concentrated in Kentucky, where it occurs as frequently as *all the farther.* Both expressions are completely absent in New England and relatively infrequent in the Northern dialect areas of the North Central and Upper Midwest States.

As far as is standard usage in all the areas considered here; it is almost always preferred in formal and informal written English, as in (". . . *as far as* I can go," from James Hagerty's news conference reported in *The New York Times,* Nov. 30, 1957, 8). A study

(Hartz) based on written English found only *as far as* in formal written English.

See also THE FARTHEST, THE FURTHEST.

Other evidence: Kurath, *LANE,* Vol. I, Pt. I, Map 49; Malmstrom, *SVTS,* 70-72, 287-92; R.I. McDavid, *AED,* 519; Mencken, *Supp. II,* 232; Pooley, *TEU,* 147-48; Wentworth, 15.

ALMOST, adv. See ONLY, adv.; MOST, ALMOST.

ALTHOUGH. See THOUGH, ALTHOUGH.

AM I NOT? AIN'T I? AREN'T I?

Summary: Although speakers of all types use the expression ain't I? *freely, it lacks upper-class social approval. In general,* am I not? *is the form preferred by most Type III (cultivated) speakers. Relatively rare in all areas,* aren't I? *is used by speakers of all types.*

Theoretically there is an argument for *ain't* or *aren't* in the first person inversion for questions because there is no regular contraction of *am not* (such as *amn't*) paralleling *aren't* for *are not* and *isn't* for *is not.* Though *aren't* and *ain't* in this context predate the American Revolution, both have been so strongly and effectively (if mistakenly) condemned that they have little widespread upper-class social approval, *aren't* less so than *ain't* because *aren't* is used by educated Britishers. Hence, it is advisable for a speaker unsure of the social situation to avoid the issue by saying, "I'm lucky today, don't you think?" or ". . . am I not?"

Data: According to one study (Malmstrom) of the Linguistic Atlas records for New England, the Middle Atlantic, the South Atlantic, the North Central States and the Upper Midwest, *ain't I?* is used by all types of informants, except in the Upper Midwest where it is avoided in Type III (cultivated) speech. Cultivated informants in all other areas use it freely: 20% in New England, nearly 33% in the Middle Atlantic and South Atlantic States and about 73% in the North Central States. Usually in Type III speech, *ain't I?* is not the only form. In Type II (the speech of those with some secondary education) it is strongly predominant in New England, almost universal in the Middle Atlantic and South Atlantic States and used by about 50% of the Type II's in the North Central States and the Upper Midwest.

Hain't I? is much less common than *ain't I* and is characteristic of Type I (uneducated) usage.

Aren't I? is relatively rare in all areas and occurs most frequently in Northern speech areas, New England, and the Upper Midwest. It is not concentrated in Type III usage but occurs about equally in all types.

Am I not? is most common in southern New England, where all types use it. Elsewhere, it is predominant mainly in cultivated speech, except in the North Central States, where no cultivated informants use it. About two-thirds of the Type III's (cultivated speakers with college education) in the Middle Atlantic and South Atlantic States and in the Upper Midwest use it.

Studies (Flannery, Hansen, McGill, Michalski) of modern literature show that *ain't I?* or *ain't he?* occurs in dialogue or in "character" stories. (*See* AIN'T, AM NOT, IS NOT, ARE NOT)

Other evidence: Atwood, 30-31; Kurath, *LANE,* Vol. III, Pt. 2, Map 676; Malmstrom, *SVTS,* 212-13; Marckwardt and Walcott, 48, 95-96; R.I. McDavid, *Lang.,* 17 (Jan.-Mar., 1941), 57-59; V.G. McDavid, 55-57; Mencken, *Am. Lang.,* 202; Newsome, *AS,* 13 (Feb., 1938), 28.

AMONG. See *BETWEEN* WITH MORE THAN TWO.

AND (*BUT, OR, .NOR*) AT THE BEGINNING OF A SENTENCE

Summary: This construction is used in the best writing.

The objection to opening a sentence with *and* (*but, or,* or *nor*) has no basis in usage. It is exclusively a matter of stylistic taste.

Data: In a statistical study of 3,400 sentences (Christensen), 200 samples were chosen from writers who could be regarded as expert in exposition or narrative. Of these sentences, 4.03% began with *and, but, or,* or *nor* (the percentage in expository writing was 6.4%). The percentages ran as high as 15% in Edmund Wilson's *The Triple Thinkers.* In another study (Stolzberg) of 600 pages in present-day magazines, including *Harper's, Time, Reader's Digest,* and *The Atlantic Monthly,* 46 sentences were found to begin with *and* (*but, or,* and *nor* were not included), or one in every 13 pages. A third investigation (Russell) found in reading 58 pages 34 sentences beginning with *and.* The selection, however, was a short story from the *Saturday Evening Post.*

AND WITH THE INFINITIVE. See TRY AND.

ANTICIPATORY IT. See IT (1).

ANY. See AGREEMENT, INDEFINITE PRONOUNS.

ANYBODY, ANYONE. See AGREEMENT, INDEFINITE PRONOUNS.

ANYHOW, ANYWAY, adv.

Summary: In the sense of "in any case, at any rate," both are standard usage, but anyway *occurs more than four times as often as* anyhow.

Data: Anyway, like *anyone,* is written as one word when no syllable receives strong stress and when *way* receives medium stress ("I won't be there *anyway*" [ɛnɪˌwe]) but as two when the stress is about evenly divided: *"Any way* ['ɛnɪ 'we] I make the cake will not be right for the contest"; "Of course *any way* you look at it, it's unpleasant" (James M. Cain, *Mildred Pierce,* 1948, p. 85, cited by Winburne).

A recent study of current literature and the speech habits of children (Hochberg) reveals that *anyway* is used by all types and ages of people, while *anyhow* appears more often in writing than in speech, as in ". . . and—the ultimate riposte—that nobody reads the scholar's books *anyhow*" (*Virginia Quarterly Review,* Summer, 1958, 471, cited by R. Thomas).

Anyways is sometimes heard in Type I (uneducated) and Type II (with some secondary education) speech, as in this representation of it: *"Anyways,* he happens to go under the name Joe . . ." (A. Kober, *The New Yorker,* Oct. 17, 1942, 19).

Other evidence: Wentworth, 24, 26.

ANY MORE, adv.

Summary: Any more *is standard English in a negative, interrogative or hypothetical context; in an affirmative sense, it is standard regional.*

Any more, employed in affirmative, noninterrogative, and non-hypothetical statements to mean "now, presently, at present, from now on," occurs in cultivated speech in certain parts of the country, as in "They are making the booths that way for some reason *any more."* Placed either at the beginning or the end of utterances, this construction occurs sporadically over a large part of the country, more often in the Middle Atlantic and Midland areas, presumably derived from the usage of Scotch-Irish immigrants of the eighteenth century who carried the phrase with them as they moved inland, to the South, and later westward along the Ohio River valley. However, the expression is very rare in serious writing.

    Data: Two studies (Holihan, Winburne) failed to turn up the affirmative usage in writing. On the other hand, used adverbially in a negative context, *any more* was found frequently by investigators (Bowden, Hickey): "It seemed to her . . . no one would ever age *any more* or die" (*Mademoiselle,* Jan., 1958, 111); "Pat and Peggy never came crying home from school *any more"* (*Reader's Digest,* Dec., 1957, 54); and "The Webster type of gang . . . is hardly in existence in this area *any more"* (Samuel Perlmutter, "News of the Week in Review," *The New York Times,* Jan. 12, 1958, Sec. 4, 4).

Other evidence: Bryant, *EJ,* XLV (Dec., 1956), 556; Dunlap, *AS,* 20 (Feb., 1945), 13-15; Gibbens, *AS,* 19 (Oct., 1944), 204; Menner, *AS,* 21 (Apr., 1946), 151; Sackett, *Word Study* (Dec., 1957), 4; Tucker, *AS,* 19 (Feb., 1944), 39; Wentworth, 24-25.

ANYPLACE, adv.

Summary: Anyplace (*and* everyplace, no place, someplace) *is colloquial when used as an adverb instead of* anywhere (*and* everywhere, nowhere, somewhere).

Data: Used as an adverb, this locution generally occurs in dialogue, "character" stories, or informal conversation (Benardete, Krupitsky, W. R. Moore, Pyles), as in "They didn't go *any place* without them" (John Steinbeck, *Sweet Thursday,* 1954, p. 56); "We argued and argued and got *no place*" (Fred Allen, in *Saturday Review,* Oct. 2, 1954, 20); and "I just thought you'd like to go *someplace* where I could give it to you" (William O'Farrell, *The Devil His Due,* 1955, p. 97).

When place is employed as a noun, it may occur with *any, every, no,* or *some* preceding it in formal English: "You may select *any place* that appeals to you"; "*Every place* that I have seen is undesirable" and "*Some place* can be found." In these examples, the noun *place* is always a separate word. As adverbs, however, *anyplace, everyplace,* etc. are often written as one word.

Other evidence: Kurath, *LANE,* Vol. III, Pt. 2, Map 709.

ANYWAY. See ANYHOW, ANYWAY, adv.

ANYWAYS. See ANYHOW, ANYWAY, adv.

ANYWHERE, ANYWHERES

Summary: In formal written English, only anywhere *is found; in current speech, however,* anywheres *occurs, but it is a receding form.*

Data: One investigator (Kurtz) found, in 8,000 pages of reading, only one instance of *anywheres,* uttered by an uneducated cowhand in a Western: "If you need to sleep *anywheres,* [sleep here]" (Clarence B. Kelland, *Desert Law,* 1949, p. 25). Like *anywhere, everywhere* and *somewhere* occur in standard writing: "One can find a desirable home *somewhere* in the suburbs."

A study of the Linguistic Atlas records (Malmstrom) reveals that in spoken English, *anywhere* predominates strongly among all types of informants in the New England and the Middle Atlantic, the South Atlantic, the North Central States, and the Upper Midwest, as in "You can find that *anywhere.*" *Anywheres* occurs also, especially before *else,* very often along with *anywhere,* among all types in all these areas. It is completely absent from Type III (cultivated) and Type II (those with at least some secondary education) speech only in New York City, Washington, D.C., Indiana, and Ohio. *Anywheres* is probably a receding form for three reasons: 1) its highest percentage of occurrence in Type III speech is among the older and more old-fashioned groups in New England; 2) it occurs proportionately with greater frequency in Type I (uneducated) than in Type II or III speech; 3) it is absent from the speech of all types of informants in two major urban and prestige centers of the Atlantic seaboard.

Other evidence: Kurath, *LANE,* Vol. III, Pt. II, Map 709; Malmstrom, *SVTS,* 63-64, 279-81; Wentworth, 26.

AREN'T I? See **AM I NOT? AIN'T I? AREN'T I?**

ARITHMETICAL FORMULAS

Summary: Usage is divided between singular and plural verbs agreeing with subjects such as eight *and* four *and* two fours *and other arithmetical expressions.*

As with collective nouns, the number of the expression may now be singular, now plural. If the speaker, for example in the illustration given above, pauses slightly after *eight* and after *four* so that each is an entity, he will probably use a plural verb, but if there is not this pause or juncture after the words he may elect a singular verb.

Data: In all periods of the history of the English language, one may find examples of divided usage in statements similar to "How much *are* (*is*) two fours?" Recent studies in Modern English (Hotchner, Kashtan, Schuchat) reveal that the singular was used in 56% and the plural in 44% of the examples compiled. As illustrations, we have ". . . Air Force estimates that 15 minutes *is* all the warning the L.S. . . ." (*Time,* Nov. 25, 1957, 27); ". . . two and two *make* four" (*McCall's,* Nov., 1957, 114); and "Then he will remember that 3 plus 2 plus 2 *equals* 7, and 9 plus 5 *equals* 14, and 14 plus 7 *equals* 21 . . ." (*Saturday Evening Post,* May 17, 1958, 105).

Other evidence: Bartlett, *CE,* 15 (May, 1954), 477; Jespersen, *Ess.,* 210-18; *MEG,* Pt. II, 6.34.

AS . . . AS, SO . . . AS

Summary: As . . . as *is usually employed in positive comparisons, but usage is divided between* as . . . as *and* so . . . as *in negative comparisons.*

Data: About the middle of the last century, one study (Rucks) shows, only 11.7% of the writers used *as . . . as* in negative statements whereas 88.3% used *so . . . as* ("She is not *so* pretty *as* her sister"); but today the situation is quite different: there has been a substantial shift to 53.6% using *as . . . as* and 46.4% using *so . . . as.* Two other studies (Winburne, Tavin) cited evidence such as the following: ". . . efficiency does not always pay *as* well *as* chance . . ." (*The Atlantic Monthly,* May, 1956, 16) and "There is not *as* much of it *as* there was . . ." (*Yale Review,* Autumn, 1955, 114); on the other hand, "But the effect was not quite *so* 1910 *as* it may sound" (*Harper's,* March, 1956, 82) and "Never had Great Britain been *so* prosperous *as* in 1955 . . ." (*The Atlantic Monthly,* May, 1956, 10).

The use of *as . . . as* in the affirmative is well established. *As . . . as* has also become involved in an almost uncountable number of word patterns or stereotypes: *as* bright *as* day, *as* clean *as* a bone, *as* cunning *as* a fox, *as* dry *as* dust, *as* easy *as* not, *as* good *as,* *as* soon *as,* *as* sure *as* fate, *as* tight *as* a drum, not *as* young *as* she used to be (to mention a few). Occasionally one also encounters *so . . . as* in the affirmative, as in "Seldom has a novel opened *so* laboriously . . . and yet carried *so* forceful an impact . . . *as* this fictionized chronicle . . ." (*The New York Times Book Review,* Apr. 1, 1956, 17, cited by Rucks). Perhaps the inverted verb selects *so . . . as,* because the head word in the sentence, *seldom,* inverts the subject-verb order in the manner of *never.*

Divided usage also occurs in the constructions *as* (*so*) *far as* and *as* (*so*) *long as*. In the former, usage slightly favors *so far as* (58%); in the latter, *so long as* is preferred, according to one study (Rucks), by an eight to one count; but according to another (Winburne), *as long as* occurred 76% of the time. Illustrations are: "*As far as* the shocks were concerned he is almost exclusively interested in two types . . ." (*American Economic Review,* Mar., 1955, 205); ". . . no one, *so far as* I know, has as yet worked out a practical policy . . ." (Walter Lippmann, *Tuscaloosa News,* Apr. 26, 1956, 4); "I've got no objection *as long as* it's a step forward." (Drew Pearson quoting I. Davidson, *Tuscaloosa News,* Apr. 23, 1956, 4); "All sorts of community services may be introduced . . . *so long as* they do not prevent the school from being an effective school." (*The Atlantic Monthly,* May, 1956, 74).

Spoken usage, however, of *so* (*as*) *long as,* if New England is typical, sharply diverges from the written. The *Linguistic Atlas of New England* shows that cultivated informants used *as long as* much more frequently (19) than *so long as* (7), 73% of the time. Also in fourteen other studies of literature, *as long as* occurred in 84% of the cases and *so long as* in 16%. The average, therefore, for written material shows *as long as* used 47% of the time, *so long as* 53%.

Other evidence: Bryant, *CE,* 17 (Feb., 1956), 313; Kurath, *LANE,* Vol. III, Pt. 2, Map 728; Marckwardt and Walcott, 23, 27, 111.

A S, Causal

Summary: Though far less frequent, causal as *is found in standard usage along with* since *and* because.

As has many meanings and, like many other words, may be ambiguous unless the writer makes his intended meaning clear through the context. For instance, in the sentence "*As* we were sitting there, we could view the boats on the river," *as* may mean *while, when,* or *because.* It has been suggested that *since* or *because* be substituted for the causal *as,* but Fries found that it occurred frequently in the standard English letters that he examined, and that about half the time *as* was used, it was used in the causal sense.

Data: A study of current usage (Geist) contains these illustrations: "Her dinners can become intellectually exhausting, *as* the guests are expected to be as knowledgeable as the hostess . . ." (*Harper's,* Feb., 1957, 36); "It is best to smell it in sunshine, *as* all good things are even better when the circumstances are toward" (*ibid.,* Mar., 1957, 98); and ". . . *as* he is on duty he cannot accompany her now . . ." (*ibid.,* Apr., 1957, 35). Of the 931 *as*-clauses encountered in this study, about 2% were causal.

In two other studies (Newsome, Teitelbaum), causal clauses introduced by *because* occurred 75% of the time, by *since* 18%, and by *as* 7%, including such magazines as the *Yale Review*. Other work in this area bears out this proportion.

Other evidence: Fries, *AEG,* 221-22; Geist, *CE,* 19 (Apr., 1957), 321-22; Newsome, *CE,* 20 (Mar., 1959), 298, 303.

AS (SO) FAR AS. See AS . . . AS; SO . . . AS. See ALL THE FARTHER (FURTHER), AS FAR AS.

A-SINGING AND A-LAUGHING

Summary: Evidence indicates that the a-prefix is characteristic of uneducated rather than archaic speech; it does not occur in written English except in represented speech.

Data: According to a study of literature (S. M. Smith) and a study (Malmstrom) of the records of the Linguistic Atlas in the New England, the Middle Atlantic, the South Atlantic, the North Central States, and the Upper Midwest, the *a*-prefix before present participles (in the context "She was *singing* and *laughing*") is rare in Type III (cultivated) speech in all areas and in all writing. In other types of speech, the *a*-prefix occurs more often before the second verb when the two are combined: *"singing* and *a-laughing."* Used facetiously, it appears in "But, as Americans say, time was *a-wasting"* (*Saturday Evening Post,* Oct. 18, 1958, 92).

Other evidence: Atwood, 34-35; Kurath, *LANE,* Vol. II, Pt. 2, Map 671; Malmstrom, *SVTS,* 228-29; V.G. McDavid, 60, 71.

AS (SO) LONG AS.   See AS . . . AS; SO . . . AS.

AS (SO) LONG AS, conj.

Summary: For expressing comparison or similarity, as long as *is used in standard formal English; it also occurs as a conjunction meaning* while, *sometimes* because *or* provided that. So long as *also occurs as a conjunction, but less frequently than* as long as.

As long as is used when physical comparison is expressed, as in "The panel is *as long as* that mirror" or when the comparison is in time intervals, as in "He has been in business *as long as* I have." At other times, it is used as a conjunction, meaning *while, because,* and *provided that.*

Data: One extensive study prepared for this book (Hotchner) found that *as long as* in the meaning of *while* occurred in 53.5% of the examples, *while* occurred 44.2%, and the variant *so long as* 2.3%. This usage is illustrated in ". . . he succeeded in blocking the Compromise of 1850 *as long as* he lived" (*American Heritage,* Summer, 1953, 11).

Textbooks warn against the use of *as long as* in the sense of "since; because; inasmuch as," but it occurs in ". . . but it did not matter *as long as* you were not sorry for yourself . . . (John P. Marquand, *So Little Time,* 1943, p. 332); "We . . . decided it was all right to keep going *as long as* there were crowds" (Ernie Pyle, *Brave Men,* 1944, p. 457, cited by Winburne); and *"As long as* both the extreme Right and the extreme Left attacked it, one felt in honor bound to stand by it" (*The Atlantic Monthly,* Apr., 1958, 45, cited by Hotchner). The study mentioned above found *since* occurring 59% of the time; *because* 26%; *for* 10.4%; *inasmuch as* 2.8%; *as long as* 1.4%; and *as* .4%—all variants.

As long as has also developed other meanings that are in current usage. For example, it means "provided that" in "I do not object to extended debate *as long as* the discussion is pertinent to the issue" (Radio: CBS, "Domestic Affairs Session," Dec. 31, 1956) and ". . . *as long as* he attends the games and does not libel the manager, he is pretty much left alone" (*The Nation,* Aug. 3, 1957,

50). The aforementioned study found *as long as* used 11.69% of the time; *provided that* 6.49%; *so long as* 6.49%; *assuming that* 3.9%; and *if* 71.43%.

According to quantitative evidence gathered in fifteen studies (Blomquist, Carswell, Chapnitsky, Edgerton, Fries, Hotchner, Kindschi, Klinner, O'Brien, Postraw, Ramsey, Ramsted, S. Smith, Speitz, Winburne), *as long as* occurred 71% of the time meaning "while," 16% of the time meaning "since," and 13% of the time meaning "provided that" when it was used as a conjunction.

The same studies show that *so long as* also occurs as a conjunction (16% of the time) but not so often as *as long as* (84%). Like *as long as,* it most often had the meaning of "while" (56.25% of the time), as in *"So long as* I thought you had loved him I didn't have a word to say"; or " '. . . *so long as* I am U. S. Ambassador, [never] will a news story go out which does not contain mention of the U. S. position' " (*U. S. News & World Report,* Aug. 1, 1958, 10). It has the meaning of "since" 12.5% of the time, as in *"So long as* Morgan was willing to call the meeting, the presidents . . . were eager to attend" (*American Heritage,* June, 1957, 35) and the meaning of "provided that" 31.25% of the time, as in *"So long as* it was legally prepared and served you could be held . . ." (*Good Housekeeping,* June, 1958, 177).

Other evidence: Fries, *AEG,* 222.

AS . . . THAN. See COMPARATIVE, INCOMPLETE.

AS TO

Summary: As to *is standard English in phrases that emphasize or point out.*

Data: As to almost always has the meaning of "concerning." It may appear in an introductory phrase, as in *"As to* the truth of his words, I am not in a position to say," or as in *"As to* permanent damage, chronic asthma . . . can result in . . ." (*McCall's,* Dec., 1957, 95).

In other instances, it may be embedded in the sentence with the meaning of "about," "on," or "concerning": "Did the doctor make any statement *as to* (*about*) the new vaccine?" or "Exact information *as to* (*about* or *on*) the time of a launching is rarely common knowledge . . ." (*The New York Times Magazine,* Dec. 22, 1957, 9). In these sentences, the choice is a matter of stylistic taste.

As to also occurs before words like *whether, when, where, why, how,* as in ". . . there have been speculations *as to whether* Lucy Isabelle Marsh sang at the Metropolitan" (*Hobbies,* Sept. 1957, 27) and "I have been in constant touch with . . . the city engineer . . . *as to how* to best proceed . . ." (*The Capital Times,* Madison, Wis., Jan. 15, 1958). Nine studies (Chapnitsky, Edgerton, Hotchner, Kilimnik, Pfankuch, Ramsey, S. Smith, Speitz, Winburne) showed that *as to* was placed before words of this kind 28% of the time, *whether* occurring 14%. Some people frown upon this construction on the grounds that *as to* is unnecessary, but it occurs in standard English sources from newspapers to fiction, even though it adds nothing to the meaning of the sentence.

Other evidence: Bryant, *CE,* 17 (Feb., 1956), 313; Curme, *Syntax,* 300.

AT ABOUT

Summary: In informal usage, at about *is a normal English expression, similar to* at almost, at around, at approximately, *and* at exactly.

Data: Frequently the *at* can be omitted without changing the meaning, as in "We arrived (*at*) *about* three o'clock," but this choice is a matter of style. Sometimes the *at* cannot be omitted: "The manager offered them all to me *at about* the normal price" (Walter B. Pitkin, *On My Own,* 1944, p. 284); "Draw a . . . line *at about* the western border" (Bernard De Voto, *Harper's,* Oct., 1946, 314). *About* cannot be omitted without changing the meaning.

The phrase *at around* is similar in meaning: ". . . you were going to place the call *at* somewhere *around* ten-thirty" (Earle Stanley Gardner, *The Case of the Rolling Bones,* 1947, p. 196) and "The pressure . . . stays *at around* twenty millimeters . . ." (*Harper's,* Dec., 1957, 65).

At approximately is, however, more formal than *at about:* "We shall arrive *at approximately* three o'clock"; *"At approximately* this point in our careers . . ."* (*New York Post,* Dec. 31, 1957, M2). A quantitative study (Hotchner) showed *at about* occurring 71.42% of the time and the variants *by about, at almost, at approximately, at around, around, at something like* 28.58%. Other studies (Bowden, Brant, Hotchner, Winburne) showed its use in standard English.

Other evidence: Fletcher, *AS,* 22 (Oct., 1947), 192-95; Harlan, *AS,* 23 (Feb., 1948), 70-71; Shewmake, *AS,* 23 (Feb., 1948), 71-72.

AT ALL, adv.

Summary: At all, *to mean "to the slightest degree" or "in any way" is used frequently in informal standard English.*

Data: In interrogative, negative, and conditional statements, such as "Are you considering the position *at all?*" and "I am not considering the dress *at all,*" the usage is unquestionably standard. So is it when used as an intensive, as in: "He didn't have to come over there *at all*" (Ernie Pyle, *Brave Men,* 1944, p. 221); " 'I'm not worried *at all,*' he said" (John P. Marquand, *So Little Time,* 1943, p. 451) and "No mistake, no mistake *at all*" (James M. Cain, *Mildred Pierce,* 1948, p. 216), all cited in a study by Winburne.

The affirmative use, meaning "absolutely, altogether, wholly," is regional, found in the South with some frequency and occasionally in the Midland area: "Edith is the finest girl *at all (of all).*" This archaic usage has disappeared from standard English, but is retained regionally in speech, usually after a superlative.

Other evidence: Brewster, *AS,* 17 (Apr., 1942), 130; Bryant, *EJ,* XLVI (Jan., 1957), 54; Dunlap, *AS,* 20 (Feb., 1945), 15-16; Laubscher, *Dial. Notes,* 4:302; Lyman, *AS,* 11 (Feb., 1936), 63; *OED.*

AT ALMOST. See AT ABOUT.

AT APPROXIMATELY. See AT ABOUT.

AT AROUND. See AT ABOUT.

AT EXACTLY. See AT ABOUT.

AT HOME. See HOME.

AT PRECISELY. See AT ABOUT.

AT SOMETHING LIKE. See AT ABOUT.

(A)WAKE, (A)WAKEN

Summary: Of the four forms, wake *is used most frequently (46.5%),* with awaken *next in frequency (31.8%),* awake *next in frequency (20.2%),* and waken, *always used transitively, least frequently used.* (A)wake *and* awaken *are used intransitively and transitively, while* awake *and* wake *most often intransitively.*

Awake is generally an intransitive verb, with the preterit form of *awoke* or *awaked* and the past participial form of *awaked* (the archaic *awoken* is heard occasionally in speech). One may say, "I *awake* at six every morning," "I *awoke* at three this morning," and "I have just *awaked.*" This verb is sometimes employed transitively as well: "He *awaked* (or *awoke*) me about one o'clock," but with less frequency.

  Data: One study (Hotchner) shows that *awaken* (principal parts: *awaken, awakened, awakened*) occurs transitively 61.5% of the time, intransitively 38.5%. Examples of each usage are: "The excitement that *awakened* him so early was still growing" (*McCall's,* Nov., 1957, 88) and ". . . that is why we *awaken* naturally . . ." (*Coronet,* Nov., 1957, 60).

  The verbs *wake* (principal parts: *wake, waked* or *woke, waked* and rarely *woken*) and *waken* (principal parts: *waken, wakened, wakened*) are likewise transitive. The study cited shows *wake* as transitive 28%, *waken* 100% of the time. One may say "I *waked* (or *woke*) him at five," or "His own muttering *waked* him more" (Wilbur Daniel Steele, "How Beautiful with Shoes," cited by Kehl) and "I *wakened* him at five." *Up* is often attached to *wake,* as in "I *woke* him *up* at five," or "I *waked up* [intransitive] at five," common in the South and eastern New England in informal English. Another study (J. Jacobson) found seven examples of *woke,* five of which were used intransitively, as in "I *woke* at half past five" (*The New Yorker,* Sept. 17, 1960, 38) and two transitively as in "He *woke* her" (*Reader's Digest,* Aug., 1960, 105).

Wake is more often used intransitively, as in "Whether I *wake* or sleep," a more literary expression than the usual "Whether I am *awake* or asleep." *Wake up* is also employed as an intransitive verb, as in the example above and "Isn't it time that school boards, parents, and taxpayers *wake up* to such waste . . . ?" (*Reader's Digest,* Sept., 1957, 39). It is used this way 90% of the time (Hotchner). Another study found one example of the past participle used intransitively, none used transitively (M. Richardson).

In the passive, the more common forms are *waken* and *awaken:* "I was *wakened* (or *awakened*) by the fire engine."

The common form in the preterit is (*a*)*woke* and in the past participle (*a*)*waked.* One sometimes hears, however, (*a*)*waked* in the preterit. In British English, the past participles (*a*)*woke* and (*a*)*woken* are still used: "They *had woken* her from a deep sleep." The past participle (*a*)*woke*(*n*) is employed in American English only in speech, and most American dictionaries regard it as an archaic or rare form. Three studies (Bowden, Hotchner, Wittman) revealed that *wake* was used most frequently, the average being 46.5%. Next in frequency was *awaken,* (31.8%), then *awake* (20.2%). The verb that occurred least often was *waken.*

In addition to these numerous forms of the several verbs is the adjective *awake,* as in "The baby is *awake* (*not sleeping*)." In a recent study (Wittman) thirteen examples of the usage were found, as in "He arose before they were *awake*" (*Harper's,* Mar., 1958, 73).

Other evidence: Atwood, 25, 97; Bryant, *CE,* 18 (Nov., 1956), 111; Curme, *PSA,* 306, 318; Galinsky, II, 419-22; Kennedy, *Cur. Eng.,* 457; Kurath, *LANE,* Vol. III, Pt. 2, Map 668-69; R.I. McDavid, *AED,* 516; V.G. McDavid, 22, 50, 68, 69; R.I. and V.G. McDavid, *AS,* 35 (Feb., 1960), 14-15.

AWAY. See WAY, AWAY, adv.

AWFUL, adj., adv.; **AWFULLY,** adv.

Summary: Awful *is used in colloquial English as an adjective meaning* "ugly; very bad; ludicrous; shocking; disagreeable; very great; great." *It is also used colloquially as an adverb meaning* "exceedingly; very." *The adverb* awfully *occurs in informal English also with the meaning of* "exceedingly; very." Awful *was used as an adverb 31.25% of the time,* awfully *68.75%.*

Data: Sometimes *awful* is used to mean "great," as in "an *awful* lot of them" or "an *awful* bore," but it is generally used with the meaning above, in such statements as "You look *awful*" or "That's *awful.*" Four studies (Basse, Ethel Berkowitz, Pérez, Siegel) revealed that these meanings occur in conversation, on television, on the radio, or in written dialogue, as in ". . . let some fresh air in. It must be just *awful* in there" (*Collier's,* Dec. 13, 1952, 10). Forty-five examples of this usage were found.

Awful also may substitute for *awfully* in expressions like "It's *awful* good of you"; "This room is *awful* cold"; and "I was *awful* scared . . ." (*Collier's,* Nov. 29, 1952, 32). Used as an intensive to mean "very," *awful* occurred about one-third of the time, *awfully* the other two-thirds. The Linguistic Atlas survey of New England also shows divided usage for that section.

Other evidence: Bryant, *CE,* 16 (Feb., 1955), 310; Fries, *AEG,* 202-6; Krapp, 63; Kurath, *LANE,* Vol. III, Pt. 2, Map 716.

BACK OF. See (IN) BACK OF, BEHIND.

BAD, BADLY

Summary: Usage is almost evenly divided between feel bad *and* feel badly. *In spoken English, more examples of* feel badly *occurred; in formal written English, more examples of* feel bad. *With verbs like* look *and* sound, bad *is almost always preferred.*

Data: Some speakers differentiate between the two, as in "I felt *badly* when the old place burned" and "I felt *bad* because my stomach hurt," but quantitative studies (Elroy Berkowitz, Bowden, Conciglia, Haggerty, H. B. Levine, Mindlin, S. Silverstein, R. Thomas) reveal that among cultivated speakers usage is about evenly divided. This proportion holds also for the cultivated informants interviewed for the *Linguistic Atlas of New England,* but in three centers (Boston, Providence, and Portland) where there were five, four, and three informants respectively, only the cultivated informants used *badly* and it was the only form they used. The two cultivated informants in Newport were divided and one in Springfield used both.

In formal English, one will generally find *bad.* Ernest Hemingway, however, writes in *The Old Man and the Sea:* "At one time he was feeling so *badly* toward the end, he thought perhaps it was a dream." He uses both forms in *Green Hills of Africa:* "feel so *badly*" (p. 62); "feel *bad*" (p. 86); "feel *badly*" (p. 121); "feel *bad*" (p. 137); "felt very *badly*" (p. 190). Other striking examples are: ". . . the boys weren't too *badly* off" (Ernie Pyle, *Brave Men,* p. 289) and "It seems to me that the President and his genuine friends and supporters need not feel too *badly* because the Republicans have lost control of Congress" (Walter Lippmann, *Marquette* [Michigan] *Mining Journal,* Nov., 8, 1954, 6).

Other evidence: Feinsilver, *AS,* 24 (Oct., 1949), 161-70; Kurath, *LANE,* Vol. III, Pt. I, Map 493; Marckwardt and Walcott, 36, 103.

BARELY. See HARDLY.

BARREL(S). See LOT(S), HEAP(S).

BARRING. See PROVIDED, PROVIDING, conj.

BECAUSE. See AS, causal.

BECAUSE, ON ACCOUNT OF

Summary: On account of *occurs as a substitute for* because *only as a regional colloquialism.*

Data: In a context such as "I like him *because* he's so funny," a study (Malmstrom) based upon the Linguistic Atlas shows that *because* is practically universal in New England, the Middle Atlantic, the South Atlantic, the North Central States, and the Upper Midwest in the speech of all types of informants.

In Virginia, North Carolina, South Carolina, and Georgia, *on account of* occurs along with *because* in the speech of both the educated and the uneducated informants, but this usage is not expanding. In written English, only *because* occurs, except in represented speech.

Other evidence: Kurath, *LANE*, Vol. III, Pt. II, Map 729; Malmstrom, *SVTS*, 39, 264-65.

BECAUSE OF. See DUE TO, BECAUSE OF, OWING TO.

BEGIN, v.

Summary: Began *is the preferred preterit form in standard formal English, but both the nonstandard preterit forms of* begun *and* begin *are found in regional and British colloquial usage.*

Data: In standard formal and informal English, *began* is the preterit form of *begin* (principal parts: *begin, began, begun*), heavily preferred, according to Linguistic Atlas records, in New England, the Middle Atlantic, the South Atlantic, the North Central, and the Upper Midwest States by all types of informants (studies by Allen, Hotchner, Kehl, Malmstrom, Stevens).

The nonstandard *begun* occurs most frequently in New England and the Middle Atlantic States; the nonstandard *begin,* most frequently in the South Atlantic and North Central States, particularly in Kentucky. Both nonstandard variants are relatively rare in the Upper Midwest States. *Begun* also occurs in the common speech of England. More than half the 200 informants interviewed for the Linguistic Atlas of England used *begun* in the context, "It —— to rain." (W. Nelson Francis)

This particular variation, the old preterit plural, is common in verbs containing a nasal as in *sang/sung; sank/sunk; stank/stunk; shrank/shrunk; rang/rung.*

Other evidence: Atwood, 6; Bryant, *CE,* 17 (Feb., 1956), 313; Kurath, *LANE,* Vol. III, Pt. 2, Map 635; Malmstrom, *SVTS,* 92-93; R.I. McDavid, *AED,* 515; V.G. McDavid, 22-23; Menner, *AS,* 1 (Jan., 1926), 232; Pooley, *TEU,* 46-49.

BEHIND. See (IN) BACK OF, BEHIND.

BETTER. See HAD BETTER (BEST).

BETWEEN WITH MORE THAN TWO

Summary: In standard English between *is used in reference to two (80.7% of the time); or to more than two (19.3% of the time) in expressing the relation of a thing to other surrounding things severally and individually, as "an agreement* between *three persons"; to indicate intervals between similar objects or events which occur repeatedly: "between* songs," *"between* meals"; *to refer to the specific relation of a thing (or things) to separate specific things: "a number* between *ten and twenty"; to express joint participation or action: "between* us lawyers."

The *OED* states positively that in all senses *between* has been, from its earliest appearance in Old English more than a thousand years ago, extended to more than two, even in those utterances in which *among* is now considered better. It is still the only word available, according to the *OED,* to express the relation of a thing to many surrounding things severally and individually, *among* expressing a relation to them collectively and vaguely: we should not say "the space lying *among* the three points," or "a treaty *among* three powers," or "the choice lies *among* the three candidates in the select list," or "to insert a needle *among* the closed petals of a flower."

Data: Examples from recent studies (Benardete, Fisch, Haase, R. Thomas) include: "Let us go one step further and suppose that *between* the United States, Canada, and a vast rich country such as Brazil, there could be established an agreement under which . . ." (Louis Bromfield, *A New Pattern for a Tired World,* 1954, p. 90). In *The Atlantic Monthly,* Walter Macken writes, *"Between* sobs and groans and the streaming tears" ("The King," June, 1951,

37). Another illustration is "There are more tensions than ties *between* India and Pakistan, Burma, East Africa, and those other Indian Ocean countries where the Indian merchant and laborer set up a number of disturbing problems" (*ibid.,* Mar., 1951, 17). Other illustrations from this magazine may be cited, but it may be well to illustrate from a different type of periodical, such as *High Points* (New York City Board of Education Publication), where one may find "to show the interrelationship *between* peoples, races, and cultures" (Jan., 1952, 25); "To promote friendly . . . relations *between* U.S.A. and our 20 sister republics of Latin America"; "But the important difference *between* these compositions and those written last year and those by the present seventh-grade pupils is in the awareness of the dangers. . . ." Many other illustrations may be cited to show that *between* may refer to more than two in specific usages. The proverbial expression *between you and me and the lamppost* (*gatepost*), meaning "in confidence," helps to establish and preserve this usage. So does *between us,* which often includes more than two persons. On the other hand, when more than two is considered collectively as a group, the preposition *among* is regularly employed (Sternberg), as in "They distributed the books *among* the foreign students."

There is also another use of *between* involving more than two. It indicates intervals between similar objects or events which occur repeatedly: *between dances; between the acts; between songs; between meals.* Another like usage refers to the specific relation of a thing (or things) to separate specific things: "the opening *between* the shutters"; "a number *between* one and ten." Similar to this usage is the expression *between each,* equivalent to "between each two," when speaking of a series, as in "The concert consisted of twelve numbers with a short intermission *between each.*"

In a recent reading in periodicals one investigator (Vilardi) found that out of sixty-nine examples of *between,* fifty-five (79.7%) examples were used with two and fourteen (20.3%) were used with more than two. In three of the aforementioned studies *between* was used with two in 80.7% and with more than two in 19.3% of the cases. One can therefore see that *between* may be used with two or with more than two.

Other evidence: Jespersen, *MEG*, Pt. II, 7.761; Marckwardt and Walcott, 36, 107; Pooley, *TEU*, 135-37; Rice, *EJ*, XXVI (Jan., 1937), 66-68.

BETWEEN EACH. See *BETWEEN* WITH MORE THAN TWO.

BIT. See BITE, v.

BITE, v.

Summary: The preterit bit *and the past participle* bitten *are standard English, but the form* bit *(past participle) is a regional colloquialism.*

Data: One study (Rosenthal) shows that "He was *bit* by a dog," "He got *bit* by a dog," *dogbit, snakebit* occur in speech and represented speech, but not in formal English.

Another study (Malmstrom) shows that *bitten* predominates in Type III (cultivated) speech in New England, the Middle Atlantic, the South Atlantic, the North Central States, and the Upper Midwest, and in Type II (people of some secondary education) speech in the Northern dialect areas. It shows, further, that *bit* is distinctly a South Midland colloquial form, a fact underlined by the even more evident parallel occurrence of *dogbit* almost universally in Type II speech in the South Midland areas of the East and frequently in Type II in Kentucky, south Ohio, and Indiana, as well as in South Carolina.

Other evidence: Atwood, 6; Kurath, *LANE*, Vol. III, Pt. 2, Map 636; Malmstrom, *SVTS*, 95-96; R.I. McDavid, *AED*, 521; V.G. McDavid, 23; R.I. and V.G. McDavid, *AS*, 35 (Feb., 1960), 14; Wentworth, 59.

BLACK. See COMPARISON, ILLOGICAL.

BLAME . . . FOR (ON)

Summary: Both locutions occur in standard English with about equal frequency.

Although some writers avoid *blame* followed by *on,* preferring "Do not *blame* him *for* the accident" to "Do not *blame* the accident *on* him," nevertheless the latter construction appears regularly in standard usage, as several studies demonstrate (Benardete, Hook, Horn, Sloan, R. Thomas, Winburne).

Data: In a reading of *Time* (Feb. to May, 1957), one investigator found *blame . . . on* five times, *blame . . . for* three times. From daily newspapers come the following illustrations: ". . . [he] *blamed* this *on* 'poor planning and wasteful practices' " (*New York Herald Tribune,* Nov. 20, 1957, 1) and this headline from that newspaper: "DORIA SINKING *BLAMED ON* FAULTY SAFETY RULES (Jan. 4, 1957, Sec. II, 1). In *The New York Times,* Peter Kihss writes: "The Communist national convention *blamed* the party's political isolation here chiefly *on* Left-sectarian errors." (Feb. 12, 1957, 3).

Both locutions are used by James M. Cain in one work: ". . . there was no sense *blaming* him *for* things that were rapidly becoming too much for her" (*Mildred Pierce,* 1948, p. 30) and "She was quite explicit about *blaming* this all *on* Bert . . ." (p. 18).

BLOW, v.

Summary: The preterit blew *and the past participle* blown *are formal standard English; the form* blowed *is limited to Type I (uneducated) and II (those with at least some secondary school education) speech.*

Data: Studies (Allen, Kehl, Malmstrom, Rothman) show that *blew* is the standard form, as in the context "The wind *blew* hard." According to the Linguistic Atlas records, it is universally preferred in Type III (cultivated) speech in New England, the Middle Atlantic, the South Atlantic, the North Central, and the Upper Midwest States.

Blowed (always heard in the expression "I'll be *blowed*") is very frequent in the speech of Type II informants in the Midland dialect areas of the Atlantic coast and predominates heavily in Type II in the South Atlantic States. In other areas, it is generally limited to Type I speech.

Other verbs in which the use of the preterit and past participle follows the same regional pattern are: *grow, know, throw, draw.* A study of the verb *know* (Garey) found eighty-four examples of the preterit *knew,* six of the variant *knowed,* and one of the past participle *knowed* used by the illiterate members of society: ". . . the next time they seed him they wouldn't have *knowed* him except for the cap, the coat and them Irish britches gone now . . ." says an uneducated character in William Faulkner's *A Fable,* 1950, p. 196.

Other evidence: Atwood, 6; Eliason, 246; Kurath, *LANE,* Vol. III, Pt. 2, Map 637; Malmstrom, *SVTS,* 98-99; V.G. McDavid, 23-24; Wentworth, 63.

BLOWED. See BLOW, v.

BOIL, v. See KNEEL, v.

BOTH. See AGREEMENT, INDEFINITE PRONOUNS.

BOUGHT(EN)

Summary: Bought *is the generally accepted past participle of* buy, *but* boughten *appears in cultivated regional speech.*

Data: According to one study (Malmstrom) of the Linguistic Atlas records for New England, the Middle Atlantic, the Southern Atlantic, the North Central, and the Upper Midwest States, *boughten* as an attributive (*"boughten* bread") is distinctly a Northern and North Midland usage. Wherever this usage is part of the regional dialect, it is used by cultivated speakers as well as those less well educated. In other dialect areas, *bought* is used if this lexical variant is chosen to describe "baker's bread," especially in Type I (uneducated) and Type II (those with at least some secondary school education) speech in the South and South Midland.

Bought, however, has not become a generally acceptable adjective, but it does occur, as in "a *bought* dress" as distinguished from one made at home. The author of "Button Notes" in the magazine *Hobbies* (Hotchner) chose the variant *boughten* to describe buttons, but put it in quotation marks: ". . . most of them have associations and histories which few *'boughten'* buttons of today can boast" (Sept. 1957, 52). One extensive study (Sforza) showed that *boughten* never occurs in standard English as a past participle.

Other evidence: Atwood, 7-8; Malmstrom, *SVTS,* 104; R.I. McDavid, *AED,* 526; V.G. McDavid, 25; R.I. and V.G. McDavid, *AS,* 35 (Feb., 1960), 11-12, 16, 17; Wentworth, 70.

BREAK, v.

Summary: The preterit broke *and the past participle* broken *are standard English;* broke *as a past participle is found in nonstandard English.*

Data: Several studies (Abowitz, Hotchner, A. M. Smith, Strong) show that *broken,* rather than *broke,* occurs as standard usage in this context: "The glass is *broke/broken.*" However, in the common speech of England, usage is divided in the context "I have *broke/broken* it," with a tendency toward regional distribution. Thus in the records of the Linguistic Atlas of England, *broken* is almost universal in the North, *broke* in the Southwest, with usage mixed in the Midlands (W. Nelson Francis).

In America, the use of *broke,* meaning "without money," is standard formal English, as in ". . . Turkey is unquestionably *broke"* (*New York Post,* Aug. 16, 1957) and ". . . any United States citizen—be he wealthy or *broke"* (*The New York Times,* May 1, 1955, Sec., 1, 29).

A colloquial use of broke as an attributive occurs in the expression "a *broke* horse," referring to a tamed animal, and it occurs as a noun in the expression, "Go for *broke,"* meaning "to gamble for everything."

Other evidence: Atwood, 7; Barnhart, Files; Wentworth, 77.

BRING, v.

Summary: The preterit brought *and the past participle* brought *are standard English;* brung *and* brang *are nonstandard.*

Data: According to one study of the Linguistic Atlas records

(Malmstrom), in the context "I *have brought* your coat," *brought* as the past participle predominates heavily in the speech of all types in New England, the Middle Atlantic, South Atlantic, North Central, and Upper Midwest States. *Brung* is rare everywhere and *brang* is even more rare. *Done bring* is used by a few Southern Negroes, *broughten* occurs only once, and *bringed* is not used at all.

In written English, according to one study (Abowitz), only *brought* occurs. In speech and comedy shows, however, one may occasionally hear *brung* used for humorous effect or to indicate a person with little education, as in "See what I *brung* you," and "I didn't forget to *brung* it" ("The Honeymooners," WRCA, Nov. 6, 1958).

Other evidence: Atwood, 7; Kurath, *LANE*, Vol. III, Pt. 2, Map 638; Malmstrom, *SVTS*, 101; V.G. McDavid, 24-25.

BROADCAST, v.

Summary: The preterit and past participial form in standard English is broadcast, broadcasted *occurring rarely.*

Data: Two studies (Haase, Kennedy) found only the form *broadcast,* as in "He *broadcast* yesterday from WNYC" and "The lengthy Red Star reference . . . *was broadcast* today by Moscow radio" (*New York World-Telegram and Sun,* Jan. 6, 1957, 5). *Broadcast,* like *cast* and *forecast,* has the same form in all tenses.

BROKE. See BREAK, v.

BURST, v.

Summary: The principal parts in standard English are: burst, burst, burst (*see* bust). Bursted *and* bustin' *are nonstandard forms.*

Data: In four studies (Hotchner, Kehl, Winburne, Wittman), only *burst* was found, as in ". . . he ran at it with his shoulder; it *burst* at the latch, went slamming in . . ." (Wilbur Daniel Steele, "How Beautiful With Shoes," *Fifty Great Short Stories,* p. 312) and ". . . Monty *burst* into howls of laughter . . ." (James M. Cain, *Mildred Pierce,* 1948, p. 128).

Bustin' instead of *bursting* occurs in the semiclassical song, "Spring is *bustin'* out all over," but this is in an uneducated Western context. It occurs also in represented speech, as in "Y' know that wild steer that was always *bustin'* outta the pasture?" (*Saturday Evening Post,* Oct. 26, 1957, 62).

Other evidence: Atwood, 7; Kurath, *LANE,* Vol. III, Pt. II, Map 639.

B U S H E L (S). See LOT(S), HEAP(S).

B U S T, v., n.

Summary: Bust (*and its preterit and past participle* busted *and its present participle* busting) *occur as (1) nonstandard variants of* burst *(2) informal or special terms meaning roughly* "break." Bust *meaning* "failure" *occurs as a standard noun.*

Data: Four studies of this word (Gabel, O'Rourke, Winburne, Wittman) reveal that in its second sense, *bust* is not a variant of *burst,* but a different word: nobody says or writes *trust-bursting, block-bursting, racket-bursting, bursted in rank,* yet *bust* in each of these combinations leads to standard informal wording. An example is ". . . he is condoning their *union-busting* tactics" (*U. S. News & World Reports,* Nov. 1, 1957, 97). A *middlebuster,* a double moldboard plow used in the South, illustrates the specialized use of a variant.

In its first sense, the word *break* is often substituted as in "The dam (balloon) *broke.*" Conversely, for *break, bust* may be substituted, for example, in reference to an axle or nose: "His nose was *busted* in last week's fight" ("The Joe Palooka Story," TV program, Mar. 31, 1956). This usage is heard often when it is necessary to imply a feeling stronger than "burst" or "break," but it is an inelegant, low colloquial form.

A noun has also developed, as in *"boom* and *bust,"* illustrated in ". . . and the *boom* inevitably becomes a *bust"* (*Wall Street Journal,* Nov. 11, 1955, 6) and "Money managers figure that business showing will prevent a *bust"* (*U. S. News & World Report,* Nov. 1,

1957, 24). This usage is standard. As a noun it may also refer to a spree of any kind, as in "He was going on a *bust*."

From *bust* has developed the colloquial expression *bust up,* used both as a noun and a verb, as in "Then came the *bust up* . . . for the Prince and out he got . . ." (John P. Marquand, *So Little Time,* 1943, p. 372) and "You mean you've *busted up?*" (James M. Cain, *Mildred Pierce,* 1948, p. 20). Similar expressions are *bust out* and *bust in,* employed as verbs.

The evidence of four studies (Gabel, Hotchner, McMillan, O'Rourke) show that *bust* occasionally occurs with the meaning of "to be bankrupt," as in "When the war was over, Baltimore's good customer, the South, was *busted*" (*Saturday Evening Post,* May 11, 1956, 55). This usage is colloquial.

Other evidence: Atwood, 7; Barnhart, Files; Kurath, *LANE,* Vol. III, Pt. 2, Map 639; Mathews, *DA,* 229; Russell, *AS,* 23 (Dec., 1948), 290-93.

BUT AT THE BEGINNING OF A SENTENCE. See *AND (BUT, OR, NOR)* AT THE BEGINNING OF A SENTENCE.

BUT THAT. See BUT WHAT, conj., rel. pro.

BUT WHAT, conj., rel. pro.

Summary: *The expression* but what *is standard usage as (1) a relative pronoun meaning* "but that," "but who," *or* "that . . . not" *and (2) as a conjunction after words like* "doubt" *and* "fear" *and in negative statements.* But that *and* that *are used interchangeably with* but what.

Data: An example of the first usage is: "There is no one *but what* would consider this act unwise." The simple relative *what,* meaning "that" or "which" is no longer standard English, as in "A kitten *what* wouldn't eat.' *That* would be substituted in current standard English.

Examples of the second usage come from two studies (Karlin, M. Richardson): "We are not sure *but what* this particular police dog is in contempt . . . ("The Squirrel Cage," an editorial, *New*

York Journal-American, Mar. 5, 1958) and "There is little doubt *but what* Mr. Baruch's venture into autobiography . . ." (Charles Poore, *The New York Times,* Nov. 21, 1957, 35M). *But that* as a variant is illustrated by "I don't know *but that* I should let my son buy . . ." (Sam Shulsky's Financial Column, *Chicago American,* Oct. 15, 23). Another variant is *but,* which occurs often in New England, according to the Linguistic Atlas, in a context like "I don't know *but* (*but that* or *but what*) I'd better do it," meaning "I think I'd better do it."

Similarly, we have "I don't know *that* (*as* or *whether*) I'd better do it," which has the negative meaning "I think I'd better not do it." For instance, "I don't know *but what* (*but that*) I'd better write" signifies an intention to write, *but* "I don't know *as* (*whether* or *that*). . . ." implies doubt on the part of the speaker and does not show an intention to write.

Comparative studies (Abelack, Bowden, J. Cohen, Hotchner, Kevilin, Kovitz, Richardson, Schauer) found *but what* occurring 28.6% of the time, *but that* 23.8%, and *that* alone 47.6%, all of which were in negative statements.

Other evidence: Curme, *PSA,* 97-101; Kurath, *LANE,* Vol. III, Pt. 2, Map 731.

B U Y, n.

Summary: purchase *is the standard formal word for* "something bought," *but by means of functional shift from the verb,* buy *occurs in informal usage.*

Buy conveys succinctly and briefly the idea of a bargain, an advantageous purchase, something bought or to be bought at a gain to the buyer. It is, therefore, used for signs, in advertisements, and in colloquial speech.

Data: One study (Mindlin) did not find a single example of *buy* as a noun, but another (Levy) found a number of illustrations, among them: "Feast your eyes on the A & P *buys!*" (*New York Post,* May 28, 1956, 19) and "The most for your money! Our 17,000 excellent *buys!*" (*Linn's Weekly Stamp News,* May 28,

1956, 19). Signs may bear the words: "Best *buys* in town!" or the next-door neighbor may say: "There were some wonderful *buys* at the auction."

Occasionally, *buy* refers to the "act of buying," as in the expression "to make a *buy* of grain," but generally it conveys the idea of something bought or to be bought, especially at bargain rates.

Buy has also been used in a novel way in the title of a weekly newspaper column giving new food ideas and specifying particular brands to buy: *"Buy-Lines"* by Nancy Sassar, *New York Daily News,* Feb. 16, 1956, 54.

Other evidence: Mathews, *DA,* 233.

BY ABOUT. See AT ABOUT.

CALF, n. See HOOF, n.

CAN, MAY, v.

Summary: In formal standard English, can *expresses power or ability and* may *expresses possibility or permission. However, on all levels of speech* can *is used to express permission.*

In Old English, *may* had the meaning of "to be able" and *can* in addition to meaning "know" meant "know how to," "to be able to." Through the centuries, confusion has arisen and at present *can* is often used to express permission instead of *may.*

Data: Studies of written dialogue and speech (A. Daly, Haase, Herold, Hotchner, Silberg) produced the following illustrations of *can* meaning permission: " 'You *can* tell her for me there's nobody dangerous on this train,' he said" (Mary Roberts Rinehart, *The Swimming Pool,* 1952, p. 40); "You *can* eat up the rest of the brownies" (*Saturday Evening Post,* Mar. 21, 1953, 151).

Can is almost universally employed in negative expressions instead of the unused *mayn't.* "Why *can't* I go to the beach?" will be used rather than "Why *mayn't* I go to the beach?" and the negative answer is likely to be "You *can't.*" Even if the question is *"May I go?"* a negative answer may well be "You *can't* go today, for I want you to meet your father at the airport." *Can* is, therefore, standard usage in the negative. Children also generally employ the negative *can't* in asking permission: *"Can't* I go to the movies tonight?"

The above studies also show that *may* is used to express permission in formal written English, almost without exception.

Other evidence: Haase, *CE,* 11 (Jan., 1950), 215-16; Pooley, *TEU,* 137-39.

CAN'T HARDLY. See HARDLY.

CAN'T (CANNOT), COULDN'T (COULD NOT) HELP BUT

Summary: Can't (cannot) help but *plus the infinitive is standard English. It occurs in spoken and written English. Usage is divided between this construction and* cannot help *plus the gerund, with the latter occurring more frequently in formal written English.*

Data: Cannot help but appears to be the modern version of the older *cannot choose but* and has the same grammatical pattern. It has been employed by cultivated writers for more than fifty years, as several studies showed (Everson, Hahn, Hotchner, R. Jacobson, Kalina, McMillan, Russell, R. Thomas, Wells, Winburne) and hence is well established, as in, "Henry, deep in the guilt of his desertion, *cannot help but* regard Jim Conklin as a Christ figure . . ." (*Kenyon Review,* Spring, 1953, 313); "And *cannot help but* see him, day after day" (Stephen Vincent Benet, *Western Star,* 1943); "Mr. Wagner goes on to point out how this process *cannot help but* corrupt the reading tastes of the masses" (John Ciardi, *Saturday Review,* Feb. 16, 1957, 55).

Some authors employ *cannot help* plus the gerund and *cannot help but* in the same work, as in "We *couldn't help* liking a lot of the Italians" (Ernie Pyle, *Brave Men,* 1944, p. 218); and "One *could not help but* be moved by the colossus of our invasion" (*ibid.,* p. 465).

In edited American English, *cannot help* plus a gerund (*cannot help going*) occurs most frequently. *Cannot but* plus an infinitive (*cannot but* go) also occurs (*See* NOT . . . BUT). Other variants are: *can but* plus infinitive (*can but go*) and *cannot help but* plus infinitive (*cannot help but go*).

Other evidence: Bryant, *CE*, 17 (Apr., 1956), 414; Kadison, *AS*, 30 (Feb., 1955), 55-56; Thomas, *CE*, 10 (Oct., 1948), 38-39.

CAN'T SEEM TO

Summary: The informal expression can't seem to *occurs in standard conversational English.*

Data: Three studies (Berman, A. Collins, Lichtman) turned up no examples of this expression in formal written English, but discovered a number of illustrations in spoken English, dialogue, and interoffice communications. Examples are: "Since that time, I *cannot seem* to do anything to please her" (*Los Angeles Examiner,* June 21, 1955, II, 4). The expression is a colloquial effort to qualify or to be tentative. "I *can't seem* to find it" is less positive than "I can't find it." It is also simpler than the variants *do not seem able to, seem not to be able to,* or *seem unable to.* It probably grew up with constructions like "I don't seem to have . . ." and "He doesn't seem to be aware of . . ." Speakers who say uncertainly or worriedly, "I *can't seem* to . . ." apparently use other devices in writing, except when being deliberately informal.

Other evidence: Bryant, *CE*, 17 (Apr., 1956), 414; Marckwardt and Walcott, 40, 120.

CASE, GENITIVE OF NOUNS THAT NAME INANIMATE THINGS

Summary: Although the phrasal genitive (light of the moon) *is more common than the inflected genitive case* (moon's light) *of inanimate nouns, standard usage is variable.*

Data: From available evidence and two new studies (Baron, Emblen), three classes of nouns may be distinguished:

(1) those which always employ the -*s* case form: (a) *month's salary, minute's peace,* etc. (b) *arm's length, hair's breadth* (c)

dollar's worth, pity's sake, etc. (d) *Campbell's soups, Boeing's plant,* etc.

(2) those which never employ the *-s* case form: *cost of shoes, bat of an eye, man of determination* (not *shoes' cost, eye's bat,* etc.)

(3) those which employ either the *-s* case form or the phrasal genitive indifferently: *earth's surface, surface of the earth; war's end, end of the war,* etc. Akin to this group are collective nouns which name organizations or groups of people: *committee's work, work of the committee; Belgium's premier, premier of Belgium;* whether nouns like *committee* and *Belgium* name animate or inanimate referents is a matter of arbitrary definition. Note that some of these have a third form: *committee work,* etc., employing the common case rather than the *-s* case form of the phrasal genitive. *See* GENITIVE CASE.

Other evidence: Bryant, *CE,* 16 (Oct., 1954), 55-56; Curme, *Syntax,* 75; Fries, *Lang.,* XIV (Apr.-June, 1938), 121-23; Hall, 204; Jespersen, *MEG,* Pt. VII, 9.5ff.; Thomas, *CE,* 14 (Jan., 1953), 236-39.

CASE, OF NOUN OR PRONOUN SUBJECT OF A
GERUND

Summary: In written formal English, both nouns and pronouns almost always occur in the genitive case before a gerund.

Data: In sentences like "What was the reason for *Bennett* [or *Bennett's*] leaving the church?" and "Do you remember *him* [or *his*] making a disturbance?" prescientific grammar chose the genitive forms (*Bennett's* and *his*), ruling that the subject of a gerund must always be in the genitive. Fries found (*AEG*) only one instance of an inflected genitive noun before a gerund: "There can be no objection to Sergeant S———'s making an application. . . ." The uninflected noun was "overwhelmingly" predominant, e.g., "There is no necessity for her *son* being with her." Concerning the pronoun he found the usage almost evenly divided, the genitive occurring 52% of the time. The usage is too complicated for a simple rule, even though three studies (Drdek, Rollnick, Tidwell) support the summary above: therefore, several qualifications are necessary:

1. The genitive case is used (a) when the gerund is the subject or complement of the verb: *"Miller's* gambling was his undoing" and (b) when the gerund must be distinguished from the participle: "The doctor explained *Miller's* sneezing" in contrast to "The doctor hated to see *Miller* sneezing."

2. The genitive case is impossible when (a) the subject (like *this, these, some,* or *both*) has no specific form for the genitive: "He objected to so *few* being admitted," and (b) the subject of the gerund is a clause or a phrase or is modified by a clause or a phrase: "The miners objected to *anyone* who had a family taking the risk" and "They objected to *anyone* with a family taking the risk."

3. When the gerund is the object of a verb or preposition and its subject has a genitive form, usage is divided. In sentences like "We were aware of Mr. *Miller* [or *Miller's*] having been an athlete," both forms occur. In sentences like "We were aware of *him* [or *his*] having been an athlete" *his* is more common in written English, where the genitive of personal pronouns is preferred to the objective case. In the studies, the genitive of the personal pronoun occurred in 90.3% of the examples and the objective in 9.7%. When the subject of the gerund is a noun naming an inanimate thing or an abstraction, either the genitive or the common case is used indifferently: "There is no question of the *state* [or *state's*] having the power." But when the subject receives the intended emphasis, it may occur in the common case (if a noun) or objective case (if an inflected pronoun): "Can you imagine the *state* (or *it*) having the power?" or "Can you imagine John (or *him*) having to work all night?"

Other evidence: Bartlett, *CE,* 11 (May, 1950), 456-57; Fries, *AEG,* 76-77, 84-85; Hall, 136-43; Pooley, *AS,* 8 (Apr., 1933), 63-66; *TEU,* 113-19.

CATCH, v.

Summary: The preterit and past participle caught *occur in standard English;* catched *is nonstandard.*

Data: According to one study of the Linguistic Atlas records (Malmstrom), the preterit of *catch* in the context, "Who *caught* it?" is strongly predominant in all areas among all types, and appears to be universal in the Upper Midwest.

The nonstandard variants *catched* (almost always pronounced [kɛtʃt]), *ketched,* and *cotch* are relatively rare and widely scattered in distribution. Note, however, that the standard pronunciation of *catch* [kætʃ] has a standard variant [kɛtʃ], heard not infrequently in the speech of Type III informants (with four years of college education). One study found none of these variants in writing (Kehl).

Other evidence: Atwood, 8; Kurath, *LANE,* Vol. III, Pt. 2, Map 641; Malmstrom, *SVTS,* 107-8; R.I. McDavid, *CE,* 14 (Feb., 1953), 290-91; V.G. McDavid, 25-26; Wentworth, 100, 136.

C A T C H E D. See CATCH, v.

C H A R G E S, *sing.* **See GROUNDS,** *sing.*

C L I M B, v.

Summary: The preterit and past participle climbed *is standard English.* Clim *and* clum *are nonstandard.*

Data: According to one study of the available records of the Linguistic Atlas (Malmstrom), the preterit *climbed* in the context "He *climbed* up a tree" and the past participle in the context "I *have* often *climbed* up" are practically identical in proportion and distribution, and practically universal in Type III (cultivated) speech in all areas.

Two nonstandard variants are in frequent use: *clim* and *clum.* The evidence shows that *clim* is principally Northern and dying, while *clum* is Midland and still alive. *Clim* also occurs in the South in Type I (uneducated) and Type II (those with at least some secondary school education) speech. In Eastern Virginia the form *clome* occurs in Type I speech. In written English, only *climbed* occurs (Blumengarten).

Other evidence: Atwood, 8-9; Kurath, *LANE,* Vol. III, Pt. 2, Map 642; Malmstrom, *SVTS,* 109-11; R.I. McDavid, *AED,* 515, 519, 523; V.G. McDavid, 26-27; R.I. and V.G. McDavid, *AS,* 35 (Feb., 1960), 13, 16.

COLLECTIVE NOUNS. See AGREEMENT, COLLECTIVE NOUNS.

COMBINE, n.

Summary: The noun combine, *from the verb, occurs in informal standard usage. The alternative,* combination, *occurs more frequently (63% of the time, against 37% for* combine).

Combine as a noun has long been accepted in standard English when it refers to a farm machine which harvests, threshes, and cleans grain in one series of operations as it moves over the field, but another meaning has developed, referring to an alliance of persons or organizations for the purpose of furthering their commercial, political, or other interests. This meaning, often employed interchangeably with *combination,* is accepted by the businessman, the radio and television commentator, the man in the street, and the professional writer in social studies. Therefore, though less preferable than the longer form, it is accepted usage, as one study shows (Rappa).

Data: Professional writers in the social studies use both terms without distinction. For example, Corwin D. Edward and Theodore J. Kreps in *A Cartel Policy for the United Nations* (1955) employ both terms: "This qualification was meant to distinguish cartels from *combines* or trusts" (p. 4); "The state of Kansas was more successful in an action the same year (1893) against a similar *combination*" (p. 4).

Writers in other fields also use the word, as in "But law violation has not been the biggest sin of the food *combines*" (Norman Cousins, *Current History,* Feb., 1938, 27) and ". . . Fiat, Italy's biggest industrial *combine* . . ." ("Foreign News—Italy," *Time,* Apr. 22, 1957, 40).

Some writers, particularly those writing in periodicals and newspapers, have extended the meaning to convey the idea of intrigue, as in: "The Macmillan idea of the U.S.-British *combine* against Nasser outside the U.N. is not in the cards" ("Worldgram," *U. S. News & World Report,* Mar. 29, 1957, 97); ". . . one of the three Midwest cities where the gambling *combine* operates" (George Carpozi, Jr., "Report Big Bets on 'Sugar' to Win," *New York Journal-American,* May 4, 1957, 1).

Other evidence: Bryant, *CE,* 19 (Dec., 1957), 130; Lee, 1-2; Mathews, *DA,* 363-64.

COME, v.

Summary: The preterit came *and the past participle* come *are standard English;* come *as a preterit is nonstandard.*

Data: According to one study of the Linguistic Atlas records (Malmstrom) and one other study (Edelman), *came* is the standard preterit in the context "He *came* over to see me," predominating strongly in all areas. The variant *come* occurs in all major speech areas and predominates in Type II (those with at least some secondary education) speech in the Middle Atlantic and South Atlantic States. Therefore, in these areas, it is characteristically colloquial though in other areas it is characteristic of only uneducated or old-fashioned usage.

Other evidence: Atwood, 9; Kurath, *LANE,* Vol. III, Pt. 2, Map 640; Malmstrom, *SVTS,* 113; V.G. McDavid, 27.

COME AND. See TRY AND.

COMPARATIVE, ABSOLUTE

Summary: In this construction, the comparative is employed even though the idea of comparison has practically disappeared from the expression. It is used in informal standard English.

Data: Common examples of this construction were found by investigators (Eldin, Fetouh, Hotchner) in "higher education," "the better life," "the younger generation," "at better stores everywhere," where the comparative is assumed to have greater strength than the superlative. Also, a man in years may not object to being called an "older man," whereas he may dislike very much being termed an "old man," for "older" seems less old than "old." So it is with "larger women," "lower classes," etc., where the comparative seems more polite than the simple form of the adjective.

In the business world, the absolute comparative is common, as in *"better* stores," *"better* dresses," the latter designating a special department in most of the "larger" department stores where "higher priced" dresses are sold.

With the use of the absolute comparative, the comparison is rather difficult to complete, even impossible sometimes, for the comparison is usually vague and uncertain. If forced, a complicated and awkward structure may result from "Almost all the stories . . . come from the *smaller* quarterlies . . ." (*Saturday Review,* Dec. 14, 1957, 13) and similar structures.

Similarly, an absolute superlative is observed in "You are *most* generous" and "You are *most* kind," where *most* is only an intensive, not a superlative. This usage is common in spoken English and informal written English. Examples are: "The . . . Clinic was *most fortunate* to have Arline Evans as its administrator" (Elizabeth Seifert, *The New Doctor,* 1958, p. 3); "At *best,* dieting should never be undertaken in times of stress" (*Reader's Digest,* Aug., 1958, 109); "Mr. Kramer has done so with a distinction that places him on a level with Hollywood's *best"* (*Saturday Review,* July 26, 1958, 23); ". . . it can *most* certainly become a welter of mediocrity" (*Esquire,* July, 1958, 24).

Other evidence: Sheldon, *AS,* 20 (Oct., 1945), 161-67.

COMPARATIVE, INCOMPLETE

Summary: The incomplete comparative or the implied comparison occurs in informal standard usage.

The incomplete comparative is a comparative in which the conclusion is not expressed, but is easily supplied by the reader, as in "Read in the living room; it's lighter there" ["than here"]; John is better today" ["than he was before"]. The implied comparison, as shown above, is generally with another place, time, or condition, and not with another thing or other things, unless the object with which the comparison is made is clear from the context.

Data: Five studies (S. Cohen, Eldin, Fetouh, Hotchner, A. M. Thomas) produced a number of examples of this usage typical of which is "His parents wanted a *better* standard for their son . . ." ["than that of the town"] (*Saturday Review,* Dec. 14, 1957, 12). In much advertising copy, expressions like *"Milder, better*-tasting cigarettes" are commonplace, the public expected to complete the comparison to the conclusion that the advertised article is better than that of any competitor. The advertiser favors this usage for apparently legal and psychological reasons.

There is a tendency to use the comparative degree where a positive would do. *See* COMPARATIVE, ABSOLUTE.

Other evidence: Sheldon, *AS,* 20 (Oct., 1945), 161-67.

COMPARISON, DUAL

Summary: The dual comparison ("as well or better than"; "as heavy if not heavier than") *occurs in standard English.*

Since the eighteenth century, textbooks have frowned upon such locutions, suggesting that the writer insert *as* after "well" and "heavy" or to write, "as heavy as George, if not heavier."

Data: Quantitative evidence is lacking on alternatives to dual construction, but studies (Golub, Hotchner, Russell, R. Thomas) of sources such as *Harper's, Life,* and *The New York Times* support the usage. An editor writes: "In Philadelphia she lived on Chestnut Hill, which considers itself *as good if not better than* the Main Line . . ." (*Life,* Apr. 15, 1940, 5-6). A college professor writes: ". . . the prospects for the fall are *as good or better than* they were last year" (*The News Letter of the College English Association,* Sept., 1942). A columnist writes: "The President is a political fundamentalist *as much or more so than* any chief executive of recent memory" (*The New York Times,* June 25, 1950, E3). In view of this evidence, the locution can hardly be called nonstandard.

Other evidence: Leonard, *Doctrine of Correctness,* 286.

COMPARISON, ILLOGICAL

Summary: The *"superlative* + any" *in constructions like* "the greatest of any"; "the largest of any" *occurs in informal and sometimes formal English; also, many of the absolute adjectives, such as* perfect, round, dead, complete *are used comparatively in informal English.*

Data: The first construction has been employed by writers since the time of Chaucer. Examples are: ". . . because the finback has the *tallest* spout of *any* whale" (R. C. Murphy, *Logbook for Grace,* 1947, p. 147); "Its population would have remained the *most* carefully screened of *any* body of settlers ever to have come to America" (*The New York Times Book Review,* Apr. 20, 1947, 7).

This construction is a variant of the partitive genitive, an analogical development from a true partitive, as in "the best of the dresses." Similarly, a true partitive *either of them* has given rise to false partitives by analogy, such as *both of them* and *all of them,* now standard formal English, illogical as they may seem in suggesting that a whole may be a part. The superlative with *any* may at times be a true partitive when *any* is a plural: "The American people *are* the *most* conservative . . . of *any people* in the entire world" (*The Atlantic Monthly,* Sept., 1944, 77). By analogy the superlative with the singular *any* has followed: "Operating on what Cott states is the *lowest* program budget of *any* local commercial station in a major city . . ." (*Saturday Review,* Aug. 2, 1958, 21). Considering the caliber of writers who have used this construction through the centuries, one cannot call it substandard, even though many writers will avoid it. One study (Raybin) turned up no examples of it, another (Fetouh) only two, but a third study found it used 29.4% of the time, whereas the logical comparison, the superlative *all,* occurred 70.6% of the time, as in "the loveliest of *all*" (*The New Yorker,* Aug. 2, 1958, 25) (Hotchner).

Occasionally, the comparative is also used illogically with *any,* as in: ". . . 'It would be a *more intolerable* wrong of nature *than any* which man has devised' " (*Reader's Digest,* Nov., 1957, 71).

However, the study cited above found that the logical construction with *any other* occurs 93.3% of the time, as in "He has served there *longer than any other* person in history . . ." (*Reader's Digest*, Aug., 1958, 89).

In like manner, adjectives like *perfect, unique, round, straight, dead, final, black, impossible, complete* are compared freely even though some textbooks contend that these adjectives should not be compared since their meaning is absolute; i.e., they name qualities that do not vary in degree. Yet a famous example comes from the Constitution: "We the people of the United States, in order to form a *more perfect* union. . . ."

In formal usage, one finds *more nearly perfect, more nearly round, more nearly complete* as in "The day we went to Belmont was the *most nearly perfect* in the history of the New York Weather Bureau . . ." (*The New Yorker*, July 26, 1958, 15). In common, general use, however, these words are not regarded as absolute in their meanings and in actual practice are frequently compared: "Of the three, this is the *blackest*"; "That was the *deadest* party I ever attended"; and ". . . the book is certainly the handiest, *most complete*, and generally reliable introduction to its subject" (*The New York Times Book Review*, May 11, 1958, 20). One study found words of this type compared 89% of the time (Hotchner).

Other evidence: Hughes, *CE*, 17 (Mar., 1956), 360-61; Kenyon, *CE*, 18 (Dec., 1956), 171-72; Newsome, *AS*, 13 (Feb., 1938), 27; Pooley, *TEU*, 121-23.

COMPARISON OF ABSOLUTES (PERFECT, UNIQUE, ROUND, ETC.). See COMPARISON, ILLOGICAL.

COMPLETE. See COMPARISON, ILLOGICAL.

CONCERNING. See PROVIDED, PROVIDING, conj.

CONSIDERABLE, CONSIDERABLY

Summary: In formal English, considerable *occurs before a noun, sometimes before the noun modifier; as an intensive, it is nonstandard;* considerably *occurs in colloquial English.*

Data: Illustrations of the first of the above usages were found in (Spetalnick): "He nevertheless remained in *considerable* awe of his old mentor" (Dale Kramer, *Ross and the New Yorker,* 1951, p. 254) and "It expects a *considerable* national circulation . . ." (*ibid.,* 63). However, one sometimes hears *considerable* used as a verb modifier, instead of *considerably:* "My niece aided *considerable* in moving" (A Texan over WABC, "Events of the Day," Apr. 2, 1956, 7:40 P.M.), but in formal and informal writing a clear distinction is kept: "Use of the profile form . . . entailed *considerable* danger" (Kramer, *op. cit.,* 248) and ". . . the switch was *considerably* more dramatic . . ." (Noel P. Busch, *Briton Hadden,* 1949, p. 189).

Considerable also occurs in nonstandard English in such contexts as "considerable odd," "considerable more," as evidenced by R. H. Thornton in *An American Glossary* (Vol. III), *Dialect Notes* (Vol. 3:6, 184, 210), and by the *OED.* Here *considerable* is an intensive. In colloquial English, the more frequent form is *considerably,* as in *"considerably* expensive," meaning "very expensive." However, it appears more often with the comparative, as in *"considerably* more expensive," patterning with "a good deal," "a lot," etc.

Other evidence: Bryant, *EJ,* XLV (May, 1956), 285; Dunlap, *AS,* 20 (Feb., 1945), 16.

CONSIDERING. See PROVIDED, PROVIDING, conj.

CONTACT, v.

Summary: Contact *as a verb occurs in colloquial and informal usage.*

Data: Though many people frown upon the use of *contact* as a verb to mean "get in touch with" or "meet," it is greatly used on radio and television and in the business world. From the business world, this usage has made its way into all levels of speech and one may now hear a clergyman, a lawyer, a librarian, and even a professor of English say, "If you want it, *contact* the owner," or "Mr. Brown *contacted* him last night about the meeting."

One study (Haase) found that in written usage it occurs principally in advertisements, as in *"Contact* your Frigidaire dealer today," from *Time* and *Life;* in business correspondence, as in "Have your representative *contact* us"; and in dialogue. However, it sometimes appears in other contexts: "All eight Trustees *contacted* agreed with . . ." (Editor, *Columbia Alumni News,* Mar., 1957, 4) and "Committee counsel Robert Kennedy said the probers have been informed that Pastor was *contacted* in the matter . . ." *(New York Daily News,* Sept. 19, 1958, 3).

Contact was once used widely in the early days of aviation to mean "start the motor."

Other evidence: Bryant, *CE,* 16 (Jan., 1955), 247; Horwill, 81-82; Lee, 1-2; *OED.*

CONTRACTIONS

Summary: Contractions occur frequently in articles of an informal nature, in the writings of columnists, and in discussions of various topics of the day. They are standard usage.

A contraction is a word or word pattern which has been syncopated in common use. In writing, it is marked by an apostrophe which replaces the missing letter(s), as in: *"I've"* [aɪv] for "I have" [ˈaɪ hæv] "you're" [jur] for *you are* [ju ɑr], etc. Since contractions belong to spoken English, in writing they occur in informal material —the familiar, relaxed, and colloquial in style such as personal letters, informal essays, and especially in plays, stories, and novels where dialogue is used to represent conversation. They may also occur in formal English. The matter is one of option.

Data: Three studies (Geensburg and Bowman, Hirsch, Polimeros) show that editors and writers consider contractions standard usage. Another study (Macmillan) found them used 39% of the time in the *American Scholar* (Winter, 1951–52). One of the above studies (Polimeros) found them used 39.1% of the time in fifteen different magazines including *The Atlantic Monthly* and *Kenyon Review,* most often in articles of an informal nature.

In all these studies, it was found that the apostrophe is employed to indicate the dropped letter(s), long a standard practice. Some experimental writers, however, omit it. Bernard Shaw used to insist that the apostrophe was unnecessary and avoided it in his writing. It is true that except for a few contractions which would resemble other words (*he'll—hell; I'll—ill*) omitting the apostrophe would not cause confusion.

The most common contractions are those of auxiliary verbs with the preceding pronominal subject, such as *I've, we've,* and *you've* from *have; he's, she's, it's* from *is; we're, you're,* and *they're* from *are; I'm* from *am; I'd,* etc. from *had* or *would; I'll,* etc. from *will* or *shall;* and of the negative with the preceding auxiliary verb, such as *isn't, aren't, can't, don't, hasn't, won't,* etc. from *not. Ain't* is another frequently used contraction in speech. One other that is common is *let's* from *let us.*

There are also a few contractions used chiefly by poets: *e'er* (*ever*), *ne'er* (*never*), *e'en* (*even*), *o'er* (*over*), *'tis* (*it is*), and *'twas* (*it was*).

Other evidence: Kennedy, *Cur. Eng.,* 26, 256.

CORRELATIVES, EITHER . . . OR; NEITHER . . . NOR, etc.

Summary: Correlatives are used in standard English to join like sentence elements (80.5% of the time), but sometimes (19.5%) they join unlike elements. Usage is divided.

Correlatives appear in pairs, so related that each implies or complements the other, as, for example, *either . . . or, neither . . . nor, both . . . and, the . . . the.* The first word signals the relationship and the second serves as the real connective between the two items. Correlatives may be adverbs or coordinating conjunctions indicating a variety of grammatical notions, particularly addition, apposition, alteration, or contrast. The chief function of many coordinating conjunctions is merely to add. For instance, in the use of *both . . . and,* the duty of addition is performed by *and* with or without its correlative *both,* which serves to emphasize the fact that an addition is being made: "*Both* the British *and* the French

Governments were reported to have advised the United States . . ."
(*The New York Times,* Apr. 11, 1957, 3).

Data: Two studies (E. Solomon, Raybin) show that correlatives may join sentence elements of any kind. Two adjectives are joined in the example above, two nouns in: "He has fought *both* nazism *and* communism . . ." (*The New York Times,* May 7, 1957, 34); two infinitive constructions in: ". . . and refused *both* to negotiate Mr. Beck's suspension *and* to discuss in advance the procedure of the . . . committee" (*ibid.,* May 8, 1957, 36); two verbs in: "The Premier made it clear tonight that he *neither* needed *nor* wanted right-wing support . . ." (*ibid.,* Mar. 15, 1957, 3); two clauses in: "Their silence has led to speculation that *either* Israel's supply from the Persian Gulf has been cut off, *or* she had agreed to slow down her oil activities . . ." (*ibid.,* Apr. 12, 1957, 12); two phrases in: "The Brazilian was cited . . . for his achievements *both* as a composer *and* as a music educator" (*ibid,* Mar. 5, 1957, 33). The principal function of the correlative is to emphasize the fact that two ideas are involved and thus to aid the reader. Consider the last illustration, omitting *both.*

An adverb and a conjunction occasionally join together to form a correlative. Among the most common are *not (only)* . . . *but (also), not* (or *never*) . . . *nor,* as in "He sought to speak *not* as Communist *but* as Premier of Asia's largest nation" (*ibid.* Apr. 1, 1957, 24); "The greatest problem in the Middle East is *not* Egypt *nor* even Israel. . . ." (*ibid.,* Mar. 21, 1957, 30).

Correlatives are generally followed by the same grammatical construction, as in ". . . *either* for pleasure *or* for profit" (*ibid.,* May 6, 1957, 28), where both are before phrases. One of the studies cited found the correlatives occurring before the same kind of construction in 81% of the cases. In 19%, however, they were placed before unlike structures, as in: "*Either* presidential powers and duties were not discharged *or* were handled in such manner as the Cabinet, the President's family and his personal entourage could devise" (James Reston, *ibid.,* Mar. 20, 1957, 4), where *either* is placed before the subject and *or* before a verb. Another example is ". . . the most startling difference will *not* be in the numbers that attend, *but* in their sex" (*ibid.,* Apr. 4, 1957, 32), where *not* is followed by the verb *be* and *but* by a prepositional phrase. When ellipsis is involved, many types of different constructions occur, as in ". . . it was *not* the fault of the teachers entirely *but also* of the college that asked only . . ." (*ibid.,* May 2, 1957, 30) and ". . . it would place in that post a man *not only* amply qualified on other grounds, *but especially* because of his rich experience as a journalist . . ." (*ibid.,* Apr. 8, 1957, 22).

Though most sentences containing correlatives use parallel structure, this is not a requirement, since current usage has behind it a long literary history in permitting the free use of correlatives when the construction is clear and unambiguous.

Other evidence: Curme, *Syntax,* 162-64; Hall, 182; Mermin, *AS,* 18 (Oct., 1943), 171-91; Pooley, *TEU,* 96, Roberts, *UG,* 235-36.

C O T C H. See CATCH.

C R O W, v. See GROW, v.

DANGLING MODIFIER (MISRELATED)

Summary: *This construction is a sentence modifier containing a participle, gerund, or infinitive which does not modify the subject of the main clause; it has been used for centuries in cultivated English. When meaning is unambiguous, it is informal standard usage.*

Data: Five studies (Benardete, Hickey, Petit, Sloan, R. Thomas) produced these illustrations: *"Born on a farm near Salem, Indiana,* his public school education was received in the schools of that state" ("A Great Educator Passes," *Colorodo School Journal,* Apr., 1953, 4); *"Commenting on your editorial,* 'Ike and the Doctors': To my regret, Ike so far has shown himself a bundle of contradictions" (*Detroit News,* Mar. 25, 1953, "Health Insurance and the Doctors"); *"Allowing for the decline in the dollar and changes in the taste,* that is still a jump of close to $7 billion or fifty-six per cent" (*The Reporter,* Apr. 17, 1958, 11). In the first example, *Born on a farm near Salem* dangles because *education,* the subject of the main clause, was not born on a farm. Such a construction, however, usually modifies the whole main clause.

Words like *consider, hope, pend, speak, owe,* and *look* are common in this construction, as are a number of participles like *assuming, having, making, returning, turning, talking,* as in *"Turning to the economic front,* 54% of the votes are cast for national unions" (*The Nation,* May 9, 1934, 524); *"Taking into consideration the combined data on the card,* it appears that . . ." (*Scribner's,* Nov., 1934, 270). These constructions are sentence modifiers.

However, in some sentences the reader is misled into attaching the modifier to a subject which it does not meaningfully modify, e.g., *"Turning the corner,* a handsome school building appeared" and *"After finishing grammar school,* my family left Omaha." Although such statements are not actually misunderstood most of the time, they are howlers and are thus stylistically faulty. *See* SENTENCE MODIFIERS.

Other evidence: Bartlett, *CE,* 14 (Mar., 1953), 353-54; Hall, 167; Pooley, *TEU,* 107-13; *CE,* 14 (Dec., 1952), 170-71; Russell, *AS,* 10 (Apr., 1935), 113-18; Steinbach, *AS,* 5 (Feb., 1930) 181-97.

DANGLING PARTICIPLE. See DANGLING MODIFIER (MISRELATED).

DARE, v.

Summary: The preterit and past participle dared *occurs in standard English, with or without the following* to. Dare *or* dares *occurs in the third person singular.* Durst *is archaic and no longer is used in writing.*

In Old English, this verb belonged to the preterit-present group, among which were *ought, can, may, shall,* and *must.* Their original preterits acquired a present signification and by the time they were written down they were felt to be present in meaning. As a result, these verbs, once preterits, developed new presents and new preterits, as in the third person singular present in modern English: "He dare (not *dares*) not go tonight" and "He *may* (not *mays*) not go." In Old English, the new preterit for *dare* became *dorste,* which survived as *durst.*

Dare, however, by analogy with the numerous weak verbs, developed early in the sixteenth century the new forms *dares* (present) and *dared* (preterit), so that the two forms *dare* and *dares* occur in the third person present and the two forms *dared* and *durst* in the preterit.

Data: Durst has become archaic, and in written English only *dared* occurs, as several studies show (Fein, Felberbaum, Hotchner, Rosenfeld). In regard to *dare,* it was originally followed by an infinitive without *to,* as in "He *dare* not write," but in present day usage, *dare* occurs with or without *to:* "He *dared to* play a program . . ." (Howard Taubman, *The New York Times,* Jan. 5, 1955) and "But do I *dare* name names?" (Robert Frost, *Build Soil—A Political Pastoral,* 1936, 1. 43). "I *dare* say" is a common expression in modern English, often written as *daresay* and said like *maybe,* as if it were one word instead of two: "The collection is rounded out—I *daresay* there was no help for it— with . . ." *The New York Times,* Sept. 24, 1955, 115) (Barnhart's Files).

Style determines the inclusion or exclusion of the *to.* One study cited above found one example in written English of *dare* plus *to* in the negative and two examples of *dare* without *to* in the affirmative; in spoken English, the negative plus *dare* plus *to,* as in *wouldn't dare to try* occurred 25% of the time, the negative plus *dare,* without the *to,* as in *wouldn't dare* 75%. Usage is divided.

American English has no standard negative contraction but several nonstandard ones, among them *dasn't* [dæsənt] and *daresn't* [dersənt] or [dærsənt]. *Daren't* [derənt] or [dærənt] is standard British English but rare in American.

Other evidence: Abbott, *AS,* 32 (Feb., 1957), 33; Atwood, 33; Barnhart, Files; Bryant, *CE,* 17 (Oct., 1955), 52; Curme, *PSA,* 256-59; *Syntax,* 474-75; Jespersen, *MEG,* Pt. IV, 1.8 (1) *ff.,* Pt. V, 12.2, 25.2; Krapp, 179; Kruisinga, 5th Ed., Pt. II, *Eng. Accidence and Syntax,* I, 18-19, 430-33; Kurath, *LANE,* Vol. III, Pt. 2, Map 696.

DATA, DATUM, n.

Summary: *In standard usage,* datum *is always singular.* Data *occurs as both singular and plural; when a plural marker precedes* data, *the verb is always plural.*

Data: Derived from the Latin, the noun *datum* and its plural *data* mean "fact(s)" or "item(s) of information," as in "Each *datum* (fact) was checked, but the *data* (facts) are not sufficient." However, several studies (Lang, Mishelkevitz, Russell, Sloan, R. Thomas) show that *data* also occurs as a singular collective noun meaning "information" or "material," as in "While the accumulating *data piles* up in his books . . ." (*Sewanee Review,* Autumn, 1953, 682) and "No *data* is as yet available on how far this increase continues" (*The New York Times,* Aug. 10, 1958, E9). Thus, in some sentences *data* may take either a singular or plural verb indifferently.

However, when a plural marker precedes *data,* the verb is always plural: "When these *data are* to be analyzed . . ." In one of the studies cited above, where number was distinguishable, eleven examples (16%) of *data* in the singular occurred and fifty-eight (84%) in the plural. *Data* is now going the way of *stamina, opera, news, links,* originally plurals, but now singular nouns. *See* AGENDA.

Other evidence: Barnhart, Files; Bartlett, *CE,* 15 (Apr., 1954), 417; Ball, *AS,* 3 (Apr., 1928), 293-94; Fries *AEG,* 43; Pound, *AS,* 3 (Oct., 1927), 26-27; *AS,* 31 (May, 1956), 156; *WNID.*

DATE, n., v.

Summary: Date *as a noun or as a verb occurs in informal standard writing, especially that dealing with teen-agers and their social relationships, referring most often to a social appointment or engagement.*

Data: The use of *date* to mean a social engagement, especially with a person of the opposite sex, is standard usage, as in "I made a *date* for lunch." For instance, Maureen Daly and Wellington G. Pierce, who write about teen-agers, and magazines like *The Atlantic Monthly, Coronet,* and the *Reader's Digest,* when referring to young people and their social lives, employ it regularly to mean a meeting. Several studies (Holihan, Holster, Hotchner, H. Minsky, K. Moore) show that the term has established itself in the language.

Date is also used to refer to the person with whom one has a social engagement, as in "Her *date* came late"; "My *date* will undoubtedly cry . . ." (*Glamour*, Oct., 1957, 130). In one of the studies cited above, *date* with this meaning occurred in 24% of the examples. Sometimes it specifically meant "escort," "girl friend," "girlfriend," "boy friend," "boyfriend," or "lover."

Date as a verb is now being used, in connection with teen-agers primarily, to mean "make an appointment" or "have engagements with." It occurs more often in spoken English, but it sometimes appears in the written as well: "I was also dating Dick . . ." (*Saturday Evening Post*, Dec. 14, 1957, 58); and "It doesn't say don't *date* passengers or crew members" (*Holiday*, June, 1958, 187). *Date* as a noun occurs about three times as often.

Other evidence: Barnhart, Files; Marckwardt and Walcott, 36, 126.

DAYS. See ADVERBIAL GENITIVE.

'D BETTER. See HAD BETTER (BEST).

DEAD. See COMPARISON, ILLOGICAL.

DID, DONE. See DO, v.

DIDN'T USE TO

Summary: This expression occurs in the speech of all types in all areas. It is standard usage, but rarely occurs in writing.

Data: The negative form of *used to* is *didn't use to* and is heard in all areas and among all types of speakers. Other phrases that occur in different sections are *used to didn't be* (nonstandard), *used to wasn't* (nonstandard), *used not to be, used to not be, never used to be, usen't to* (nonstandard).

In some dialect areas, *use to* may also occur as an adverb of time, as in *"Use to* they lived somewhere else." Here it means "formerly." One also hears in speech *use to* as a variant of *used to,* as in "He *use to* (*used to*) live here." Two studies (Gross, Harrison) revealed only a single instance of *didn't use to* in writing.

Other evidence: Atwood, 33-34; Kurath, *LANE,* Vol. III, Pt. II, Map 700; V.G. McDavid, 58, 59, 68; R.I. and V.G. McDavid, *AS,* 35 (Feb., 1960), 14.

DIFFERENT FROM, THAN, TO

Summary: *Evidence shows that* different to *is rare in American English, that* different from *generally occurs in formal written English, that* different than *also occurs in standard usage.*

Data: In formal English *different* is usually followed by *from:* "His care is different *from* mine." However, *different* may be followed by *to* (current British usage) or more often by *than:* "Our young people are living in a world *different to* the one I grew up in" (*Winthrop Alumnae News* [S.C.], July, 1957, 30); "Roosevelt, the man of action, . . . is not a *different* person *than* the Roosevelt given us by the Secret Service men who have written . . ." (*The New York Times Book Review,* Jan. 22, 1950, 1); "However, Mr. Criswell is exploring this haunted room in the house of fiction with a *different* torch *than* that used by most writers today" (*ibid.,* Aug. 10, 1958, 19); "The case for military aid and defense support rests on a very *different* range of considerations *than* the case for economic aid" (*Yale Review,* Summer, 1958, 503); "Whittier, being of an older school, used a *different* manner *than* Whitman" (Louis Untermeyer, *Stars to Steer By,* 1941, p. 239).

One study shows *different from* used 84.4% of the time and *different than* 15.6%; another (Concool) found *different from* in 87.5% of the occurrences and *different than* in 12.5%. No examples of *different to* turned up in either study. *Different than,* however, has been used in literature since the seventeenth century, and the evidence (Benardete, Everson, Haase, Isseks, Lichtman, McMillan, Rosenbaum, Salwen, R. Thomas, Winburne) shows that it is in standard usage today along with *different from.*

The use of *different than* and *differently than* may have arisen from a confusion of *different from* with *other than*. Pooley, however, points out that *than* is a convenient shortcut for "from that which," as in "It was *different* in size *than* (from that which) he had expected." An insistence upon *different from* often leads to extra words. "That is entirely *different than* it is in other parts of the state" (Discussion program, TV, Channel 4, Jan. 16, 1955) is more economical than ". . . *different from* what it is . . ." or "*different from* that which it is. . . ."

Other evidence: Bolinger, *EJ*, XXVIII (Coll. ed., 1939), 480; *AS*, 2 (Oct., 1946), 199-200; Haase, *CE*, 10 (Mar., 1949), 345-47; Pooley, *TEU*, 166-68; Wise, *AS*, 22 (Oct., 1947), 237.

DIFFERENT THAN. See DIFFERENT FROM, THAN, TO.

DIFFERENT TO. See DIFFERENT FROM, THAN, TO.

DIVE, v.

Summary: Though the preterit dived *is more frequent in formal written English, the alternate form* dove *occurs in informal writing and is preferred in the speech of certain regions.*

Data: One study (J. Jacobson) of current literature found seven instances of the preterit *dived,* none of *dove;* another (Hotchner) discovered five of *dived,* one of *dove;* a third (Sheil) found one instance of *dived,* none of *dove;* a fourth (Winburne) discovered one example of *dived* and one of *dove;* and an investigation of three groups in Cleveland, Ohio, classified according to education (Tyson), showed *dived* occurs somewhat more frequently in all three. However, the educated group preferred *dove* in the contexts "The Boys *dived/dove* from the raft" and "He *dived/dove* for the ball." Apparently, *dive/dove* is following the pattern of the verbs *drive/drove, rise/rose,* etc. Illustrations of *dove* in writing are: "And late one afternoon an Italian . . . *dove* right down into the midst of a hundred ships" (Ernie Pyle, *Brave Men,* p. 34) and "Mr. O'Keefe stripped down and *dove* into the water" (*New York World-Telegram and Sun,* July 28, 1955, 6).

According to two studies of the Linguistic Atlas records (Allen, Malmstrom), only speakers of the Northern dialect areas preferred *dove* to *dived*. In southern and eastern Pennsylvania, through the other areas in the Middle Atlantic States and in the South Atlantic States north of the Peedee River, Type III (cultivated) informants strongly preferred *dived*. In northern and western Pennsylvania and in the South Atlantic States south of the Peedee, both forms occur, with *dove* preferred by the more modern and more educated informants. This pattern of preference is also reflected in the North Central States. Another study of speech (Sheppard) bears out these findings in substance.

Thus, evidence shows that *dove* is a northern form, expanding southward. *Div* is occasionally heard in Type I (uneducated) speech of northeastern New England, the South, and South Midland.

Other evidence: Allen, *EJ*, XLV (Apr., 1956), 188-94; Atwood, 9; Horwill, 110; Kennedy, *Cur. Eng.*, 455; Kurath, *LANE*, Vol. III, Pt. 1, Map 580; Malmstrom *SVTS*, 116-17; R.I. McDavid, *AED*, 515, 516, 526; V.G. McDavid, 27-28; Pooley, *TEU*, 139-40; R.I. and V.G. McDavid, *AS*, 35 (Feb., 1960), 12.

D O, v.

Summary: The principal parts of the verb do *are* do, did, done. *The preterit* did *and the past participle* done *are the standard forms;* done *in the preterit is colloquial and receding in use.*

Data: One study (Lipschultz) found 152 examples of the preterit *did,* as in "He *did* it so skillfully . . ." (*Holiday*, Sept., 1959, 43), 110 examples of *done,* 101 of which occurred as past participles illustrated by "Few Americans have *done* that" (*Saturday Review*, Jan. 31, 1959, 15) and 9 as preterits as in "I *done* another bad thing" (Lennie in John Steinbeck's *Of Mice and Men,* 1937, p. 113). Another investigation (Polimeros) found *did* was used 475 times and *done* 59. In only four cases was *done* used instead of *did,* three occurring in John Steinbeck's *The Grapes of Wrath* and one in *Esquire,* all used to represent speech of a nonstandard variety, as in the first study mentioned. A third study of writing (N. Fagen) reveals thirty-five examples of *did* in the preterit and one of *done,* spoken by an uneducated Puerto Rican.

According to one study (Malmstrom) of the Linguistic Atlas records for the New England, the North Central, and the Upper Midwest States, in the context "He *did* it last night," *did* in the preterit occurs universally in the Type III (cultivated) speech of New England and almost universally in the same type of the North Central and Upper Midwest States. In New England, the preterit *done* is strongly preferred by Type II informants (with at least some secondary school education) and Type I informants (uneducated); in the North Central States about half the Type II's use *done;* in the Upper Midwest about one-fourth of the Type II speakers use it. This kind of occurrence indicates that *done* is in colloquial but recessive usage.

The past participle *done* occurs also as a superfluous auxiliary in nonstandard speech: "I've *done* told you all I'm going to tell you." Sometimes, *do* is heard in northern speech to mean "cheat," as in "Did he *do* you on the trade?" *Done,* followed by the preposition *in,* means "exhausted" in colloquial English, as in "After the hikes, I'm always *done in.*"

The preterit of *do* was not investigated in the Middle Atlantic or the South Atlantic States.

Other evidence: Atwood, 9; Kurath, *LANE,* Vol. III, Pt. II, Map 690; Malmstrom, *SVTS,* 120; V.G. McDavid, 22, 28, 53, 69, 71, 72; R.I. and V.G. McDavid, *AS,* 35 (Feb., 1960), 15, 17; Wentworth, 172.

DOCTOR, v.

Summary: Doctor *as a verb is used intransitively (mainly in speech) and transitively in standard English.*

Data: The noun *doctor* has given rise to the verb *doctor* used in standard English transitively and intransitively. As a transitive verb, it means "to treat medicinally," as in *"He has been doctoring his own wife, giving her his remedies";* *"I have been doctoring my cold for a week, but it is not any better."* It is also used colloquially to mean "repair" or "mend" as in "Will you *doctor* this bag for me?" This meaning occasionally occurs in somewhat colorful writing, according to one study (McCann), as in "The incumbent, Henry Bonfig, was hustled in . . . to *doctor* CBS-Columbia's troubles . . ." (*Forbes,* Mar. 1, 1956, 18) or in the headline "If You Can't Axe It, Fix It. TV On A Mass *Doctoring* Spree" (*Variety,* Dec. 11, 1957, 29) followed by the statement, "Increasing number of contract-tied agencies and sponsors . . . have embarked on a mass *show-doctoring* spree in a desperate attempt at salvaging their properties." Another colloquial meaning, according to a second study (Strong), is "to tamper with" or "to falsify," as in "He *doctored* the evidence," or "Remaking your age has nothing to do with *doctoring* the dates on your birth certificate" (*Vogue,* Jan. 15, 1958, 96). Intransitively, it is used in colloquial English, meaning "to practice medicine," as "He has been *doctoring* in this community for a year" and "to take treatments," as "I've been *doctoring* for about six months and I am still far from well."

DON'T, v.

Summary: Does not *is standard usage in formal written English;* don't *in the third person occurs regularly among cultivated speakers in parts of the East, but rarely appears in writing.*

Data: Don't is the contracted form of *do not,* used colloquially in all persons, a variant of *doesn't* in the third person singular. In positive constructions, *does* still prevails, although some speakers in the South and South Midland use "He (She) (It) do." Cultivated speakers may say, "If *he don't* . . ."; "*It don't* matter"; or "Why *don't she?*" This form may be following the pattern of preterit-present verbs in Old English, which now do not add -*s* in the third person singular, as *can, may, shall. He does, he don't* are analogous to *he needs, he needn't.* Professor John S. Kenyon suspects that *don't* in the third person singular is merely the correct subjunctive continued in use after our sense of the subjunctive has become dimmed.

In informal speech, *don't* is well established along with *doesn't.* From investigations made (Garron, Halbrecht, Rosenblum), come these examples: "That *don't* mean the problem was done correctly" (a college professor); ". . . it *don't* need any rubbing" (a radio commercial advertising a miracle cleaner, WABC, Nov. 9, 1954). Anyone listening to radio and television programs often hears this use of *don't*. C. C. Fries, in *American English Grammar,* found that the slightly lesser educated group substituted *don't* 30% of the time and the group with little formal education used it generally, *doesn't* being exceedingly rare.

According to one study of the Linguistic Atlas records (Malmstrom), *he don't* occurs 75% of the time for cultivated speakers (Type III) in the Middle Atlantic States and about 50% for those in the South Atlantic States. In these areas, Type III informants rarely say *he doesn't* along with *he don't.* In the Middle Atlantic States, those who use both forms live near New York City or Philadelphia, which, like other urban cultural centers, radiate influence upon their surroundings by replacing local with national or literary forms. (See Kurath's *Word Geography,* p. 2.) In New England, the North Central, and the Upper Midwest States, where again many Type III informants use *he don't, he doesn't* occurs more often as a companion form. In addition, in these areas *he don't* becomes more frequent in direct ratio to the lack of education and social and economic advantages.

Thus the Atlas reveals a distinctively regional use of *he don't* in the Midland and Southern areas of the East, which is not expanding northward or westward.

Other evidence: Atwood, 28; Fries, *AEG,* 52-53; Kurath, *LANE,* Vol. III, Pt. 2, Map 688; Malmstrom, *SVTS,* 199-200; Malone, *EJ,* XXXIX (Feb., 1950), 104-5; Marckwardt and Walcott, 45, 46; V.G. McDavid, 53-54; McMillan, *CE,* 5 (Nov., 1943), 100-1.

DOUBLE GENITIVE

Summary: The double genitive occurs in standard English.

Such expressions as *a friend of mine* and *a friend of Jane's* occur alongside *my friend, Jane's friend,* and *a friend of Jane* in standard English. The construction may include names of people and personal pronouns, but we do not find inanimate nouns as the objects of the double genitive phrase. For example, *earth's surface* and *surface of the earth* are both standard, but not *surface of the earth's*.

Data: One comparative study (R. Jacobson) found the periphrastic genitive (the *of*-phrase) and the inflected genitive, as in *New York's skyscrapers,* occurring 99.6% of the time and the double genitive .4%. Nevertheless, it does occur, as in "Neither the natural rose *of Razalja's* nor the . . ." (*Saturday Review,* Jan. 18, 1958, 16) and ". . . to the Court *of St. James's* in London" (Aileen Pippett, *The Moth and the Star,* 1953, p. 1, cited by Strong).

In speech *friend of the teacher's* may be confused with *friend of the teachers.* In writing, however, one may use *friend of the teachers, friend of the teacher's,* or *teachers' friend.* One should also remember that *a picture of John* refers to his likeness and *a picture of John's* means a picture belonging to him. When the inflected genitive represents ownership, as in *a dog's bone,* it keeps its form even when it follows the preposition *of,* as in *a bone of the dog's.* "He found *a bone of the dog's*" is quite different from "He found *a bone of the dog.*"

When *the* modifies the head noun, the double genitive is not so common: *a cousin of Fred's,* but usually *the cousin of Fred.* However, it occurs often after the demonstratives *this, that, these and those:* "*This (That, Those, These) book(s)* of Hazel's." This construction has a long history of standard usage.

Other evidence: Bryant, *FEG,* 146; *CE,* 17 (Dec., 1955), 178; Curme, *PSA,* 135-36; *Syntax,* 75-77; Fries, *AEG,* 76-77; Hatcher, *Word,* 6 (Apr., 1950), 1-25; Jespersen, *Ess.* 145-46; Poutsma, II, I, A, 50-58.

DOUBLE NEGATIVE

Summary: Some double negatives, such as "I ain't got none," are nonstandard, but a number of pseudo-double negative constructions are standard usage in speech and writing.

The double negative, which goes back to Shakespeare at least, consists of a negative adverb (*not* or *never*) or a negative verbal contraction like *ain't, can't, won't,* and a negative pronoun *none, no one,* or *nothing,* the negative adjective *no,* or a negative connective like *but,* as in "I don't gain nothing." No one misunderstands the double; nor does one cancel out the other to make an affirmative. The double negative is simply out of style. The comics and cartoons, however, emphasize its use in nonstandard English.

Data: Three investigations (Kalina, McMillan, Sloan) found the double negative representing uneducated speech or used in humorous situations. Pseudo-double negatives, like *can't hardly, can't barely, not but* are colloquial in nature and at times are used by well-known writers. In educated speech one hears "For two hours we *couldn't scarcely* see a thing" instead of *"could scarcely see"* or "We *haven't but* one left."

Two negatives may be applied to the same word or idea, as in *not infrequent, not uncommon, not without reason.* In these expressions, the two negatives do make an affirmative, an unemphatic one, in standard usage.

Two negatives occur in informal English and even in formal English in the same sentence when one negative statement depends upon the other in order to give a qualified meaning or special emphasis to an idea. "She is *not* sure she *won't* write in" does not mean "She will not write in," but that she may possibly write in. Also *"Don't* you think she *isn't* a good teacher!" with stress on the word *teacher* means not merely she is a good teacher but that the speaker has discovered that she is a good teacher or that the listener had better think she is a good teacher.

In sentences like "I *shouldn't* wonder if it *didn't* snow tonight," the second *not* is redundant. "I *shouldn't* wonder if it snowed tonight" is preferable. See also *cannot (can't) help but; hardly.*

Other evidence: Bernstein, *CE,* 7 (Dec., 1945), 167-69; Bryant, *CE,* 19 (Feb., 1958), 229; Kurath, *LANE,* Vol. III, Pt. 2, Map 718; Marckwardt and Walcott, 98-99; Pooley, *TEU,* 98-100.

DOVE. See DIVE, v.

DRAG, v.

Summary: *The preterit and past participle* dragged *is standard English.* Drug *as a preterit and past participle occurs widely in nonstandard speech.*

Data: *Drug* is heard on rare occasions in cultivated speech (Type III), but three studies (Hartdegen, Hotchner, Schauer) give evidence to the conclusion that it never appears in formal written English, except in represented speech: ". . . He practically *drug* me in here to sit with him." (Dan Cushman, *Stay Away, Joe,* 1953, p. 166).

Other evidence: Atwood, 9-10; Barnhart, Files; Wentworth, 182.

DRANK. See DRINK, v.

DRAW, v.

Summary: *Preterit* drew *and past participle* drawn *are standard English. The form* drawed *as preterit and past participle is rustic and rapidly becoming obsolete. It is not found in cultivated speech.*

Data: According to one study (Malmstrom) of the Linguistic Atlas records for the Middle Atlantic and the South Atlantic States of the preterit *draw* in the context "He *drew* it out" and of the records for the North Central and Upper Midwest States in the context "The apron *drew up*," *draw up* being one of several lexical variants for *shrink,* the form *drawed* is rustic and is rapidly becoming obsolete. It was not recorded in New England, or in Wisconsin and in parts of Michigan and Illinois.

Drew is the standard form, predominating in Type III (cultivated) and Type II (with at least some secondary school education) speech in all areas. The evidence also shows that *drawed* is a Southern and South Midland form, occurring mainly in old-fashioned speech and rapidly receding. Two studies made (Kaye, Kehl) show that the preterit *drew* and the past participle *drawn* are the only forms found in formal written English.

Other evidence: Atwood, 10; Malmstrom, *SVTS,* 124; V.G. McDavid, 29-30; Wentworth, 179.

DREAM, v.

Summary: *The preterit and past participle dreamed* [drimd] *or* dreamt [drempt] *occur in standard English as both transitive and intransitive. In written English,* dreamed *is the more common form, whereas in speech the reverse is true.*

Data: In two studies (M. Hartman, Hotchner), *dreamed* occurred in written English 96% of the time and *dreamt* in 4%, but in conversation and direct interviewing *dreamed* occurred 7% and *dreamt* 93% of the time.

An investigation of three groups (Tyson), classified according to educational level in Cleveland, Ohio, showed that upon direct questioning, only the group with the least education preferred *dreamt* to *dreamed* in the context "I *dreamt/dreamed* last night." All three types preferred *dreamed* in the past participle, a suggestion that *dreamed* is encroaching upon *dreamt* in spoken as well as in written English.

Other evidence: Atwood, 10; Kurath, *LANE,* Vol. III, Pt. 2, Map 643; V.G. McDavid, 22, 29, 30, 72.

DRINK, v.

Summary: *The preterit* drank *and the past participle* drunk *or* drank *both occur in standard spoken English, but* drunk *is the past participle in formal written English;* drunk *and* drinked *are nonstandard preterits.*

Data: Three studies (Hotchner, Nemser, Stevens) of standard written English showed only the preterit *drank* and the past participle *drunk.* An investigation, however, of three groups in Cleveland, Ohio, classified according to education (Tyson), showed the preterit *drank* used 95% of the time and *drunk* only 5% among the uneducated in the context "I *drunk/drank* too much water." On the other hand, the past participle *drunk* occurred only 56% of the time and *drank* 44% in the context "I had *drunk/drank* too much beer." The best-educated group, however, preferred *drunk,* but the middle group employed *drank* much more often. For spoken English, the Linguistic Atlas records the preterit and past participles of *drink* in the contexts "I *drank* a lot of it" and "How much *have* you *drunk?*"

According to a study of these records (Malmstrom), *drank* is the standard preterit, predominating in Type III (cultivated) speech and Type II speech (informants with at least some secondary education) in all areas. The nonstandard preterit *drunk* is principally a Midland and South Midland usage; the nonstandard *drinked* occurs in scattered fashion throughout the East, most often in New England, and is found in the South Midland and Kentucky.

The past participle of *drink* shows divided usage. In Type III, *drunk* predominates strongly only in the South Atlantic States, but is infrequent in other types of this area. In New England and the Upper Midwest, usage is almost equally divided between *drunk* and *drank* in Type III speech. In the North Central States, *drunk* occurs twice as often as *drank* in Type III speech, but in the Middle Atlantic States the reverse is true, *drank* occurring twice as often as *drunk*. Type II informants in all areas strongly prefer *drank*. In the Pacific Northwest, *have drank* is also common in speech but it rarely occurs in written English.

Drunken is now obsolete as a past participle, but it has become a full-fledged adjective in standard English: "a *drunken* brawl." The nonstandard *drinked,* however, occurs as a South Midland usage in Type I speech.

Other evidence: Abbott, *AS,* 32 (Feb., 1957), 38, 40; Allen, *CE,* 18 (Feb., 1957), 283-85; Atwood, 10-11; Avis, *AS,* 28 (May, 1953), 110-11; Kurath, *LANE,* Vol. III, Pt. 2, Map 644; Malmstrom, *SVTS,* 126-28; R.I. McDavid, *AED,* 521; V.G. McDavid, 30-31; R.I. and V.G. McDavid, *AS,* 35 (Feb., 1960), 14, 17.

DRIVE, v.

Summary: *The preterit* drove *and the past participle* driven *are standard English. Other forms are nonstandard.*

Data: Two studies of written English (Chovan, Polonsky) failed to turn up any forms but the standard, and the Linguistic

Atlas, according to one study (Malmstrom), shows that these forms, in the context "I *drove* a nail" and "I *have driven* many nails" occur in all areas.

The nonstandard preterit *driv* is a Southern, South Midland and northeastern New England usage and is receding. The nonstandard preterit *druv* is the most common one in the North Central and Upper Midwest States, occurring most often in Kentucky, but it is rare and scattered in the East. Uneducated informants who use one or the other of these forms tend to level the past participle to the same form.

Other evidence: Atwood, 11-12; Kurath, *LANE*, Vol. III, Pt. 2, Map 645; Malmstrom, *SVTS*, 132-34; R.I. McDavid, *AED*, 516; V.G. McDavid, 31-32; R.I. and V.G. McDavid, *AS*, 35 (Feb., 1960), 15.

DROWN, v.

Summary: The preterit drowned *and past particle* drowned, *both transitive and intransitive, are standard English; the form* drownded *is nonstandard.*

Data: According to one study (Malmstrom) of the records of the Linguistic Atlas, the past participle *drowned* in the context "He was *drowned"* is used almost universally by Type III (cultivated) informants everywhere and predominates also in Type II (those with at least some secondary school education) informants in New England, the Middle Atlantic, and the South Atlantic States, and in the speech of all types in the North Central and the Upper Midwest States. Three studies (Hotchner, Toback, Wein) of written English revealed only the standard English forms with the variant *drownded* occurring once in dialogue.

Other evidence: Atwood, 12; Kurath, *LANE*, Vol. III, Pt. 1, Map 522; Malmstrom, *SVTS*, 135-36; V.G. McDavid, 32; Wentworth, 182.

DRUG. See DRAG, v.

DRUNK. See DRINK, v.

DRUNKEN. See DRINK, v.

'DRUTHER. See HAD (WOULD) RATHER.

DUE TO, BECAUSE OF, OWING TO

Summary: All three of these locutions introducing an adverbial phrase, as in, "Due to (Because of) (Owing to) lack of courage, he failed," *occur in writing produced and edited by unquestionably educated persons.*

Data: In six studies (Fisch, Frankel, Hider, Hotchner, Winderbaum, Wolkoff), *due to* in a context such as that cited occurred 34% of the time as an alternative to the possibility of *because of* or *owing to.* In two studies, which considered only written variants, *due to* occurred 30%, *because of* 62%, and *owing to* 8% of the time. Examples of *due to* introducing an adverbial phrase are: "So far, *due to* engineering controls, more precise than any known to industry, this has never happened" (*Saturday Evening Post*, Dec. 5, 1953, 173); and *"Due to* ill health it became necessary for him . . ." (*Colorado School Journal*, Apr., 1953, 4).

Some textbooks object to this use of *due to* on the grounds that it should be reserved for such a sentence as the following, where *due* comes after the verb *to be:* "Their success is *due* largely *to* first-rate writing . . ." (*Saturday Review*, Mar. 14, 1953, 59). In the six studies cited above, this pattern prevailed 65% of the time, but 35% of the time *due to* introduced an adverbial phrase. Those who do not care to use *due to* in adverbial phrases can no longer condemn those who do. It is established in the language.

Another expression that is now being used similarly is *thanks to,* as in *"Thanks to* his knowledge of physics, he was able to accomplish the task." Here one may substitute *due to, owing to, because of.*

Other evidence: Bryant, *CE,* 15 (May, 1954), 478; Fries, *AEG,* 118, 126; Kenyon, *AS,* 6 (Oct., 1930), 61-70; Newsome, *AS,* 13 (Feb., 1938), 29; Pooley, *TEU,* 14, 140-41.

DURST. See DARE, v.

EACH. See AGREEMENT, INDEFINITE PRONOUNS.

EACH AND EVERY

Summary: This expression, characteristic of officialese, is redundant but acceptable in informal English; it does not occur in formal written English.

Data: *Each* points to the individual, considered as such, while *every* points to the total number of individuals, emphasizing the completeness of the list. It is a perfectly normal and useful expression, as, for example, in a sentence such as "Principals are to report the name, age, sex and address of *each and every* county pupil," where the principals are told to get several facts about each pupil and to be sure that all pupils are included; or in "Conformists themselves, the American students see little need to insist that *each and every* person be and behave just like themselves" (*Swarthmore College Bulletin,* Oct., 1957, 1); or in "But he gave that one hour *each and every* day . . ." (*The New York Times Book Review,* Nov. 23, 1958, 3). According to two studies (Rashkin, Weiss), this expression does not occur in formal written English.

Other evidence: McMillan, *CE,* 9 (Apr., 1948), 394; *OED.*

EACH OTHER, ONE ANOTHER

Summary: The two terms are used interchangeably in standard English.

Data: From evidence of studies (Adams, Cahill, M. Daly, Hotchner, R. Thomas, Winburne) it is impossible to establish a difference in meaning between *each other* or *one another;* modern writers interchange them indifferently: "The recognition of this fact does not prevent speakers who represent different levels of usage from mixing in the daily contacts of life and communicating with *each other*" (Albert C. Baugh, *A History of the English Language,* 2nd ed., 1957, p. 380); "And it was in the individuality of the individual men, in their differences from *each other,* that the founders of this Republic put their trust" (Archibald MacLeish, *American Scholar,* Autumn, 1953, 394); "The major ethnic differences were no longer confined to national entities in their hostile or friendly dealings with *each other"* (Norman Cousins, *Saturday Review Reader No. 3, 1954,* p. 18); "It seems less surprising that Davis and Bragg . . . had such an affinity for *one another"* (*The Sewanee Review,* Summer, 1956, 493). The quantitative evidence shows *each other* referring to two in 57.4% of the occurrences and to more than two 42.6% of the time. As a variant of *one another,* one study showed *each other* referring to more than two in only 40% of the cases.

Other evidence: Jespersen, *MEG,* Pt. II, 7.751-53; Kruisinga, II, 567; Newsome, *AS,* 13 (Feb., 1938), 27; Pooley, *TEU,* 143; Thomas, *CE,* 18 (May, 1957), 422-24.

EAT, v.

Summary: Preterit ate *and past participle* eaten *are standard English;* et *and* eat *as preterits are nonstandard except in limited areas.*

Data: The Linguistic Atlas for New England, the Middle Atlantic, the South Atlantic, the North Central, and the Upper Midwest States recorded the preterit and past participle of *eat* in the contexts "We *ate* at six o'clock" and "How often have you *eaten* today?"

According to one study of the records (Malmstrom), the standard preterit *ate* and past participle *eaten* are almost universal in cultivated speech in all areas.

The nonstandard preterit *et* is characteristic chiefly of New England; the nonstandard preterit *eat* shows increasing frequency in the Atlantic Coast northward and is the most common variant in the Middlewest. In certain areas of the East (notably in the Valleys of Kanawha and the upper Ohio and its tributaries, in a deep coastal area from the James River to Rhode Island, in north and west New York, and in South Carolina and east Georgia), the two nonstandard variants *et* and *eat* occur about equally. In these areas, especially along the coast, *eat* is more old-fashioned and less favored; *et* is preferred, or even a prestige form, in the speech of many older Type III (cultivated) informants. Informants of this type who use *et* normally use *eaten* as the past participle. Informants of other types who use one or the other of the nonstandard preterit forms usually level the past participle to the same form.

In Great Britain the past tense *ate* is pronounced *et* [ɛt].

Two studies (Agress, P. Minsky) show that except in represented speech, *ate* and *eaten* are the only forms that occur in writing.

Other evidence: Atwood, 12-13; Kurath, *LANE,* Vol. III, Pt. 2, Map 646; Malmstrom, *SVTS,* 137-40; V.G. McDavid, 32-34.

EITHER. See AGREEMENT, INDEFINITE PRONOUNS.

EITHER (NEITHER) WITH MORE THAN TWO

Summary: In written English, either *and* neither *usually refer to one of two, not one of three or more; but on rare occasions, the reference is to more than two.*

Data: If more than two items, say dresses, are being considered for a particular occasion, one might say *"Either (Neither) of the dresses will do."* The more usual structure, however, would be *"Any one (Not any) (None) of these dresses will do." Either* and *neither* normally refer to alternatives, but a strict interpretation would rule out sentences like: "I shall elect *either* Spanish, French, or Italian." One can easily imagine a situation with any number of substantives, as in "You make take *either* A, B, C, D, or E." Here one has the awkward alternative of using the coordinate *or* three more times.

Quantitative evidence (Naddell, Silverton, R. Thomas) shows that this usage is extremely rare in standard written English. However, it does occur: ". . . but is trained for *neither* thinking, leisure, livelihood, nor citizenship" (*Harper's,* Apr., 1957, 532); "To date, *neither* its 'Hansel and Gretel,' 'Boheme,' 'Butterfly,' 'Fledermaus,' or 'Faust' will satisfy the taste that seeks . . ." (*Saturday Review of Literature,* Nov. 24, 1951, 52).

Other evidence: Hall, 86; Jespersen, *MEG,* Pt. II, 7.731-2; Kurath, *LANE,* Vol. 3, Pt. 2, Maps 610-11; Pooley, *TEU,* 144-45.

EMPHATIC IT. See IT (5).

EQUALLY, EQUALLY AS, JUST AS

Summary: Equally *occurs far more frequently in written English than* equally as *or* just as, *but the latter two do occur, particularly in the structure* as . . . as.

Data: The expression *equally as* has arisen through the confusion of *equally* with *just as*. For instance, one may say "It's *equally* important for me to go" or "It's *just as* important for me to go." In studies of fiction, periodicals, and newspapers (Basner, Blomquist, Church, Donkle, Edgerton, Fink, Fries, Hearden, Hosig, Kindschi, Lerdahl, Nusbaum, O'Brien, Pfankuch, Postraw, Ramlow, Scribner, Shim, Speitz, Tatham, A. M. Thomas), *equally* occurred 80% of the time, as in *"Equally* important is the fear . . ." (*The New York Times,* "News of the Week in Review," Nov. 10, 1957, Sec. 4, 3E). In 34.4% of the examples, it modified verbs, as in "is *equally* marked"; in 65.6% it modified adjectives, as in *"equally* important." *Just as,* in the *just as . . . as* structure, occurred 10% of the time, as in "Middle-income men are *just as* hopelessly addicted *as* millionaires . . ." (*Better Homes and Gardens,* May, 1957, 227). *Equally as* occurred 10% of the time in the same structure, as in "Their house . . . was *equally as* original *as* Mrs. Stowe herself" (Helen Pillsbury, *Chicago Daily Tribune,* Dec. 22, 1957). *Equally as* occurs in other structures, like: *"Equally as* vital, she generates . . ." (*Commonweal,* July 19, 1957, 393); "His steps are . . . *equally as* unwavering" (*Sheboygan* [*Wisconsin*] *Press,* Dec. 21, 1957, 13).

Several studies (Church, Postraw, Speitz, Tatham) revealed that *equally as* occurred in newspapers and magazines; *equally* and *just as* occurred in fiction as well as in these media.

EVEN, adv. See ONLY, adv.

EVEN THOUGH. See THOUGH, ALTHOUGH.

EVENINGS. See ADVERBIAL GENITIVE.

EVER, adv. See ONLY, adv.

EVERY, adv.

Summary: Every *is more often employed as an adjective* ("every day") *in standard written English, but it does occur as an adverb* ("every so often") *in spoken English and informal writing.*

Data: Two studies (Hewitt, Hotchner) show its use as an adverb, as in "She lectures from time to time . . . and *every now and then* she startles her readers with blank verse reviews of Shakespeare or Molière" (*Theatre Arts,* Mar., 1957, 71).

Every often occurs before an adjective, before numerals and ordinals, and even before an adverb preceding an adjective, as, for example, "*Every* colonial system . . ." (*Current History,* Feb., 1958, 76); ". . . can land only once *every* two or three weeks" (*Reader's Digest,* Mar., 1958, 188); "*Every* third woman you passed . . ." (Edna Ferber, *Saturday Review,* May 24, 1958, 4); ". . . *every* significantly new philosophy has . . ." (*Science and Society,* Winter, 1958, 64). In the studies cited above, forty-five examples were found preceding adjectives and fifteen preceding numerals and ordinals. Undoubtedly the noun preceded by the adjective, the numeral, the ordinal, or the adjective and also preceded by an adverb is thought of as a unit.

Other evidence: Krapp, 231-32; Perrin, *CE,* 5 (May, 1944), 451.

EVERYBODY, EVERYONE. See AGREEMENT, INDEFINITE PRONOUNS.

EVERYPLACE. See ANYPLACE, adv.

EVERYWHERES. See ANYWHERE, ANYWHERES.

EXACTLY, adv. See ONLY, adv.

EXCEPT (THAT). See WITHOUT, UNLESS.

EXCEPTING. See PROVIDED, PROVIDING, conj.

FAILING. See PROVIDED, PROVIDING, conj.

FARTHER, FURTHER

Summary: Further, *meaning* "in addition" *or* "more" *occurred in formal written English 53% of the time; referring to distance,* farther *is used 62% of the time and* further *38%. Usage is divided.*

Data: In actual practice, according to four studies (Etkin, Flick, Simon, Trapp), the two words are interchangeable in all uses, except that *further* is always used in the sense of "more" or "in addition," as in ". . . as weapons to fight off *further* inquiry" (*The New York Times,* Sept. 1, 1954, 18) and "They might be *further* astonished to learn . . ." (*Collier's,* Nov. 26, 1954, 32). Examples of *further* and *farther* referring to distance are: "If the *Saturday Review* would like to carry this a little *farther,* it might try to find out . . ." (*Harper's,* June, 1955, 19) and "Paris was such fun, but it's getting *farther* and *farther* away" (*American Magazine,* Nov., 1954, 116); ". . . Nothing could be *further* from the truth" (*Reader's Digest,* July, 1952, 15).

Other evidence: Curme, *Syntax,* 501-2; Kemp, *CE,* 17 (Oct., 1955), 53; Marckwardt and Walcott, 28, 105-6; Pooley, *TEU,* 146-47.

FEEL, v. See KNEEL, v.

FEEL BAD. See BAD, BADLY.

FEWER. See LESS, FEWER.

FINAL. See COMPARISON, ILLOGICAL.

FINE

Summary: Fine *may substitute for* well *in spoken English or in written English representing conversation, but in standard written English, its use is limited to an adjectival term of approval.*

Though *fine* is standard usage, like *nice, wonderful,* and *lovely* it has become a counter word and is overused. As a result, it has lost its force and become a vague modifier, as in "He has developed into a *fine* teacher." It would be more effective but not more correct to use another word, such as *able, competent, effective,* or *excellent.*

Data: One study (Fischler) shows that *fine* is sometimes used after verbs where *well* generally occurs in formal English, as in "I tried it on and it fit *fine"* (Donald Hough, *Captain Retread,* 1944, p. 16) and frequently one hears "I'm doing *fine"* or "I could see *fine."* In reference to inanimate things, one also may hear "It works *fine"* instead of "It works *well."* "He did *fine"* is as well established in spoken English as "Play *fair"* and "Hold *tight." Finely* seems a little precious and is rarely heard except before a participle, as in "a *finely* woven material." In another study (Burke), no example of *fine* to replace *well* was found in a reading of more than 4,000 pages of literature and periodicals, but it was heard once in conversation.

Other evidence: Marckwardt and Walcott, 101; Mathews, *DA,* 606-7.

FIT, v.

Summary: *The preterit forms of* fit *and* fitted *in standard English alternate without any distinction, although social and regional preferences exist.*

Data: An investigation of three groups classified according to educational level (Tyson) showed that in the context "The suit *fitted/fit* badly," the group with least education preferred *fitted* (12 to 3), the group with most education, *fit* (10 to 5). All three groups preferred *fitted* in the past participle, in the context "The plumber had *fitted/fit* the pipe expertly before I arrived."

According to the Linguistic Atlas survey, in New England *fitted,* in the context of "His coat *fit/fitted* me," is more common in cultivated speech, whereas in the Upper Midwest (Allen), *fit* is preferred by all classes of speakers, and used by 80% of the culti-vated speakers. Another investigation (Dickson) shows that *fit* occurred frequently in written English. Both *fit* and *fitted,* like *knit/knitted,* are standard.

Other evidence: Atwood, 14, 17; Barnhart, Files; Berkeley, *AS,* 30 (Dec., 1955), 311; Dickson, *AS,* 31 (Oct., 1956), 225-26; Kurath, *LANE,* Vol. III, Pt. 2, Map 647; V.G. McDavid, 35; R.I. and V.G. McDavid, *AS,* 35 (Feb., 1960), 18; Wentworth, 219.

FITTED. See FIT, v.

FIX, n., v.

Summary: In addition to its well-established meanings, in informal English, fix *as a verb may mean* "to repair," *or* "to punish," *or* "to bribe," *or* "to prepare," *or* "to arrange"; *as a noun, it may mean* "pre-dicament," *or* "a dose of narcotics," *or* "position in navigation or avia-tion."

In formal usage *fix* has a number of well-established meanings: "to fasten firmly," as *"Fix* the table to the floor"; "to direct steadily," as *"Fix* your attention on the trapeze artist"; "to make permanent," as *"fixing* color in dyeing"; "to settle definitely," as "He *fixed* the rent at fifty dollars"; "to place definitely on," as "He *fixed* the blame on Charles."

Data: Investigations (Bryant, Goldberg, Winburne) show that *fix* has a wide spectrum of informal meanings. *Fix,* meaning "to repair," has now become established in American English (the British generally say *mend* or *repair*). It is found in a variety of magazines, especially in those catering to home improvement and in "Do It Yourself" handbooks and manuals, often following the words *how to* in the title of articles, as: "How to *Fix* a Win-dow" (*Better Homes and Gardens,* June, 1947, 133). This mean-ing has become so common that the verb is occasionally employed in a colloquial manner as a noun, as in the title "Quick *Fixes*" (*Coronet,* May, 1955, 14), meaning "Quick Repairs." The verb is also sometimes joined to *it* to form a new word *fixit,* as "Eton's

Fixit Shop"; "Daddy, the *Fixit* Man" (*Parents' Magazine,* Sept., 1945, 36). Another combination is *fixup,* as in ". . . any painting, papering, or *fixup* expenses that might be needed to make the house saleable . . ." (*Wall Street Journal,* Feb. 11, 1954, 2). One often hears statements like "John should *fix up* the house" or "I must *fix up* the car before summer."

In informal English or in special fields, *fix* has a number of other usages. Used with *in,* it means "predicament," as "He will be in a *fix* if the supervisor returns"; ". . . there is a sameness and repetition to the *fixes* he continuously finds himself in" (*The New York Times,* June 4, 1955, 9). It also refers to "a dose of narcotics," as in "He took a *fix* out of curiosity and had never since been able to control the urge" (*Newsweek,* May 2, 1955, 51). *Fix,* likewise, occurs as a verb with this meaning, as "I blew the joints for mor'n a year before I ever *fixed* . . ." (*Time,* June 9, 1952, 50). Another meaning of *fix* is "a position in navigation or aviation determined from the bearing of two or more known points": "As navigator he must figure continuous *fixes* . . ." (*Harper's,* Oct., 1955, 41).

As a verb it means "to revenge oneself on" or "to punish," as in "I'll *fix* that cleaner for ruining my dress"; "to arrange matters, by trickery, bribery, or other means, in one's favor," as "The race (jury) (election) was *fixed*" (*Fix* also occurs as a noun with this meaning, as in "It wasn't until the game was actually under way that he learned the *fix* wasn't in" in *The New Yorker,* Mar. 5, 1955, 52. A derivative noun from this meaning is *fixer,* referring to the one who does the arranging.); "to prepare (for, to be, to do)," as in "He's *fixing* to go fishing," or "She's *fixing* to cook a cake"; "to arrange" or "put in order," as "She should *fix* her hair differently."

Fixed is also used colloquially in the expression *well-fixed,* to mean "having sufficient money or supplies" and in a question like "How are you *fixed* for blades?" meaning "Do you have sufficient blades?" Then there is the expression to *fix up with,* meaning "to arrange with" or "to clear up any difficulty," as in "I'll *fix* it *up with* him before I leave the city," as well as *to fix up,* meaning "to arrange an engagement for a boy with a girl," as in *"Fix* me *up* with a beautiful girl for tonight."

A derivative noun from the verb *fix,* employed colloquially in the plural, is *fixings,* referring to "trimmings, embellishments, accompaniments," as in "The *fixings* for the turkey were under way."

Other evidence: Barnhart, Files; Hench, *AS,* 30 (Dec., 1955), 309-10; Mathews, *DA,* 621-22; Mencken, *Supp. I,* 497-98; Wentworth, 220.

FOLK(S)

Summary: Folk, *meaning* "people; persons," *has two plurals in standard usage:* folk *and* folks, *as* "rural folk" *and* "folks say."

Data: Two studies (Breiter, B. Levine) show that, in informal English, *folks* is used to refer to "relatives," immediate family, "parents," as in "My *folks* went away last week" or ". . . I couldn't sleep if I didn't do what I could to help my *folks"* (*New York Daily News,* Feb., 24, 1957, 9). The Linguistic Atlas survey of New England found *folks,* along with *people,* sometimes referred only to one's immediate family (parents, brothers, and sisters) to the exclusion of more distant relatives. Otherwise, it was usually synonymous with *relatives, relations, connections, kin folks, home folks, kinsmen.*

Folks, meaning people, is also employed colloquially on radio and television (Breiter), as in "Good morning, *folks!"* or "Maybe you *folks* would like to hear a song" ("Ed Sullivan Show," WCBS, Apr. 20, 1957, 8:00 P.M.). *Folk*s is the much more common form in spoken English. It is also used as the plural of *you: "you folks,"* as in "I saw *you folks* on the porch." Likewise, it occurs in the intimate type of story in magazines, newspaper columns, children's books, and the work of a certain kind of author who wants to be familiar, friendly, and confidential.

Linked with *folks* are *folksy* and *folksiness,* meaning "friendly," "sociable." *Folk* is frequently compounded with other words: *folklore, folksay, folkways,* written as one word. *Folk music, folk dance, folk tale, folk song, folk story, folk tune, folk laws, folk air,* however, are always written as two words.

Other evidence: Bryant, *CE,* 21 (Oct., 1959), 38; Kurath, *LANE,* Vol. II, Pt. 2, Map 388; Marckwardt and Walcott, 120; Wentworth, 225-26.

FOR TO

Summary: For to, *as in* for to tell, *is chiefly colloquial usage;* to *followed by the infinitive is the standard usage in educated and written English.*

Data: One investigator (Malmstrom), drawing from the Linguistic Atlas records for the New England, the Middle Atlantic, the South Atlantic, the North Central, and the Upper Midwest States, studied the infinitive of purpose in the context "He came over *(for) to tell* me about it."

To followed by the infinitive is the most common construction and is universal in Type III (cultivated) speech in the North Central and the Upper Midwest States and practically so in the same type in the New England, the Middle Atlantic, and the South Atlantic States.

For to tell occurs in all areas but does not predominate in the speech of either Type III or Type II informants (those who have at least some secondary school education). In New England it is clearly an older form. According to two studies (Harris, Swetsky), it does not occur in formal written English.

Other evidence: Atwood, 34; Kurath, *LANE,* Vol. III, Pt. 1, Map 572, Pt. 2, Map 703; Malmstrom, *SVTS,* 226-27; V.G. McDavid, 59; R.I. and V.G. McDavid, *AS,* 35 (Feb., 1960), 17.

FORMAL IT. See IT (2).

FREEZE, v.

Summary: The preterit froze *and the past particple* frozen *are standard English;* freezed *is nonstandard.*

Data: According to a study (Malmstrom) of the Linguistic Atlas records, in the context of "The lake *froze* over last night," *froze* is the standard preterit form, universal everywhere in Type

III (cultivated) speech. With rare exceptions in the New England, the Middle Atlantic, and the North Central States, and with no exceptions in the Upper Midwest States, it is universal also in the other types. The nonstandard variants, *freezed, frozed, friz,* and *frez,* are limited to the South Atlantic States, where they are definitely older forms, rapidly receding. In two studies of written English (Brown, Hotchner), there was only one deviation from the standard form, in Ernest Hemingway's "A Man of the World": "Even his smell was *froze* . . ." (*The Atlantic Monthly,* Nov., 1957, 65), but this is represented speech.

Other evidence: Atwood, 14-15; Kurath, *LANE,* Vol. III, Pt. 2, Map 648; Malmstrom, *SVTS,* 142-43; V.G. McDavid, 35.

GENERAL IT. See IT (4).

GENITIVE CASE

Summary: In standard usage, the genitive case designated by the apostrophe or apostrophe and s *occurs with inanimate nouns, as in* New York's finest *and* science's *influence.*

The *of-phrase* rather than the inflected genitive (the so-called *s*-genitive) is frequently asserted to be the correct form with inanimate objects, as in the *president of the college* (instead of *the college's president*), but such obvious idiomatic exceptions as expressions of time, distance, and value (*ten days' grace, a dollar's worth*) as well as others (*heart's content, at his wit's end, at swords' points*) show that the rule is not accurate.

Data: One study (Baron) based upon a reading of about a thousand pages of *Life, Time, Newsweek,* and *Coronet* (August, 1953, through January, 1954) disclosed 272 examples of the *s*-genitive with inanimate objects distributed over the following areas:

(1) political, 40%: *Germany's rearming, the nation's social security.*
(2) physical objects, 16%: *turnpike's stations, book's main divisions, car's performance.*
(3) periods of time, 14%: *four hours' ascent, by the week's end.*
(4) commercial products, 7%: *GM's patents,* etc.
(5) publications, 6%: *Newsweek's article, Time's staff.*

(6) organizations and institutions, 5%: *Harvard's School of Public Health, U.N.'s Korea Civil Assistance Command.*

The other 12% occurred in connection with collective nouns, as in *the U. S. Bureau's 30-day outlook* (6%); abstract nouns, as in *freedom's ring* (.8%); with personifications, as in *Death's head* (.4%); and with the word *world*, as in *the world's greatest adventure* (5%). Another study (R. Thomas) found a total of 489 examples with a similar distribution.

Though the *of*-phrase is the more common with names of inanimate objects, either form may be used. One study (Helen Henry) found the periphrastic, or the *of*-phrase, used 61% of the time as compared to the inflected genitive.

Although the uses of the *s*-genitive are in the highest degree varied and subtle, its most common function is to indicate possession, as in *the man's hat* and *Sam's book*. It does not, however, occur with the partitive genitive, which names the whole of which a part is taken. *A dress of silk* and *a piece of pie* are *of*-genitives, but *silk's dress* or *pie's piece* would be impossible.

Frequently, however, the noun-adjunct construction (a noun used as a noun modifier, as in *road map, chair cushions*) will occur instead of the genitive. A study (Gerdy) of current prose showed that the *of*-phrase occurred 677 times, the noun-adjunct, 617, and the inflected genitive, 611. Usage is almost equally divided among the three. *See* CASE, GENITIVE OF NOUNS THAT NAME INANIMATE THINGS; CASE, OF NOUN OR PRONOUN SUBJECT OF A GERUND.

Other evidence: Bryant, *CE*, 16 (Oct., 1954), 55-56; Fries, *Lang.*, XIV (Apr.-June, 1938), 121-33; Hall, 202-7; Thomas, *CE*, 14 (Jan., 1953), 236-39.

GENITIVE CASE BEFORE THE GERUND. See CASE, OF NOUN OR PRONOUN SUBJECT OF A GERUND.

GENITIVE OF NOUNS THAT NAME INANIMATE THINGS. See GENITIVE CASE.

GET, v.

Summary: Preterit got *and past particple* got *or* gotten *occur in stand-ard English. In formal written English* got *occurs 76.6% of the time, invariably preferred in the senses "possess," or "have" and "must," or "be able." In spoken English both* got *and* gotten *occur about equally in the senses "acquire," "receive," and "become," in verb-adverb com-binations, and as a passive auxiliary in place of* to be.

Data: The many meanings and shades of meaning are too numerous to list here, but usage principles concerning a few of them are discussed in the following paragraphs. The discussion is based upon nineteen investigations (Algeo, Asman. Benardete, Billias, Bowden, Coxe, Donkle, Feeney, Gross, Hook. Hotchner, Kovitz, McMillan, Pregenzer, M. Richardson, R. Thomas, Watson, Whalen, Winburne).

1. got ("acquired," "received," "become")

The use of the forms of *get* in the sense "acquire," "receive," or "become" is never questioned. Both *got* and *gotten* occur for these meanings, as in "I have already *gotten* (or *got*) my books"; "It has *gotten* very good reviews universally . . ." (*American Scholar,* Spring, 1954, 204); "Relations between the two gentlemen have *gotten* (or *got*) worse as the years have passed." The choice here, as in the other uses where *gotten* is acceptable, depends upon style.

2. got ("possess," "have")

In both standard and nonstandard English *have got* and *has got* (often contracted, as in *I've got, we've got, he's got, she's got, they've got*) are simply alternatives for *have* and *has* in the sense "possess" and in certain auxiliary uses, as in "Elvis has *got* the best . . ." (*Harper's,* Jan., 1958, 46); "He *hasn't got* a ten-gallon hat or a chromatic shirt or even a pair of chaps . . ." (Bernard De Voto, *Harper's,* Nov., 1958, 59); ". . . and there must be something to talk to and to love. And if you *haven't got* it you'll make it in your head, or out of a stone in a canyon wall" (Loren C. Eiseley, "Buzby's Petrified Woman" [the educated narrator speak-ing], *ibid.,* 79). The use of *got* in such constructions is characteristic of conversational or informal English. One study found that in formal written English *have* and *has* are much more common (74% of the time) than *have got* and *has got* (26%). Note that in all these examples we find *got* rather than *gotten*.

In colloquial English one also finds the omission of *have* and *has,* letting *got* carry the sentence, as in ". . . we *got* more of it . . . better of it than anywhere, anytime" (*Miami Herald,* Dec. 31, 1957, 18B); "You *got* power" (*Ladies' Home Journal,* Dec., 1952, 148). Here one has an example of obscuration to the point of inaudibility. That is, children and others learning the language fail to hear the slight *'ve* and therefore do not pronounce it. For instance, in *"You've got* power" [juv gɑt 'pɑuɚ] the [v] is likely to be so reduced that it remains unheard so that "you *got* power" results. In a sense the construction may be one on paper alone, for the [v] of *have* may be completely gone. In speech our expectation of [v] in *you've* makes us think we hear it.

In the usage of *have (has) got* or of *got* alone, the idea of the present time overshadows that of the past time. For example, the present perfect tense has the force of a present tense, as in "Jane has a blue dress, but look at Louise; she *has got* a bright red one."

The British extend this usage to the past tense as well as to the present affirmative and negative, as in "He *hadn't got* a dollar for the fare." An American would say, "He *doesn't have (hasn't)* (*hasn't got*) a dollar for the fare" in the present negative and "He *didn't have* . . ." in the past negative.

In interrogative statements the *got* creeps in by analogy to the word order in the ordinary question, as in "Have you *got* it here?" The word order parallels other questions like "Does he wish a statement?" or "May I have a statement?" where a weak auxiliary is at the beginning of the question. Similarly, "What *have* you *got* to say about it?" (*American Scholar,* Spring, 1954, 197) has an alternative "What do you have to say about it?" If, however, there is no object expressed, *have* is not expanded into *have got.* The question would be "Has he?" not "Has he *got?*"

3. got ("must")

Have got is also used in America and even more in England with the meaning of "must," denoting obligation, as in "I *have got* to go to work now" or "You've *got* to explain that last thing a little bit" (*American Scholar,* Autumn, 1955, 474). The *got* adds more emphasis and vigor to the statement, as *have,* often employed as an auxiliary in compound tense forms (*have written, spoken,* etc.), has gradually lost its force as an independent verb. "I *have got* to go" is exceedingly common, even among careful speakers. Note that this construction consists of *have₊got₊to₊*infinitive. *Got* is never prefixed to the infinitive without *to*. In nonstandard English *got₊ to₊*infinitive is also employed with the meaning of "must" in expressions like "You *got to* go," originally "You*'ve got to* go." "You *got to* go" is more often heard without juncture, a pause, between *got* and *to* as [gatə]: "You *gotta* go."

A comparative study of *have* and *have got* with the meaning of "must" showed *have* employed 56% of the time and *have got* 44%. Usage is divided.

4. get (got) ("to be able" with infinitive)

In standard colloquial English *get* (*got*), meaning "to be able," often precedes an infinitive, as in "I *get to go* tomorrow and "I *got to talking* with him and in the course of the conversation . . ." (*Coronet,* Jan., 1958, 72).

5. get (got) ("begin," "began" with *-ing* form of verb)

Get and *got* also occur in the sense of "begin" and "began" with the *-ing* form of a verb, e.g., "Let's *get going*" (Comment of President Eisenhower, *The New York Times,* Nov. 16, 1957, 60) and "He *got thinking* maybe Mike hadn't searched" (Hillary Waugh, *Hope to Die,* 1948, p. 184). "He *got thinking*" presumably derives from "*He got to thinking,*" where the phonetic development would be [gattə > gat-t > gat]. The conventional transcription of *got thinking* may be misleading; in actual speech the lengthening of the [t] may still be present, but the writer has been unable to recognize the conventional spellings his speech requires. As a result *got* appears with the *-ing* form of the verb following, as in *got going, got thinking,* etc.

6. get (got) as passive auxiliary

Often added to a past participle in informal English, *get* has become a passive auxiliary used in place of the verb *to be,* as in "They went to City Hall and *got married*"; "The man *got hurt* on his way home"; "I shouldn't care if I did *get sent* home."

7. get (got) in verb-adverb combinations

In Modern English, *get* is often joined with adverbs to form verb-adverb combinations such as *get ahead, get around, get at, get by,* etc., all good colloquial English, but of varying degrees of currency. *Get ahead,* for example, is higher up the scale of usage than *get at* or *get by.* They occur in both standard and nonstandard English.

Other evidence: Atwood, 26-27; Barnhart, Files; Bartlett, *CE,* 10 (Feb., 1949), 280-82; Bryant, *CE,* 19 (Jan., 1958), 171; Crowell, *AS,* 34 (Dec., 1959), 280-86; Fries, *AEG,* 170-71; Galinsky, II, 412-13; Hatcher, *MLN,* 64 (Nov., 1949), 433-46; Marckwardt, *CE,* 16 (Feb., 1955), 309-10; *OED;* Rice, *AS,* 7 (Apr., 1932), 280-96; Robertson, *AS,* 14 (Dec., 1939), 247-48.

GET, GOT, AS PASSIVE AUXILIARY. See GET, v., 6.

GET, GOT, IN VERB-ADVERB COMBINATIONS. See GET, v., 7.

GET, GOT ("TO BE ABLE" WITH INFINITIVE). See GET, v., 4.

GET SICK. See TAKE SICK.

GIVE, v.

Summary: The preterit gave *and the past participle* given *are standard English;* given *as a preterit is nonstandard.*

Data: According to a study of the Linguistic Atlas records (Malmstrom), in the context of "That's the one you *gave* me," *gave* is the standard form, nearly universal in Type III (cultivated) speech and strongly predominant in the speech of Type II informants (those with at least some secondary school education) in all areas investigated: the New England, the Middle Atlantic, the South Atlantic, the North Central, and the Upper Midwest States. The most common nonstandard variant of *gave* is *give,* chiefly characteristic of Type I (uneducated) speech but occurring in the speech of about 80% of the Type II informants in West Virginia. One study (Downing) turned up *given* in the preterit: "They never *given* them back to me," spoken by an uneducated Negro boy (Carson McCullers, "The Heart Is a Lonely Hunter," p. 429, in *The Ballad of a Sad Café*, 1951).

Other evidence: Atwood, 15; Kurath, *LANE*, Vol. III, Pt. 2, Map 649; Malmstrom, *SVTS*, 144-45; V.G. McDavid, 35-36.

GO AND. See TRY AND.

GOBS. See LOT(S), HEAP(S).

GOOD AND

Summary: Good and *occurs as an intensive before adjectives and adverbs in colloquial English and occasionally in written English. Very occurs much more often (about 80% of the time) but* good and *is also acceptable usage.*

Good and is a colloquial intensive placed before an adjective or adverb, as in "I am *good and (very)* tired." The *and* is omitted before an adjective that precedes its noun (*good black coffee*), but inserted before a predicate adjective ("The coffee is *good and black*") or any adjective after its noun ("coffee, *good and black*") or before an adverb ("He is running *good and fast*").

Data: One study (Rosenthal) found two examples of *good and* in *The New York Times Magazine,* May 25, 1958, 19: ". . . it can be said with reasonable accuracy that South Americans are *good and* mad at the United States"; and as a caption under a picture accompanying the article by Szulc, *"Good and* Angry Neighbors." Another study (H. D. Levine) showed *good and* employed about 17% of the time by students 12-13 years of age and also caught the expression on radio and television, in the theater, in general conversation, and occasionally in written material. A third investigation (Winburne) found similar evidence in his reading. Like *good and* (in the context *"good and* hungry"), the expressions *"good and* ready," *"good and* strong," and *"good and* warm" were recorded by the Linguistic Atlas of New England.

Other evidence: Byington, *AS,* 19 (Oct., 1944), 229; Fries, *AEG,* 203-4; Kurath, *LANE,* Vol. III, Pt. 2, Map 716; *OED.*

GOOD AT. See GOOD, WELL.

GOOD MANY. See GOOD, WELL.

GOOD, WELL

Summary: In formal standard English, good *occurs in such contexts as "the* good *man" or "The man is* good*." Well, meaning "in good health," may be used in the same way: "the* well *man" or "The man is* well*." In nonstandard English,* good *is often substituted for the adverb* well, *as in, "Do it* good*"; on the other hand,* good *in reference to the functioning of inanimate things is becoming increasingly common in standard English, as in "The car runs* good*."*

These two words have been traditionally used after the verb *feel,* also with different connotations. In "He feels *good,*" or "I like this suit; it feels *good,*" *good* designates a generalized state of goodness, but in "He feels *well,*" *well* refers to a state of health, a specific meaning; the man is free from disease or ailment. However, in a sentence such as "Things are *well* with us these days," meaning "things are in a favorable condition," one may easily substitute *good,* suggesting that "things are as they should be or perhaps even better." Here the words are interchangeable. Verbs with which *good* alone is used are *taste, sound,* and *smell:* "His cooking tastes (smells) very *good.*" *Well* also occurs in such contexts as "He played *well* yesterday," in which *well* tells that he performed satisfactorily. *Good* in this context is nonstandard, though verbs like *run, play,* and *work* often pattern after *taste, feel, sound, act, seem,* which permit *good* to follow, as "The radio plays *good,*" "This machine works *good.*"

Data: Two studies (Fischler, Malanaphy) found examples of *good* instead of *well,* as in "The car runs *good*" and "I can talk pretty *good* to a couple of people . . . but. . . ." Another (Hotchner) found *good* used in 13% of the illustrations, as in

"The dance was going *good*" and "It seems he's faring pretty *good,*" (*New York Times Book Review,* Oct. 4, 1953, 8).

One investigation (Winburne) shows *good* also used in the colloquial expression *make good,* meaning "to make recompense for," as in "If there's not enough money to pay the depositors, then the stockholders have to *make* it *good*" (James M. Cain, *Mildred Pierce,* 1948, p. 141); "to keep an agreement," as in "He's *making good* on that promise now, having recaptured northern Burma . . ." (*The Best from Yank,* 1945, p. 131); "to succeed in doing," as in "I'd been joking and bragging . . . about what a crack rifle shot I was, so I had to *make good* . . ." (Ernie Pyle, *Brave Men,* 1944, p. 188); "to become successful," as in "He *made good* in that job." One would hardly say "made well" here; on the other hand, "Do well" is perfectly good standard English.

Good has likewise joined itself to *do* in the verb *do-good,* from which the noun *do-gooder* has been formed, referring to an earnest humanitarian determined to promote reform or welfare work, whether the beneficiaries want it or not.

In spoken English, *good* may function as an intensive, as in "a *good* long time." Katherine Anne Porter has one of her characters in *Noon Wine* (1936) say, "I've been waiting to speak to him for a *good* long spell now . . ." (*Six Great Modern Short Novels,* 1954, p. 185, cited by Rosenthal). Here *good* means "very," as it does when joined to *and* and placed before an adjective, as in *"good and* cold," *"good and* sweet," *"good and* hot." Other examples (Winburne) are ". . . he was good and *mad* . . ." (Ernie Pyle, *Brave Men,* p. 202) and "It was *good* and dark . . ." (*The Best from Yank,* 1946, p. 168). The *OED* cites *good and* as colloquial American, giving 1834 as the earliest use. These constructions attain a certain emphatic quality through the use of the word *good,* whereas the word *very* would seem less strong. *See* GOOD AND.

Another combination including *good* is *good at,* meaning "having ability in," which is standard English: ". . . Madge was always *good at* language" (John P. Marquand, *So Little Time,* 1943, p. 22).

In standard English, *a good* is also used with *many* to designate an indefinite number: *"A good many* of us feel we have failed . . ."* (Pyle, *op. cit.,* p. 457) and *". . . a good many* veterans had gone away . . ." (*The New Yorker,* Sept. 13, 1947, 25). *A good many* seems especially inviting since the speaker in no way obligates himself to be specific about quantity when he uses the idiom. The idiom does not mean "more than many" or "a great many," for it may actually denote " a very few."

Other evidence: Barnhart, Files; Fries, *AEG,* 203-4.

GOT ("ACQUIRED," "BECAME," "RECEIVED"). See GET, v., 1.

GOT ("BEGAN," WITH -ING FORM OF VERB). See GET, v., 5.

GOT ("MUST"). See GET, v., 3.

GOT ("POSSESS," "HAVE"). See GET, v., 2.

GOTTEN. See GET, v.

GRADUATE (FROM)

Summary: In current American English the idiom to be graduated from *in the context "He* was graduated from *Princeton University" has generally been replaced by* graduated from. *"He* graduated Princeton" *is nonstandard English.*

Data: Graduated from is now the standard idiom, as examples from two studies (Flannery, Hotchner) show: "He was born in Staten Island and *graduated from* Harvard College in 1908" (*The New York Times,* May 13, 1958, 29); "She *graduated from* Sarah Lawrence College" (*ibid.,* May 15, 1958, 32); "At seventeen he *graduated from* high school . . ." (Ernie Pyle, *Brave Men,* 1944, p. 129); "Chet Allen . . . just *graduated from* high school . . ." (*Newsweek,* Dec., 23, 1957, 12). One may occasionally hear the telescoped expression *to graduate college,* as: "He *graduated college* (high school) this year." This nonstandard construction is more common in the Middle Atlantic area, especially in Philadelphia and New York City; however, it is heard in other sections, especially in larger cities such as Chicago. If the name of the institution or some substitute word does not follow, *graduated* without *from* occurs, as in "He graduated in May, 1958."

Other evidence: Bryant, *CE,* 17 (Apr., 1956), 415; Curme, *Syntax,* 440; Dunlap, *AS,* 20 (Feb., 1945), 17; Hall, 113.

GROUNDS, sing.

Summary: The formal plural grounds, *in the expression* on the grounds that, *followed by a single* "ground" (*a valid reason, motive, or cause*), *is in common use today in magazines, newspapers, books, and speech.*

Data: From one study (Pound) came the following examples: "In his last years in high school he was expelled, he says, on *grounds* of general rowdiness" (*Time,* Aug. 29, 1955, 54); "The prosecution objected to the proposal on *grounds* that Alley is required to be present during all phases of his trial before a general court martial" (*Baltimore Sun,* Oct. 18, 1955, B, 36/2); "She sued me for divorce later, on *grounds* of mental cruelty" (William Inge, *Bus Stop,* 1955, p. 47). This plural has become singular.

Similarly *charges* has become singular: "The Roman Catholic bishop of Shanghai and 'his principal accomplices' have been arrested by Chinese Communist authorities on charges of espionage [a single charge], Radio Moscow announced" (United Press dispatch in Lincoln [Neb.] *Evening Journal,* Dec. 10, 1955, 10).

Grounds and *charges* have followed the path of other plural nouns that have become singular; *bodice, gallows, innings, news, politics, shambles, trace, truce.* We also have the established expression: *a means to an end,* where *means* is singular.

Other evidence: Pound, *AS,* 31 (May, 1956), 154-56.

GROW, v.

Summary: *The preterit* grew *and the past participle* grown *are standard English;* growed *is nonstandard.*

Data: The Linguistic Atlas for the Middle Atlantic and the
South Atlantic States records only the preterit of *grow,* but for the
New England, the North Central, and the Upper Midwest States it
records both the preterit and the past participle. The contexts are
"Bob *grew* a lot in one year"; "Bob *grew* a lot last year"; "You*'ve
grown* big"; and "You*'ve grown* a lot since I last saw you."

According to one study (Malmstrom), *grew* is universal in Type
III speech (cultivated) in all areas, and prevails strongly in the
speech of those with at least some secondary school education
(Type II). In Type I speech (uneducated), the main variant is
growed. Grown predominates in all types in all areas. Nearly all
informants who use *grew* in the past used *grown* as the past participle. One study of writing (Katzman) found no variants from these
forms.

Unlike *grow,* the verb *crow,* which once had the principal parts
of *crow, crew, crown,* has now established as usage *crow, crowed,
crowed.* One may occasionally still hear "The cock *crew,*" but "The
man *crowed* (not *crew*) over his success."

Other evidence: Atwood, 15-16; Kurath, *LANE,* Vol. III, Pt. 2,
Map 650; Malmstrom *SVTS,* 147-48; V.G. McDavid, 36-37.

HAD BETTER (BEST)

Summary: Had better, *meaning* "would be wiser, safer, to one's advantage, *"is often substituted for* should *or* ought *in standard English;
the contraction* 'd better *and the shorter form,* better, *both occur in
informal English;* better had *is substandard.*

Data: According to three studies (Cahn, Samkoff, Tanderjian),
this idiom is used for suggestions, advice, commands given indirectly at times or emphatically in threats: "You *had better* retract
that statement." *Would better* occurs occasionally but *had better*
is much more frequent.

Another variant is the contraction *'d better:* "You*'d better* leave
that alone" (*New York Herald Tribune,* Mar. 10, 1957, Sec. 10,

29) and "You'*d better* take the picture down" (John Steinbeck, *The Moon is Down,* 1942, p. 54). In one study (Samkoff), *had better* occurred 52% of the time in written and spoken English, *'d better,* 48%. Similarly, in informal speech, the *had* is sometimes dropped entirely as in, "You [   ] *better* go to school now"; "If he writes you, you [   ] *better* answer immediately." One study (Tanderjian) showed *better* alone occurring twice as often as *had better* or *'d better* in writing, but *had better* is generally employed in most writing unless the direct words of a speaker are being recorded.

The inverted form, *better had,* is used in substandard speech, especially for emphasis; e.g., if one says idly, "I think I'll go to class today," the response might be: "You *better had!*"

Another idiom that follows *had better* is *had best:* "We *had best* call him before six o'clock." One study revealed the same number of written examples of it as *'d better;* another found half as many in spoken English.

Other evidence: Marckwardt and Walcott, 118; Mathews, *DA.* 109.

HAD(N'T) OUGHT. See OUGHT NOT.

HAD (WOULD) RATHER

Summary: Had rather *and* would rather *are used interchangeably in standard English to indicate preference; in formal English, the contraction* 'd rather *is not used.*

Data: One study (Cahn) showed *had rather,* in statements like "I *had rather* go to the theater than to the beach," occurring in 32% of the examples from speech and writing and *would rather* in 68%. In speech, the unstressed *had* or *would* yields the contraction *'d rather:* "I'*d* much *rather* stay home." In one study (Samkoff), *had rather* occurred 55% of the time and *'d rather* 45%. In nonstandard speech the form *'druther* occasionally occurs.

Other evidence: Kurath, *LANE,* Vol. III, Pt. II, Map, 717; Marckwardt and Walcott, 117.

HAIN'T. See I HAVEN'T.

HALF. See AGREEMENT, INDEFINITE PRONOUNS.

HANG, v.

Summary: *The preterit and past participle* hung *or* hanged *both occur in standard English, usually in a particular sense.*

Data: Two studies (Hotchner, Leon) reveal that the form *hanged* is used only with reference to execution; that *hung* is also used in this sense but that *hanged* is more common in standard formal English. In other senses only *hung* is used. In the sense of "delayed," *hung* is used with *got* and *up* in the colloquial sense: "I *got hung up* by the red light on my way over."

Other evidence: Atwood, 16; Kurath, *LANE,* Vol. III, Pt. 2, Map 651.

HARDLY

Summary: Hardly, *meaning "barely; not quite; not probably,"* joined *with a negative does not occur in formal English;* followed *by* when, *it occurs in standard usage.*

Data: Occasionally, one hears in speech a statement like "I *can't hardly* wait to get home . . . ," but as an intensified negative, it is used only in colloquial English. A reading of 3,000 pages of prose (Roslin) turned up only one example of *can't hardly,* which was quoted speech: "I *can't hardly* wait to go back on TV" (*Look,* Oct. 19, 1954, 21). Similar to *can't hardly* is *haven't hardly,* as in, "I *haven't hardly* any left."

Along with *hardly,* the words *barely* and *scarcely* are somewhat negative in character and are not added to another negative in formal standard usage. It must be said, however, that certain phrase patterns of nonstandard English, in which the double negative makes the negative notion much more emphatic ("I ain't got hardly any" or "I ain't got none"), make the acceptable patterns

("I have hardly any" and "I have none") seem pale by comparison.

Hardly also occurs in formal English followed by *when* (not *than*), as in *"Hardly* had the surface rock been removed *when* three great beryl masses . . ." (*Reader's Digest,* May, 1957, 169). So does *scarcely,* but in informal English one may find *scarcely . . . than* and *hardly . . . than,* as in, *"Scarcely* had the clatter of the carts died away *than* a carriage raced through . . ." (*ibid.,* September 1940, 120) and "Jack [Paar] had *hardly* misfitted into his army khaki *than* he was assigned to an entertainment unit . . ." (*Mc-Call's,* Aug., 1958, 105). This usage, according to one study (Hotchner), is rare. Three studies (Kalina, Roslin, S. Schwartz) failed to find *barely* joined with a negative and only found one in the affirmative; the word is apparently not frequently used.

Other evidence: Curme, *Syntax,* 274; Jespersen, *Ess.,* 302-3; *MEG,* Pt. V, 454; Marckwardt and Walcott, 53, 99.

HARDLY THAN. See HARDLY.

HAVEN'T HARDLY. See HARDLY.

HE DON'T. See DON'T, v.

HEAP(S). See LOT(S), HEAP(S).

HEAVE, v.

Summary: The preterit and past participle heaved *or* hove *occur in standard English, but* hove *is chiefly used as a nautical term.*

Data: One study based upon 544 pages of reading in current literature (J. Jacobson) found the preterit *hove* only twice, both times nautically, as in "And now we *hove* to with engines stilled" (*Holiday,* June, 1960, 22). The common preterit is *heaved,* as in "He *heaved* a sigh" or "He *heaved* the rock with a mighty effort."

HERSELF. See MYSELF.

HIMSELF. See MYSELF.

HOME

Summary: Home *may be used after the verbs* go *and* get *without a preposition in standard English; in colloquial English,* home *occurs instead of the formal expression* at home, *often after* to be.

Data: One investigator (Winburne) encountered several illustrations of the first rule, illustrated by "Herbert . . . if you are not willing to welcome the boy gracefully, *go home*" (*The New Yorker,* Sept. 6, 1947, 22) and "You can *go home* now . . ." (Erle Stanley Gardner, *The Case of the Rolling Bones,* 1947, p. 80). Similarly, *get* does not require a preposition, as in "Will you *get home* by ten o'clock?" Another investigator (Passamonti) found seventeen examples of *home* following *go* and *get,* 59% of the time with *go* and 41% with *get.*

In colloquial English, *home* occurs instead of the formal expression *at home,* often after the verb *to be,* as in "He is *home* tonight." Another variant is *to home,* employed in the same way, as in "They weren't *to home* last evening."

According to two studies (Atwood, Malmstrom) the Linguistic Atlas survey, in a context such as "He isn't *at home,*" *at home* predominates strongly everywhere in the speech of all types except the most old-fashioned, east-educated informants in New England. *To home* is a Northern form, occurring most frequently in New England and the area of Northern settlement in the North Central States, although it is found also in one sub-area of the South Atlantic States, the Savannah River valley. It is probably receding in the Inland Northern dialect area since no Type III (cultivated) informant in the Upper Midwest States uses it. *Home,* without a preposition, is a minority form everywhere, but occurs in Type III speech in all the areas considered here: New England, Middle Atlantic, South Atlantic, North Central, and Upper Midwest States.

In a study (N. Fagen) based on written material, *at home* was employed 90% of the time, and *home* without a preposition was used in the other 10%, as in "He arrived *home* earlier than usual . . ." (*Saturday Evening Post*, Nov. 17, 1956, 96). No example of *to home* was found.

The expression *back home*, meaning "at home," "at one's home," "at one's home town," "in one's home country," also occurs. It implies that the speaker is not at his house or in his native city or land, as in *"Back home* . . . he and Mrs. Bradley probably took one drink a month . . ." (Ernie Pyle, *Brave Men*, 1944, p. 307) and "He had married a beautiful Indian girl *back home"* (*ibid.*, p. 48). *Back home* has yet another meaning, as in "Her husband was . . . *back home* after two years and a half as a German prisoner" (*ibid.*, p. 457, all cited by Winburne).

Other evidence: Kurath, *LANE*, Vol. II, Pt. 2, Map 403; Malmstrom, *SVTS*, 59-60, 277-79; Marckwardt and Walcott, 109; R.I. McDavid, *AED*, 515; R.I. and V.G. McDavid, *AS*, 35 (Feb., 1960), 11-12.

HOOF, n.

Summary: The plural of hoof *is generally* hoofs, *although* hooves *occasionally occurs.*

Data: One investigator (J. Jacobson) found in his reading of 544 pages of contemporary prose eight examples of *hoofs* and one of *hooves:* "With a clatter of *hooves* and a spatter of mud they passed him" (*Better Homes and Gardens*, Dec., 1960, 33). He also saw the plural *hooves* in a subtitle to the Swedish motion picture, *The Virgin Spring*, directed by Ingmar Bergman: "I hear the horse's *hooves* in the distance." The subtitle was added in the United States. The common usage is illustrated in "He heard the sound of *hoofs* and wheels on the trail." (*Saturday Evening Post*, Nov. 12, 1960, 70).

The plural of *calf*, however, is always *calves*. The study cited above encountered no instances of any other plural form of this word. By the same token, this study reveals that the only plural of *knife* is *knives*, and the study cited above shows that the only standard plural of *wolf* is *wolves*.

HOVE. See **HEAVE,** v.

HUMAN, n.

Summary: Human *is used as a noun to indicate one of the* human race, a human being, *especially in technical and semitechnical writing, but other variants such as* person, man, people *are used predominantly in formal English. It is used widely in speech.*

Data: The word *human* is generally employed as an adjective, as, for example, *human nature, human race, human affairs, human beings;* however, two studies (Hickey, Cooper) contain these examples of *human* as a noun: "There is every reason to use data for mutations in mice in calculating the results for *humans*" (Dr. H. J. Muller, "Radioactivity and Children," *U. S. News & World Report,* May 13, 1955); "Radioactive fallout is a threat not only to *humans* but also to animals, crops, and unpackaged food" (*Radioactive Fallout,* Federal Civil Defense Administration, Booklet No. 7, 13). It is used elsewhere too, as "Like *humans,* animals are clannish" (*Coronet,* Jan., 1958, 97); "The son's struggle symbolizes that of all *humans* who are conscious of their double heritage . . . " (*Theatre Arts,* Nov., 1957, 93). One hears it on radio and television, as in "We *humans* have a way of hurting those we love" ("Jane Wyman Theatre," WNBC, Apr. 7, 1957, 9:00 P.M.) or in an advertisement: "Lions don't smoke—*humans* do; so if you're human, smoke Chesterfield" ("Dragnet," WNBC, Mar. 21, 1957, 9:00 P.M.). Professors, clergymen, journalists, and the general public employ it. Many, however, still object to it.

In formal written English, the use of *human* as a noun is far outweighed by other variants, such as *human beings, persons, man, people,* and *human race.* In one study (Hickey) *human* as a noun occurred seven times, whereas the alternatives appeared fifty times, the most common being *human being.* Yet the study showed that *human* is coming into use in serious writings, in such periodicals as *Newsweek* and *Coronet* and in such publications as *The New York Times, Theatre Arts,* and *Current History.*

Other evidence: Jespersen, *Ess.*, 190.

HUNG. See HANG, v.

HYPERCORRECT USE OF WHOM. See WHO, WHOM.

I HAVEN'T

Summary: I haven't *is the standard English form, but* I hain't, *a variant of* I ain't, *is popular but recessive in Eastern speech; it rarely occurs in cultivated speech and never occurs in written English except to represent speech.*

Data: In the Linguistic Atlas records for the New England, the Middle Atlantic, the South Atlantic, the North Central, and the Upper Midwest States, according to one study (Malmstrom), the present tense form of *to have* is recorded in the contexts *"I haven't* done it" and *"I haven't* done nothing."

The Eastern records show that nearly all informants there know and use *haven't* along with *ain't* or *hain't* in this context. *Hain't* is a little more common than *ain't* and slightly more old-fashioned, and both forms occur with high frequencies in both Type I (uneducated) and Type II (those with at least some secondary school education) speech, but usually not in Type III (cultivated) speech. In the Middle West, *ain't* is much more common than *hain't* but is not a majority form in any group. Thus the usage, while colloquial in the East, is also recessive.

Atwood notes (p. 31) that in the East the distribution of *hain't* in "I haven't done nothing" is entirely different from that in "I am not going to hurt him." He concludes that many informants use *ain't* in both contexts but those who use *hain't* use it only to mean "have not," and thus distinguish it from *ain't,* "am not." This idea seems to be reflected in the field records of the Upper Midwest where *hain't* is found only in the *have* context.

Hain't does not occur in written English except in represented speech, as was shown by one study (Billias).

Other evidence: Atwood, 31; Kurath, *LANE*, Vol. III, Pt. 2, Map 684; Malmstrom, *SVTS*, 213-14.

IF, WHETHER

Summary: Usage is divided between whether *and* if *in introducing noun clauses that indicate doubt or uncertainty and function as the object of such verbs as* ask, doubt, know, see, wonder.

Data: Either *if* or *whether* can begin a noun clause that indicates doubt or uncertainty and functions as the object of a verb like *ask, care, doubt, know, learn, matter, mind, recall, remember, report, say, see, show, tell,* and *wonder,* e.g., "Some Americans will want to know *if* the African Negro problem . . . has anything to tell them about the American Negro problem" (*Saturday Review,* Mar. 26, 1955, 16); "We cannot know for sure why Matusow did any of it, *whether,* as some say, it was a deep plot all along or *whether* . . ." (*ibid,* Apr. 2, 1955, 26); "I wondered *if* the press of the great golden magnum of vintage urbanism had lost any of its sparkle while I was away . . ." (*The New Yorker,* Oct. 29, 1955, 97); "I wondered, idly, *whether* this was because the Republicans were in now or because Howard had sold the yacht" (*ibid.,* 102). Investigations made (Abbott, Benardete, Bruno, Gellman, Hotchner, McMillan, Stearns, R. Thomas) reported 187 noun clauses introduced by *if* and 128 of them functioning as objects of verbs. Of the object clauses, 49% were introduced by *if* and 51% by *whether.* Most of the clauses introduced by *if* followed *ask, doubt, know, see,* and *wonder,* but a few followed other verbs.

In formal written English, *whether* is the more common form when the clause is followed by a correlative *or* or *or whether,* as in the preceding examples. In conversational English, however, *if* occurs in such constructions, e.g., "I couldn't tell *if* the singer was a man or a woman . . ." (*The New Yorker,* Oct. 29, 1955, 33); ". . . he does not know *if* he is more happy or more wretched" (*Harper's,* Dec., 1954, 72). *Whether* is usually followed by *or,* but not consistently. "I don't know *whether* I can (*or* not)"; "Let's see *whether* you can type." Likewise, *if* may be followed by *or* to express an alternative: "I don't know *if* I can (*or* not)." Both *if* and *whether* may be employed in one sentence: "When we hear their double talk, we wonder *if* they are fooling us or *whether* they are wasting time until the President gives his consent"; "Nevertheless, Mr. Wilson does picture the type of decent postwar man who has a conscience and wonders *if* he should permit his conscience to rule him . . . or *whether* he should become a yes-man . . ." (*The New York Times Book Review,* July 17, 1955, 18). As corroboration of these findings, a study conducted in 1961 (Berg) found nineteen examples of clauses introduced by *whether,* fifteen of which were noun clauses used as objects of verbs (*ascertain, ask, decide, predict, see, wonder*) and 15 examples introduced by *if,* all of which were noun clauses acting as objects of verbs (*ask, doubt, see, wonder*).

In the negative, along with *if* and *whether, as* and *that* occur: "I don't know *as* (*that, if*) he will do it"; "I don't know *whether* he will do it or not." *As* occurs in informal English after the verb *know,* but *that* is common in both informal and formal English following the verbs listed in the first paragraph: "I do not doubt *that* he will be there." *As* and *that,* however, do not occur correlated with *or* as do *if* and *whether.*

Other evidence: Bryant, *CE,* 17 (Nov., 1955) 113-14; Fries, *AEG,* 224-25; Kurath, *LANE,* Vol. III. Pt. 2, Maps 731, 734; Steinbach, *AS,* 4 (Feb., 1929), 161-65; Zieglschmid, *AS,* 5 (Oct., 1930), 50-51.

IMPOSSIBLE. See COMPARISON, ILLOGICAL.

(IN) BACK OF, BEHIND

Summary: Once frowned upon as colloquial, (in) back of (*as a sub-stitute for* behind) *now occurs in both spoken and written English; in formal writing,* behind *is used.*

Data: One investigator (Winburne) cites this example of the usage: "The artillery was usually a few miles *back of* the front line infantry . . ." (Ernie Pyle, *Brave Men,* 1944, p. 97). *In back of* has likewise struggled up to standard usage and now one hears it employed on all sides, by performers on radio and television, by graduate and undergraduate students, by teachers, professors, and college presidents (Bongiorno) as in ". . . he was aware of a presence *in back of* him" (*McCall's,* Nov., 1959, 88). However, a study conducted in 1961 (Roach) found twenty-two examples of *behind* in writing, only one of *in back of,* suggesting that most writers, if not speakers, prefer *behind* in formal situations. Four other studies (Gross, Hotchner, Karlin, R. Thomas) also found more examples of *behind.* Nevertheless, *in back of* is standard usage now, patterned on *in front of.*

According to a study of the Linguistic Atlas records (Malmstrom), in the context of "The broom is *behind* the door," *behind, back of,* and *in back of* are used by informants of all types in all areas: New England, Middle Atlantic, South Atlantic, North Central, and Upper Midwest States. *Behind* strongly predominates but the other forms are frequent also, especially in Northern areas. *Back of* is used much more often than *in back of,* especially in Type III (cultivated) speech, but evidence points to divided usage, nationally distributed.

Other evidence: Bryant, *CE,* 16 (Jan., 1955), 247; Curme, *Syntax,* 564; Kurath, *LANE,* Vol. III, Pt. 2, Map 723; Malmstrom, *SVTS,* 48-50; 271-73; Marckwardt and Walcott, 39, 109.

INCLUDING. See PROVIDED, PROVIDING, *conj.*

INCOMPLETE COMPARATIVE. See COMPARATIVE, INCOMPLETE.

INDEFINITE IT. See IT (3).

-ING, -IN (PARTICIPIAL ENDINGS)

Summary: Both the -in and -ing endings of present participles are standard usage in speech; in written English, only the -ing ending occurs, except in represented speech.

Data: The Linguistic Atlas recorded the present participial forms in the context "She was *singing* and *laughing*" for the New England, Middle Atlantic, South Atlantic, North Central, and Upper Midwest States. Usually the field workers ignored the specific context and recorded all present participles heard.

The evidence, according to one study (Malmstrom), shows that the present participial endings *-in* and *-ing* alternate in both Type III (cultivated) and Type II (with at least some secondary school education) speech, probably as a phonological difference. In written English, only the *-ing* ending occurs except in dialogue.

Other evidence: Atwood, 34-35; Kurath, *LANE,* Vol. II, Pt. II, Map 420; Vol. III, Pt. II, Maps 671-72; Malmstrom *SVTS,* 229-30; V.G. McDavid, 60, 71.

IN REGARD(S) TO

Summary: In regard to *is the standard English idiom;* in regards to *is characteristic of nonstandard English.*

Data: The following example from one study (Gabel) typifies standard usage of this idiom: "But she gave an honest answer, at least *in regard to* Sally" (Margaret Maze Craig, *Three Who Met,* 1958, p. 129). The locution *as regards to* shows the influence of *as regards,* another variant which occasionally occurs, as in "I should be very grateful to you if . . . you would not mislead me *as regards* the weather . . ." (William Saroyan, *Love, Here is My Hat,* p. 37, cited by Brazeau).

According to one reader (Winburne), *with regard to,* as in ". . . a situation of some sort existed *with regard to* Veda . . ." (James M. Cain, *Mildred Pierce,* 1948, p. 229) occurred along with the more common *in regard to.* Another reader (Gabel) found only *in regard to* in his study of modern fiction and criticism. Other variants are *concerning* and *regarding.*

Other evidence: Fries, *AEG,* 44.

INSIDE, INSIDE OF

Summary: Inside of *occurs as a standard variant for* inside *in contexts denoting time or place.*

Data: Two investigators (Lightcap, Zemlock) found examples denoting place: "Delving *inside of* one's own mind for psychological purposes is very difficult . . ." (*Look,* Dec. 25, 1956);

"She was then taken *inside of* a closed car back to her home . . ." (*New York Daily News,* Jan. 6, 1958, 3).

Inside of also occurs in contexts with reference to time, as in examples from one investigator (Winburne): "You play it right, and *inside of* a week your financial situation will be greatly eased . . ." (James M. Cain, *Mildred Pierce,* 1948, p. 25); ". . . it seemed to me that they should all be down with pneumonia *inside of* a week" (Ernie Pyle, *Brave Men,* 1944, p. 253).

The patterning of *inside of* is similar to that of *in front of* and *in back of*. For greater formality than the standard *inside (of)*, *within* is preferred, as in "He will be there *within* ten minutes."

INVITE, n.

Summary: Invite *is normally a verb, but it is frequently used humorously as a noun in speech. In formal written English, however, invitation is usual.*

Data: One study (Gitter) recorded as an example Bob Hope's remark on the "Colgate Comedy Hour" (Apr., 1956): "There's no need for a book of Who's Who! You're somebody if you got an *invite* to the Grace Kelly wedding." Ed Sullivan also greeted Kate Smith on "Toast of the Town" (May 27, 1956) with: "You have a standing *invite* to be on our show." A principal speaking to his teachers said, "Have the pupils take home these P.T.A. *invites.*" One often hears sentences like: "Did you get an *invite* to the party?" "We sent out thirty invites"; "A formal *invite* to the center will be sent to all prospective members." The study cited above found this use of *invite* in 18% of the written occurrences and in 38% of the spoken ones.

IT

Summary: In written English, it *occurs in four main senses, in the following order of frequency: 1) anticipatory, 2) formal, 3) indefinite, 4) general. In the emphatic sense,* it *appears only in spoken English.*

Data: 1. Anticipatory *it.* In this use, *it* is placed first in the sentence and followed by a singular verb and a group of words (an infinitive with its complements, a clause, etc.) which may be substituted for it in a more forceful, direct statement, as in "So *it* was only sensible to take precautions" (*Harper's,* Jan., 1958, 12). Here one may say, "To take precautions was only sensible" and omit the *it.* This *it* has been called variously the anticipatory or provisional subject, the expletive, the "filler-in," the pattern-filler, since it may be left out of the sentence. Beginning a sentence with *it* in this manner is a common pattern in current English, particularly in standard English. One study (Faust and Beauchamp) found this usage in 20.3% of 589 examples of *it* occurring in 29 different magazines, and another study (Hotchner) encountered this usage in 47% of the examples.

2. Formal *it* (situation *it* and impersonal *it*). Formal *it* may occur either first in the sentence or embedded in it. This *it* cannot be omitted without recasting the whole sentence, for it does not refer to a succeeding clause or to anything expressed in the context. Many such sentences begin: "*It* is that . . . ," "*It* seems (appears) that . . . ," "*It* looks as if (though) . . . ," etc. For example, in a sentence like "*It* seems to me that Eudora is lonely" (*The Atlantic Monthly,* Jan., 1957, 6), we cannot make *that Eudora is lonely* the subject of *seems* in a more emphatic statement, as can be done in some sentences beginning with *it,* e.g., "*It* does not matter whether you write the letter or not," where *whether you write the letter* . . . may be substituted in a more forceful and economical assertion. In a sentence like "In a way he is, *it* may be noted, a great deal like his father," *it* is embedded in the sentence and refers to nothing expressed in the context. *It* is only a pattern-filler in the clause *it may be noted,* serving as the subject of *may be noted.*

Formal *it* is often employed in an impersonal sense, as in "*It* is said that . . ." or ". . . *it* can rain on one side of the street and not on the other . . ." (*Harper's Bazaar,* Nov., 1957, 68). Since *it* does not refer to a definite person or thing, it is termed "impersonal." Almost all idioms concerning weather fall into this pattern, as in "*It* is thundering." One cannot say, unless poetically, "The thunder thundered."

The verbs pertaining to weather, for the most part, have always been impersonal in English. The sentence "*It* is freezing" in Old

English would have been "Hit frēoseð (frīest)." Speakers of Old English seemed to feel the need of an expressed subject even though it had no meaning. The insertion of *it* made the statement fit into the ordinary pattern of the declarative sentence with an expressed subject in its normal position before the verb. This use of *it* is good current usage. One study (Hotchner) showed that this usage occurred in 1.5% of the examples.

Formal *it* is also used as a subject in a sentence to designate a person or thing faintly presented by the situation but later identified, as in "*It's* Andy" or "*It* was late November and the day was bleak" (*McCall's,* Jan., 1958, 32), or "*It* is a ship." This use of *it* is sometimes called "situation *it*" since the *it* points to someone or something in the general situation. In the study of formal and informal writing cited above, this usage occurred in 9% of the examples.

Formal *it* is often used to emphasize a particular fact by introducing a relative clause, as in "*It* was *Mary* who did it," where *who did it* follows *Mary*. This statement is more emphatic than the statement "Mary did it." It is also employed for emphasizing what would be the object in a simple sentence by bringing *it* forward, as in "*It* was *David* they admired," instead of "They admired David."

One study (Faust and Beauchamp) found all three usages of formal *it* occurring in 10.1% of the material read, another (Hotchner) in 27.3% of the material.

3. Indefinite *it*. There are many uses of *it* that do not belong to the impersonal category. They may be termed "indefinite," as in "After thinking *it* over . . . she decided that she wanted the professional training" (*Mademoiselle,* Sept., 1957, 191) and "*It* is a long distance." In one study (Hotchner) of current writing in magazines and newspapers, this usage occurred in 18.3% of the examples.

In a number of idiomatic colloquial expressions, *it* functions as the object of the verb: "You two must have *it* out some day"; "Go *it*"; and "He hoofed *it* across the cornfield." Also, in a number of prepositional phrases the indefinite *it* functions: "Make a night of *it*"; "Make a clean breast of *it*"; "He is in for *it*." Some people frown on this usage in utterances like "*It* says here that . . ." or

"It says in the paper that . . ." The *OED Supplement* to 1927 cites illustrations of this usage and the Leonard survey labels as "established" the example *"It* says in the book that. . . ." This expression is in standard usage.

4. General *it.* The general *it* refers to a preceding group of words and not to one specific thing, as in "You judge your family's shopping ability by what it gets for what it spends. *It's* an excellent way to judge your community, too" *(Better Homes and Gardens,* Oct., 1949, 214). One study (Faust and Beauchamp) cited this usage in 5.9% of the examples found, another (Hotchner) in 9% of them. *See* REFERENCE, VAGUE OR INDEFINITE: THIS (PRONOMINAL).

5. Emphatic *it.* Emphatic *it* often functions as the subjective complement (predicate noun): "He thinks he is *it."* Here *it* is pejorative in meaning, suggesting a pretentious individual who overrates himself. The emphatic *it* in the "he is *it"* pattern may also refer to one who is the ultimate authority in a special field, or one who has reached the highest point in some particular achievement or activity: "For the best diving in this country you are *it."*

The *it* in the foregoing examples refers to a person, but the predicate pronoun may refer to a crisis, the inevitable, a culmination beyond which no one can go, as, for example, D-Day or any serious attack of any kind. This usage is illustrated in the Air Force play by Moss Hart *(Winged Victory,* 1945, Act II, Scene 2):

> FIRST BOY: You know it ain't exactly unimportant.
> From today on—we're a crew. This is *it.*
> PINKY: Yep. This is the day, fellers. It's the big day.
> Me, I'm glad it's here. This is *it.*

The meaning of "This is *it"* has been extended and has been adopted by the advertisers and now may be seen referring to some brand of perfume or the latest Hollywood pictures. The pattern, however, has not been changed. In this usage, *it* is standard spoken English.

Other evidence: Beauchamp, *AS,* 26 (Oct., 1951), 173-80; Bryant, *FEG,* 42-43, 119-20, 171, *213-14; CE,* 17 (Apr., 1956), 414-15; Curme, *PSA,* 149-50; *Syntax,* 7, 9-1; Fries, *AEG,* 140-141, 228, 230-32, 241-44; Jespersen, *Ess.,* 154-55, 328, 330, 349; Kruisinga,

Handbk., §§2077, 2252, 2421 *ff.;* Marckwardt and Walcott, 35, 72; Mathews, *DA*, 892; Pooley, *TEU*, 124; Pound, *AS*, 6 (Apr., 1931), 313-14; *AS*, 29 (Dec., 1954), 263-67; Roberts, *UG*, 251-52; Wyllie, *AS*, 31 (Oct., 1956), 230.

IT DON'T. See DON'T, v.

IT IS BECAUSE. See REASON . . . IS BECAUSE *(REASON IS THAT).*

IT'S HER. See IT'S I/ME, IT'S WE/US, IT'S HE/HIM, IT'S SHE/HER, IT'S THEY/THEM.

IT'S HIM. See IT'S I/ME, IT'S WE/US, IT'S HE/HIM, IT'S SHE/HER, IT'S THEY/THEM.

IT'S I/ME, IT'S WE/US IT'S HE/HIM, IT'S SHE/HER, IT'S THEY/THEM

Summary: In edited expository writing, the nominative forms (I, we, *etc.) are generally, but not always, employed; in reported conversation and in fiction, the objective forms* (me, us, *etc.) occur with some frequency.*

Data: A great deal has been made of these locutions, especially *It's I/me,* as shibboleths of correctness, and much has been written about it. Given the facts of usage, however, one can resolve the problem fairly simply.

One investigator (Rosenzweig) reveals that in edited expository writing, the nominative forms are almost always used, as in: "*I* couldn't believe that woman was *I* . . ." (*Saturday Evening Post,* Sept., 22, 1956, 122) and "It was *I* who hated" (Lucy Freeman, *Fight Against Fears,* 1951, p. 243). On the other hand, one finds such examples as "And as this actor speaks his meditated words, they find a growing response in a certain invisible audience, which is not simply *us,* the readers or listeners." (Louis L. Martz, *Yale Review,* Summer 1958, 529.) and "If the people who happen to be fools are *us,* we are nonetheless funny" (Walt Kelly, *Saturday Review,* Aug. 30, 1958, 28). Conversation and represented speech afford many examples of the objective forms, as evidenced by two studies (Tilkin, Winburne). Illustrations are: "She said *it was him*"; and "Dammit, *it is him!*" (Erle Stanley Gardner, *The Case of the Rolling Bones*, 1947, p. 207).

The use of *I* gives a more formal effect, whether it be in speech or in writing. In some dialects, however, it merely gives a snobbish effect.

That the objective forms are appropriate in spoken English receives abundant support from the considerable amount of evidence available from the Linguistic Atlas records of cultivated informants (Type III); this evidence at the same time, according to one study (Malmstrom), shows some significant regional variations. For example, in *It's I/me, It wasn't I/me* (*we/us* was not covered in the survey), *me* predominates over *I* in all areas but New England, where usage is divided. Likewise, *him, her,* and *them* (these pronouns were recorded only in the Eastern United States) predominates over *he, she,* and *they* in the Middle Atlantic and South Atlantic States; even in New England, the exception, more than a third of the cultivated informants consistently use the objective forms.

Among the inconsistent users, there is some interesting variation. For example, *It's them* is not recorded by any user in New Hampshire and Maine. In the Middle Atlantic States, *It's she* occurs more often than *It's her*. West Virginia informants consistently use only the objective forms of all the personal pronouns recorded for that area. In the South Atlantic States, usage in *It's he/him* is divided, *them* occurs slightly more often than *they*, but *she* is always used instead of *her*.

Other evidence: Dykema, *AS*, 24 (Feb., 1949), 46; McMillan, *C.E.*, 9 (Apr., 1948), 394; Kurath, *LANE*, Vol. III, Pt. 2, Maps 603-5; Mencken, *Supp. II*, 371-73; Rice, *AS*, 8 (Oct., 1933), 58-63; Sapir, 165-82; Stageberg, *CE*, 16 (Mar., 1955), 376-78; Sweet, *NEG*, Pt. I, §§1076-85.

IT'S ME. See IT'S I/ME, IT'S WE/US, IT'S HE/HIM, IT'S SHE/HER, IT'S THEY/THEM.

IT'S THEM. See IT'S I/ME, IT'S WE/US, IT'S HE/HIM, IT'S SHE/HER, IT'S THEY/THEM.

JELL, v.

Summary: The verb jell, *a back formation from the noun* jelly, *occurs in current American usage, with the meaning* "to crystallize" *or* "to take or cause to take definite form." *As a noun meaning* "jelly or like jelly," *it is colloquial.*

Data: From one study (Hartz) come the following examples of *jell* as a verb: "I am waiting for my plans to *jell"* and ". . . in the hopes that his offspring's marital plans will *jell* . . ." (*The New Yorker,* Dec. 14, 1957, 89-90) and "The ingredients that were present on paper simply failed to *jell"* (*Saturday Review,* Dec. 21, 12-13). This figurative use probably derives from the original meaning of the verb, "to congeal like jelly," a term often applied to the making of jelly: "This juice won't *jell"* and "The gelatin won't *jell"* (*Ladies' Home Journal,* Dec., 1957, 4). Another investigator (Taub) found an example of a noun function: "The pudding will harden into a delicious *jell* when cooled" (*The New York Times,* Apr. 13, 1957, 35). This use is colloquial.

Other evidence: Mathews, *DA,* 902.

JUST, adv.

Summary: The adverb just *occurs in standard English in the meanings of* "exactly" *and* "shortly before." *It also means* "only," *but in formal English* only *is the preferred form.*

Data: Today *just* is a versatile adverb, appearing in various kinds of writing from fiction to journalism, as evidenced by three studies (L. Cohen, R. Cohen, Goldstein). According to one study (L. Cohen), its meanings fall into three categories:

1. "exactly, precisely" (27.4%) as in "*Just* what is it that excites Europeans . . ." (Irwin Shaw, *Holiday,* Jan., 1954, 103); ". . . and sure enough, *just* as Lizzie had said, Madge's Uncle Judson . . ." (John P. Marquand, *So Little Time,* 1943, p. 95).

2. "at the moment spoken of, or a very short time before" (16.6%), as in "Yet, as these words are written, bills setting up Fair Employment Practices Commissions have *just* died . . ." (Richard L. Neuberger, "Decay of State Government," *Harper's,* Oct., 1953, 40).

3. "only, merely, simply" (56%), as in *"Just* take your national political conventions" (Edwin O'Connor, "British TV," *Life,* Nov. 2, 1953, 116) and "I could run for *just* a minute" (Erle Stanley Gardner, *The Case of the Rolling Bones,* 1947, p. 103).

Another study (R. Cohen) found that *just* occurred more often in narrative fiction than in other forms of prose and predominates in both fictional and actual conversation. As a variant of *only,* it occurred 77.3% of the time in dialogue and *only* 22.7%; in actual conversation, *just* occurred 81.8% of the time and *only* 18.2%. On the other hand, *only* occurred 88% of the time in fictional narrative and *just* 12%; 90% in textbook prose and *just* 10%.

Just may occur as the first word in a sentence or be embedded in the sentence, but rarely is it placed at the end, except in a context like "Have you got the dishes done yet?" "Yes, but only *just."* In one study (L. Cohen), *just* appeared at the beginning in 23% of the examples and within the sentence 77% of the time.

As a movable modifier, *just* is generally placed immediately before the word it modifies. For example, compare "I'll *just* listen for a minute" ("I'll not do anything else") with "I'll listen for *just* a minute" ("for no longer than a minute"). In the first instance, *just* modifies the verb *listen;* in the second, *a minute.*

In speech, *just* is an intensive, as in "It's *just* beautiful" or "It's *just* glorious," etc. One also hears in informal English *"just* the same" for *nevertheless,* the more formal expression, as in *"Just the same,* she was annoyed" (James M. Cain, *Mildred Pierce,* 1948, p. 116). Of course, as an adjective, *just* has a totally different meaning.

Other evidence: Bryant, *CE,* 16 (Jan., 1955), 246-47.

KILL, v. See KNEEL, v.

KIND (SORT) OF (A, AN)

Summary: Kind of a *and* sort of a *are colloquial; the more commonly used* kind (sort) of *as an intensifier is also colloquial.*

Data: In expressions like "in an open, frank *kind* (*sort*) *of* way" and "Is this the *kind* (*sort*) *of* book that you like?" *kind* (*sort*) *of* seems to qualify the word following. From this construction there developed expanded ones like *all kind* (*sort*) *of, other kind* (*sort*) *of, these* (*those*) *kind* (*sort*) *of, this* (*that*) *kind* (*sort*) *of.* Two studies (L. Gold, Hook) show that in formal English the demonstrative or other word modifying *kind* (*sort*) is in the singular: "*This* (*that*) *kind* (*sort*) *of* picture is good"; "America's officials are fully conscious of the need for *this kind of program*" (*The New York Times,* "News of the Week in Review," Jan. 6, 1952, Sec. 4, 1). The plural forms *these* and *those,* however, occur where a plural noun follows the *of:* "*These* (*Those*) *kind* (*sort*) *of* cars have their use." This usage is colloquial. *See* THOSE (THESE) KIND (SORT) OF.

In formal English when *kind* (*sort*) *of* is employed to express a class, it is not followed by *a* or *an.* "It is that *kind* (*sort*) *of* book" —not "*kind* (*sort*) *of a* book"; "Shakespeare was a . . . *kind of* artist who . . ." (*Catholic World,* Oct., 1955, 170). Studies (Benardete, J. Fagen) show that *kind* (*sort*) *of a* (*an*) *is colloquial,* as illustrated by a panelist on "What's My Line?" (WCBS-TV, Dec. 16, 1951) who asked, "Would I be the *kind of a* person who would come to you?" A second panelist asked, "Are you that *sort of a* person?"

Another investigator (Winburne) reveals that *kind* (*sort*) *of,* meaning "rather, somewhat, to some extent, in a way" modifies the word following: "He shook hands *sort of* timidly," (Ernie Pyle, *Brave Men,* 1944, p. 194); "I'd *kind of* like to take a look at Jim myself" (John P. Marquand, *So Little Time,* 1943, p. 518). This usage has led to the development of *kinda* [kaɪndə] (*sorta* [sɔrtə]), as in, "We can *kinda* determine which is more important."

According to two studies of the Linguistic Atlas survey (Allen, Malmstrom), in a context such as "It's *rather* cold," the combined occurrences of *kind of* and *sort of* in the speech of all types of informants far outnumber those of *rather. Rather* is a majority usage only in cultivated New England speech, particularly in northeast New England, a relic area, and among the older, more old-fashioned group there. Even there, however, many cultivated informants use *kind of* or *sort of* along with *rather*. This evidence shows that *rather* is a recessive form, while *kind of* and *sort of* are standard usage in all these areas. Of the two latter forms, *kind of* is a majority usage among all types of informants in all areas (New England, Middle Atlantic, South Atlantic, North Central, and Upper Midwest States), while *sort of* is not a majority usage in any area although it occurs with considerable frequency in all areas. One investigator (R. Kleinman), in her reading and listening, found *kind of* preferred in all situations.

Other evidence: Bryant, *CE,* 17 (Dec., 1955), 178; Fries, *AEG,* 51; Malmstrom, *SVTS,* 77-79, 293-94; *EJ,* XLIX (Oct., 1960), 498-99. Marckwardt and Walcott, 41, 193; Rice, *EJ,* XXVI (Apr., 1937), 326-27.

KNEEL, v.

Summary: The preterit and past participle knelt *or* kneeled *occur in standard English.* Knelt *is dominant among all types of speakers, but* kneeled *as an alternate is neither local nor nonstandard. The preferred preterit forms of the similar verbs* feel, kill, spill, spell, spoil, boil *in writing are* felt, killed, spilled, spelled, spoiled, *and* boiled. *In formal English the participial form is* felt, killed, spilled, spelled, spoiled, *and* boiled.

Data: These six verbs involving divided usage were the subject of six studies based upon contemporary readings (Garey, Hotchner, Karlin, Kehl, Rosenthal, Wolf). It was learned in two of them that both *knelt* and *kneeled* occurred as standard written preterits, as in "He *knelt* in the driveway and prayed" (*Reader's Digest,* June, 1957, 53) and ". . . the Moslem spread his rug, *kneeled,* and bowed . . ." (*ibid.,* Jan., 1958, 77), but that *knelt* is heavily favored in cultivated speech. A study (Allen) of the Linguistic Atlas material of the Upper Midwest found it the majority form in all levels of speech. Two of the studies (Hotchner, Kehl) also found that the preterit and past participle of *feel* is *felt,* whereas of *kill* it is *killed* in written English, with the *t-* ending, *kilt,* as a dialect form. On the other hand, usage is divided between *spilled* and *spilt,* *spelled* and *spelt.* In ordinary conversation, one may say, "I *spilled* (or *spilt*) the milk," but usually in the proverbial setting it is: "No use crying over *spilt* milk." The written form, however, is generally *spilled* in American English.

So it is with *spelled,* although one may hear in spoken English, "He *spelled* the word correctly" or "He *spelt* the word correctly." Similarly, usage is divided between *spoiled* and *spoilt* in conversation. In New England, about one-fourth of the cultivated informants use *spoilt,* in the Middle Atlantic States about one-eighth, and in the South Atlantic States more than one-third. The preferred written form, however, according to two studies (Hotchner, Karlin) is *spoiled.* On the other hand, the preterit and past participle of *boil,* according to three studies (Hotchner, Karlin, Wolf), is *boiled* in both standard spoken and written English. According to the Linguistic Atlas survey, the form *boilt* occurs mainly among Type I (uneducated) speakers of the Middle Atlantic and South Atlantic States.

Other evidence: Atwood, 6, 17, 21-22; Kurath, *LANE,* Vol. II, Pt. I, Map 306; Pt. 2, Map 652; V.G. McDavid, 22, 24, 38, 45, 68, 72.

KNIFE, n. See HOOF, n.

KNIT, v. See FIT, v.

KNOW, v. See BLOW, v.

KNOW-HOW, n.

Summary: Know-how *as a noun meaning "technical or professional competence" is now standard English, used particularly in business reports, in patent law, and in informal situations.*

Data: Examples of this usage are: "A bank, merely with its 'know-how,' may save an estate the equivalent of . . ." (In a leaflet issued by the Chase National Bank of New York in May, 1943); "Similarly the sharing of technological knowledge—the *know-how*

—is illustrated . . ." (Forty-first Annual Report of the U. S. Steel Corporation, Mar., 1943). Popular in industry, commerce, and advertising, the usage has been given impetus by newspapers and magazines, as in "Electronics *know-how*" (*"The New York Times,* Apr. 1, 1956, Sec. 10, 6); "engineering *know-how*" (Everett C. Smith, "Industry Views the Teaching of English," *The English Journal,* Mar., 1956, 128). First used in 1857, according to the *Dictionary of Americanisms,* it is now very common in informal English. From the study that shows this (Maldou) comes this example: Ed Murrow on "See It Now" (WCBS, June 9, 1957, 6 P.M.) commented, "We have no monopoly of *know-how.*" The compound is so well established that we find the noun appearing in the noun-adjunct construction (a noun used as a noun modifier) as evidenced in the newspaper headline "Test Your Camera *Know-How* Rating" (*New York World-Telegram and Sun,* Apr. 27, 1956, 50) and in ". . . *know-how* knowledge for the whole family" (advertisement on Radio-WRCA, Mar. 14, 1956).

Other evidence: Barnhart, Files; Bryant, *CE,* 19 (Oct., 1957), 38; Byington, *AS,* 19 (Oct., 1944), 229-30; Fletcher, *AS,* 19 (Dec., 1944), 265: Mathews, *DA,* 941; Pound, *AS,* 19 (Feb., 1944), 65-66.

LAY. See LIE, LAY, v.

LEARN. See TEACH, LEARN.

LEAVE, LET

Summary: The verb leave (*principal parts:* leave, left, left) *in the sense of* "permit" *or* "allow" *is nonstandard;* let (*principal parts:* let, let, let) *in the sense of* "permit to remain" *is also nonstandard, though less common.*

Data: Leave usually means "depart from" or "go away from," as in ". . . I *left* the theater deeply shaken" (*Holiday,* Oct., 1957, 88, cited by Aviles), whereas that of *let* is "permit" or "allow," as in "Once we get softhearted and *let* the doctor bring the mercury along . . ." (*The Atlantic Monthly,* Oct., 1957, 52, cited by Aviles). Even though the meanings differ, these two words are often confused, largely because *leave* is employed in both senses, as in *"Leave* me go with you" (instead of *"let* me") or "Please *leave* him come home" (instead of *"let* him"). From one study (Polimeros) comes this example from John Steinbeck: *"Leave* me salt the meat" (*The Grapes of Wrath,* 1939, p. 146) and from another (Kehl): ". . . you wouldn't *leave* nobody else hug and kiss you . . ." (Wilbur Daniel Steele, "How Beautiful with Shoes," *Fifty Great Short Stories,* p. 315). The confusion results because another meaning of *leave,* "permit to remain," overlaps with *let,* meaning "permit," as in ". . . and sometimes it was set on a shelf . . . and *left* there" (Shirley Jackson, "The Lottery," *Prize Stories of 1949,* p. 174). This usage of *leave* in the sense of "permit" or "allow" is nonstandard.

The reverse confusion, *let* meaning "permit to remain," is less widespread, but common in the eastern part of the Midland area (eastern Pennsylvania, except the Philadelphia area), where "Don't close the door; *let* it open" may be heard even from educated speakers. This usage, however, is low colloquial even in this region. The confusion of *leave* and *let* apparently derives from usage by speakers of German background, where *lassen* overlaps both words.

In this confused construction, although either verb may take an object and although a noun or pronoun may intervene between the verb and the infinitive, only *let* is followed by an infinitive without *to: "Let* me *have* it" (*"Permit* me *to have* it"). There are, however, certain parallel constructions in which either verb may be employed, but each yielding a different meaning.

For instance, *"Let* it in" means "allow it to come in" (as a dog), but *"Leave* it in" means "do not remove it" (as a word in a sentence). Similarly, *"Let* me alone" generally means "don't bother me or interfere with me," as in "He wishes the newspaper boys, as he calls them, would *let* him *alone* . . ." (John P. Marquand, *Melville Goodwin, U.S.A.,* 1951, p. 131, cited by Aviles), whereas *"Leave* me alone" means "go away and allow me to remain in solitude." These two expressions, however, are both in standard usage and often employed one for the other. Consider this sentence by Henry Seidel Canby in a letter to the editor: "But write to the Concord, Massachusetts, Chamber of Commerce and beg them to *let* Walden

Pond *alone"* (*Saturday Review,* Aug. 31, 1957, 22). Originally, an early meaning of *let* was "leave behind," now found in the expression, *"Let* me alone." According to the *OED,* this expression is synonymous with *"Leave* me alone."

Let alone, meaning "not to mention," occurs also, as in "Not even seeing the wire against which they lay, *let alone* anything beyond it" (William Faulkner, *A Fable,* 1954, p. 131); ". . . little room or energy for even minimum class preparation, *let alone* unassigned but recommended reading" (*Harper's,* Apr., 1957, cited by Hotchner). *Leave alone* as an alternative here is nonstandard.

Other evidence: Bryant, *EJ, XLVI* (May, 1957), 300; Fries, *AEG,* 131; Kurath, *Word Geography,* 33, 79, Figs. 155, 156; Marckwardt and Walcott, 42, 56, 123-24.

LESS, FEWER

Summary: Less *occurs with countable items in magazines and formal texts. In one study,* less *was so employed in 20% of the examples; in another, in 33% of them. Evidence shows that usage is divided.*

Less and *fewer* both indicate a comparison with something larger, either in number or amount. *Fewer* is used only with countable items, as in "There are *fewer* apples in this barrel than in that one. *Less,* on the other hand, is generally employed in referring to quantity, material in bulk, as in "There is *less* milk in the pitcher than I thought," but it is now often being substituted for *fewer.*

Data: Formal English, as studies show (Anderson, Rose, Watkins), makes a distinction between the two words in most instances, but other studies (Bowden, Christensen, Gross, Hotchner, Rothman, R. Thomas) reveal that *less* does occur as a substitute for *fewer,* as in "Out of the 170 million people in the country, *less* than 8 million have IQ's that are high . . ." (*Harper's,* Mar., 1958, 14); "Rejoice then that no *less* than thirty-four of the eighty-one past volumes . . . are back in print . . ." (*The New York Times Book Review,* Mar. 30, 1958, 24). In advertising, one usually hears or sees *less* substituted for *fewer,* as "98% *less* calories," promised for one of the salad dressings. Mayor Robert Wagner of New York City in a television address (WABC, Mar. 18, 1956) spoke of *"less* accidents, *less* deaths, and *less* complaints" as well as of "giving out *less* tickets."

Less is appearing in such formal texts as the following: "English, for example, has *less* than forty-five phonemes" (B.F. Huppé and Jack Kaminsky, *Logic and Language*, 1956, p. 58).

L E T. See LEAVE, LET.

LET'S, LET US, LET'S US

Summary: Let us *is the formal English expression, but* let's *occurs more frequently in informal written English;* let's us *is colloquial.*

Data: Let *us* is the formal English expression, as in *"Let us* not delude ourselves . . ." (*The New York Times Magazine,* Dec. 22, 1957, 5). In informal English, *let's,* originally a contraction of *let us,* is often substituted, as in *"Let's* say one fourth of the kill was unreported" (*The Atlantic Monthly,* Oct., 1957, 51), where *let's say* is used instead of *let us say. Let's us,* on the other hand, is a confusion of the two former expressions, as in *"Let's* go" and *"Let us* go," giving *"Let's us* go."

In five studies (Anderson, Aviles, Hotchner, Nanos, Sapienza) *let's* occurred 99 times and the contraction *le's* once, making 100 occurrences, 77%; *let us,* 28 times, 21.5% of the examples; and *let's us* once with *le's us* once, totalling 2, or 1.5% of the occurrences.

In speech *let's* is occasionally heard as *le's,* illustrated in *When the Whippoorwill* by Marjorie Kinnan Rawlings (1940, p. 79): *"Le's us* go down to the gulf. . . ." The other alternative for *let us* (that is, *let's us*) is also illustrated here. This construction, however, rarely occurs in print; if it does, it is in dialogue.

It should be noted here that expressions like *"Let us* pray" with medium stress on *us* belong to ecclesiastical language and are quite distinct from *"Let's* pray."

Other evidence: Fries, *The Structure of Eng.,* 103-4; Krapp, 360; Van Krimpen, *CE,* 17 (Jan., 1956) 241.

LET'S DON'T. See LET'S NOT, LET'S DON'T.

LET'S NOT, LET'S DON'T

Summary: Let's not *occurs in standard written English; both* let's not *and* let's don't *occur in colloquial English.*

Data: In negative statements, both locutions are used: *"Let's not* upset the plan"; *"Let's not* talk about it please" (J.D. Salinger, "Just Before the War with the Eskimos," *Prize Stories of 1949,* p. 260); *"Let's not* excuse ourselves from responsibility . . ." (Agnes E. Meyer, *PMLA,* Apr., 1957, 13); *Let's not* be late . . ." (Max Schulman and Robert Smith, *The Tender Trap,* 1955, p. 101); and "Now *let's don't* go at it like it was our last New Year's on earth" (*Saturday Evening Post,* Dec. 31, 1955, 43). The emphatic *let's don't* did not appear in three studies (Aviles, M. Levine, R. Thomas) of written English, but it is used in spoken English as the emphatic counterpart to "I do want to go."

Another expression that occurs in colloquial speech is *don't let's,* as in *"Don't let's* go there." The long-suffering soap opera heroine says to her short-tempered fiancé, *"Don't let's* quarrel."

Other evidence: Bryant, *CE,* 17 (Jan., 1956), 241; Curme, *Syntax,* 433; Krapp, 360.

LIE, LAY, v.

Summary: In written English, the verb lie (*principal parts:* lie, lay, lain) *is not confused with* lay (*principal parts:* lay, laid, laid); *only in spoken English is* lay *substituted for* lie.

Through the centuries, *lie* and *lay* have been confused because the preterit of the intransitive *lie* (lay) is the same as the present tense of *lay* (lay), which once meant "to cause to lie."

Data: In the nineteenth century, *lay* was used in place of *lie* rather often, as indicated by examples from such writers as Lord Byron ("There let him *lay*"); Willkie Collins ("The look . . . which *underlaid* her expression"); and Anthony Trollope ("I have *laid* awake upon it"). However, in seventy occurrences of *lie* and fourteen of *lay* in readings of Modern English (Bowden, Hotchner, Kehl, Zarcone), there was no confusion of the two verbs.

Speech is another matter. Most of the difficulty is with *lay,* for *lie* is intransitive, with little tendency to be used transitively. On the other hand, *lay* may be used both ways, depending upon meaning. *Lay* not only means "to put or place," where a direct object is necessary, but it has also developed several intransitive meanings. In nautical language one hears: "The sailors *lay* forward" and "The sailors *laid* out along the yards." A newspaper correspondent describing a sinking ship on WNBC said: "She was *laying* out at sea" (Jan. 6, 1952, 1:18 P.M.). Likewise, "A hen *lays*" or a "worker *lays* to his oars," that is, "applies himself vigorously." Because *lay* may be either transitive or intransitive, it is often used for both verbs in speech, as in *"Lay* (Lie) down, Tricksie" or "He *laid* down for an hour." An investigation of three groups in Cleveland, Ohio, classified according to education (Tyson), showed the preterit *laid* used 58% of the time in the context "I *laid/lay* down yesterday" and *lay* 42%. The best-educated group employed *lay* two-thirds of the time, whereas the other two groups used *laid* 71% of the time. In the context "He was so tired that he *lay/laid* right down," *lay* was employed 51% of the time and *laid* 49%. In this instance *laid* was used by the best educated group 73% of the time and *lay* by the other two groups 64% of the time.

In the context of "I'm going to *lie* down" and "He *lay* in bed all day," Linguistic Atlas evidence, according to one study (Malmstrom), shows that, although *lie* predominates as the present form in the speech of Type III (cultivated) informants everywhere and is practically universal among the Eastern ones, 20% of the Type III informants in the Middle-West and 40% to 50% of the Type II informants (with some secondary school education) in all areas use *lay* instead of *lie* in the present, both transitively and intransitively. In the preterit, the Atlas evidence shows that in all areas except southwest New England, the eastern shore of Virginia, and North Carolina, *laid* and *lay* occur about equally in Type III speech and that *laid* occurs more frequently in Type II speech. The evidence thus reveals a clear case of divided usage, especially in the preterit.

As a noun, *lay* has become standard usage in America. We speak of "the *lay* of the land," whereas the British say "the *lie* of the land."

Other evidence: Atwood, 18; Bryant, *EJ,* XLV (Jan., 1956), 39; Fries, *AEG,* 289; Kurath, *LANE,* Vol. III, Pt. I, Map 494; Pt. 2, Map 653; Malmstrom, *SVTS,* 149-51; Marckwardt and Walcott, 24, 55, 82; V.G. McDavid, 39-40; R.I. and V.G. McDavid, *AS,* 35 (Feb., 1960), 18; Pooley, *TEU,* 163-65.

LIGHT, v.

Summary: The preterit and past participle lighted *or* lit *alternate in standard English without any distinction.*

Data: One investigator (Stevens) reports these examples from his reading of *The New York Times* of Sunday, Nov. 6, 1955: ". . . where it *lighted* up everything in sight" (Sec. VI, 14) and "It is *lighted* up by bits of informal folksy writing" (Sec. VII, 1), but no examples of *lit.* Nevertheless, the latter form occurs in such statements as "He *lit* a cigarette" and "He *lit* out for home." With *up, lit* in colloquial English means "intoxicated," as in "He was *lit up* on three drinks."

LIKE, conj.

Summary: Like *as a conjunction rarely appears in formal written English, but occurs in spoken English and in conversational written English.* As *is the preferred conjunction in formal English, with* as if *and* as though *fairly common variants.*

Like has had a long history as a conjunction. It was used so by Shakespeare and Keats, and in the Bible we find: *"Like as* a father pitieth his children, so the Lord pitieth them that fear him" (*Psalms,* 103:13), where *like* and *as* appear together. Since then, the *as* has been dropped; the *like* remains.

Data: In modern usage, professors, lawyers, clergymen, radio and television commentators, and journalists employ *like* as a subordinating conjunction to introduce clauses in standard English situations. From two of the fifty-two studies undertaken for this entry (Erickson, Ramsted), one finds these examples: "We don't

BLAIRSVILLE SENIOR HIGH SCHOOL
BLAIRSVILLE, PENNA.

take abuse *like* our mother would have" (F. Scott Fitzgerald, *The Last Tycoon,* 1941, p. 68); " 'All clear?' he asked, *like* he was getting ready to roll up the maps again" (Walter Van Tilburg Clark, *The Ox Bow Incident,* 1940, p. 125); and "The situation here is beginning to look more *like* it did in the days immediately following Pearl Harbor" (David Lawrence, *Detroit Free Press,* July 4, 1950, 4). Advertisers use it widely, as in the slogan "Winston tastes good/*Like* a cigarette should." The expressions *"like* I say (said)" and *"like* I told you" are common in speech: *"Like* I said, they won't find a clue"; *"Like* I told you, it is difficult to do."

In one study (Brachfeld), *like* as a substitute for *as* was found in spoken English two and one-half times as often as in written. Investigators (Brazeau, Chapnitsky, Class, Coxe, Donkle, Everson, Kehl, Lerdahl, Meerdink, Meinell, Postraw, Searles, Sloan, S. Smith, Thiele, R. Thomas, Winburne) found it in advertisements, quotations from speakers, dialogue, or informal English of a folksy nature. In fifty-two studies of contemporary fiction, newspapers, and periodicals, investigators (Hansen, McMillan, Middleton, Nusbaum, Perrin, Ramlow, J. G. Schwartz, Scribner) found 109 examples, 50 of which were substitutes for *as,* which occurred 571 times. Comparing these two figures, one sees that *like* occurred only 8% of the time for *as* and *as* occurred 92%, mostly in newspapers and magazines. The evidence of seventeen studies (Blomquist, Church, Dalles, Edgerton, Erickson, Fries, Hearden, Klinner, C. Krauss, O'Brien, Pfankuch, Remes, Shim, Skeris, Speitz, A. M. Thomas, Wetzler) supports the traditional contention that *like* is rarely used for *as* in formal written English.

In informal English, however, *like* substitutes not only for *as,* but for *as if* and *as though,* as in "He stood there *like* he didn't know what to do" (Nathaniel Lamar, "Creole Love Song," *The Best American Short Stories*—1956, p. 238) and "It sounded *like* the whole fort was groaning" (Niel H. Swanson, *Unconquered,* 1947, p. 331). One investigator (Ramsey) found, in reading 9 short stories, 6 examples of *like* as a conjunction, 5 of which were variants of *as if* or *as though.* In the 109 examples mentioned above, 59 were substitutes for *as if* and *as though,* which occurred 242 times, *as if* 164 and *as though* 78. *Like* was used 19.6% of the time and *as if* and *as though* 80.4%. Most of these examples of *like* were in dialogue or in quoted speech, not in formal English.

According to two studies (Allen, Malmstrom) of the Linguistic Atlas records, in the context of "It seems *as if* he'll never get well," New England informants use *as if* and *as though* without distinction. *Like* is of rare and scattered occurrence. In the Upper Midwest, *like* and *as though* are used with almost equal frequency, *as if* being relatively rare. In the North Central States, *like* predominates heavily over *as though* and *as if* combined; the two latter forms occur about equally. In the North Central and Upper Midwest States, *like* is used by almost half of the Type III informants (cultivated), and from half to almost three-fourths of the Type II informants (with some secondary school education). Though no investigation was carried out in the Middle Atlantic or South Atlantic States, the evidence available suggests that *like* is standard usage in the speech of all areas except New England and is expanding vigorously to the South and West.

Studies (Bodoh, Carswell, Fink, Hosig, Tatham) show that *as if* or *as though* is usual in formal English, one interchangeable with the other. In certain constructions, like "The dress looks *like* new" and "He ran *like* mad," *like* has been acceptably substituted for *as if*.

Hypercorrectness accounts for the substitution of *as* for *like,* as in "She sings *as* a bird," or "The freeways, *as* pipes which carry water, were designed to and can only carry as much traffic . . ." (cited by Christensen), where the preposition *like* is correct in standard English.

Other evidence: Kurath, *LANE,* Vol. III, Pt. 2, Map 732; Malmstrom, *SVTS,* 40-42, 266-68; R.I. and V.G. McDavid, *AS,* 35 (Feb., 1960), 18; Pooley, *TEU,* 153-55; Roberts, *UG,* 239, 321, 330; Simpson, *CE,* 13 (May, 1952), 463-64.

LIKE FOR

Summary: This expression followed by an infinitive and its subject, as in, "We would like for *you to have it" is used by cultivated speakers throughout the country, especially in the South; however, it rarely occurs in formal written English.*

Data: Though three studies recorded no use of this expression in writing (Anderson, Haase, Watkins), it occurs in represented speech, as in: "I'd *like for* you to have it, sir" (Leland Jamieson, "Attack," *Saturday Evening Post,* June 22, 1940, 64); and ". . . the economic situation . . . is not what the people would *like for* it to be . . ." (*Decatur* [Alabama] *Daily,* as quoted in the *Tuscaloosa* [Alabama] *News,* Oct. 7, 1940). Considering its frequency in speech, one can only wonder at its rarity in edited writing and surmise that editors must disapprove of what some textbooks call the redundant *for.* Actually, *like for* occurred in literary English as early as 1474, a fact which gives further weight to the view that the locution is an idiom in standard English speech.

Other evidence: Curme, *Syntax,* 250; Dunlap, *AS,* 20 (Feb., 1945), 18-19; Haase, *CE,* 12 (Oct., 1950), 38-39; Jespersen, *MEG,* Pt. V, 300 *ff.*; Kurath, *LANE,* Vol. III, Pt. II, Map 703; Perrin, *CE,* 3 (Mar., 1942), 591; Russell, *AS,* 16 (Feb., 1941), 17-18; Wentworth, 360-61.

LIKE TO, ALMOST

Summary: The phrase like to *for* almost *is a regionalism; in written English,* almost *is used.*

In the Middle Atlantic and South Atlantic States, one hears "I *liked to* burned myself" instead of "I *almost* burned myself." Another variant heard in the Middle Atlantic States is "I *like to* have burned myself"; "*It liked to* have burned him." *Like* grows out of the earlier *had like. I had like* became *I'd like,* then *I like.* One study (Lederman) found this: "I *like to* starved, said Al" (John Steinbeck, *The Grapes of Wrath,* 1939). One investigator (Donkle) found *like t'* instead of *almost* in a comic strip. See OED, s.v. *like,* adj., A9b.

Other evidence: Atwood, 36; *OED;* Wentworth, 360.

LIT, v. See LIGHT, v.

LOADS. See LOT(S), HEAP(S).

LOAN, v.

Summary: The verb loan *occurs in American standard English;* lend, *however, is used more frequently in formal written English.*

Data: Despite attempts to keep *loan* as a noun ("I should like a *loan*"), it has now established itself in accepted usage as a verb, especially in relation to money. Two studies (Hotchner, Weber) found that it is interchangeable with *lend,* as in: "We have been accused of faltering in our plans *to loan* substantial sums of money to many of the nations of Europe" (*The New York Times,* Feb. 20, 1957, 19) and "We *loan* the fruits of our wisdom and see it repaid to us tenfold" (H. V. Kaltenborn on the radio, Mar. 11, 1957, 10:00 P.M.).

Other evidence: Lee, 1-2.

LOT(S), HEAP(S)

Summary: A lot, (a) lot of, lots of *are found principally in spoken English or in advertisements; in newspapers, usually in informal columns; in dialogue in fiction; in articles including or representing speech. Similarly,* (a) heap of *and* heaps *are found in spoken English or in dialogue representing an adolescent or rural speech.* (A) heap of *and* heaps *are not so common as* (a) lot of *and* lots of. (A) heap of *and* heaps of *seem to be recessive forms, whereas* (a) lot of *and* lots of *are standard.*

Data: In informal English the nouns *lot(s)* and *heap(s)* mean "a great quantity" or "a large number," as illustrated by "I've made quite *a lot* of money" (John P. Marquand, *So Little Time,* 1943, p. 279, *"Lots* of times I've filled my mess kit" (Ernie Pyle, *Brave Men,* 1944, p. 194) (both cited by Winburne); *"A lot* of commotion . . . is flying around Eisenhower's proposed $71.8 billion budget . . ." (*Life,* Apr. 15, 1957, 57, cited by Guskin); "I had *heaps of* fun"; *"A heap* of people will be there." More often one hears "I had *lots* of fun" and *"A lot* of people will be there," as evidenced by two investigations (Sawyer, Winburne). *Heap* is still used, especially among adolescents, but *lot* is more frequent. According to one study (Goldman), *(a) lot of* and *lots of* were used in 79% of the examples found and *(a) heap of* and *heaps of* in

21% of the examples. In formal English one may find "I had a *great deal of* fun" and "A *great many* people will be there."

An occasional variant of *a lot* is *a lots,* as in "It will save *a lots* of young people from killing themselves." One study (Abowitz) of teen-age speech found evidence of this expression.

Both (*a*) *lot* and (*a*) *heap* are also used informally as adverbs, as in "She is *a lot* better today" or "I had *a heap* (*lot*) rather live in the West." In formal English *much* may be substituted in each case. Similarly, one hears "I like her *a lot,*" "He talks *a lot* but doesn't say much," where *a lot* modifies a verb. Here *a great deal* may be substituted in formal English.

Where *a lot of* is followed by a plural noun, a plural verb is selected, as in "*A lot of* letters were lying on the desk," but "*A lot of* milk was given to the children."

Another usage similar to that of *lots* and *heaps* is *loads,* as in "I had *loads* of fun"; "*Loads* of big red apples were on the ground." One also hears in informal English "Thanks *loads*" along with "Thanks *a lot.*"

The Linguistic Atlas survey in New England based on the context "*a lot* of fun" found in addition to *a lot* the following variants as well: *a pile, piles; stacks; a barrel, barrels; a bushel, bushels; slews; gobs; scads; oodles; oceans;* and *scollops.* The first noun means "a large quantity." It is used either with words to express abstract ideas, as in the context "*a lot* of fun" or with words designating concrete objects, as "*a lot* of papers." Certain synonymous expressions, such as "no end of fun," also occurred.

Other evidence: Fries, *AEG,* 44; Kurath, *LANE,* Vol. II, Pt. 2, Map 416; Marckwardt and Walcott, 36, 126.

LOUD, LOUDLY. See SLOW, SLOWLY.

MAY. See CAN.

MAY CAN. See MIGHT COULD.

MIGHT COULD

Summary: Might could *is a colloquialism, confined principally to the South, where it is often used by Type II speakers (with some secondary school education).*

Data: One study (G. Thomas) revealed that this expression and its variants do not occur in written English except in dialogue. However, it is used in Southern speech and may also be heard in the South Midland section and the German area of Pennsylvania, chiefly in Type I (uneducated informants) and Type II speech. Along with *might could, may can* occurs. Nonstandard usage includes *oughta could* and *useta could.*

Other evidence: Atwood, 15, 35; R.I. McDavid, *AED,* 526; V.G. McDavid, 62, 67, 69; R.I. and V.G. McDavid, *AS,* 35 (Feb., 1960), 17; Wentworth, s.v., *could,* 135.

MIGHTY, adv.

Summary: *As an intensifying function word meaning* "very; to a great degree," mighty *occurs in standard speech and in informal written English.*

Data: Formerly synonymous with "powerful," *mighty* in its modern sense occurs in such combinations as *mighty glad, mighty good, mighty useful, mighty nice, mighty fine.* Though Type III (cultivated) speakers use it, some people avoid this use of *mighty.* However, it has appeared in quality magazines, as in ". . . the problem is *mighty* difficult," from *The Atlantic Monthly* of May, 1953, and in Mackinlay Kantor's *"The Romance of Rosy Ridge."* These were stories about rural, provincial folk and of an earlier period. One investigator (Kennedy) found nine occurrences of *mighty,* thirty-eight of *very,* three of *highly* and one of *awfully,* all used as intensifiers.

The Linguistic Atlas survey of New England in the context "I'm *mighty* glad to see you" shows that it occurs along with such variants as *very, awful(ly), terribly, real, certainly, so, damn, darn(ed).* Older forms, such as *dreadful, right, more than, tickled to death,* and *sure am glad,* also occurred. *Mighty* in the above context occurs less commonly with *happy, delighted,* and *pleased.*

Other evidence: Fries, *AEG*, 201; Kurath, *LANE*, Vol. II, Pt. 2, Map 426.

MISRELATED MODIFIER. See **DANGLING MODIFIER.**

MORE. See **AGREEMENT, INDEFINITE PRONOUNS.**

MORE, MOST PERFECT. See **COMPARISON, ILLOGICAL.**

MORE, MOST PLUS ABSOLUTES. See **COMPARISON, ILLOGICAL.**

MORE, MOST ROUND. See **COMPARISON, ILLOGICAL.**

MORE, MOST UNIQUE. See **COMPARISON, ILLOGICAL.**

MORE THAN ONE

Summary: More than one *is usually singular in standard English.*

Data: Though the sense of the expression is plural, it is generally treated as a singular that agrees with a singular noun and that takes a singular verb, as in these examples from two studies (Bowden, Speitz): "More than one lawyer *was* (not *were*) present"; *"More than one* New England family still cherishes the . . . tea set . . ." (*House and Garden,* Mar., 1957, 40) and *"More than one* case has been noted . . ."* (*The New York Times Book Review,* Sept. 29, 1957, 41). The noun agrees in number with the nearest part of the phrase and the verb agrees with the noun. One usually hears, however, *"More lawyers than one were* present," where *more lawyers* is the subject. If *more than one* occurs alone as the subject, it may be singular or plural, depending upon whether *more* or *one* has the greater stress, as in *"More than one* is (are) going." One study (Gershowitz) of current periodicals turned up no instances of *more than one.*

Other evidence: Jespersen, *MEG,* Pt. II, 180; *OED;* Perrin, *CE,* 4 (Dec., 1942), 196.

MOST. See AGREEMENT, INDEFINITE PRONOUNS.

MOST, ALMOST

Summary: In colloquial English most *occurs occasionally as a substitute for* almost. *In expository prose the standard form is* almost.

Data: In formal written English, *most* is an adverb meaning "in the greatest degree or to the greatest extent" (a *most* beautiful evening); *almost* is an adverb meaning "nearly": *"Almost* all people like music." In informal colloquial English *most* is frequently substituted for *almost,* as in "John likes *most* all sports" instead of *"almost* all." This use of *most* is found especially in the combinations *most all, most anybody* (*one*) (*thing*), *most everybody* (*one*) (*thing*), and before *always, surely, certainly:* "That music should please *most everybody* (*one*)"; *"Most anybody* (*anyone*) can go without questioning"; *"Most all* the books are gone"; " 'We've been having arguments—*most every* day—about our new furniture . . .' he said" (*Reader's Digest,* Oct., 1956, 27); "He *most always* goes to the country for the weekend"; "She will *most certainly* (*surely*) want to buy a dress." This usage is the result of syncopation, not of confusion. For example, in rural areas one may hear "He was *a'most* ready," or "God A'mighty." Then the loss of *a'* would result in *most.* According to three studies (Bowden, Hotchner, G. Thomas) this use of *most* is rare in formal written English, but not in standard spoken English. In one of these studies (Hotchner) there was one instance of *most* along with six of *almost,* the one (*most every*) being used in conversation. It does not occur in a context such as "She was (*al*)*most* beautiful," for the two meanings are quite different.

Other evidence: Barnhart, Files; Bryant, *CE,* 17 (Jan., 1956), 241; Horwill, 206; Leonard, *AS,* 4 (Feb., 1929), 254; Pooley, *Gram. and Usages in Textbooks on Eng.,* 136-37; *TEU,* 156.

MUCH. See AGREEMENT, INDEFINITE PRONOUNS.

MYSELF

Summary: Myself *is most often employed as a reflexive pronoun or as an intensive in standard English, but it has a number of other standard uses: 1) as an emphatic member of a compound subject or object; 2) as a subjective complement; 3) in comparison; 4) in absolute constructions. The same conclusions apply to the other persons of the reflexive pronouns:* yourself, himself, herself, *etc.*

Myself is familiar as a reflexive pronoun (or direct object), as in "I hurt *myself*" and as an intensive (or subject appositive), as in "I *myself* did it" and "I did it *myself*." However, it has a number of other established uses in standard English, according to two extensive studies of modern prose and speech (Cherney, R. Thomas).

Data: 1. As the emphatic member of a compound subject or object. Except in poetry (*"Myself* will to my darling be/Both law and impulse"—Wordsworth), *myself* is rarely used as the simple subject in place of *I,* but the emphatic form is used as part of a compound subject, especially in informal conversational English. It has been employed in this way since the Middle English period, as Chaucer's *Canterbury Tales* testify: "Ther was also a Reve and a Millere,/. . . A maunciple, and *myself* . . ." The locution is frequent in Shakespeare ("My father and my uncle and *myself*/Did give him that same royalty he wears" (*I Henry IV,* IV, iii, 54-55). Citations may also be given from Benjamin Franklin, Ralph Waldo Emerson, and Nathaniel Hawthorne, but more recent illustrations are: "After the frames are on the beach another fellow and *myself* ought to carry them and stack them" (E. B. White, *Harper's,* Dec., 1941, 105); "Why have Walter Hampden, Victor Jory, Ernest Truex, June Duprez, Richard Waring, Philip Bourneuf, Margaret Webster and *myself* . . . banded together and signed up . . . ?" (Eva Le Gallienne, *The New York Times,* July 21, 1946, Sec. II, 1). One commonly hears statements like: "The gang, John, and *myself* are going home" or "My wife or *myself* will attend to the matter."

Myself also occurs in a compound object, in an enumeration, not occupying first place. Two investigators (Hook, Pooley) of contemporary prose found two such usages, similar to "He invited

Jane and *myself* to the play" and "Are you going to call Pat, Jane, and *myself* before you go?" *Myself,* of course, is firmly established as a reflexive object ("I cut *myself*"), an indirect object ("I bought *myself* a new bag"), and the object of a preposition ("This scene between Johnny and *myself* will explain everything"), but as a sole object of a verb, except in the reflexive sense, it is not acceptable English, according to the findings of the above-mentioned investigations.

2. As a subjective complement (predicate nominative). This construction is a common one, as in "I am (not) *myself* today." It is also used in a series, thus: "The members of the . . . force were Ronnie Green, . . . Bill Moss . . . and *myself*" (George X. Sand, *Ford Times,* Jan., 1952, 2); or in a compound subjective complement: "The other two are Mr. Stein and *myself,* and we . . . are the 'conventional' or 'traditional' prosodists" (John Crowe Ransom, *Kenyon Review,* Summer, 1956, 460).

3. In comparison. In informal English, one hears *myself* after *than* and *as:* "It was not easy for as poor a typist as *myself*"; "A force greater than *myself* had picked me up and was disposing of me" (Whittaker Chambers, *Witness,* 1952, p. 282); "They are . . . quite as capable as *myself* in answering questions" (Louis Bromfield, *From My Experience,* 1955, p. 51).

4. In absolute constructions. Examples of this kind are not frequent, according to one study already cited (Cherney), but they occur: "A number of ranchers here, *myself* included . . ." (*Wall Street Journal,* Jan. 14, 1955, 11).

The same conclusions apply to the other persons of the reflexive and intensive pronouns (*yourself, himself, herself,* etc.), but *hisself* and *theirselves,* forms of *himself* and *themselves,* are nonstandard usage.

Other evidence: Barnhart, Files; Bryant, *EJ, XLVII* (Feb., 1958), 98; Burnham, *AS,* 25 (Dec., 1950), 264-67; Hall, 175-77; Marckwardt and Walcott, 37, 71-72; *OED;* Pooley, *TEU,* 156-59; *AS,* 7 (June, 1932), 368-70; *Word Study,* 16 (Mar., 1941), 1.

NEARLY, adv. See ONLY, adv.

NEITHER. See AGREEMENT, INDEFINITE PRONOUNS.

NEITHER WITH MORE THAN TWO. See *EITHER (NEITHER)* WITH MORE THAN TWO.

NIGHTS. See ADVERBIAL GENITIVE.

NO ACCOUNT. See NO GOOD, WORTHLESS.

NOBODY. See AGREEMENT, INDEFINITE PRONOUNS.

NO GOOD, WORTHLESS

Summary: While these expressions are not identical in meaning, they are generally alternated without distinction, except that worthless *is reserved for formal English;* no good *is used colloquially.*

Data: In situations where the two are interchangeable, *worthless* seems to describe the quality of a particular object, whereas *no good* applies to a situation of less specific nature, as in this business man's comment about a television set: "Those indoor aerials are *worthless.* Just look at that picture. It's *no good.*" *No good* describes the entire situation and is less specific in reference than *worthless,* which refers to indoor aerials. This broader meaning is apparently intended in "I tell you those fascists are *no good*" (*The Best from Yank,* 1945, p. 27, cited by Winburne) and "I'm just *no* damn *good . . .*" (James M. Cain, *Mildred Pierce,* 1948, p. 188, Winburne). One investigator (Cutler) found both *no good* and *worthless* were used as adjectives in speech.

No good and *worthless* are not always used interchangeably. Sometimes, *no good* expresses displeasure, as in "My working hours are *no good.*" It may also mean "no benefit" or "no value," as in "It is all too easy to conclude that the youth of today is thundering downhill on a bobsled and that *no good* can come of it" (R. C. Hendrickson with F. J. Cook, *Youth in Danger,* 1956, p. 4, cited by Rosenfield). Here *no good* functions as a noun, whereas in the previous examples it acted as an adjective.

Other uses of *no good* are found in the expressions *come to no good,* meaning "end in failure" and "to do *no good,*" meaning "not to help," as in ". . . after seeing that arguing with Kane did absolutely *no good,* he decided . . ." (Kenneth P. Kempton, *Short Stories for Study,* 1953, p. 155).

An expression similar to *no good* is *no account,* used to mean "worthless," as in "He is *no account,*" and probably a short form of the more formal *of no account.* Like *no good,* it may be placed before a noun to describe it: "A *no account* (*no good*) dog was around here this morning," meaning "a worthless dog." Paul Green has as the title of a play: *"The No 'Count Boy,"* where *account* has been clipped to *'count.*

Similarly, *no use* is a second expression employed informally in some ways like *no good,* as in "It's *no use* to go to the library today" and "We tried to duck the challenge but it was *no use*" (*The Best from Yank,* 1945, p. 186), where it means "of no advantage to" or "useless." The more formal expression is *of no use,* as in "It is *of no use* to ask." In such a sentence, British usage prefers *no good.* In these examples, *no use* serves as a complement following the verb *to be.* It is not placed before a noun as are *no good* and *no account.*

No use may also be employed as a noun with its modifier, as in "There is *no use* in getting excited"; " '. . . and it's *no use* saying it wasn't . . .' " (*New Yorker,* Aug. 2, 1958, 27). The expression *to have no use for* means in formal English "to have no need or occasion for," as in "I have *no use* for a piano since I do not play." The same expression is used colloquially to mean "to have no liking or tolerance for," as in " 'I've got *no use* for a motor that . . .' he once declared" (*Reader's Digest,* Apr., 1958, 204, cited by Hotchner).

Other evidence: OED.

NO PLACE. See ANYPLACE, adv.

NO USE. See NO GOOD, WORTHLESS.

NOMINATIVE ABSOLUTE

Summary: The nominative absolute, usually consisting of a noun plus a participial modifier and at times including a complement and/or modifiers of the participle, as in *"We stayed at home,* the play having been canceled," *is a well-established construction, useful in exposition and almost necessary in description and narration.*

Data: Three studies (Christensen, Hickey, Hotchner) showed that the principal use of this construction is to add narrative detail, giving a picture of an action, as in "The mockingbird sang in a tree by a farm gate, *her notes coming in a high trill";* or descriptive details, giving appearance rather than action, as in "Sister and her beau occupied the front parlor, *the beau wearing his natty new suit* with the peg-top trousers and his highest collar" (Marian Castle, "Give Me a Home I Can Hide In," *Better Homes and Gardens,* May, 1951). The governing clause nearly always precedes the absolute, which fills in the details of the action, picture, or statement merely sketched in general terms by the preceding clause.

Instead of a weakness, the loose attachment of the absolute construction is really an advantage, especially in descriptive-narrative writing, where a cumulative effect can be achieved by adding details in this way.

The absolute construction generally consists of a subject (usually a noun, sometimes a pronoun) and a modifier (an infinitive or participle, past or present), as in "Meanwhile the cardinal is in jail, the sentence *to be pronounced* tomorrow" (Lowell Thomas, Feb. 7, 1949) and "The younger girl wore the simple ankle-length organdy of a schoolgirl, her hair *tied* back by a ribbon" (Nina Brown Baker, *Big Catalogue,* 1956, p. 40); "That *done,* he gave the downbeat for a resounding triad . . ." (*Musical America,* Apr., 1958, 14). The construction may lack either of these, as in "The man sat there weeping, *his feet on the floor and his head in his hands"* or "Across the room he gazed at the woman, *her face like a death mask beneath the wide-brimmed hat."*

Other evidence: Christensen, *CE,* 11 (Apr., 1950), 401-3; Curme, *PSA,* 79, 84, 85, 98, 128; *Syntax,* 152-58; Jespersen, *MEG,* Pt. V, *Syntax,* 9, 75 *ff.;* Kruisinga, 5th ed., Pt. II, *Eng. Accidence and Syntax,* 3, 2099 *ff.*

NONE IS (ARE). See AGREEMENT, INDEFINITE PRONOUNS.

NOR AT THE BEGINNING OF A SENTENCE. See *AND*
(BUT, OR, NOR) AT THE BEGINNING OF A SENTENCE.

NOT . . . BUT

*Summary: The construction, always with a numeral following, as in
"Don't take but one," is standard American English, principally used
in speech.*

Data: One may hear "I *didn't* bring *but* two," but not "I *didn't*
bring *but* this"; or "I *didn't* hear *but* four or five songs on the air,"
but not "I *didn't* hear *but* Bing Crosby." In Modern English an indefinite pronoun has been added, as "I didn't hear *anything but*
(I heard *nothing but*) the wind" or the *not* has been eliminated:
"The sheep is *but* an animal."

Occasionally this construction is found in writing, as in "The
government last year could *not* raise *but* $3,000,000,000" (*Con-
gressional Record,* Jan. 25, 1935, 1037). Here *not but* means
"only," as do the formal English *none but* in *none but the brave*
and *nothing but* in *nothing but the best.* The construction *not but*
goes back to the earliest English. Formal written English, however,
generally uses *only:* "Get *only* one"; "I want *only* one" instead of
"Do *not* get *but* one"; "I do *not* want *but* one."

Another pattern, according to one study (Hotchner), in which
not . . . but occurs is: "He *cannot* help *but* run" (See CAN'T
HELP BUT); ". . . I could *not but* remember an anecdote" (*The
New Yorker,* Dec. 28, 1957, 25); ". . . those who knew and re-
membered Joanne could *not* help *but* think back . . ." (*Coronet,*
Jan., 1958, 102). This construction is not from Old English, but
grew up after the late Renaissance, according to the *OED,* based
on Latin *non possum non.* See CAN'T (CANNOT), COULDN'T (COULD
NOT) HELP BUT.

Other evidence: Bryant, *CE,* 17 (Apr., 1956), 414; Hatcher, *AS,* 24
(Feb., 1949), 49-53; *OED.*

NOT, ILLOGICALLY PLACED

Summary: The all . . . not *expression, as in* "All *men are* not *alike," is standard English.*

Data: Despite the logical argument for *"Not all* men are alike," this idiom has a long and reputable history, dating back to Hamlet's "All is not well." In Modern English, these typical examples suggest that the construction is fairly widespread: "The building of dykes and fill is *not* considered practical by many . . ." (*Coronet,* Apr., 1958, 145), where *not* logically modifies *practical* (the building of dykes is considered, but considered impractical); and ". . . that he did *not* criticize in anger or in malice, but in love and affection" (*The New York Times Book Review,* July 27, 1958, 6), where *not* logically should precede in *anger* (he did criticize, but not in anger).

The placing of the modifier *not* frequently results in illogical statements, but two studies (Goetz, Hotchner) show that generally the context removes any chance of ambiguity, as in "Our parents did *not* think it suitable that we should drive home to the country, with boys or without them" (*The New Yorker,* Jan. 4, 1958, 19), where not logically modifies *suitable* (the parents did think).

Writers of formal English prefer to place the modifier *not* logically, whereas most speakers determine its position by context rather than by logic.

Other evidence: Russell, *AS,* 9 (Apr., 1934), 115-19.

NOTWITHSTANDING. See PROVIDED, PROVIDING, conj.

NOWHERE NEAR

Summary: This expression is used in standard English.

Data: An informal phrase meaning "not nearly," as in "It is *nowhere near* twelve o'clock," *nowhere near* is carried in standard dictionaries with no restrictive label. One investigator (Hotchner) reports these examples: "These figures need not frighten us since

they are *nowhere near* what we now spend on military affairs . . ."
(*Educational Forum,* Nov., 1956, 51) and ". . . and he knew
that she was *nowhere near* asleep" (*The New Yorker,* July 19,
1958, 34). The expression *nowheres near,* however, is not standard
English. Four investigators (Banschick, Bowden, Fuhr, Lederman)
found no examples of *nowheres near* in writing.

Other evidence: OED.

O C E A N S. See LOT(S), HEAP(S).

OF IN COULD OF, COULDN'T OF, SHOULD OF,
SHOULDN'T OF, WOULD OF, etc.

Summary: These expressions are nonstandard English.

Data: The normal pronunciation of unstressed *have* in many
positions is [əv], identical with the pronunciation of *of* in many positions. In standard written English, it is spelled *have* or *'ve,* as in
could have or *could've.* Writing *could of,* etc. is a misspelling
unless it represents dialect speech. A recent example appears in
conversation in Walter Bernstein's "A Reporter at Large": "He
could of blowed you right apart with that gun!" (*The New Yorker,*
Sept. 21, 1957, 151, cited by Rothman). Three studies (Algeo,
Bernstein, Ramsey) found only two examples of *of* for *have* in
writing representing dialect speech, and only three examples in
conversation. The proper spelling of this sound would be *uv,* but
that combination of letters does not look like English while *of*
does. Compare the spelling *wuz,* found in "dialect" writings for
unstressed *was,* which is phonetically meaningless because everyone
says *wuz.* Such manipulations of spelling are literary conventions.

Other evidence: Kenyon-Knott, *have* and *of;* Wentworth, 422.

OF-GENITIVE. See GENITIVE CASE.

OF WHICH. See WHOSE, OF WHICH.

OFF, OFF OF, OFFEN, FROM, OFF FROM

Summary: Off of *and* off from *occur in informal English in all principal speech areas of the country. Formal usage employs* off *alone.*

Data: Some speakers use the two expressions in standard English contexts, as in "I stepped *off of/from* the platform"; "I can make a lunch *off of* cottage cheese and an apple"; "We were able to get *off from* writing the paper." *Off of,* at times reduced to *off o'* ['ɔfə] in colloquial speech, is the more frequent of the two. A nonstandard usage is *offen* ['ɔfən], as in "He bought it *offen* a street peddler."

Two studies (Allen, Malmstrom) of the Linguistic Atlas records reveal that in a context such as "He fell *off* the horse," *off* predominates in the speech of informants of all types in New England and the Middle Atlantic, the South Atlantic, the North Central, and the Upper Midwest States. *Off of* also occurs in Type III (cultivated) and Type II (those with some secondary school education) speech in all these areas, although it is more characteristic of Midland and Southern usage than of Northern. *Offen* is characteristic of Type II and Type I (uneducated) speech in all these areas; *off from* is essentially a Type I usage. *From* occurs only in New England and the Upper Midwest, predominantly in old-fashioned speech.

The evidence thus shows that *off* and *off of* are standard usage in these areas; *offen* is uneducated and low colloquial usage; *off from* is characteristically uneducated usage; and *from* is typically old-fashioned usage.

Five studies (Anderson, Hotchner, Kehl, Miskel, Sandler) reveal that in formal usage *off* occurs without *of* or *from,* as in "I . . . tried . . . to peel the green hide *off* the white pith . . ." (*The New Yorker,* Dec. 28, 1957, 25).

Similar to the usage of *off, off of,* and *offen* is that of *out, out of, outen,* in the sense of "through," as in "He went *out* (*out of*) (*outen*) the door," or in the sense of *from,* illustrated by "He fell *out* (*out of*) (*outen*) the window." Formal usage employs *out* alone. In the sense, however, of "away from" *out of* occurs, as in "He went *out of* her life, never to return." *Outen* is nonstandard.

Other evidence: Dunlap, *AS,* 20 (Feb., 1945), 19-20; Kurath, *LANE,* Vol. III, Pt. 2, Map 724; Malmstrom, *SVTS,* 52-54, 274-76; R.I. McDavid, *AED,* 522.

OFF FROM. See OFF, OFF OF, OFFEN, FROM, OFF FROM.

ON ACCOUNT OF. See BECAUSE, ON ACCOUNT OF.

ON CAMPUS, ON LINE, ON STAGE

Summary: On campus *and* on stage *are found in standard spoken and written English;* on line *is a regionalism for the formal expression* in line.

Data: Usage is divided between *on campus* and *on the campus.* One study (Trinneer) showed *on campus* employed 43% of the time and *on the campus* 57%, as in the subtitle and title of two articles, "Big Man *on Campus*" (*Business Week,* May 7, 1960, 28) and "New Man *on the Campus,*" (*The Nation,* May 21, 1960, 444). *On campus* seems to be following other accepted expressions, such as *on land, on foot, on edge.*

The same tendency to drop the article is seen in *on (the) stage.* In a study (Alloco) of *on stage* versus *on the stage, on the stage* occurred 61% of the time, as in "No German wants to hear illiterate speech *on the stage*" (Edward Mangum, "A White-face 'Green Pastures' for Germany," *Theatre Arts,* Nov., 1958, 66). Other substitutions were *on stage* (generally written as two words), *upon the stage,* and *onto the stage. On stage* occurred 22% of the time, illustrated by "He overcame his defect entirely, *on stage* and off" (Alice Griffin, "Community Theatre, GI Style," *ibid.,* 76). It also occurs in speech, in practical theatrical circumstances, and in informal writing about the theatre. No doubt it is formed by analogy with *off-stage,* which is, according to the dictionaries, standard English.

On line, as in "He stood *on line,*" is almost universal in all types of speech in New York City and the Hudson Valley. *In line* is found in all other areas and generally in formal written English.

Other evidence: R.I. McDavid, *AED,* 518.

ON, ONTO, ON TO

Summary: Similar to on *and* upon, on *and* onto *are used interchangeably (but only in the sense of* "to a position on") *without much distinction except for stylistic reasons.*

The basic earlier meanings of *on* were "in contact with" and "in motion toward," but as *on* developed uses in contexts other than the physical, its old meaning of "direction toward" became lost. This meaning was later supplied by the preposition *to,* as in "climb *on to* the wagon."

Data: One study (B. Kleinman) based on current publications found *on* employed 61% of the time, as in ". . . in the belief that it will be put *on* a pedestal . . ." (*Look,* Aug. 16, 1960, 30) and *onto* in 39% of the occurrences, as in "The designated agent followed him *onto* the bus" (*ibid.,* 42) and ". . . hopped up *onto* the table" (*Harper's,* 1960, 62).

Onto at times occurs as two words, *on to,* but generally it is felt to be a single preposition when an object follows. When *on,* however, is part of the verb or modifies the verb, it is written separately, as in ". . . the decision to hold *on to* the price line . . ." (*Fortune,* Dec., 1960, 127).

ON, UPON

Summary: Usage is divided betweeen on *and* upon *in numerous senses, but the tendency in current written English is to employ the simpler word* on.

Data: In the reading of about 100,000 words in newspapers, periodicals, and fiction, one investigator (Bauer) found *on* employed 92% of the time. Examples of *upon* are: ". . . sitting *upon* a platform of grass . . ." (*The New Yorker,* Oct. 1, 1960, 54); ". . . Castro's impact *upon* Latin America" (*Commonweal,* Dec. 23, 1960, 334); and ". . . to march *upon* Albany . . ." (*The New York Times,* Dec. 14, 1960, 38).

ON LINE. See ON CAMPUS, ON LINE, ON STAGE.

ON STAGE. See ON CAMPUS, ON LINE, ON STAGE.

ONE ANOTHER. See EACH OTHER, ONE ANOTHER.

ONTO. See ON, ONTO, ON TO.

ON TO. See ON, ONTO, ON TO.

ONE IN (OF, OUT OF) FOUR (EIGHT, TWENTY, etc.)

Summary: The verb may be either singular or plural after one *qualified by such a phrase as* "out of four" *in statements like* "*One out of (in) four* was/were *badly damaged.*"

Data: One investigator (Russell), in casual observation over a five-year period, turned up only sixteen examples of this construction, almost all from newspaper writing. Of these, ten contain a singular verb, as in "Spot check-ups on 1,000,000 cars over the country disclosed that *one of four was* dangerously defective . . ." (*The New York Times,* June 19, 1955, 67). Of the six plurals noted, one occurs in an article by a university professor: ". . . it is estimated that *one in every three* people *harbor* the germs" (*This Week,* Nov. 6, 1955, 14). Another investigator (Adams) reported one instance of it in the plural form: "Only *one out of 5* U.S. homes *are* in soft water areas . . ." (*Saturday Evening Post,* May, 1952, 87).

Other evidence: Barnhart, Files.

ONE OF THOSE WHO (WHICH, THAT) IS (ARE). See
   AGREEMENT, NUMBER OF VERB AFTER *ONE OF THOSE WHO
   (WHICH, THAT).*

ONE . . . ONE

Summary: The locution one . . . one *is generally avoided as awkward or unpleasant in speech, but in formal, edited English, the repetition of* one *occurs more often than the alternative, the personal pronoun.*

Data: One investigator (Lucke) found that in informal American English, *one* is often followed by different forms of the pronoun *he* to avoid repetition of *one* a number of times, as in *"One* should protect *one's* voice, for *one* never knows when *one* may lose it."* Instead of this awkward locution (frequently used to avoid *I*), one may hear: *"One* should protect *his* voice, for *he* never knows when *he* may lose it," or *"You* should protect *your* voice, for *you* never know. . . ."

In written English, as one study (J. Richardson) showed, this construction is common, as in: *"One* was or *one* was not there. If *one* was there, it behooved *one* to be at *one's* superlative best . . ."* (William Carlos Williams, *The Autobiography of William Carlos Williams,* 1951, p. 58); "From one end of the country to another, *one* recognizes this party line the moment *one* enters avant-garde circles, just as *one* recognizes the master list" (Van Wyck Brooks, *The New York Times Book Review,* Dec. 30, 1956, 10). Here, however, is the shift from *one* to *you:* "At every juncture . . . *one* encountered fellow pilgrims. *You* went into the dining cars for breakfast . . . and sitting at a table opposite was . . ."* (Roland Gelatt, *Saturday Review of Literature,* June 24, 1950, 50).

In a study of six issues of *Harper's* (M. E. Krauss), *one* was followed by *one, one's* and *oneself* in 84.6% and by *his* in 15.4% of the examples found. Another study (Lucke) showed *one . . . one* in 58.9%, *one* followed by the third personal pronoun in 17.5%, *one . . .* first person in 21%, and *one . . . you* in 2.6% of the examples from contemporary magazines and nonfiction. There were, in this same material, 164 examples of *you . . . you,* nearly two and one-half times as many as of *one . . . one* (67). In less formal writing, *you . . . you* frequently occurs.

Other evidence: Jespersen, *Ess.,* 150; *MEG,* Pt. VII, *Syntax,* 4.7₅; Kruisinga, 5th Ed., Pt. II, *English Accidence and Syntax,* 2, 1266; Roberts, *UG,* 88-89.

ONLY, adv.

Summary: The position of only *with respect to the word it modifies is not fixed in standard usage. However, in written English, where word stress and intonation are lacking,* only *is usually placed immediately before the word or words it modifies.*

Data: The construction "Well, you *only* had breakfast an hour ago," though regarded by some as "slovenly," is never misunderstood. No one thinks that you and no one else had breakfast an hour ago. The intonation pattern of *only* meaning "just you" would differ from the one meaning *"only* an hour." *Only* before the verb occurs both in written and in spoken English. According to one study (Haase), it occurred 14% of the time in written English. Since the meaning is clear, such a sentence is acceptable. Similarly, in a statement like "I *only* saw her at school," it is unlikely that anyone misunderstands and thinks that *only* limits the subject. Nor does anyone misunderstand "I *only* had five dollars" or "We *only* saw him once."

Only may also modify a phrase or a clause introduced by the verb, as in "Its real value can *only* be understood by those using it every day," where *only* modifies *by those.* In such sentences *only* is sometimes placed before the verb in spoken and written English. In spoken English the meaning of *only* is made clear by the use of stress and intonation. For example, in "I can *only* read when I am alone," if I stress *read,* I mean that I cannot do other things when I am alone; but if I stress *alone,* I mean that I must be alone to read.

A study of contemporary magazines (Goldstein) shows that *only* is usually placed immediately before the element it modifies, as in "He had selected *only* those she would have approved" (*Saturday Review,* Oct. 11, 1958, 49), and occurs seven times more frequently than the variant modifier *just:* "This is *just* a history of the Court . . ." (*ibid.,* 40). For example, in "I can *only* read when I am alone," *only* modifies *read,* but in "I can read *only* when I am alone," *only* modifies *when I am alone."* It is well to remember the difference between spoken and written English. In spoken English the meaning of *only* is made clear by the use of stress and intonation, but in written English where word stress and intonation are lacking, *only* is usually placed immediately before the word or words it modifies.

The strictures of the textbook writers—or puristic editors—have possibly influenced American usage, because, although the pre-verbal position is common enough in speech, in the study cited, 86% of the examples show *only* placed before the part of the sentence it modifies.

The same holds true for *almost, even, ever, exactly, hardly, just, nearly, scarcely.* For instance, consider: "He *almost* convinced everyone there"; or the common "We *just* want four more dollars," where *just* is not logically placed but is perfectly clear.

Other evidence: Haase, *CE,* 12 (Apr., 1951), 400-2; Kenyon, *CE,* 13 (Nov., 1951), 116-17; Leonard, *Doctrine of Correctness,* 96-98, 183, 285; *AS,* 6 (Apr., 1931), 292-94; Marckwardt and Walcott, 35.

O O D L E S. See LOT(S), HEAP(S).

O R AT THE BEGINNING OF A SENTENCE. See *AND (BUT, OR, NOR)* AT THE BEGINNING OF A SENTENCE.

O U G H T N O T

Summary: Ought not (*contraction:* oughtn't) *occurs as a variant of* should not *in many speech areas; it also occurs in informal writing.*

Data: According to one study (Malmstrom) of the Linguistic Atlas records, the negative form of *ought* in the context "He *ought not* to" is very common in the Midland and Southern areas of the Atlantic Seaboard and is used in the southern counties of Ohio, Indiana, and Illinois, but is rare in Michigan, Wisconsin, and the Upper Midwest. It has limited use in New England.

In Old English, *ought* was part of a preterit-present verb, a verb which was originally a preterit but which took on a present meaning and developed new extensions of form—infinitives, participles, etc. Earlier, the form *ought* served as the past participle and as the preterit.

This old use still continues in *had(n't) ought.* From Sinclair

Lewis' work come these illustrations: "We've all done a bunch of things that we *hadn't ought* to" (*Babbitt*); "I *hadn't ought* to talk" (*Main Street*); "I don't think a fellow that can't get through an examination *had* hardly *ought* to be allowed to practice medicine"; and "He *hadn't ought* to be getting drunk" (*Arrowsmith*). It should be stated that the affirmative *had ought* is far less common than the negative *hadn't ought*. Except in dialogue, present-day written English does not employ *ought* as a participle, as evidenced by one study (Rivituso).

According to the Linguistic Atlas, the social and educational distribution of *hadn't ought* is nondistinctive since in the Northern speech areas all types of speakers use it, making it standard in that section. *Had ought* was recorded in the Middle Atlantic and Southern Atlantic States in the context "You *had ought* to know," but was not systematically investigated in other areas, although a few instances are recorded for New England. No cultivated speaker uses this form and it occurs much more rarely than *hadn't ought*. It is found only where *hadn't ought* also occurs; thus, it is a Northern form but an uncultivated one.

Other evidence: Atwood, 32-33; Bryant, *CE*, 13 (Apr., 1952), 398; Kurath, *LANE*, Vol. III, Pt. 2, Map 698; Malmstrom, *SVTS*, 222-23; R.I. McDavid, *CE*, 14 (May, 1953), 472-73; V.G. McDavid, 58; R.I. and V.G. McDavid, *AS*, 35 (Feb., 1960), 12, 16.

OUGHTA COULD. See MIGHT COULD.

OURSELVES. See MYSELF.

OUT, OUT OF, OUTEN. See OFF, OFF OF, OFFEN, FROM, OFF FROM.

OUTSIDE, OUTSIDE OF

Summary: Outside *is standard English except in its function as a preposition meaning "except," when it is colloquial;* outside of *is standard English, but in the sense of* "other than" *it is colloquial.*

Data: Evidence shows that *outside* functions in standard English as a noun, "on the *outside* of the box"; as an adjective, *"out-*

side pitch"; as an adverb, "Go *outside,* please"; and as a preposition, *"outside* his house." The prepositional use to mean "except" is colloquial idiom, as in "I hear nothing *outside* (except) the radio commentator." One study (Hotchner) of written English revealed one example of *outside* and twenty-nine of *except.* Another (Lightcap) showed that *outside* occurs most frequently as a preposition.

Outside of often occurs as a variant for *outside.* One investigator (Zemlock) discovered, in contexts denoting place, *"Outside of* the home . . ." (*Ladies' Home Journal,* Nov., 1956); " 'It's much better to be *outside of* this business . . .' " (Harold Robbins, *79 Park Avenue,* 1955, p. 119); and " '. . . there is no life *outside of* Texas' " (Edna Ferber, *Giant,* 1952, p. 209).

Outside of is colloquial in the sense of "except for," "with the exception of," or "other than," as in *"Outside of* (*with the exception of*) my family I see no one"; *"Outside of* that I don't remember what my reactions were" (Ernie Pyle, *Brave Men,* 1944, p. 247, cited by Winburne). Otherwise *outside of* is standard usage, meaning "without the confines of," as in *"Outside of* his group he is disliked"; ". . . the trees looked barer than they ever did *outside of* New York . . ." (John P. Marquand, *So Little Time,* 1943, p. 170).

O W I N G T O. See DUE TO, BECAUSE OF, OWING TO.

O X, n.

Summary: In formal written English the only plural form of ox *is* oxen.

Data: A study based upon 544 pages of reading (J. Jacobson) revealed only this form, as in ". . . the *oxen* and cow could carry the packs of food and bedding" (*Reader's Digest,* Aug., 1960, 213). Where the animals are found, one may actually hear at times the analogical plural *oxes,* and in the colloquial expression "dumb-*ox,*" meaning "a stupid person," *dumb-oxes* is the sole plural form.

P A I R (S)

Summary: The usual plural of pair *is* pairs, *but in business and informal usage, the plural following a number may be* pair.

Data: Customary usage is illustrated in ". . . probably fewer than a thousand *pairs* of these great birds are still alive" (*The Atlantic Monthly,* Nov., 1957, 133), but two investigations (Hotchner, Winburne) revealed several examples of *pair* as plural: ". . . three *pair* of socks for a dollar and a half . . ." (John P. Marquand, *So Little Time,* 1943, p. 255) and "three *pair* of shoes" (*Charm,* Jan., 1958, 99). The uninflected form is standard in the poker term "two *pair,*" but when the noun is qualified by an adjective the inflected form is used, as in "two low *pairs.*"

Pair, meaning "a set of more than two like or equal things making a whole," now has a restricted use, considered by most dictionaries as archaic or dialectal: "a *pair* of stairs." Among stage people, however, a *pair of steps* meaning "a movable set of steps or stairs" is a common colloquial expression. This usage has persisted in "a *pair* of beads" from the Middle Ages, when Chaucer's prioress wore her "*peire* of bedes" on her fourteenth-century pilgrimage to Canterbury. Today, although a young lady may speak of "a *pair* of beads" or "a string of beads" without any religious connotation whatsoever, this expression may on occasion refer to a rosary, as in this statement from the *The New York Times* of June 23, 1944, 7: "The Vatican's stocks of rosaries were almost exhausted this afternoon after Pope Pius XII gave away more than 18,000 *pairs.* . . ."

Other evidence: Bryant, *EJ,* XLVI (Jan., 1957), 54; Palmer, *AS,* 23 (Apr., 1948), 116; Piper, *AS,* I (Apr., 1926), 442; Wentworth, 439; Williams, *AS,* 30 (Feb., 1955), 49-52.

PASSIVE CONSTRUCTION

Summary: The passive voice occurs more often in expository prose (about 10% of the time) than in narrative writing, where it occurs infrequently (less than 2%).

When a verb construction indicates that the subject is being acted upon instead of performing the action, it is said to be in the passive. Actually it is the subject that is passive: "The girls were taken to the show." The purpose of the passive is to transpose the active object into the passive subject, so that "She wrote a letter," for example, becomes "A letter *was written* by her." The added phrase *by her* can be dropped at will, so that the passive becomes a useful method of omitting the original subject. Instead of "Charles called me on the telephone," one may avoid mentioning the name by saying "I *was called* on the telephone."

Data: Generations of textbook writers have warned against the use of the passive as an enfeebling construction, but its uses have increased, particularly with the growing up of the perfect and progressive tenses. It is especially useful in scientific writing. Three studies (Friedman, Warfel, Wolf) suggest that textbook strictures are not always observed. One of these studies (Warfel), based on reading *The New York Times,* found the passive used 13% of the time, the active 87% (participles and infinitives were not included). Another study (Friedman), this one based on reading the *Harvard Business Review,* showed the passive used in 8% of the examples and the active in 92%. A third study (Wolf), of twenty different magazines, disclosed the passive in use 7.5% of the time, the active 92.5%. One of the studies revealed that the passive occurred 4.8% of the time in advertising, 1.8% in the short story, and .9% in the novel.

The passive is used when the receiver of the action is more important than the doer: "The child *was struck by* the car." The doer may be unknown or unimportant or perhaps obvious: "The store *was robbed* last night" (unknown); "Plows *should* not *be kept* in the garage" (unimportant); "Kennedy *was elected* president" (obvious). It also permits varying degrees of emphasis. One may place the doer or the action done at the end or at the beginning of the sentence: "The car *is being repaired,*" or "The car *is being repaired* by Jack." The active construction is "Jack *is repairing* the car."

The passive occurs in both formal and informal English. Fries (*American English Grammar*) found the passive used much more frequently in standard English than in vulgar. For example, the *to*-infinitive with a substantive subject, all serving as object of the verb, as in "They *directed me to return,*" occurred fifty-three times (71.6%) in the vulgar and only twenty-one times (28.4%) in the standard, whereas the *to*-infinitive depending upon a main verb in the passive, as in "I *was directed to return,*" occurred very infrequently in the vulgar, but more than three times as often in the standard. The passive has established itself and found its uses in Modern English, probably because of its impersonality.

The passive is generally formed by adding the verb *to be* to the past participle of the verb, as *am, was, shall* (or *will*) *be, have been, had been, shall* (or *will*) *have been ordered.* In colloquial English, the passive sometimes employs other verbs like *get* (See GET, v., 6) and *become,* as in "He *got* acquainted with her at Tom's" or "The theater *became filled* with smoke." This pseudopassive with *get* or *become* often suggests the idea of process, as contrasted with state, suggested by the *be*-passive. Compare "The house *was built* of stone" with "The house *got built* in record time."

Other evidence: Bryant, *Mod. Eng. and Its Heritage,* 256-57, 260, 276; *FEG,* 66-69, 140-44; *CE,* 21 (Jan., 1960), 230; Curme, *PSA,* 217-23; Dennis, *PMLA,* 55 (Sept., 1940), 855-65; Fries, *AEG,* 136-38, 144-45, 187-93; Jespersen, *Ess.,* 120-23, 252-54; Warfel, *CE,* 15 (Nov., 1953), 129.

PENDING. See PROVIDED, PROVIDING, conj.

PERFECT. See COMPARISON, ILLOGICAL.

PHENOMENON

Summary: In formal written English, phenomena *is the usual plural; in informal English, this form occasionally occurs in the singular by analogy with words like* opera, operas.

The word *phenomenon* is a singular form from the Greek neuter noun, the plural of which is *phenomena.* One also finds *phenomenons,* as in "infant *phenomenons,*" where the plural is being regularized or anglicized.

Data: Five studies (Edward Berkowitz, Bowden, Hotchner, Schecter, Stone) support the above conclusion, but in two of them, *phenomena* occurred as a singular in formal writing: "The basic principle of the magnetic pickup is familiar to any high school physics student who has experimented with this *phenomena*" (*Pop-*

ular Mechanics, Aug., 1957, 26) and "I used to observe the same *phenomena . . . ," phenomena* here referring to a "social hierarchy" (Max Eastman, "How Human Are Animals?" *Saturday Review,* June 22, 1957).

Other evidence: WNID; Pound, *AS,* 3 (Oct., 1927), 26-27.

P I L E (S) . See LOT(S), HEAP(S).

PLEAD, v.

Summary: In standard English, pleaded *and* pled *are both used as preterit and past participle, and occur with about equal frequency.*

Data: One study (J. Jacobson) found in the reading of 544 pages of magazine prose and of fiction that *pleaded,* as in "I *pleaded* with members of both groups to stick to a peaceful course" (*U.S. News & World Report,* Mar. 23, 1959, 134), occurred about 50% of the time and *pled* 50%, as in "The British *pled* to let them evacuate the Jews" (Leon Uris, *Exodus,* 1958, p. 490).

P L E D . See PLEAD, v.

PREPOSITION AT END OF CLAUSE OR SENTENCE

Summary: In spoken standard English, the preposition frequently comes at the end of a clause or sentence; in written English, where there is a choice, the preposition is generally placed before its object. It does, however, occur at the end.

When John Dryden in the seventeenth century decided, on the analogy of Latin, against the propriety of placing a preposition at the end of a clause or a sentence, he set up a prejudice which has persisted to the present time.

Data: Actually, a number of constructions require the final preposition:

1. The final preposition may be part of the verb, especially in passive constructions, as in ". . . hardly any wind for us to *contend with"* (*Holiday,* June, 1953, 70); ". . . a recess *was* tacitly *agreed to"* (*New York Post,* May 28, 1953).

2. If the relative pronoun serving as the object of a preposition

is omitted, the preposition invariably comes last, as in "It was the lumber company's watchman I went up there to call *on*" (*Holiday,* June, 1953, 45); *cf.* ". . . watchman *on whom* I went up there to call"; "Pride, dignity, conventionality became poor rags *to wrap* one's loneliness *in*" (*Ladies' Home Journal,* Mar., 1953, 110); *cf.* ". . . *in which to wrap* one's loneliness."

3. If *that* or *as* is the relative, the preposition comes last: ". . . plans *that* he really does not look *at* . . ." (*Saturday Review,* Apr. 2, 1955, 30). Observe that if *at* is removed from the end of the preceding example, *that* must be replaced by *which:* ". . . plans *at which* he really does not look. . . ."

4. The preposition may come last because the clause it is in may be the object of a preposition, as in "Many a marriage might be saved by a timely look at what it was built *on*" (*Ladies' Home Journal,* Apr., 1953, 25), where the clause *what it was built on* is the object of the preposition *at*.

One construction, however, on which usage may vary, is illustrated in "News . . . is . . . those things that happen *about* which people are curious" (*Saturday Review,* Jan. 1, 1955, 9). Here the preposition could have come at the end, thus: ". . . which people are curious *about*," as it actually does in the sentence "I recognized one which three of my partners had been working *on* . . ." (*ibid.,* Oct. 2, 1954, 18). This sentence, likewise, could have been written: "*on* which three of my partners had been working. . . ." Quantitative evidence on this construction, as it occurs in a study of formal written English (Russell), shows an overwhelming preference for the preposition before its object: in almost 94% of the instances. In informal written English and in conversation, other studies (Dunlap, Frost, Hessel, Spanier, R. Thomas, Zavin) show that one finds more instances of the preposition at the end of the clause or sentence than in formal English. One also frequently finds the preposition at the end in questions: "But isn't this exactly what the ostrich was counting *on?*" (*New York Herald Tribune,* Nov. 30, 1952) and "What are we afraid *of?*" (*Life,* May 18, 1953, 172).

Other evidence: Bryant, *CE,* 8 (Jan., 1947), 204-5; Charnley, *AS,* 24 (Dec., 1949), 268-77; Curme, *Prin. & Prac.,* 133-34, 163-65, 284-

86; Leonard, *Doctrine of Correctness*, 98, 184; Pooley, *AS*, 7 (June, 1932), 387-88.

PRETTY

Summary: Pretty *as an adverb, meaning* "moderately, somewhat, tolerably, in *or* to some degree," *is well established in informal standard English.*

Data: Pretty, originally an adjective meaning "cunning" or "crafty," then "clever," "skillful," and later "pleasing," "comely," "attractive," has since the sixteenth century been employed as an adverb in the above sense. One book (J. Lesslie Hall) cites two hundred instances from fifty-two well-known writers, covering a period of two and one-half centuries. So frequently is it used in this sense now that some handbooks warn against its overuse. Yet we have these examples, taken from three investigations (Bongiorno, R. Thomas, Winburne): "She's *pretty* good that way" (John P. Marquand, *So Little Time,* 1943, p. 550); "We Americans are, for the most part, a *pretty* moral people . . ." (Dean Acheson, *Yale Review,* Summer, 1958, 482); and ". . . *pretty* soon we were in the thick of conversation" (Ernie Pyle, *Brave Men,* 1944, p. 409).

Pretty is used to modify adjectives and adverbs, as *pretty old, pretty well, pretty late, pretty soon.* In this construction, *pretty* has lost much of its original meaning, now indicating "to some degree, somewhat." Its use at times lessens the force of the following modifier. For instance, if a person says, "That picture is pretty good," with less stress on *pretty* and more on *good,* he means that it could be better.

In written English, because of the lack of stress, the use of *pretty* may result in ambiguity, as in "She talked with a *pretty* American accent." One does not know whether *pretty* modifies *American* or *accent.*

The expression *sitting pretty,* "in good circumstances," is colloquial, used informally, as in ". . . there was a German in the foxhole, *sitting pretty* . . ." (Ernie Pyle, *ibid.,* p. 450).

In the southern and southeastern parts of the United States, *pretty* is also employed as a noun, meaning "something pretty, as a jewel, a ribbon, a toy, or the like," illustrated in the quotation "I'd give a *pretty* if you was making that one for me" (James Still, "Snail Pie," *American Mercury,* June, 1940, 211).

Other evidence: Barnhart, Files; Fries, *AEG,* 201; Hall, 217-19; Kurath, *LANE,* Vol. III, Pt. 1, Map 497; Marckwardt and Walcott, 28, 99; Wentworth, 475-76.

PRICE

Summary: Though price *generally occurs as a noun, it is also a standard English verb meaning* "ask or set the price of"; *as an infinitive following a verb,* to price *is colloquial.*

Data: The noun usage of *price* is illustrated in "The *price* is low." It also occurs as a noun-adjunct, as in "There will be a *price* increase soon," and as a verb, meaning "to set or fix the value of," as in "These dresses are *priced* higher." A study conducted by one investigator (Hochberg) showed that *price* occurred as a verb meaning "to set or fix the value of" 63.6% of the time and as a verb meaning "to ask the price of," as in "She wants to *price* the table at another store," 36.4% of the time. The latter meaning was found only in spoken English.

Other evidence: Lee, 1-2; Marckwardt and Walcott, 96.

PROVE, v.

Summary: The preterit proved *and the past particples* proved *and* proven *occur in standard English.*

Data: According to eight studies (Abbott, Choven, Cook, Desberg, Hook, Palmer, Sheil, Stevens), *proved,* as in "He has *proved* his worth," is used 81% of the time in formal English, and *proven,* as in "He has *proven* his point," 19% of the time. A ninth investigation (Sheppard) concerning the context "He has (*proved* or *proven*) his point" showed *proved* was employed 83% of the time and *proven* 17%. Usage is therefore divided between *proved* and *proven* in the past participle. *Proven* has long been common in legal usage: "That is not yet *proven*."

Proved is more frequently used in a verb phrase, as in "has *proved* the point," or "It will be *proved*," whereas in a position before a noun, *proven* is more common, as "a *proven* fact"; "One penalty inevitably attached to the purchase of *proven* performers is a high price" (Robert D. Merritt, *Financial Independence Through Common Stocks,* United Business Service, Boston, 1952, p. 16); "They hold that whereas *proven* reserves in 1939 were sufficient . . . in 1955 were enough for only 11 years" (*The New York Times School Weekly,* Apr. 28, 1957, 7). *Proven,* however, does occur in a verb phrase, as in "Nothing on this score *had* so far *been proven*" (*The Reporter,* May 30, 1957, 13); "Since the beginning of residential rent control under O.P.A. the problem of brokerage commissions *has proven* troublesome" (*New York World-Telegram and Sun,* Feb. 26, 1957, 32).

Other evidence: Bryant, *EJ,* XLV (Dec., 1956), 555; Galinsky, II, 517-18; Marckwardt and Walcott, 38; Pooley, *TEU,* 159-61.

PROVEN. See PROVE, v.

PROVIDED, PROVIDING, conj.

Summary: Both forms are used in standard English, with a slight preference for provided.

Data: One study (Kanner) shows *provided,* as in "He will write, *provided* (that) he is well," occurred 59% of the time and *providing,* as in "He will play, *providing* (that) the weather is good," occurred 41%, each usually with the meaning of "on the condition that."

Providing follows along with *barring, concerning, including, pending, excepting, respecting, failing, regarding, considering, notwithstanding, saving, seeing,* etc., which are other historical participles that have assumed connective function. Examples from another investigator (R. Thomas) are ". . . but this doesn't make any difference *providing* the teller uses plenty of high hard words" (*Saturday Review,* Aug. 30, 1958, 8) and ". . . such a program was possible—*providing* an official project could be established . . ." (E. Bergaust and W. Beller, *Satellite,* 1956, p. 33).

An example of *provided* may be found in Howard Mumford Jones, *The Pursuit of Happiness* (1953, p. 22): ". . . that the people have a right to regulate, alter, and abolish their constitution . . . *provided* the results were not repugnant. . . ." *Provided* occurs frequently in legal work, especially in contracts and other agreements.

Other evidence: Bryant, *CE*, 10 (Nov., 1948), 109; *Word Study*, XXV (May, 1950), 4-5; Fries, *AEG*, 207, 216.

QUICK, QUICKLY. See SLOW, SLOWLY.

QUITE A (AN)

Summary: In informal English quite a (an) *has firmly established itself, especially in idioms like* quite a few *and* quite a bit, quite a little, quite a lot; *it is occasionally employed in formal English by some textbook writers.*

Quite a (an) is an idiom or word pattern serving as an inexact quantifier for purposeful vagueness or as a quantifier signifying "some" when the exact amount, degree, etc. is not essential for the meaning.

Data: From two investigations (Salzberg, Winburne) come these illustrations of this usage of *quite a (an)*: ". . . there are *quite a* few of them . . ." (*The Best from Yank,* 1945, p. 108); "I've found out *quite a* bit of family history" (Erle Stanley Gardner, *The Case of the Rolling Stone,* 1947, p. 121); "You kids like each other *quite a* lot, don't you?" (John P. Marquand, *So Little Time,* 1943, p. 552). It occasionally occurs in formal English, as in "Of these, *quite a* few are first declension Latin nouns . . ." (J. N. Hook and E. G. Mathews, *Modern American Grammar and Usage,* 1956, p. 158).

Quite a (an) may precede a noun, or a noun immediately preceded by an adjective, or an adverb, as "*Quite a* number are present today"; "Sally's *quite a* girl" (Marquand, *op. cit.,* p. 442); "*quite an* impressive building," where it means "very"; "You've known my husband *quite a* while, haven't you?" (Marquand, *op. cit.,* p. 391).

168   QUITE A FEW

Other evidence: Jespersen, *Ess.,* 17.5₂; Newsome, *AS,* 13 (Feb.,
1938), 27.

QUITE A FEW. See QUITE A (AN).

RAISE, v., n.

Summary: Raise *in the sense of* "bringing up" *(verb) or in the sense
of* "an increase" *is standard American usage.*

Data: One raises corn, pigs, and children in America, as illustrated in "Is the heir apparent going *to be raised* like a hothouse
rose? Or is he going to be exposed to the rough-and-tumble of a
normal life?" (*Look,* Dec. 11, 1956, 51). *Bring up* is another
term often used, as in "He was *brought up* in Georgia." *Rear* is
employed in formal contexts, sometimes where *raise* might ordinarily occur, as in ". . . the young of the flock were *reared* in
captivity year after year" (Louis and Margery Milne, *The World
of Night,* 1956, p. 88, cited by R. Thomas). One study
(O'Rourke) indicated that *raise* appears in newspapers and magazines far more often than *rear.*

The Linguistic Atlas survey of New England, based on the contexts "She has *brought up* three children" and "She has *brought up*
a large family," found all three terms in use, the most common being *brought up.* An old-fashioned variant that occurred was *fetched
up.*

Raise, meaning "an increase," as in wages, appears often: "Another *Raise* on the Long Island [Railroad]" (headline in *The New
York Times,* Dec. 16, 1956) and "Urges Bigger Teacher *Raise*"
(*ibid.,* Jan. 4, 1957, 3). According to one study (Rinaldi), usage
is divided between *raise* and *rise,* as illustrated by these headlines:
"UPA Asks New Teacher Pay *Rise*" (*New York Post,* Dec. 28,
1956, 7); "ICC Examiner Favors Rail Fare *Rise* in East" (*ibid.,*
Dec. 18, 1956, 32). Either may be used, *raise* occurring 55% of
the time, *rise* 45% in one study (Rinaldi) and 48.6% and 51.4%
in another (O'Rourke).

Raise appears as an element in many idioms: "*raise* bail";
"*raise* a doubt"; "*raise* a glass to"; "*raise* money"; "*raise* one's

stick" (to begin conducting a musical organization); *"raise* one's voice." However, *raise* in expressions like *"raise* Cain (merry Ned, the devil, old Harry, hell, hell with, a rumpus, the roof)," meaning "to create a disturbance," is limited to colloquial contexts.

Other evidence: Barnhart, Files; Kurath, *LANE,* Vol. II, Pt. 2, Map 395; Lee, 1-2; Mathews, *DA,* 1354.

RANG. See RING, v.

RARELY EVER

Summary: This expression is now established in colloquial idiom. In formal English, the ever *is omitted.*

Data: The expression *rarely if ever,* as in "I *rarely if ever* play," has been telescoped in spoken English to *rarely ever,* as "I *rarely ever* play." According to the *Thorndike-Barnhart Comprehensive Desk Dictionary,* this locution is good idiom.

In formal situations, *ever* is omitted, as in "Schumann's six little intermezzi, *Opus 4,* which *rarely* appear on recital programs . . ." (*Musical America,* Dec. 15, 1958, 31). Two studies (A. Cohen, S. Schwartz) showed that *rarely* occurs alone in writing.

Another expression in formal English is "I *rarely or never* play," but not "I *rarely or ever* play" or "I *rarely or hardly ever* play." A written example occurs in James Gould Cozzens' *By Love Possessed* (1957): "A powerful instinct, *rarely or never* lacking . . ." (p. 315, cited by Cohen).

Rarely is also followed by *if at all,* as in "Certainly a wife *rarely if at all* thinks of herself in these practical terms . . ." (*The American Home,* Jan., 1959, 35).

Other evidence: Jespersen, *MEG,* Pt. III, 396.

REAL, REALLY

Summary: In formal English, real *precedes a noun, as in* "real courage"; *in colloquial English,* real *serves as an intensifier, meaning* "very"; really, *an adverb meaning* "truly" *or* "genuinely," *is employed in both formal and informal English.*

Data: Real as an adverbial intensifier of adjectives or adverbs is common in informal, cultivated speech, as illustrated by "I had a *real* good time"; "Will everyone be *real* quiet so that I can hear the sound of a pin when it drops?"; "Run *real* fast"; "I thought it was a *real* good time to invite over someone . . ." (Margaret Arlen, *WCBS,* Jan. 12, 1952, 8:50 A.M.). It sometimes finds its way into informal writing, as in "I've needed to remember that lesson a few times since, and it's been *real* helpful" (*Reader's Digest,* Nov., 1960, 47). Though frequently employed in this way by speakers of standard English, adverbial *real,* according to three studies (P. Hartman, Speitz, Webb), does not occur in formal written prose. One extensive study (Rappa) of current periodicals and fiction showed *really* used 85% of the time and *real* 15%. When *real* occurred, it was in either conversation or conversational writing.

Nevertheless, a sentence like "The boy is *really* bad" is not the exact equivalent of "The boy is *real* bad," nor would anyone use "I will write *really* soon" for "I will write soon." *Really,* an adverb meaning "genuinely" or "truly," as in "a *really* extraordinary person," is not always an adequate substitute for *real.*

Other evidence: Barnhart, Files; Curme, *Syntax,* 140; Jespersen, *MEG,* Pt. II, 15.26; Pooley, *AS,* 8 (Feb., 1933), 60-62; *TEU,* 161-63; Wentworth, 496.

REAR. See RAISE, v., n.

REASON . . . IS BECAUSE (REASON IS THAT)

Summary: Reason . . . is because *occurs in standard usage. In formal English* reason is that *occurs somewhat more frequently, but* reason . . . is because *is a variant, which occurs more often in speech than in writing.*

Data: In seven comparative studies (Everson, Greene, Heisler, Hotchner, Porcelli, Sloan, R. Thomas) made, twenty-eight examples, or 32.6%, of *reason . . . is because* occurred in written English and fifty-eight, or 67.4%, of *reason is that.* In spoken English *reason . . . is because* occurs even more frequently than in written English; the studies found 108 examples, 60.7%, and only seventy of *reason is that,* 39.3%.

The locution occurs more often with intervening words between *reason* and *is because,* as in "The *reason* the new Leedsians will keep their appointment with Samarra, as Miss McCarthy sees it, *is because* they have traded every traditional ethic and set of values for a half digested belief in promiscuous 'scientific' rationalization" (Alice S. Morris, *The New York Times Book Review,* Nov. 6, 1955, 5); "Perhaps the *reason* that this projected rational man may at first seem bloodless *is because* we have been concentrating on the negative side . . ." (*The American Scholar,* Spring, 1952, 160); ". . . but looking back, he had decided the only *reason* he married her *was because* every male in town . . ." (Robert Penn Warren, *At Heaven's Gate,* 1943, p. 10). The natural connective stressing the idea of reason is *because.*

This type of sentence will occur as long as the following type is also found: "That *can be* only *because* he wants it to be" (*Saturday Review,* Mar. 12, 1955, 19). "*That,* I thought, *is because* Joe Maas taught me to . . ." (Clinton P. Anderson, "The Best Advice I Ever Had," *Reader's Digest,* July, 1953, 52). Psychologically, this latter construction with *that* (*this*) is equivalent to the *reason . . . is because.* No handbook writer has ever objected to it, but has concentrated on the *reason . . . is because,* which continues to be employed by many reputable writers.

A frequent variant of *reason . . . is because* is *reason why . . . is because:* "But the third great *reason why* history is rewritten *is* simply *because* the constant discovery of new materials necessitates a recasting of our view of the past" (*Saturday Review,* Feb. 6, 1954).

Following the same pattern is the commonly used *it is because:* "When it . . . attracted attention *it was because* of its varied usefulness, and it was mentioned favorably" (Wallace Rice, *"Get* and *Got," American Speech,* Apr., 1932, 280).

Other evidence: Cherry, *AS,* 8 (Feb., 1933), 55-60; Leonard, *Doctrine of Correctness,* 83; Marckwardt and Walcott, 31; Pooley, *TEU,* 135; *CE,* 18 (Nov., 1956), 110-11; Thomas, *CE,* 10 (Dec., 1948), 168-69.

REASON IS THAT. See REASON . . . IS BECAUSE (REASON IS THAT).

REASON WHY. See REASON . . . IS BECAUSE (REASON IS THAT).

REFERENCE, VAGUE OR INDEFINITE: IT. See REFERENCE, VAGUE OR INDEFINITE: THIS (PRONOMINAL).

REFERENCE, VAGUE OR INDEFINITE: THAT. See REFERENCE, VAGUE OR INDEFINITE: THIS (PRONOMINAL).

REFERENCE, VAGUE OR INDEFINITE: THIS (PRONOMINAL)

Summary: In standard English, this *occurs more often without a summarizing noun that refers to a preceding clause or sentence than it does with a definite antecedent or reference;* that, it, which *are used in the same manner, but less frequently.*

The pronoun *this* may be used with either a substantive or a "notional" antecedent; that is, it may refer to a preceding group of words, an entire sentence or clause, or to several sentences, as in "But I remember that his father had once told me that Ved would never attempt anything beyond his capacity. Apparently *this* meant he could do just about everything . . ." (*Saturday Review,* Aug. 17, 1957, 11). This usage has been common from the time of Shakespeare: "*This* above all: to thine owne self be true."

Data: Among present-day professional writers *this* is used with a "notional" antecedent more often than with a substantive. Five studies (Edelstein, Hotchner, Nelson, Russell, Statham), ranging over different kinds of material, such as fiction, nonfiction, magazines, and newspapers, indicate that *this* occurs more often without a summarizing noun, in 57⅔% of the cases, as in the example "If a yacht-owner decides to wander into foreign waters during a war and wants coverage on *this,* he gets, for an additional fee, a third clause, reinstating the war perils" (*The New Yorker,* Aug. 6, 1949, 16); and "The rugs in the bedroom are rolled and sent to

the cleaner, and *this* brings up a discussion on . . ." (Edward
Weeks, *The Atlantic Monthly,* July, 1955, 75); and "Let your
reason dominate your desires, and you will see that there is nothing
in *this* for you but trouble . . ." (*Look,* Jan. 22, 1957, 36).

Professional writers sometimes use the phrase *all this,* especially
when the pronoun is used very inconclusively: "Even when, loving
him, she is unfaithful—in her fashion—the narrator nobly understands, forgives and loves. Eventually he marries Suzie and makes
a pot of money as an artist. *All this* happens because . . ." (*The
New York Times Book Review,* July 28, 1957, 4); "*All this* at a
time when our schools are already bulging with pupils . . ."
(Agnes E. Meyer, *The Atlantic Monthly,* Jan. 1958, 29); "*All
this* induces a kind of numbness at the base of the skull . . ." (Edward Weeks, *op. cit.*).

The pronoun *that* is employed in the same manner, though much
less frequently: "What they actually got was Stalin's pledge in 1943
to enter the war . . . and, of course, his continued war effort
against Germany, though probably he had little choice in *that*"
(*The New York Times Book Review,* July 28, 1957, 17). In one
study (Edelstein) where fifty-seven instances of *this* occurred with
a "notional" antecedent, there was only one of *that,* and compared
to 180 instances of *this* with a definite antecedent, there occurred
only four of *that.*

Occasionally in Modern English, *this* occurs in reference to a
following statement, as in " 'Now tell me *this:* is it too unthinkable
that Amélie . . .' " (Francis Parkinson Keyes, *Dinner at An-
toine's,* 1948, p. 152). One often hears comments like "*This* is
what she said: 'I am not going, no matter what you do' " or " 'I'm
not going, no matter what you do.' *That* was what she said."

As with *this* and *that, it* and *which* are used with a "notional"
antecedent, as in "Militarily, Stalin wanted an immediate second
front in France. . . . This was agreed on, but *it* took time" (*The
New York Times Book Review,* July 28, 1957, 17) [the pronoun *it*
refers to the idea of obtaining and achieving a second front]; "You
judge your family's shopping ability by what it gets for what it
spends. *It's* an excellent way to judge your community too" (*Better
Homes and Gardens,* Oct., 1949, 214) [*It* refers to the idea of the

preceding sentence]; "He asked me to describe the jacket to him and the typography of the book, *which* I did" (*Saturday Review,* Aug. 17, 1957, 36) [*which* refers to the idea expressed in "me . . . book"]. However, one study (Roberts) based upon 603 examples of *which* showed that it occurred with a substantive antecedent 95.5% of the time. In formal prose *which* generally has a definite antecedent. Four other investigators (Hotchner, Nelson, Russell, Wilson) conducted studies for this entry.

Other evidence: Bartlett, *CE,* 11 (Oct., 1949), 40-41; Beauchamp, *AS,* 26 (Oct., 1951), 173-80; Bryant, *EJ,* XLV (Dec., 1956), 556; Drake, *AS,* 35 (Dec., 1960), 275-79; Rice, *EJ,* XXV (Mar., 1936), 245; Roberts, *AS,* 27 (Oct., 1952), 171-78.

REFERENCE, VAGUE OR INDEFINITE: WHICH. See
REFERENCE, VAGUE OR INDEFINITE: THIS (PRONOMINAL).

REGARD(S). See IN REGARD(S) TO.

REGARDING. See PROVIDED, PROVIDING, conj.

RELATIVE PRONOUNS AND CLAUSES

Summary: In standard English, relative clauses in which the relative pronoun is absent but understood (called "contact" clauses) occur frequently; however, relative clauses containing the expressed overt relative pronoun occur almost four times as frequently. In these clauses, who almost always refers to "person" antecedents and which to "thing" antecedents; that usually refers to "thing" antecedents but it may refer as well to "person" antecedents.

A relative pronoun normally introduces a clause following a noun which is said to be the antecedent. Relative pronouns differ from all other connectives in having a function within the clause. This description fits *that, which,* and *who* (*whom, whose*); where there is no relative pronoun ("contact" clause), we may either suppose a relative pronoun to be added or treat the noun to which the clause relates as having a double function. This first alternative has been chosen for this entry.

Data: An extensive investigation of a reputable mass-circulation magazine (Faust) produced 519 instances of clauses with expressed (overt) relative pronouns and 152 with the relative pronoun omitted. *That, which,* and *who* appeared with the following constructions within the clause:

1. (a) As the subject: ". . . mothers *that* protect them . . ."; ". . . the mile *which* separated us . . ."; "It was Cyrus *who* came. . . ."

(b) After a preposition within the subject (modifying it): ". . . real estate, some of *which* was leased . . ."; ". . . the youth, all of *whom* were supposed to be . . . communists . . ."; "53,000 workers, of *whom* 52,200 . . . are Mexicans. . . ."

2. As the object of a verb: ". . . words *that* he suggested . . ."; ". . . wiles *which* she recognized . . ."; ". . . sleuth *whom* he brought. . . ."

3. (a) With a preposition preceding: ". . . compulsion against *which* there is no defense . . ."; "people to *whom* he's not really drawn. . . ."

(b) With a preposition following (at the end of the clause): ". . . something *that* they were pushed into . . ."; ". . . two sayings *which* his heirs . . . have subscribed to . . ."; ". . . no Yugoslav *whom* he could depend upon. . . ."

4. As a modifier: ". . . figures *whose* legs and arms worked . . ."; "forty-seven minutes at the end of *which* time he saw a girl. . . ."

Relative pronouns added to the parallel contact clauses would show the following constructions within the clause:

1. As subject: ". . . to the hotel room [　] he'd thought was so lush . . ."; "The first one [　] makes a move . . . I'll cut him down. . . ." (in dialogue).

2. (a) As object of a verb: ". . . he had done everything [　] he could . . ."; ". . . the . . . costume [　] she wore. . . ."

(b) As predicate nominative: ". . . to testify to the red [　] they once had been. . . ."

3. With preposition following (at end of clause): ". . . any deal [　] he gets into. . . ."

That, which, and *who* (*whom, whose*) appeared most often by far as subjects (407 of 519 instances); by contrast, the understood relative pronouns of contact clauses would have been most frequent as verb objects (135 of 152 instances). The expressed (overt) pronouns were distinguished from each other by constructions in which they were next most frequent: object of a verb for *that* (27); object of a preceding preposition for *which* (38) (*that* never follows a preposition, but may be governed by a final one in the clause, as "The place *that* he sent it to," not "The place to *that* he sent it"); and modifying position for *who,* in the form of *whose* (14) (*whom* occurred only 10 times in all; *who* and *whom* never replaced each other in material examined).

Contact clauses and those introduced by *that* refer to very similar kinds of terms: "thing" words, whose singulars are replaceable by *it,* in well over 90% of the instances; and "person" words, whose singulars are replaceable by *he* or *she,* for the rest. *Which* and *who* refer virtually always to "thing" and "person" words, respectively. However, in at least ten instances *which* had no single-term reference, or definite antecedent, as in "She was very pretty, *which* did not surprise him."

Relative clauses occur after some words traditionally classified as either pronouns or adjectives: e.g., *that* after *something* and *everything; which* after (*the*) *first* and *anything; who* after *those* and *he;* and contact clauses after *all* and *something.* The proportions have a wide spread, from 2% of all occurrences of *which* through 10% for *who* and 11% for *that* to 26% for the contact clauses. The most frequent combination is *all* with a contact clause (seventeen instances), as in *"All* [   ] he wants is. . . ."

Other evidence: Menner, *AS,* 6 (June, 1931), 341-46; Roberts, *UG,* 68-78, 263.

RESPECTING. See PROVIDED, PROVIDING, conj.

RIDE, v.

Summary: The preterit rode *and the past participle* ridden *are standard English;* rode *as a past participle is nonstandard.*

Data: According to two studies (Allen, Malmstrom) of the Linguistic Atlas records for New England, the Middle Atlantic, the South Atlantic, the North Central, and the Upper Midwest States, in the context "I have never *ridden* a horse," ridden is the standard form, universal in Type III (cultivated) speech on the

Atlantic Coast and a majority form in Type III and Type II speech (of informants with at least some secondary school education) in the North Central and Upper Midwest States.

Rode, as in "I *have* never *rode* a horse," is the main nonstandard variant and has wide currency in Type II speech in almost all areas, particularly among older informants. *Rid* is an archaic form, occurring mainly in the speech of older informants in typically relic areas such as northeast New England and the coastal and mountain areas of the South and South Midland. It is also used in the preterit, as in "He *rid* into town at a gallop."

One investigation of written matter (Hotchner) reports forty-eight examples of the preterit *rode,* three of the past participle *ridden,* and no variants for either.

Other evidence: Atwood, 19; Kurath, *LANE,* Vol. III, Pt. 2, Map 655; Malmstrom, *SVTS,* 155-56; V.G. McDavid, 41.

RING, v.

Summary: The preterit rang *or* rung *and the past participle* rung *occur in standard English.*

Data: Field workers for the Linguistic Atlas found *rang* and *rung* with about equal frequency in the context "Who *rang/rung* the bell?" in New England. However, only about one fifth of the cultivated informants used *rung* in the preterit. According to three studies (Abelack, Fleming, Hotchner), *rang* is the usual form in formal English. The past participle *rang* occurs sometimes, but *rung* is the common form.

Other evidence: Atwood, 19; Kurath, *LANE,* Vol. III, Pt. 2, Map 656; Poutsma, Pt. II, § II, 585.

RISE, v.

Summary: The preterit rose *and the past participle* risen *are standard English.*

Data: According to one study (Malmstrom) of the Linguistic Atlas records, in the context "The sun *rose* at six," *rose* is the standard form, almost universal in Type III (cultivated) speech in the North Central and Upper Midwest States, prevailing throughout New England, New York, New Jersey, and Pennsylvania, and common among younger informants in other areas of the Middle Atlantic and South Atlantic States.

Many informants use a form of the lexical variants *come up* or *raise* in the above context. "The sun *raised*" is a South Midland usage, characteristic of Type I (uneducated) speech but occurring also in Type II (with at least some secondary school education). "The sun *riz*" is a northeastern New England, South Midland, and Southern form, occurring in Type I speech. *Rised, arose,* and the uninflected *rise* are minor variants showing distinctive regional distribution.

One study (Rinaldi) of 1,355 pages of magazines, newspapers, and fiction found thirty-nine examples of *rose* in the preterit, ten examples of the past participle *risen,* and no variants for either. Another study of 4,957 pages (Bonander) found twenty-six examples of *rose,* and one variant, *riz,* in the dialogue of William Faulkner, eight examples of *risen,* and one of *arisen.*

Other evidence: Abbott, *AS,* 32 (Feb., 1957), 35; Atwood, 19-20; Kurath, *LANE,* Vol. III, Pt. 2, Map 657; Malmstrom, *SVTS,* 158-59; R.I. McDavid, *AED,* 516, 525; V.G. McDavid, 41-42; R.I. and V.G. McDavid, *AS,* 35 (Feb., 1960), 14, 15.

ROUND. See COMPARISON, ILLOGICAL.

RUN, v.

Summary: The preterit ran *and the past participle* run *are standard English; in some areas,* run *is acceptable in the preterit.*

Data: According to one study (Malmstrom) of the Linguistic Atlas records for New England, the Middle Atlantic, the South Atlantic, the North Central, and the Upper Midwest States, in the context "He *ran,*" the standard preterit is *ran,* strongly predominant or almost universal in Type III (cultivated) speech everywhere.

Run, however, occurs normally in Type II speech (informants with at least some secondary school education) on the Atlantic

Coast northeast of the Merrimack River and South of the Potomac River. In the Middle West it is frequently found in both Type II and Type III speech, especially in the North Central States. In these areas, it is, therefore, acceptable usage in speech.

In one investigation of twenty-four periodicals, newspapers, short stories, and a novel (Bring), 109 examples of the preterit *ran* were found, with no variants.

Other evidence: Abbott, *AS*, 32 (Feb., 1957), 35; Atwood, 20; Kurath, *LANE*, Vol. III, Pt. 2, Map 658; Malmstrom, *SVTS*, 162-63; V.G. McDavid, 42.

R U N G. See RING, v.

S A N K. See SINK, v.

S A T. See SIT, SET, v.

S A V I N G See PROVIDED, PROVIDING, conj.

S C A D S. See LOT(S), HEAP(S).

S C A R C E L Y. See HARDLY; ONLY, adv.

S C A L L O P S. See LOT(S), HEAP(S).

S E E, v.

Summary: The preterit saw *and the past participle* seen *are standard English;* seen *as a preterit is nonstandard.*

Data: According to one study of the Linguistic Atlas records (Malmstrom) for New England, the Middle Atlantic, the South Atlantic, the North Central, and the Upper Midwest States, in the context "He *saw* me," *saw* is practically universal in Type III (cultivated) speech in all areas. Two extensive studies (Cahill, Rothberg) of modern prose reveal that the variant *seen,* which is used frequently by Type II informants (those with at least some secondary school education) in the Midland areas and with increasing frequency in the North Central States, is found only in dialogue representing characters of little education or foreign birth.

The variant *see* is clearly a regular northern and southern form in uneducated speech, while the variant *seed* is the most common preterit form in Type I (uneducated) speech in certain areas of the South Atlantic States and South Midland.

Other evidence: Atwood, 20; Kurath, *LANE,* Vol. III, Pt. 2, Map 659; Malmstrom, *SVTS,* 165-66; R.I. McDavid, *AED,* 516, 519, 523, 526; V.G. McDavid, 43; R.I. and V.G. McDavid, *AS,* 35 (Feb., 1960), 12.

S E E D. See SEE, v.

S E E I N G. See PROVIDED, PROVIDING, conj.

S E E M. See CAN'T SEEM TO.

S E E N. See SEE, v.

S E N D A N D. See TRY AND.

SENTENCE MODIFIER

Summary: Most sentence modifiers occur at the beginning of the sentence; the conjunctive adverb is the most common of them.

Data: One of the important functions of the adverb is to modify a sentence as a whole. This is a very different function from modifying the verb or any other word in the sentence, as can easily be seen my comparing *"Happily* he did not die" and "He did not die *happily,"* where the first *happily* modifies the whole sentence and the second the verb only. Compare *"Perhaps* you will stay," *"Evidently* that remark was made for my benefit," *"Fortunately,* there was one more train that day." The italicized words in the preceding sentences influence the whole statement and not any one word. Other adverbs which often apply to a whole idea are: *surely, certainly, probably, simply, even, positively, definitely.* In addition to words, there are infinitive and participial constructions as well as prepositional phrases that modify the whole idea. For example, in *"To come to the point,* the material available is not suitable," *to come to the point* is a sentence-modifying infinitival group, as are the participial constructions in *"Judging from his appearence,* he is not ill" and *"Considered from your side and mine,* the course is not a good one," and also the prepositional phrase in *"In writing an article,* the outline is a major considera-tion." Such constructions are equivalent to a subordinate clause be-ginning with *if:* "*If* you judge . . . ," etc. Likewise the somewhat literary nominative absolute, deriving its name from the parallel Latin introductory construction and employing a participle with its subject, functions as a sentence-modifying adverb, as in *"He being dead,* the daughters moved away"; or *"The father being dead,* the daughters . . . ," or *"The father dead,* the daughters . . . ," where *being* is understood. One of the more frequent sentence modifiers, however, is the subordinate clause introduced by such conjunctions as *if, after, since, so, because, although,* as in *"If this be true,* what then is left of the claim that American society has no place for the intellectual?" (*Southwest Review,* Winter, 1958, 66) where *If this be true* influences the whole question. It is evident from these illustrations that the sentence-modifier is not uncom-mon.

In a study (Hickey) made from samplings in twenty-three peri-odicals, two newspapers and two pieces of fiction, 600 sentence modifiers occurred, 78% of which were at the beginning of the sentence, 9.33% at the end and 12.67% within the sentence. The largest number of sentence modifiers were conjunctive adverbs (53.2%), as in *"Perhaps* the most famous pre-Revolutionary Lutheran was John Peter Zenger" (*Look,* Apr. 1, 1958, 81); "That would be too simple, *of course,* and maybe too permanent" (*The Reporter,* Apr. 17, 1958, 10). Then came adverbial clauses (39.3%) introduced by such conjunctions as *if, when, although, after, since,* as in "But it would have been more in accord with accepted standards of scholarship *if* he had shared his information with his readers" (*Saturday Review,* Mar. 29, 1958, 17). Follow-ing were prepositional phrases (3%), as in *"With the Assembly scheduled to recess this week for a month,* the Premier was playing

for time" ("Editorial," *The New York Times,* Mar. 23, 1958, 2E);
the present participial construction (2.2%), as in "But *allowing
progress its due and then some,* the fact remains that much of the
science of packaging is essentially a concerted assault on the eye,
touch, and psyche of the consumer" (*The Reporter,* Apr. 17, 1958,
8); the infinitival construction (1%), as in *"To make all this more*
comprehensible, Dr. Lucius Roy Wilson . . . cites the case of a
man who underwent major surgery in 1938 . . ." (*Coronet,* May,
1958, 58); the nominative absolute (.8%), as in *"The Cause being sacred,* that great war for the Cause was, in all particulars,
sacred, too . . ." (James Gould Cozzens, *By Love Possessed,*
1957, p. 203); past participial construction (.5%), as in "What
proportion of our wealth and energy should be put into defense,
given the present international political context?" (*Current History,*
Oct., 1957, 212).

Other evidence: Bryant, *CE,* 17 (Oct., 1955), 53; Kruisinga, 5th
Edit., II, *English Accidence and Syntax,* 2, 123-24; 3, 253-55; Perrin,
CE, 5 (Mar., 1944), 342.

SET. See SIT, SET.

SHALL, WILL

Summary: While the usage of shall *and* will (*including* 'll, shan't,
and won't) *is highly complex, all the complexity is within the area of
standard English; there is no* shall-will *"error" like, for example,* "He
done it" *to make the speaker or writer conspicuous.*

Data: In a study made some years ago, the American Telephone and Telegraph Company found that *shall* occurred six times
in six conversations, *will* 1,305 times in 402 conversations. In a
later study (Henderson), *will* occurred in all persons 93.5% of the
time and *shall* 6.5%; in another (Schaller) *shall* 41% of the time,
will 59%. A third study (Winthrop) found 101 examples (92.7%
of *will* in its various forms and 8 uses of *shall,* 7.3%), all in the
first person and half of them from the same article.

The Linguistic Atlas recorded *shall* and *will* in the contexts "I
shall be disappointed if he doesn't come," "I *shall be going* next

Saturday," and *"We shall be glad* to see you." Field workers of the North Central and Upper Midwest States generally recorded the future forms whenever they heard them in conversation.

Will or *'ll,* according to one study (Malmstrom), is universal in the speech of all types in the Upper Midwest States and practically so in the North Central States. In the East, with the exception of northeast New England, a relic area, both *will* or *'ll* and *shall* occur in the speech of all types, with the younger and more modern informants strongly preferring *will* or *'ll.* Only in northeast New England is *shall* decidedly more frequent than *will* or *'ll,* particularly in Type III (cultivated) speech of the older generation. In the *we* context *will* or *'ll* is much more frequent than in the *I* context, probably because textbooks (and, therefore, teachers) emphasize *I shall* more than *we shall.* In the second and third persons *shall* usually indicates obligation, as in "The duties of the treasurer *shall be* . . . ," and in the first person *shall* sometimes indicates determination, as in Douglas MacArthur's famous promise, "I *shall* return."

Valiant efforts by many textbooks to make *I, we shall* indicate simple future and *I, we will* indicate determination have not succeeded. To indicate determination unmistakably in the first person, a writer may use a modifier (*I certainly will, I will indeed,* etc.) or a different construction (*I promise to* . . . , *I am determined that* . . . , etc.). The speaker may also make use of stress. In most declarative statements, where one need not distinguish between simple future and determination, either *shall* or *will* in the first person will pass unnoticed. To some, the choice of *shall* or *will* has rhetorical importance, changing the style somewhat. *Shall* gives a more or less formal effect.

Other evidence: Bartlett, *CE,* 15 (Oct., 1953), 55-56; Fries, *AEG,* 150-54, 158-59, 161-62; Kurath, *LANE,* Vol. III, Pt. 2, Maps 694, 702; Malmstrom, *SVTS,* 232-33, 304; V.G. McDavid, 61; Mencken, *Am. Lang.,* 200; Roberts, *UG,* 146; Robertson, *AS,* 14 (Dec., 1939), 251-53; Whyte, *CE,* 5 (Mar., 1944), 333-37.

SHE DON'T. See DON'T, v.

SHOW, v.

Summary: The preterit showed *and the past participle* shown *occur in standard English. The past participle* showed *appears very infrequently.*

Data: Four studies (Cook, McDavid, Sheil, R. Thomas) reveal that *shown* is employed more frequently than *showed* as a past participle, as in "Moreover, one could sense in . . . the picture that he was *shown* the intense nostalgia for western civilization . . ." (*The Reporter,* May 17, 1956, 16). In an investigation (Sheppard) of eighteen students from New York, Ohio, Massachusetts, and Pennsylvania concerning the context "I've *showed/ shown* my picture before," *shown* occurred seventeen times, *showed* only once (in the speech of a Bostonian). *Showed* occurs infrequently in formal written English. One reader found only one example in his reading since 1949: "But practically all the other figures . . . were better than in May, which in turn *had showed* improvement over April" (E. L. Dale, *The New York Times,* July 9, 1958, 1).

Other evidence: Thomas, *CE,* 11 (Dec., 1949), 157-58.

SHOW OFF. See SHOW UP.

SHOW UP, v.

Summary: Show up, *meaning chiefly* "to expose" *or* "to appear," *occurs frequently in informal English.*

Data: An investigation of these usages (Gitter) revealed that in thirty-seven cases where the possible meaning "to appear" was implied, *to show up* was used twenty-six times, or 70.3% of the time, and in twenty-six possible cases where "to expose" might have been employed, *show up* was the choice fourteen times, or 54% of the time. The phrase occurs principally in spoken English as in "I'm glad he *was showed up* (exposed) for what he really is," and "To *show up* (appear) should be everyone's goal" (a principal of a school to students). One study (Winburne) listed forty examples of the usage, as in "If he were in uniform, he could *show up* as well as the lot of them . . ." (John P. Marquand, *So Little Time*, 1943, p. 570) and "They *showed up* wonderfully at night . . ." (Ernie Pyle, *Brave Men*, 1944, p. 137).

Similarly, *show off* is another combination which occurs mainly in spoken English. It means "to display ostentatiously," as in "He *shows off* whenever a guest arrives." It may also occur as a noun, as in "He is only a *show off*," referring to one who behaves so as to attract attention.

SHRANK. See SHRINK, v.

SHRINK v.

Summary: The preterit shrunk *or* shrank *and the past participle* shrunk *or* shrunken *occur in standard English;* shrinked *is nonstandard.*

Data: One study of the Linguistic Atlas records (Malmstrom) for New England, the Middle Atlantic, the South Atlantic, the North Central, and the Upper Midwest States with the exception of Wisconsin and parts of Michigan and Illinois reveal that in the context of "The collar *shrank/shrunk*," *shrunk* is the preferred form everywhere among all types of speakers. However, *shrank* occurs also everywhere among all types, though less frequently. *Shrinked* occurs in the South Midland States among the uneducated, both as a preterit and as a past participle.

The New England records show that *shrunk* is the usual form in the past participle. About 13% of the informants, including a fair number of Type III (cultivated), use *shrunken*. A differentiation, however, is often made between the two forms, depending upon the auxiliary used: "It *has shrunk*," but "It *is shrunken*." *Shrunken* is also often employed as a pure adjective, particularly when placed before a noun: "a *shrunken*, old man," with the meaning "contracted in size, shriveled." Minor variants in speech are *shrank, shrinked*, and *shrunk*.

A study of three groups of students (Tyson) in Cleveland, Ohio, showed that the first (elementary education) preferred *shrank* in the context "The fawn *shrank/shrunk* back when the tiger passed"; the second (high school education) preferred *shrunk;* and the third (one or more years of college) used *shrank*. In the past participle, all three groups strongly preferred *shrunk*. Two studies of contemporary prose (Collins, Winters) found *shrank* in the preterit with no variants, *shrunk* in the past participle with no variants.

Other evidence: Abbott, *AS*, 32 (Feb., 1957), 35; Atwood, 20-21; Kurath, *LANE*, Vol. III, Pt. 2, Map 660; Malmstrom, *SVTS*, 170-71; R.I. McDavid, *AED*, 521; V.G. McDavid, 43-44.

SHRUNK, SHRUNKEN. See SHRINK, v.

SINCE. See AS, CAUSAL.

SING, v.

Summary: The preterit sang *and the past participle* sung *occur in formal written English.*

Data: According to the *OED, sung* was a common preterit form in the eighteenth century, but two studies (Fleming, Stevens) show that at the present moment, *sang* is the preferred form, as in "Anton Dermota *sang* the part of . . ." (*The New York Times,* Nov. 6, 1955, 22). *Sung* occurs occasionally in spoken English, as "She *sung* well last evening."

Among certain people of Type I (uneducated) speech, *sing* has a specialized meaning, "to inform to the police," as in "Did he *sing* when he got caught?"

Other evidence: Kennedy, *Cur. Eng.,* 455; Marckwardt and Walcott, 48, 85; Poutsma, Pt. II, § II, 587.

SINK, v.

Summary: The preterit sank *and the past participle* sunk *occur in formal written English.*

Data: In formal written English, the preterit *sank* and the past participle *sunk* are generally found, as in "The ship *sank* yesterday" and "The ship has *sunk*." Three investigations (Fleming, Hotchner, Stevens) of written English found no variants for the preterit *sank* or the past participle *sunk*. *Sunk,* however, occurs occasionally in the preterit as does the old form of the participle *sunken,* as in "It has *sunken* to the bottom." *Sunken* usually occurs before a noun, as in "the *sunken* garden."

Other evidence: Kennedy, *Cur. Eng.,* 455.

SIT, SET, v.

Summary: The verbs sit (sat, sat) *and* set (set, set) *are not synonymous but they have been confused for centuries in speech; while the preterit form* sat *predominates in Type III* (cultivated) *usage,* set *also occurs as a standard regionalism in the preterit of* sit. *In formal written English, only* sit *occurs in the present and* sat *in the preterit and past participle.*

Both of these verbs are used transitively and intransitively. The chief distinction between *sit* as an intransitive and *set* as a transitive verb is in stress patterns when an adverb follows: "Will you *sit* down?" and "Will you *set* the pitcher down?" In each case *down* has the primary stress, but *set* has a heavier stress than *sit*.

Sit was originally intransitive, meaning "to take a seat" or "to be seated," and *set* transitive, meaning "to cause something to sit," as "to set a pot on the stove"; that is, "to put or place the pot on the stove." Although this distinction was once observed, each verb has developed other uses which are now standard English. *Sit* is used transitively to mean "to seat (oneself)," as in *"Sit* yourself on the bench"; "to keep one's seat upon," as "She *sits* her horse well"; "to place in a seat; cause to sit," as *"Sit* the baby up," meaning specifically "to cause the baby to sit."

Similarly, *set* is intransitive in the following instances: "to sit on eggs," as "The hen *set* for one week and left the nest" or "the *set-*.ting hen" (*cf.* "a *setting* of eggs"); "to pass below the horizon," said of heavenly bodies, as "the *setting* sun" or "The moon *sets* tomorrow at four o'clock"; "to become hard or solid," as "The cement *set* after four hours"; "to become fast or permanent," said of colors, as "The color *set* in the material"; "to assume a rigid state," as "The muscles in his face *set*"; "to hang or fit," as "The coat *sets* (or *sits*) well"; "to have a certain direction or course," as "The current *sets* to the east." The name of the hunting dog, the *setter,* derives from "setting" or pointing out game by standing in a rigid position. On the other hand, *"set* down for a few minutes and rest" or "come and *set"* are nonstandard usage. One can see that, with the exception of these two usages, *set* has good standing as an intransitive as well as a transitive verb. Since its latter occurrence is more frequent, perhaps it will be safe to say that *set* is generally transitive and *sit* intransitive, so long as one remembers the other meanings each has developed as standard usage.

Data: Of the two verbs, *set* has demonstrated by far the greater vigor, as any dictionary will testify, especially as it has become a component of many idioms, such as *set about, set aside, set back, set down, set in, set off, set on, set to, set up.* The *OED* devotes eighteen pages, each of three columns, to this word.

The Linguistic Atlas records the present imperative and the preterit of *sit* in the contexts *"Sit* down," and "I *sat* down" or "He *sat* down" for New England, the Middle Atlantic, the South Atlantic, the North Central, and the Upper Midwest States.

According to one study (Malmstrom), two present forms are current: *sit* and *set,* as in "I *sit*" and "I *set,*" both meaning "to take a seat." *Sit* predominates in New York City, northern New Jersey, the lower Hudson Valley, Pennsylvania east of the Susquehanna, and the North Central and the Upper Midwest States. On the Atlantic Coast south of Pennsylvania, except in the large cities, *sit* is uncommon except in Type III (cultivated) speech. *Set* occurs also in Type II (informants with some secondary school education) and Type III speech in the North Central and Upper Midwest States. It approaches geographic concentration only in Kentucky and Ohio, especially in Type I (uneducated) speech.

Of the Eastern informants who use *sit* in the present, those on the Coast prefer *sat* in the preterit. The *sit-sat* combination predominates also in Type III and Type II speech in the North Central States and the Upper Midwest inland States. Eastern users of the preterit *sit* tend to use the leveled combination *sit-sit* (in the present and preterit), although the combinations *sit-set* and *sit-sot* also occur. Of the Eastern informants who use the present *set* ("I *set* here every day"), most prefer the preterit *set*. The combinations *set-sat* and *set-sot* also occur. *Sot*, however, is definitely an archaism. In South Midland usage, *sot down* occurs for *sat* in Type I speech.

According to three studies of contemporary prose (Hotchner, Kehl, R. Thomas), only *sit* occurs in the present and *sat* in the preterit and past participle; the verb *set* was used in the transitive 89% of the time and in the intransitive 11%.

Other evidence: Atwood, 21; Bryant, *CE,* 17 (Feb., 1956), 312; Kurath, *LANE,* Vol. II, Pt. I, Maps 318, 324; Vol. III, Pt. 2, Map 661; Malmstrom, *SVTS,* 174-75; Marckwardt and Walcott, 58, 83; R.I. McDavid, *AED,* 521; V.G. McDavid, 44-45; R.I. and V.G. McDavid, *AS,* 35 (Feb., 1960), 14; McMillan, *CE,* 4 (Nov., 1942), 137; Pooley, *TEU,* 163-66.

SLEW(S). See LOT(S), HEAP(S).

SLOW, SLOWLY

Summary: Slowly *occurs much more frequently in formal written English than* slow, *and* slow *occurs more often in spoken English than in written English.*

In Old English, adverbs were formed in two ways: by adding *-lice* (*-lic* + *e*), which developed into *-ly;* by adding *-e*, which later dropped off. *Slow* and *slowly* are the two forms of the adverb which have come down to us. Used in English literature throughout the centuries, they are recognized by all respectable dictionaries as adverbs. Observe the use of both forms in one poetic line from Arthur Hugh Clough: "In front the sun climbs *slow*, how *slowly*" ("Say Not the Struggle Naught Availeth").

Data: Today we generally say "Drive *slow*" but "The man walked *slowly* down the road." The shorter form is usually employed in imperative sentences (Go *slow*), whereas in declarative sentences the longer form is more common. In speech one often hears statements such as "Don't walk so *slow*" or "He speaks too *slow,*" but in written English the *ly* form occurs more frequently, as in "The program went very *slowly* . . ." (*The New Yorker,* Jan. 4, 1958, 24); ". . . and it moved *slowly* behind the trees" (Ernest Hemingway, *Across the River and into the Trees,* 1950, p. 24). In the reading done by five different persons (Hazel Henry, Hotchner, Meder, Nanos, Whitesell) concerning this usage, twenty-eight examples of *slowly* were found but none of *slow* with the exception of the sign "School—Drive *Slow.*" The Linguistic Atlas survey of New England, on the other hand, found nearly two hundred informants using *slow* in the context "Go *slow*" and only three using *slowly.* Seven used both forms.

What is true of *slow, slowly* is also true of a few other adverbs like *loud, loudly; quick, quickly;* and *soft, softly.* A well-known example employing the adverb that developed into *loud* comes from an early English lyric written about 1240: "Summer is icumen in;/Lhude sing, cuccu!" Often one hears in spoken English remarks like "I'll do it *quick,* by return mail" (Nina Brown Baker, *Big Catalogue,* 1956, p. 68) or "Come *quick* . . ." (*Ladies' Home Journal,* Apr., 1958, 160). The Linguistic Atlas survey of New England also found *quick* in the context "Come *quick*" used nearly two hundred times, *quickly* twenty times, and both forms ten times. In written English, however, a quantitative study (Meder) found eight examples of *quickly* and four of *quick,* three of which were in colloquial slogans, such as "Get rich *quick*" and "Sow thick, thin *quick,*" and one in dialogue.

Other evidence: Bryant, *CE,* 18 (Oct., 1956), 47; Kurath, *LANE,* Vol. III, Pt. 1, Map 493; Marckwardt and Walcott, 29, 36, 99, 100; Pooley, *TEU,* 10-11, 59-62; Rice, *AS,* 2 (Sept., 1927), 489-91.

S O, adv.

Summary: In standard English, adverbial so is generally used in three ways: 1) as a quasi-intensifier with the idea expressed in a preceding clause or sentence; 2) as a full intensifier modifying an adjective, adverb, or verb; 3) as an intensive meaning "very."

Data: The adverb *so* is often used as a modifier indicating degree, with the degree specified in a following *as* or *that* clause, e.g.,

"The state was not *so* prosperous *as* it once had been" and "The farmers were *so* prosperous *that* they voted the party back into power"; "Resolve to live a life *so* full and satisfying that . . ." (*New York Journal-American,* Dec. 30, 1957, 12) (See AS . . . AS; SO . . . AS). Some textbooks insist that the *as* or *that* clause is necessary. But, according to three studies (Hotchner, McMillan, R. Thomas), there are several such uses of *so* without a completing clause following:

(1) As a quasi-intensive with the idea expressed in a preceding sentence or clause, e.g. (28.3% of the time), "It comes then as something of a shock to realize that the *Southwest Review* has endured forty years. . . . Why, one wonders, has the *Southwest Review* been able to preserve its vitality and its prestige and its readership for *so* long?" (*Southwest Review,* Autumn, 1955, 281) [i.e., for so long as forty years]; "Fourteen years ago it seemed incredible that he was eighty, his mind was *so* active and his pen *so* sharp" (Brooks Atkinson, *The New York Times,* Nov. 5, 1950, Sec. 2, 2). This use of *so* is common in all types of English.

(2) As an intensive modifying adjectives, adverbs, or verbs (29.3% of the time), "In short, all three novels were probably a long way beyond what one would expect from *so* young a writer" (Granville Hicks, *College English,* Jan. 11, 1950, 178); "Why was this generation which had been *so* ill used, which had *so* many grievances—why was it *so* lacking in youthful energies?" (Oscar Handlin, *The Atlantic Monthly,* Jan., 1951, 26); "But he was also, by the same token, incapable of the conventional postures that enter into *so* many cases of Nineteenth Century *Weltschmerz*" (*Yale Review,* Summer, 1955, xxiv). This use of *so* is also standard English.

(3) As an intensive meaning "very" (42.4% of the time), "Make haste slowly with your first typewriting lessons and learn the touch system. It will save you *so* much time and work later on" (*The Denver Post,* Feb. 22, 1955); " '. . . it would make me *so* happy' " (Frank Yerby, *The Devil's Laughter,* 1954, p. 120); " 'I'm *so* happy!' she cried" (Eric Heath, *The Murder Pool,* 1954, p. 216). This use of *so,* meaning "very," is common in conversational English but rare in formal written English. It receives un-

usual stress in speech, ranging from a statement like "I'm *so* glad
you like it" to the common schoolgirl expression "I'm *so* thrilled,"
"He is *so* handsome," and "She is *so* beautiful." In informal writing
one may find this usage, as in these sentences from articles from
the *Woman's Home Companion*, July, 1952: "Two-piece dress
with a softly draped halter and full skirt, made up here in a brilliant
floral print. *So* pretty for evening parties" (p. 56); "You'll like
Mrs. Wiese's favorite refrigerator meal, a sure hit for a warm day
and *so* easy" (p. 78). Advertisers also make use of this *so,* as in
an advertisement from the *Seattle Times,* June 27, 1952: "Pure
orange flavor makes this specialized aspirin *so* easy to take."

Other evidence: Fries, *AEG,* 206; Thomas, *CE,* 12 (May, 1951),
453-54.

S O, conj.

Summary: In formal English, so *does not occur frequently as a conjunctive variant of* so that, *but it is common in spoken English, often
in place of more specific words.*

Data: In speech, *so* is used to introduce clauses of purpose:
"He went late *so* he could avoid the crowd." Though investigators
(Anderson, Baker, Gross, Hotchner, Kehl, Nanos) found fifty-
seven examples of this usage in modern popular prose, in formal
English one generally finds: "He went late (*so*) *that* he might (in
order to) avoid the crowd." One of these investigators found *so*
used 14.3% of the time and *so that* 85.7%. An example of the *so*
usage is: "The Governors' Conference [*sic*] have repeatedly de-
manded that Congress curtail grants and proportionately reduce
federal taxes *so* the states could pay their own way . . ."
(*Reader's Digest,* Dec., 1956, 34).

So is likewise employed in speech to introduce clauses of result
which in formal English would usually be introduced by *so that*
or changed to a construction introduced by *since* or *because.* For
example, the colloquial "The letter was lost, *so* I had to write another" would be in formal written English "The letter was lost, *so
that* I had to write another" or *"Since (Because)* the letter was lost,

I had to write another." An investigator (Watkins) reading the *Chicago Sun-Times* for about three weeks in 1957 encountered six instances of conjunctive *so* in result clauses, as in "After a few experiences they decided that the headgear was too cumbersome for comfort, *so* they gave up the practice" (Nov. 14, p. 58).

While *so* is employed in formal written English in each of the two uses above, it is used more frequently in spoken English. According to Fries (*AEG*, p. 226), it occurs six times more frequently in nonstandard English than in standard. In the standard English letters which he examined, he found 17 instances; in the vulgar English letters, 105. An example from written prose is: "He is an adventurer in his own right, *so* this excursion into romantic cloak-and-sword drama was something more . . ." (*Theatre Arts*, Dec., 1957, 83).

The frequent use of *so* as a coordinating conjunction to connect ideas, particularly in narrative accounts, is known as the "*so*-habit." One may hear: "Jane wanted to continue her college career, *so* she decided to get a job. *So* she looked at the papers every day, *so* she could find out what positions were available for the summer."

Other evidence: Fries, *AEG*, 207, 208, 226-27, 239, 287-88.

SO . . . A S. See AS . . . AS; SO . . . AS.

SO FAR AS. See AS . . . AS; SO . . . AS.

SO LONG AS. See AS . . . AS; SO . . . AS.

SOFT, SOFTLY. See SLOW, SLOWLY.

SOME. See AGREEMENT, INDEFINITE PRONOUNS.

SOMEBODY, SOMEONE. See AGREEMENT, INDEFINITE PRONOUNS.

SOMEPLACE. See ANYPLACE, adv.

SOMEWHERES. See ANYWHERE, ANYWHERES.

SORT OF (A, AN). See KIND (SORT) OF (A, AN).

SPED. See SPEED, v.

SPEED, v.

Summary: In standard spoken English, both sped *and* speeded *occur as preterit and past participle; in formal writing,* sped *is preferred.*

Data: Examples of each form are: "With all due speed, investigators *sped* to the crash sites" (*The Nation,* Dec. 31, 1960, 516); "Industry is *speeded* up"; "They *speeded* up as we passed." Two recent studies (J. Jacobson, Stevens) found only the form *sped* in written English. *Speeded* is generally used in reference to exceeding the speed limit, as in "They *speeded* for a short time on the highway."

SPELL, v. See KNEEL, v.

SPILL, v. See KNEEL, v.

SPLIT INFINITIVE

Summary: The split infinitive ("to openly examine," "to fully express") occurs more commonly in standard informal writing than in formal writing. Whether to avoid or to use this construction is a matter of style. A split infinitive may eliminate awkwardness or ambiguity or add emphasis or clarity. On the other hand, it is advisable not to place too many words between to *and the infinitive as in "I planned* to, *after consulting my friend,* buy *one." The result is awkwardness.*

Data: An infinitive is said to be split if an adverb or an adverbial construction comes between the word *to* and the infinitive "*to* accurately *count*"; "*to* in some manner *compensate*"; "*to* either *write* or forget." This construction has occurred in the works of the best of writers since the beginning of the fourteenth century and has continued to the present time. Those who consider this construction to be nonstandard might consider Willa Cather's "I've heard enough *to* about *do* for me" or Booth Tarkington's "The truth is I have come *to* rather *dislike* him." More recent examples are: ". . . fresh approaches created in order *to* effectively *reach* the multi-billion dollar . . . market" (*New York World-Telegram and Sun,* Dec. 2, 1957, 14); ". . . it took until about 1910 for the phonograph *to* entirely *supersede* the music box" (*Hobbies,* Aug., 1957, 80); ". . . where it takes a password *to* even *gain* entrance" (*ibid.,* Dec., 1957, 39).

Since the Old English period, the relative frequency of the infinitive with *to* has increased over that of the simple infinitive. In the material examined for his *American English Grammar,* Fries found simple infinitives used only 18% of the time. With the increasing use of this infinitive combination has come the placing of other words between the *to* and the infinitive, so that the so-called "split infinitive" has become rather common in modern writing.

A contributing influence to the rising practice is, undoubtedly, the use of *to* with two infinitives, the second of which has an adverb directly before it, as in "He has the ability *to understand and* fully *sympathize* with others" and "All that you have to do is *to write and* patiently *wait* for an answer." Here *fully* and *patiently,* placed before the second infinitive in each instance, come after the *to.*

A second contributing factor may be found in word order. In Modern English, modifiers are usually placed directly before the words they modify, as in "She *successfully* finished the book" or "She delighted in *successfully* finishing the book." As a result, there is pressure to put the adverbial modifier of an infinitive immediately before the infinitive and after the *to.*

Then there are other split expressions which have not gained the publicity of the split infinitive. In a sentence such as "He is as clever in his writing as his sister," one observes a split comparison. Often one sees a split subject and predicate, as in "He, instead of writing me, called in person." Furthermore, the split finite verb phrase is constantly used, as in "I have never heard him"; "If the desired result is ever reached . . ."; "He will be highly recommended." So by analogy one finds words placed between the *to* and the infinitive.

The split infinitive is used to avoid ambiguity, to gain emphasis or the desired shade of meaning, or to attain the most natural and effective word order. In "If Mr. Smith will find time *to* completely *examine* the papers, he will discover what the facts are," placing *completely* before the infinitive will give the awkward *time completely to examine,* as well as what is called "a squinting modifier," one that may be interpreted in two ways (modify *find* or *examine*). Putting it after *examine* separates *examine* from its object and produces the clumsy *examine completely the papers.* In another sentence, such as "I desire *to* actually *learn* to read Arabic," if the intent is to have *actually* modify the infinitive *learn* and to avoid a split infinitive one may write: "I desire actually to learn to read Arabic," where *actually* may be considered as modifying *desire* rather than *learn,* or one may write: "I desire to learn actually to read Arabic," where it may be considered as modifying *read.* In either statement the author has a squinting modifier, for each may be interpreted in two ways. This is particularly true when another verbal construction precedes an infinitive. On the other hand, the sentence is clear if the infinitive is split. There is no ambiguity whatever.

In some sentences a split infinitive is hard to avoid unless the idea is completely rearranged or rewritten. Take Theodore Roosevelt's "His fortune having been jeopardized, he hoped *to* more than *retrieve* it by going into speculations in the Western Lands" (*The Winning of the West,* Vol. 1, Ch. II). The word order of this sentence cannot be changed without modifying the author's meaning. Consider also "The men in the district are declared *to* strongly *favor* a strike."

In one comparative study based on the reading of a daily newspaper (Kovitz), the split infinitive occurred 21.7% of the time. In another based on miscellaneous reading (Hotchner), it occurred 17.9% of the time. The average of the two shows the split infinitive occurring 19.8% of the time. Three additional studies (Lindsay, Nass, M. Richardson) encountered the split infinitive twenty times, giving a total in the five studies of thirty-nine instances.

Other evidence: Bryant, *CE,* 8 (Oct., 1946), 39-40; Curme, *MLN,* 29 (Feb., 1914), 41-45; *Syntax,* 1931, 458 *ff.;* Fowler, *MEU,* 558-60; Fries, *AEG,* 130-33; Jespersen, *MEG,* Pt. V, *Syntax,* IV, 330; Pooley,

TEU, 100-6; Rice, *EJ*, XXV (Mar., 1937), 238-40; Roberts, *UG*, 204-6.

S P O I L, v. See KNEEL, v.

S T A C K S. See LOT(S), HEAP(S).

S T A N K. See STINK, v.

S T I N K, v.

Summary: Preterit stank *or* stunk *and past participle* stunk *are standard spoken English. In written English the preterit* stank *generally occurs.*

Data: A recent example of *stank* was found in the *Magazine of Fantasy and Science Fiction:* "Her white dress, tattered and white no longer, *stank*" (Apr., 1958, 67). One hears *stunk,* for example, in "It *stunk* to high heaven." The Linguistic Atlas survey of New England shows *stunk* in the preterit for that region. This form seems to occur rather infrequently in written English. Two extensive readings (Hotchner, A. M. Smith) produced only one form in the preterit: *stank.*

Another variant of *stank* and *stunk* heard occasionally is *stinked,* as in "His pigs *stinked* up the room." This form is nonstandard.

Other evidence: Kennedy, *Cur. Eng.,* 455; Kurath, *LANE,* Vol. II, Pt. 1, Map 306.

S T O M P, v.

Summary: Stomp *as a verb is standard English, a variant of* stamp.

Data: Though dictionaries customarily label this word "dialectal," apparently on the assumption that *stamp* is the only standard form, it is quite generally used in the specialized sense "to beat down forcibly, as with the foot," to borrow Mencken's phrase, occurring not only in speech but in such publications as *Downbeat, Ladies' Home Journal, Musical America, Saturday Evening Post,*

Time, and the daily papers, as in "The Farmer boy . . . was knifed, *stomped* and clubbed . . ." (*New York Herald Tribune,* Apr. 16, 1958, 11). Three recent investigators (Kerner, Loos, Sloan) found scattered examples of it in writing. *Stomp,* according to the Linguistic Atlas records, is employed by all types in the Upper Midwest, according to one study (Allen), and in New England, especially to describe movements of a horse: "The horse *stomped* nervously" (compared to "The child *stamped* angrily").

Other evidence: Barker, *AS,* 5 (Aug., 1930), 494; Kurath, *LANE,* Vol. III, Pt. 1, Map 583; Mencken, *Am. Lang., Sup. II,* 76; Randolph and Wilson, 10; Russell, *AS,* 30 (Dec., 1955), 287; Wentworth, 592.

STRAIGHT. See COMPARISON, ILLOGICAL.

STRICKEN. See STRIKE, v.

STRIKE, v.

Summary: The preterit struck *and the past participle* struck *or* stricken *are standard English; though obsolete in England,* stricken *has special meanings in standard American usage.*

Data: The form *struck* is employed exclusively when the word is given its literal meaning, as ". . . when you are *struck* on the back of the head" (*Reader's Digest,* Sept., 1957, 144) or "He was *struck* by a car." Obsolete in England, *stricken* is preserved in a few instances in American English, three studies reveal (Hotchner, Loos, Sheil). It may mean "afflicted, as with disease, trouble or sorrow," as in ". . . who *was stricken* by polio last year while the New York City Ballet was performing in Denmark" (*The New York Times Magazine,* Dec. 1, 1957, 43), "*stricken* with grief," "*a stricken* animal," referring to one that has been wounded. The phrase "*stricken* in years" meaning "advanced" likewise remains in the language. *Stricken* has also been retained in the sense of "deleted," generally with the addition of *out,* as in "I move that . . . be *stricken* (or *struck*) from the minutes" or "The unsatisfactory clauses of the bill were *stricken out* (or *struck out*)." In British English the phrase would be *struck out. Stricken* is still often employed in the pure adjective function, particularly when placed before a noun: "He *was struck* with horror," but "the *horror-stricken* man."

Other evidence: Abbott, *AS*, 32 (Feb., 1957), 42; Bryant, *EJ*, XLV (Feb., 1956), 109; Curme, *Parts of Speech and Accidence*, 316-17; Galinsky, II, 413; Horwill, 310-11.

STUNK. See STINK, v.

STRIVE, v.

Summary: The preterit strove *and the past participle* striven *usually occur in standard English;* strived *occurs only occasionally.*

Data: One study (Sheil) of *The New York Times* encountered only *strove,* as in "Diplomats *strove* today to break the deadlock between Yugoslavia and the Philippines . . ." (Dec. 18, 1955, Sec. 2, 1), and *striven,* as in ". . . among those you have *striven* for, for years" (Sec. 1, 11). *Strived* is found in statements like "He *strived* to succeed," interchangeable with *strove.* In the past participle, *strove* occurs rarely in standard usage.

Other evidence: OED.

SUCH, SUCH A (AN), adj., adv.

Summary: Though they have other traditional functions, such *and* such a (an) *are used as pure intensifiers and are unquestionably standard English; in the negative,* no such *is standard,* no such a *nonstandard.*

Data: The use of *such* and *such a* (*an*) as quasi- or as pure intensifiers has paralleled the use of *so* (q.v.) and in current English is frequently employed by well-known writers and in the quality magazines. Some textbooks insist that an *as-* or a *that*-clause must follow, as in "It was *such a* hot day *that* we went to the beach" or "There can be many young men with *such* training *as he has."* However, *such* and *such a* (*an*) need not be followed by a completing clause. In some instances a following *as-* or *that*-clause may be implied; in others such a clause cannot be too readily supplied; and in others it is impossible to supply a clause. In this last type *such* and *such a* (*an*) have become pure intensifiers. According to one extensive study (R. Thomas), examples are found:

(1) Where *such* is followed by one or more nouns, as in "The force of *such an* idea [as the foregoing] depends upon the force of the two emotions . . ." (Lionel Trilling, *The American Quarterly*, Fall, 1949, 196). Here the following *as*-clause can be implied.

(2) Where *such* is followed by one or more adjectives plus one or more nouns: "Man, who had *such* high hopes, is now deeply in trouble, and Niebuhr quotes the Psalms" (E. R. Goodenough, *Yale Review*, Autumn, 1949, 163); ". . . and the shore birds of which he had *such* expert knowledge" (Edward Weeks, *The Atlantic Monthly*, Aug., 1955, 75).

(3) Where *such a* (*an*) is followed by a noun; one or more adjectives plus one or more nouns; an adverb, one or more adjectives plus one or more nouns: ". . . his active nature and his gift for rendering it which made *such an* impression on the Hawthornes one evening in their parlor in Lenox" (W. E. Sedgewick, *Herman Melville: The Tragedy of Mind*, 1944, p. 5); "He [Beethoven] went to work for the future, showing in the process how terribly he had needed the language he launched; he had *such a* great deal to say" (*The Atlantic Monthly*, Oct., 1953, 43); "Sales were lagging a bit, and it would be *such a* help" (*Saturday Review of Literature*, Mar. 26, 1949, 20); "If Shakespeare was the most popular playwright of his time, it was partly because he was *such an* amiable fellow with *such* generous instincts" (Brooks Atkinson, "Twelfth Night," *The New York Times*, Oct. 9, 1949, Sec. 2, 1); "And yet Henri Michaux himself is *such a* deceptively gentle, gracious man, distinguished in every gesture and every articulation; perhaps this merely proves that his catharsis is effective" (Justin O'Brien, *Saturday Review of Literature*, Dec. 29, 1951, 1); "This must be a good book—it puts *such a* fervour into a reader" (R. L. Duffus, *The New York Times Book Review*, June 30, 1957, 3). All of these uses are standard.

The negative should be mentioned here. *No such* is standard usage instead of *no such a,* as in "There is *no such* [not *no such a*] machine as that."

Other evidence: Thomas, *CE,* 15 (Jan., 1954), 236-38.

S U C H, pron.

Summary: Such *as a pronoun referring to person(s) or thing(s) is standard usage;* such *as in similar references is colloquial.*

Data: One study (Malanaphy) found in reading fiction and newspapers and listening to conversation, radio, and television, that *such* as a pronoun generally refers to person(s) or thing(s) indicated, as in "He said he was a lawyer, but he was not *such"* or "A professor, as *such,* should have the respect of his students." The frequent use occurs in sentences like *"Such* was the case in 1957" or *"Such* is my proposal."

In some constructions *such* can be substituted for *this* and *that,* as in "He assumed I was going to write the letter; that (this) was not my thought." One may as well say ". . . *such* was not my thought."

Those uses of *such* are standard. *Such as* in the sense of *those who* (*which*), or *all who,* as in *"Such as* are able to bring their own cars may go" is colloquial.

Other evidence: Roberts, *UG,* 82.

S U N K. See SINK, v.

S U P E R L A T I V E, A B S O L U T E. See COMPARATIVE, ABSOLUTE.

SUPERLATIVE WITH TWO OBJECTS

Summary: In comparing two objects the superlative is frequently employed as a form of emphasis in speech and in informal English; in formal written English, however, the superlative with two objects rarely occurs.

Data: The Linguistic Atlas survey of New England found this usage, as in "Of the two plays, his first one is best," in spoken English. Fries states in his *American English Grammar,* "The use of the superlative rather than the comparative for two, thus ignoring a dual as distinct from a plural, is a fact of Standard English usage . . ." (p. 101). Either the comparative or superlative may be used. Two quantitative studies (Eldin, Fetouh) found 537 uses of the superlative, but did not find one example comparing two objects. On the other hand, there is this example from an editorial in *The New York Times:* "Each of these memorials would supplement and add meaning to the other, but of the two, the documents project would seem to be the *most* immediately feasible" (May 18, 1958, Sec. E, 12); and Ernest Hemingway has a character say, "Crane wrote two fine stories, *The Open Boat* and *The Blue Hotel.* The last one is the *best*" (*Green Hills of Africa,* 1935; Permabooks, 1954, p. 16).

Other evidence: Curme, *Syntax,* 504; Fries, *AEG,* 99-101; Hall, 279-80; Jespersen, *MEG,* Pt. II, 203-4; Kurath, *LANE,* Vol. III, Pt. 1, Map 497; Leonard, *Doctrine of Correctness,* 61, 75; Pooley, *TEU,* 119-21; Thomas, *EJ,* XXIV (Dec., 1935), 821-29.

SURE, SURELY

Summary: In formal written English, sure *is an adjective and* surely *is an adverb; in colloquial English, however,* sure *frequently functions as an adverb.*

Data: Illustrations of formal usage are: "There is no *sure* way of gaining popularity" (adjective) and "She *surely* is a popular young girl" (adverb). As a colloquial adverb, *sure,* meaning "yes" or "certainly," occurs in statements like "Am I coming? *Sure* (or *Sure,* I'm coming"); "It *sure* was good to get in out of the cold"; "I *sure* have" (Senator Duff, WNBC, Jan. 20, 1955, 9 A.M.) and " '*Sure* I am,' he said lightly" (spoken by a young executive, *Ladies' Home Journal,* Nov., 1958, 151).

Some people may not employ *sure* in this way, but the use of it as an intensive affirmative answer is more firmly established than the use of it in such a sentence as "This *sure* was a good book." The standard dictionaries now include this colloquial usage. *Sure* is always used in such expressions as *sure enough* and *as sure as fate:* "And *sure enough* the accident occurred"; "I suspect that . . . and *sure enough* it turns out that his 'last January' was a month ago . . ." (Dwight L. Bolinger, " 'Next and Last,' " *American Speech*, Oct., 1955, 232); "That will happen as *sure* as fate." Two investigations (Kane, Speitz) were used in this entry.

Other evidence: Bryant, *CE*, 17 (Feb., 1956), 312-13; Pooley, *AS*, 8 (Feb., 1933), 60-62; *TEU*, 161-63.

SWIM, v.

Summary: The preterit swam *and the past participle* swum *are standard English;* swum *and* swim *in the preterit are nonstandard.*

Data: The Linguistic Atlas recorded the preterit of *swim*, in the context of "I *swam* across," for New England, the Middle Atlantic, the South Atlantic, the North Central, and the Upper Midwest States. According to one study (Malmstrom), *swam* is the standard form, practically universal in Type III (cultivated) speech and predominant in Type I (uneducated) and II (informants with some secondary school education). It is used transitively as well as intransitively, as in "He *swam* the horse across the lake."

Swum as a preterit is probably a recessive form since it is a common alternate form in the relic areas of northeast New England and North Carolina, and since it is more common in the speech of the older informants in the other areas where it is found. The nonstandard form *swim* occurs in the preterit in the South Midland area. A study based on *The New York Times* (Stevens) revealed only *swam* in the preterit.

Other evidence: Atwood, 23; Kurath, *LANE*, Vol. III, Pt. 1, Map 579; Malmstrom, *SVTS*, 179-80; R.I. McDavid, *AED*, 521; V.G. McDavid, 46-47.

SYLLABUS

Summary: Both plural forms of this word, syllabuses *and* syllabi *occur in current standard English.*

Data: The word *syllabus* originated from a mistake: it was an erroneous reading of *sittybas,* the accusative plural of Greek *sittyba,* referring to a piece of parchment used as a label (the error appeared in a fifteenth-century edition of Cicero). Then *syllabus* came to be considered as a Latin second declension noun ending in *-us,* with a plural in *-i. Syllabus* has now been anglicized so that the plural is *syllabuses,* but *syllabi* continues in use. One study (S. Solomon) showed *syllabuses* used 80% of the time in written material as a variant of *syllabi.* Another (Winburne) conducted at Michigan State University revealed that usage there is divided.

TAKE, v.

Summary: The preterit took *and the past participle* taken *are standard English;* taken *as a preterit is nonstandard.*

Data: The Linguistic Atlas records for New England, the Middle Atlantic, the South Atlantic, the North Central, and the Upper Midwest States recorded the preterit and past participle of *take* in the contexts "Who *took* my knife?" "I *took* it this morning," "He *took* his medicine," "He *took* sick," "He *took* cold," "He was *taken* sick," "Haven't you *taken* your medicine yet?"

According to one study (Malmstrom), the standard preterit *took* is practically universal in Type II (informants with at least some secondary school education) speech in all areas.

The preterit form *taken* is a South Midland and Southern form occurring with some frequency south of the Pennsylvania-Maryland line in the Eastern areas in Type II and Type I (uneducated) speech. In Southern and South Midland communities where the nonstandard *tuck* also occurs, there is considerable evidence that *taken* is the newer form.

Taken is the standard past participle, by far the most common form everywhere among all types of informants. The nonstandard *tuck,* however, occurs in Southern and South Midland Type II and Type I speech.

A study of modern prose (Cooperman) revealed that preterit variants such as *tooked, taked,* and *taken* do not occur in formal written English, but only in represented speech in dialogue. However, she found, these forms in the uneducated speech of immigrant and Negro children in New York City.

Another colloquialism is *take on,* meaning "to show extreme emotion, especially anger or sorrow."

Other evidence: Abbott, *AS,* 32 (Feb., 1957), 40; Atwood, 23-24; Kurath, *LANE,* Vol. III, Pt. 1, Map 492; Pt. 2, Map 664; Malmstrom, *SVTS,* 183-85; R.I. McDavid, *AED,* 526; V.G. McDavid, 47-48; R.I. and V.G. McDavid, *AS,* 35 (Feb., 1960), 16.

TAKE SICK

Summary: The expression take sick *is a regionalism for* become ill *or* sick; *it does not occur in formal written English.*

Data: This expression is a colloquial lexical variant of *become ill (sick),* heard commonly in New England and less commonly in the South. Its frequency varies from region to region. According to one study of the Linguistic Atlas records (Allen), 16% of the informants in the Upper Midwest use *get sick.*

One investigation (Hartdegen) did not find a single instance in formal written English.

Other evidence: Kurath, *LANE,* Vol. III, Pt. I, Map 492; *OED: take,* 44b; *sick,* B3; Wentworth, 621.

TAXI, n., v.

Summary: Both taxi *(plural:* taxis) *and* cab *(plural:* cabs) *are standard English nouns; as a verb,* taxi *occurs in standard aeronautical usage.*

Data: Taxi has evolved from *taximetercabriolet,* which was first shortened to *taxicab* and now to *taxi* and *cab;* both, with their plurals of *taxis* and *cabs,* are included in all standard dictionaries without restricting labels.

Functional shift from the noun gave the verb *taxi* with the principal parts *taxied, taxiing* or *taxying, taxied.* The older meaning of the verb is "to travel by *taxi,*" but with the development of aeronautics, a specialized meaning, one study (H. M. Gold) shows, has developed in connection with aeroplanes: "to move along the ground or on the water under its own power," as in *"Taxiing* to the east end of the runway was sufficient to warm up the Continental . . ." (*Air Facts,* Dec. 1, 1956, 28), or "You could see better, *taxi* better, and the ship was . . ." (*ibid.,* Mar. 1, 1958, 3). The verb here is intransitive, but a transitive meaning has developed: "to cause (an airplane) to taxi," as in "Don't *taxi* your plane more than 15 mph ground speed."

Other evidence: Barnhart, Files; Lee, 1-2; Marckwardt and Walcott, 96.

TEACH, LEARN

Summary: Learn *as a variant of* teach *occurs widely, but mainly in uneducated speech. The standard preterit form* learnt *is receding, while* learned *is advancing.*

The principal parts of *teach* are *teach, taught, taught,* and of *learn* are *learn, learned* or *learnt, learned* or *learnt. Learn,* meaning "to acquire knowledge," is sometimes used in place of *teach,* "to impart knowledge."

Data: According to one study (Malmstrom), the Linguistic Atlas records for New England, the Middle Atlantic, the South Atlantic, the North Central, and the Upper Midwest States, concerning the preterit usage, show that in the context "Who *taught* you that?" *learn* is substituted for *teach* by about 50% of the New England informants, and by from about 50% to 75% of the informants in the Middle Atlantic and the South Atlantic States. In the North Central States about 38% of the informants use *learn* instead of *teach,* and in the Upper Midwest about 19% do so. Although this substitution is characteristic of Type I (uneducated) speech, many Type I and Type II (those with at least some secondary school education) informants employ both verbs.

The standard preterit *taught* is almost universal in the speech of informants who use *teach* in this context.

There are two important variants of the preterit of *learn: learned* and *learnt.* In the East *learnt* predominates strongly. In communities of divided usage *learnt* is used by the more old-fashioned in-- formants. In the Middlewest *learned* is the only form used in Type III (cultivated) speech and predominates over *learnt* in Type II speech. From this evidence, one may conclude that *learnt* is receding while *learned* is advancing. Two studies of contemporary prose (D'Ambrosio, Geekie) indicate that the substitution of *learn* for *teach* does not occur in writing, except in represented speech.

Other evidence: Atwood, 17-18, 24; Kurath, *LANE,* Vol. III, Pt. 2, Map 666; Malmstrom, *SVTS,* 187-88; V.G. McDavid, 38-39, 48-49.

TEAR, v.

Summary: The preterit tore *and the past participle* torn *are standard English;* tore *as a past participle is nonstandard.*

Data: According to one study (Malmstrom) of the Linguistic Atlas records for New England and the Middle Atlantic, the South Atlantic, the North Central, and the Upper Midwest States, in the context "The road *was* all *torn* up," *torn* is almost universal in Type III (cultivated) speech in New England, the Middle Atlantic, and the South Atlantic States and predominant in both Type III and Type II (those with at least some secondary school education) in-- formants in the North Central and Upper Midwest States.

Tore is used as the past participle by about half the Type II in-- formants in the Midland areas of the Middle Atlantic States and dominates in Type II speech in the South Atlantic States. In these areas, therefore, it has the status of a colloquial form. In the Middlewest it is characteristic of Type I (uneducated) speech. Two studies of informal writing (Daughton, McDermott) revealed only the standard forms in use.

Other evidence: Atwood, 24; Kurath, *LANE,* Vol. III, Pt. 2, Map 665; Malmstrom, *SVTS,* 190-91; V.G. McDavid, 49.

THANKS TO. See DUE TO, BECAUSE OF, OWING TO.

THAT, adv. See THIS, THAT, advs.

THAT(PRONOMINAL). See REFERENCE, VAGUE OR INDEFINITE:
THIS (PRONOMINAL).

THAT, sub. conj.

Summary: Standard usage generally requires the use of the conjunctive that for subordination; though it appears in a variety of situations in formal written English, it is often omitted in informal spoken English; formal spoken usage lies between.

That is one of the most frequently used subordinating conjunctions, serving to connect a noun or an adverb clause to a sentence element in another clause, as "I know *that* he is coming" (noun clause); "He went to college *that* he might become a doctor" (adverbial clause). Even though it connects only two types of clauses, it appears in different places in the sentence and after different types of words.

   Data: For example, it may appear (1) with the subject: "*That* it continues to flourish is remarkable"; (2) with the object of a verb: "They think *that* the Army will be the answer"; (3) after adjectives: "He was sure *that* she was in the house"; (4) after nouns (no other connective possible) which generally correlate with the verbs following the clause: ". . . the hope *that* she would continue was in the minds of all"; (5) after nouns replaceable by *when, where, to which,* and the like: ". . . at the time *that* Howe was honored . . ."; (6) in apposition with clauses: ". . . let people know you had arrived, *that* your tent was up . . ."; (7) with subjective complement (predicate nominative): "His idea was *that* he should go . . ."; (8) after *except* and *in:* ". . . except *that* they weren't going"; ". . . in *that* it only reminded him of the episode"; (9) after *not* and *now:* "He could only hope that he had not been seen; not *that* there would have been any harm in it"; "I am looking forward to my going, now *that* I have accepted the position"; (10) with *it* as subject or in other positions: "It was possible *that* you might know"; "See to it *that* no harm comes to her"; "I found it amusing *that* you are going"; (11) to express result after *so* or *such,* as in: "He was so angry *that* he left without his money";

"It was such a scandal *that* Ward had to leave home"; "He would study before dinner *so that* he could go to the theater in the evening"; "He was mowing the lawn *so that* he could be free to go." Other constructions may also appear. One can easily see that there is much variety in the use of *that* as a subordinating conjunction, not to mention its versatile function as a demonstrative adjective or pronoun, and as a relative pronoun introducing an adjective clause. It is also often omitted, especially in speech.

One study (Faust) of a single issue of a mass-circulation magazine produced 811 instances of relevant clauses where *that* was used or could be inserted, 474 of them with *that*. In nondialogue, clauses with the conjunction outnumbered those without by about three to one (325 to 115); dialogue favored clauses without *that* by two to one (185 to 93). An examination of a taped interview also found 57 clauses introduced by *that* and 37 without *that*. From this study it appears that the conjunction occurs most often in formal written English, that it is omitted most often in informal spoken English, and that relatively formal spoken English lies between. This study also found that five verbs accounted for about half the total of all clauses without a conjunction, but for only about a sixth of those using *that: think, know, say, hope,* and *tell.*

Fries's *American English Grammar* shows that in the written materials he used, *that* is much more frequent in standard English than in nonstandard English.

Other evidence: Fries, *AEG*, 207-11, 226-32, 235, 239-40; Roberts, *UG*, 236-38, 242, 318, 323-26, 334-52.

THAT (THOSE) THERE. See THIS (THESE) HERE, THAT (THOSE) THERE.

THE FARTHEST, THE FURTHEST

Summary: Both these forms occur in speech, but not in writing except in represented speech. In speech, speakers on all levels prefer the farthest *to* the furthest.

Data: In a context such as "Two miles is *the farthest* he can go," according to one study (Malmstrom) of the Linguistic Atlas for New England, the Middle Atlantic, the South Atlantic, the North Central, and the Upper Midwest States, the informants of all types in all areas prefer *farthest* to *furthest*. See also ALL THE FAR-THER (FURTHER), AS FAR AS.

Other evidence: Kurath, *LANE*, Vol. I, Pt. I, Map 49; Malmstrom, *SVTS*, 70-72, 287-92.

THE WAY, JUST AS, AS, sub. conj.

Summary: The way *and* just as *occur as variants of the subordinating conjunction* as *in speech, but* as *is heavily preferred in formal English.*

Data: In spoken English the first construction occurs frequently, as in "Write *the way* you were told"; "Raise your arm *the way* I showed you"; "She continued *the way* her mother did." Ernest Hemingway has a character in *Green Hills of Africa* say: "I believe he feels just *the way* you do about it." (Permabook Edit., 1956, p. 54). One investigator (Kaufman) found this construction in a line of dialogue representing uneducated speech: "Jus' tell 'em what happened *the* same *way* you told me" (Budd Schulberg, *A Face in the Crowd*, 1957, p. 64). It also occurs in written English, as in ". . . touching the speaker's stand *the way* a musician's hand touches his instrument . . ." (*The Nation*, May 17, 1958, 441); ". . . he can divine a master performer much *the way* a dowser finds underground water" (*Reader's Digest*, Apr., 1958, 122).

Another variant of *as,* the expanded form *just as,* occurs chiefly in conversation, speeches, and dialogue exemplified in ". . . but *just as* one swallow does not make a summer, I am certainly not going to show that . . ." (Dwight D. Eisenhower, quoted in *The New York Times*, "The News of the Week in Review," June 1, 1958, 2); ". . . but now it seemed natural, no longer to be italicized, *just as* all the words came to seem the proper and natural words," (Ernest Hemingway, *Green Hills of Africa*, 1935, Permabooks, 1954, p. 36); "in spite of the efforts I've made to keep this most precious relationship *just as* it used to be . . ." (*Coronet*, May, 1958, 64).

In formal English, *as* is the usual form: "Painting and sculpture continue *as* they always have in the past . . ." (*Art News,* Feb., 1958, 65). One study (Krug) revealed one instance of *the way* (4%), two of *just as* (8%), and twenty-two of *as* (88%). Another (Hotchner) reported *the way* occurring 14% of the time, *just as* 26%, and *as* 60%.

Other evidence: Bryant, *CE,* 17 (May, 1956), 489; Bryant and Aiken, *Psychology of Eng.,* 168; Marckwardt and Walcott, 28, 109.

THEMSELVES. See MYSELF.

THERE IS (ARE), WAS (WERE). See AGREEMENT, THERE IS (ARE), WAS (WERE).

THESE. See THOSE, THEM; THIS (THESE) HERE.

THESE KIND (SORT) OF. See THOSE (THESE) KIND (SORT) OF.

THEY, INDEFINITE

Summary: Indefinite they *is established on all levels of informal English, and occurs in formal writing, but not frequently.*

Data: The indefinite *they,* as in *"They* say that he froze to death," *"They* make automobiles in Detroit," or *"They* don't have air-conditioning in that town," is very common colloquially. Three studies (Amster, Sola, R. Thomas) show that written examples are also frequent, evidenced by these passages from *Harper's:* "Some of the books *they* read at St. John's are very old" (Milton S. Mayer, "Socrates Crosses the Delaware," June, 1939, 70); *"They* say that fifty years ago the Liberty tree was dying" (*ibid.,* 64); "dynamite, *they* say" (*ibid.*); by the first sentence in a *New York Times Magazine* article: *"They* are feeding antibiotics to pigs and poultry now" (H. Borland, Aug. 31, 1952, 10); and by "Billy is one of those fascinating fellows who has won and lost fortunes, as *they* say" (*Saturday Review,* Aug. 30, 1958, 5); "In Rumania *they* tell this one . . ." (*Saturday Review,* Nov. 5, 1952, 13). This indefinite use of *they* serves different purposes.

It is often employed to represent public opinion or the opinion of a group which either condemns or supports the actions of the speaker, as in *"They* say it's hard for Germany to rearm." Here the speaker cites public opinion or the ideas of his own group since he probably does not have enough confidence in his own ideas. Also, in *The Man Who Came to Dinner* by Moss Hart and George S. Kaufman, Professor Metz says: "Here in Roach City *they* play, *they* make love, *they* mate, *they* die. See—here is the graveyard. *They* even bury their own dead" (Bennett A. Cerf, *Sixteen Famous American Plays,* p. 869). *They* in this speech refers to the provincial inhabitants of a small town. It is employed in a derogatory manner. Another example comes from a short story: *"They* called her the American Girl and sold smuggled post cards of her in the elevated stations" (P. V. Cassill, "The Sleeping Beauty," *The Best American Stories 1953,* p. 87).

At times *they* is employed when the speaker sees or imagines definite problems but refers to them without mentioning what they are, as in "And *they* want us to send our children to school in that district."

Another generalized *they* is frequently used when a person becomes emotionally involved and transfers the action of one to a group. General judgments are based upon particular incidents. For example, a college professor, annoyed by a particular student who does not know a noun from a verb, may disgustedly say, *"They* don't know any grammar today," thereby condemning all his students because one lacks this knowledge. Where there is prejudice, *they* is used often to condemn the whole group for the action of one.

We and *you,* like *they,* are also established in standard usage as indefinite pronouns in informal English, as in *"You (We)* never know what will happen when the President is away." This means "One never knows. . . ." French *on* and German *man* serve the same purpose and would be used in translating each one. See also AGREEMENT, INDEFINITE PRONOUNS and YOU, INDEFINITE.

Other evidence: Jespersen, *Ess.,* 154, 16.1₄; Marckwardt and Walcott, 72.

THEY (WAS) WERE. See WE WERE, YOU WERE, THEY WERE.

THIS, THAT, advs.

Summary: In standard usage, this *and* that *occur as adverbs, as in* this (that) far, this (that) tall, this (that) big. *The use of* that *(for* so*) with an adjective followed by a clause of result, however, is colloquial, as in "I am* that *tired I can hardly move."*

Data: According to the *OED, this* and *that* have been used as adverbs, meaning "to this (that) extent or degree," since the fifteenth century. Most of the standard dictionaries include this usage without any restricting label whatsoever.

From one study (R. Thomas) come the following examples: "We know now that things are not quite *that* simple" (Governor Averell Harriman, *Harper's,* Sept., 1958, 59); "The only kind of knowledge about himself a critic ought to have is the kind he gets by being relevant or—if he's *that* good—even wise about books and authors. If a critic is *that* good we are interested in criticism about him . . ." (Arthur Mizener, *Kenyon Review,* Spring, 1951, 218); "The Afrikaner world . . . is a world in which *this* small an act may have *this* large a consequence . . ." (Eric Larrabee, *The Reporter,* Sept. 29, 1953, 45).

Other evidence: Bryant, *CE,* 17 (Jan., 1956), 241; Curme, *Syntax,* 146; Kruisinga, 3rd ed., II, 485; Leonard, *CEU,* 129; Marckwardt and Walcott, 31, 97.

THIS (THESE) HERE, THAT (THOSE) THERE

Summary: The intensives this here *and* that there, *as in "This here (That there)* box is mine," *occur only in nonstandard usage.*

Data: In informal speech, where words are often omitted, it is possible that someone pointing out a particular box nearby may say, *"This (That)* box *here (there)* is not a good one," meaning "This (That) box, the one that is here (there), is . . ." "This here box" is nonstandard, but "This box here" is standard, patterned after structures such as *the discussion afterward, his study abroad, the noise everywhere,* and *the study hereafter,* the modifier serving to identify and following a definite intonation pattern of lowering the voice. Occasionally one hears a combination of the standard and nonstandard, as in "This here door here."

Along with *this here* goes the plural *these here.* One never hears *those there* but *them there* occurs. According to one study (Malmstrom), the Linguistic Atlas survey using the context "these fellows" found in New England that *these here* occurred in the northeastern part, a relic area, most frequently in Type I (uneducated) speech and characteristically among the older, more old-fashioned informants in all groups. This evidence indicates that in New England *these here* is receding.

That there was found only in Type I (uneducated) speech in Minnesota, Iowa, and Nebraska, and *those there* was not found in any type. This evidence indicates that informants who use the standard demonstratives *that* and *those* do not add *there* to them.

Them there occurs in Type III (cultivated) speech in New England, where about one-fifth of the cultivated speakers use it, and with much less frequency in the Middle Atlantic States, concentrated in Pennsylvania. In the South Atlantic, the North Central, and the Upper Midwest States, no Type III informant uses *them there.* In Type II speech (informants with at least some secondary school education) this usage is found in all major areas except the Upper Midwest States, with the highest frequency in New England, where about 30% of the Type II's use it. Since Type I frequencies are much higher in all areas, the evidence shows that *them there* is not standard usage in any area, although it must be considered colloquial usage in New England. It is here probably recessive since it occurs with greater frequency in the speech of the older, more old-fashioned informants in each type.

Other evidence: Fries, *The Structure of English,* 210, 226; Kurath, *LANE,* Vol. III, Pt. 2, Map 623; Malmstrom, *SVTS,* 87-88, 300-3; Wentworth, 638.

THIS (PRONOMINAL). See REFERENCE, VAGUE OR INDEFINITE: THIS (PRONOMINAL).

THOSE, THEM

Summary: Those *and* these *are the standard forms of the demonstrative adjective in written English, as in* "Those (These) *books are heavy";* them *as a variant is nonstandard.*

Data: According to one study (Malmstrom), the Linguistic Atlas evidence for New England and the Middle Atlantic, the South Atlantic, the North Central, and the Upper Midwest States shows that *them* is rare everywhere in Type III (cultivated) speech and not a majority form anywhere among Type II informants (those with at least some secondary school education).

This survey shows that *those* and *these* are standard in all areas considered.

Other evidence: Kurath, *LANE*, Vol. III, Pt. 2, Maps 624-25; Malmstrom, *SVTS*, 87-88, 300-3.

THOSE (THESE) KIND (SORT) OF

Summary: Those (these) kind (sort) of *with a plural verb and pronoun occurs frequently in speech and informal writing, but rarely in formal writing.*

Data: Fries found this construction, as in *"Those (These) kind of* books have their value," frequently employed by writers of standard English, but not once by writers of nonstandard English. *Kind of* is equivalent to an adjective and has led to the use of plural *these* and *those* with it, as in "The pitcher is supposed to stay away from *those kind"* (Harry Heilman, broadcaster for Goebel Brewing Company, Detroit, WDMJ, Marquette, Michigan, July 23, 1949). One investigator (R. Thomas) found this example in *The New York Times* (Sept. 8, 1957, Sec. E, 5) quoted from an *Atlanta Journal* editorial: "The Arkansas situation proves once more the wisdom of leaving *these kind of* things for the states and communities to decide." This construction, as three studies (J. Fagen, L. Gold, Hook) showed, rarely appears in formal written English. See also KIND (SORT) OF (A, AN).

Other evidence: Fries, *AEG,* 51; Marckwardt and Walcott, 48, 97; McMillan, *EJ,* XXXIV (May, 1945), 284; Newsome, *AS,* 13 (Feb., 1938), 28-29.

THOUGH, ALTHOUGH

Summary: In standard English though *and* although *as conjunctions are interchangeable without distinction, but* though *occurs at least five times as often.* Tho *does not occur in formal writing.*

Data: According to the *Oxford English Dictionary, although,* when used as a conjunction, was originally two words *all though* and was more emphatic than *though,* with the meaning "even though," but by 1400 it was practically only a variant. *All* had lost its independent force, and the two words had merged into one.

Today *though* and *although* are synonyms, and to express emphasis *even though* is employed, as in "Witness the plight of the airlines, which are spending billions of dollars to buy jet aircraft *even though* they have hundreds of older propeller-driven planes which are still completely air-worthy" (*The Nation,* Dec. 17, 1960, 469).

In a study based on 231 pages of reading (Ralston), *though* occurred more frequently than *although* in every category considered. Not a single instance of the spelling *tho* was found in these samplings and those of another study (Greenberg), perhaps because of the conservative influence of editors.

Of the 115 occurrences in the study of *though* and *although* as conjunctions, *though* was employed 74% of the time. A number of the subordinate clauses introduced were elliptical in nature, as in "Her face, *though* not pretty, might be called interesting . . ." (James Gould Cozzens, *By Love Possessed,* 1959, p. 137) and "In fact, operatic choruses, *although* admittedly lacking in originality . . . , are often blunt to the point of rudeness" (*High Fidelity,* Nov., 1960, 54). Often the adjective was preceded by an adverb as in this illustration. In elliptical clauses *though* occurred 90% of the time, generally to introduce an adjective qualifying the subject of the main clause (see quotation from Cozzens.) In other instances the conjunction *though* or *although* introduced a participle in both the present and the past. An illustration of the past participle may be seen in "The reason for headlines, *though* unstated, was clear . . ." (*Look,* Jan. 3, 1961, 18), where the elliptical clause *though unstated* modifies the subject *reason.* There was one instance of *though* preceding an adverb: "During the 1952 campaign, my brother Stewart Alsop proved it to me, *though* inadvertently" (*The New Yorker,* Sept. 4, 1960, 170).

Clauses, expanded or elliptical, introduced by *though* occurred in all positions in the sentence. In 64% of the occurrences the clause was imbedded within the sentence or at the end, as in "For some, this was an important protest, too, *though* for others it wasn't" (*The Nation,* Dec. 17, 1960, 472) and "I must confess that, juvenile *though* it was, I too felt a certain odd lifting of the heart" (*Saturday Evening Post,* Oct. 15, 1960, 19). In 36% of the illustrations, however, *though* occurred at the beginning, as in "*Though* Elmer plainly made some effort not to, he looked hurt . . ." (Cozzens, *ibid.,* p. 449). Of the 64% where *though* introducing the clause was embedded within the sentence or at the end, in 11% of the illustrations it appeared after a coordinating conjunction, such as *and* or *but,* generally introducing the second element of a compound-complex sentence. Examples are: "Geoffrey Moore begins by calling Sinclair Lewis a second-rate novelist, and, *though* he softens in the end towards Lewis the man, he is sparing in his praise of the books" (*Saturday Review,* Oct. 15, 1960, 20) and "Occasionally the side paths showed traces of other creatures, but *though* I saw plenty of hoof marks there were no prints of paws, and this was most reassuring" (*Holiday,* Dec., 1960, 44).

Although, likewise, introduced both expanded and elliptical clauses in all positions in the sentence, as can be seen in "*Although* the town is now surrounded by rich oil fields, it remains quiet and unpretentious" (*Holiday,* Dec., 1960, 22); in "Blue-collar employment in manufacturing output is actually falling, *although* output is rising . . ." (*The Nation,* Dec. 17, 1960, 469); and in the illustration of the use of *although* to introduce an elliptical clause cited in the fourth paragraph of this article. In 13% of the occurrences, *although* follows a coordinate conjunction, such as *and* or *but,* in a compound-complex sentence, illustrated by "America, in short, was built on a promise, and *although* we have been bothered ever since about the degree to which that promise has been fulfilled . . ." (Bruce Catton, "Morning Star," *American Heritage,* Feb., 1958, 109).

From this study it is evident that *though* and *although* as conjunctions are substituted one for the other, but from the figures one can see that *though* is employed much more frequently. In two periodicals taken at random, *The Atlantic Monthly* and *The Nation, though* occurred five times as often as *although* in each one. The reading in Cozzens' novel furnished twenty-one instances of *though,* but not one of *although.* A separate breakdown was then made of the position of each conjunction at the beginning of the sentence in order to determine whether one of the words was preferred for additional emphasis in a clause preceding the main clause. Even here the occurrence of *though* predominated. *Though* occurred 71% of the time, showing that *although* is not used in modern prose for special emphasis. Instead, *even though* is employed where emphasis is desired. From the figures, *although* seems to be slowly disappearing.

THROW, v.

Summary: The preterit threw *and the past participle* thrown *are standard English;* throwed *as a preterit is nonstandard.*

Data: According to one study (Malmstrom) of the Linguistic Atlas records for New England and the Middle Atlantic, the South Atlantic, the North Central, and the Upper Midwest States, which recorded the preterit of *throw* in the context "He *threw* a stone at the dog," the standard preterit *threw i*s preferred by practically all Type III (cultivated) informants in all areas and is used by all types in all areas. In two studies (Di Natale, McGrath) of current prose, the standard forms were always used, except by a Swedish maid testifying at a murder trial, who used the variant *throwed* (*New York Daily News,* Jan. 18, 1960, 6).

Other evidence: Atwood, 24-25; Kurath, *LANE,* Vol. III, Pt. 2, Map 667; Malmstrom, *SVTS,* 193; V.G. McDavid, 49-50.

TILL, UNTIL

Summary: Both words are in good standing and may be substituted for each other in speech or in informal writing; until *is preferred in more formal English.*

Till and *until* are not distinguishable in meaning and are used interchangeably, stylistic requirements usually determining the choice. *Till* is an older word, coming to us from Old English, whereas *until* entered the language in the Middle English period by fusing *un* (as in *unto,* with the meaning "up to") and *til.*

Data: Even though *until* is a relatively late comer, a study (Krause) of weekly magazines showed that it occurred 65.7% of the time, *till* 26.8%, *'til* 6%, and *'till* 1.5%. The latter two may be dismissed since in speech they sound like *till,* and in writing would undoubtedly pass for that word. However, an examination of the song titles in the card catalogue of the New York Public Library (Krause) showed that *till* was employed 52.6% of the time, *until* 42.1%, and *'til* 5.3%. Computing an average of the two sources, we find *until* employed 53.9% of the time and *till* 39.7%.

Until generally occurs at the beginning of sentences, whereas *till* is generally used internally: *"Until* he went to New York, he never had considered politics" and "He had never considered politics *till* he went to New York."

In addition to being interchangeable, these words are occasionally substituted in speech for *when* or *that,* as in "He had scarcely passed the corner *till* (*when*) he heard the siren"; "She had hardly reached the station *until* (*when*) the train arrived"; "It was so foggy *till* (*that*) the planes were all grounded"; "There are so many beautiful dresses *until* (*that*) it is hard to select one." In formal English, *when* is used after *scarcely* and *hardly, that* after expressions with *so,* instead of *till* or *until.*

The use of *till* or *until* in the sense "by the time that," as in *"Until* you get that done, it will be quitting time," is colloquial in central Pennsylvania from the Great Valley to the Alleghenies, and in West Virginia on the upper Potomac. This usage is of Ulster Scot origin adopted by the Pennsylvania Germans in such phrases as *bis er kommt,* "by the time he comes" (German *bis* generally means "till, until").

Till is also used colloquially in the phrase expressing time, as in "ten minutes *till* ten" (instead of *of* or *to*), in the greater part of the Midland area, especially in south central Pennsylvania and the area lying to the south.

Other evidence: Barnhart, Files; Bryant, *CE,* 16 (Nov., 1954), 131-32; Kurath, *Word Geography,* 34, 35, 79, Figs. 21, 160; R.I. McDavid, *AED,* 519; Prenner, *AS,* 24 (Oct., 1949), 232-33; Rice, *EJ,* XXV (Jan., 1936), 69.

TO HOME. See HOME.

TOO WITH PAST PARTICIPLE. See VERY WITH PAST
   PARTICIPLE.

TOWARD, TOWARDS

Summary: Usage is divided between toward *and* towards *with either form acceptable.*

Data: One may find many more instances of *toward* in the United States, but *towards,* the preferred form in England, seems to be gaining ground and is employed by reputable writers. In the four studies made (Alter, Fein, Lesser, Olkin), in written English 178 examples, or 91%, of *toward* occurred and 17, or 9%, of *towards.* In the two studies which included spoken English, 3 examples of *toward* and 6 of *towards* were heard.

Other evidence: Bryant, *CE,* 15 (May, 1954), 477-78; Kurath, *LANE,* Vol. III, Pt. 2, Map 722.

TRY AND

Summary: Try and *occurs often in speech and occasionally in informal standard English;* try to *is heavily preferred in formal writing.*

Data: In both Britain and America *try and* is a conversational alternate of *try to,* as in *"Try and* get some sleep." One study

(Tobin) found *try and* used 39.3% of the time in spoken English. It occurs also in formal written English, as in "They have long since ceased to *try and* challenge fate and have . . ." (*The New York Times Magazine,* Apr. 3, 1955, 68), but *try to* is much more common in such contexts. One systematic reading of three newspapers (Hotchner) found *try to* 97% of the time. However, as three other studies (Benardete, R. Thomas, Winburne) clearly demonstrate, *try and* is standard English on the informal level. Bennett Cerf has as the title of one of his books *Try and Stop Me* (Bantam Books, 1944).

Other verbs which follow somewhat the same pattern are *go* and *come: "Go and* get one"; *"Come and* get your book"; ". . . you'd better *go and* finish it now, dear . . ." (John P. Marquand, *So Little Time,* 1943, p. 46); "He . . . said to *go and* see my chaplain" (*The Best from Yank,* 1945, p. 170); "Some of the boys *went and* had a couple of drinks . . ." (Ernie Pyle, *Brave Men,* 1944, p. 337). However, one may say, *"Try to* do it" and *"Try* doing it," but not *"Come (Go) to* do it" and *"Come (Go)* doing it."

Other evidence: Bryant, *CE,* 17 (Dec., 1955), 178; Fries, *AEG,* 1934; Hall, 309; Leonard, *AS,* 4 (Feb., 1929), 253; Marckwardt and Walcott, 34, 192.

TYPE, TYPE OF

Summary: Type *occurs with growing frequency in popular speech and in business English; however,* type of *is preferred in formal written English.*

Data: In popular speech today one hears expressions like *better type plastic, a special type plane, that type personality* instead of the expanded forms employed in formal English: *better type of plastic, a special type of plane, that type of personality.* For example, an actress speaking on the Hi Gardner Show on television said, "I don't like that type show" (WPIX, Jan. 23, 1955, 7:05 P.M.). Four investigations (Buchbinder, Fein, R. Gold, Haase) show *type* occurring 22.8% of the time in written English and 25% in spoken English.

Type is joined to other words, often by means of a hyphen, to form adjectives, which modify nouns. *New-type,* for example, is thought of as a unit, as illustrated in the title of an article: *"The New-Type* Test in English" (*The English Journal,* June, 1931, 490). Similarly, ". . . the same *type* work" (*New York Post,* Jan. 11, 1955, 20) occurs. In *The New York Times* we may read in the headlines of *Family-Type Burlesque* or *Old-Type Format;* in advertisements, of *new-type springs, tubes,* and *motors;* in magazines, of *American-type gadgets* and *B-29 type propellers.* In the colleges and universities the professors often speak of the *academic-type man,* the *essay-type question,* and the *better-type college.* Although this usage is analogous to accepted uses of *class* and *style* (e.g., "a first-class book," "new-style clothes"), the studies cited above show that in written English *type of* is preferred 77.2% of the time. Business usage, however, seems to favor *type.*

Other evidence: Bryant, *CE,* 17 (Nov., 1955), 113; Bird, *CE,* 17 (Dec., 1955), 179; Dunlap, *AS,* 20 (Feb., 1945), 20-21; Russell, *AS,* 23 (Apr., 1948), 150; *AS,* 24 (Oct., 1949), 228; Sheldon, *AS,* 23 (Oct.-Dec., 1948), 251-56.

UNIQUE. See COMPARISON, ILLOGICAL.

UNTIL. See TILL, UNTIL.

UPON. See ON, UPON.

USETA COULD. See MIGHT COULD.

VAGUE REFERENCE: THIS, THAT, WHICH IT. See REFERENCE, VAGUE OR INDEFINITE: THIS (PRONOMINAL).

VERY WITH PAST PARTICIPLE

Summary: Very *occurs in standard English immediately before a past participle, as in "He was* very *distressed about his health," as well as before an adverb preceding a past participle, as in "He was* very *much excited."*

Data: According to evidence gathered from one reading (Hotchner), *very* was used alone before the participle 30% of the time. In many instances the verbal force of a participle, denoting a physical or mental state, is so weakened that the participle is felt to be an adjective entirely: *tired, torn, troubled, worn.* It is good usage to say, "I am *very* tired" or "a *very* tired man"; "a *very* worn book" or "He looks *very* worn." One may speak of "a pleased person," or say, "I am pleased." Since *pleased* seems to function attributively, it has come to be modified by *very,* and now one hears "I am *very* pleased." For example, the General Director of the American Association of University Women wrote in a letter (Feb. 27, 1956), "Of course we would be *very pleased* to have . . . such a member." Usage sanctions *very* when the past participle is felt to be a pure adjective, when it can be compared by employing *more* and *most* or by adding *-er* and *-est,* as *more, most troubled, tired,* etc. Since one may say, "a celebrated man," it is permissible to say, "The man was *very celebrated,*" as it is also possible to speak of a "most celebrated person." To show how both forms may be employed, here is a statement made by an English professor, reported by one investigator (P. Silverstein): "He is *very much concerned* with the state of the world and *very concerned* to help it." Three other investigations (Kovitz, McMillan, Whitesell) came upon five instances of *very* before a past participle.

Similarly, one of these studies showed, *too* may also immediately precede the past participle, as in "Mrs. Osborne confesses that she had not been *too stirred* when reading the *Iliad* as a 'classic' at the university . . ." ("Report and Summary," *College English,* Jan., 1952, 242).

Other evidence: Bryant, *CE,* 17 (Nov., 1955), 113; Marckwardt and Walcott, 43, 102-3; *OED.*

WAIT ON, WAIT FOR

Summary: Wait on *occurs in cultivated regional usage; in formal written English,* wait for *is standard.*

Data: "I'll *wait on* you" instead of "I'll *wait for* you" is a popular Midland expression, even among educated speakers. It also occurs in South Carolina and the North Central States, but it is now receding there. In other parts of the country and in formal written English, *wait for* is standard. Two studies (Ezagui, Polonsky) of current newspapers, magazines, and fiction uncovered no variants.

Other evidence: R.I. McDavid, *AED*, 519; R.I. and V.G. McDavid, *AS*, 35 (Feb., 1960), 13.

W A K E. See (A)WAKE, (A)WAKEN.

W A K E N. See (A)WAKE, (A)WAKEN.

WANT OFF

Summary: The expression want off, *as in "I* want off *at Juniper Street," is a regionalism frequent in the East Midland speech area; it does not occur in formal English.*

Data: Want off is a Midland form found among all types of speakers, but chiefly in uneducated speech. Kurath has suggested that parallel expressions in German, such as *Ich will heraus,* have exerted influence upon the locution, but this suggestion is contradicted by the North Central States records, which show that *want off* is probably of native English origin, and was localized early in Scotland and spread in the United States by the descendants of the original Scotch and Scotch-Irish settlers as they migrated southward from Pennsylvania and Southern Maryland.

The expression is heard in eastern Pennsylvania and the mountain regions of the South Midland areas. It also appeared in the southern part of the Great Lakes region and beyond the Mississippi, having been spread by further migrations. It does not occur in the North or South.

The Linguistic Atlas recorded *want off* for New England and the Middle Atlantic, the South Atlantic, the North Central, and the Upper Midwest States in the context "I *want to get off* at the next corner." In the Upper Midwest except in Minnesota, similar usages are recorded in the contexts "The dog [cat] *wants to come in* [*go out*]."

According to one study (Malmstrom), in the Upper Midwest, the short forms *want in* (*out*) are much more common than *want to come in* (*go out*) in Type I (uneducated) and Type II speech (informants with at least some secondary school education). The short forms also occur in Type III (cultivated) speech in Nebraska and South Dakota. One investigator (R. Thomas) reports an example of *want in* heard on a radio program originating in New York on August 26, 1958 ("The World Today," WDMJ, Marquette, Michigan): "And the Alaskans themselves will have to go on record as *wanting in*."

Other evidence: Kurath, *LANE,* Vol. III, Pt. 2, Map 699; *Word Geography* (pp. 30, 79, Fig. 159); Malmstrom, *SVTS,* 237-38, 305; Marckwardt, *AS,* 23 (Feb., 1948), 3-9; R.I. McDavid, *AED,* 519; R.I. and V.G. McDavid, *AS,* 35 (Feb., 1960), 13; Wentworth, 690.

WANT TO (SHOULD)

Summary: Want to *is used instead of* should *in colloquial speech but rarely in informal or formal writing.*

Data: In colloquial English this expression occurs in statements like "You *want to* (*should*) learn to type so that you can get a better position," or "Ellen *wants to* work harder if she expects to enter Smith College." It occurs also in the negative, as in "You *don't want to* wear that dress if you expect to work." One study (Hotchner) reported no examples in writing, another (Bryant) encountered this usage in a letter written by an English professor: "You *will want to* write a memorial. . . ."

Other evidence: Pound, *AS,* 7 (Aug., 1932), 450-51.

WAY, AWAY, adv.

Summary: Way *occurs commonly in colloquial and educated speech as a variant of* away; *it also occurs in informal writing.*

Data: Colloquially *way* is used as an adverb, as in "He went *way* around by Lincoln"; "He went *way* to Labrador"; "He is *way* behind in production"; "That is *way* over my head." Here *way* has been substituted for *away*. It is common in educated speech, and it was marked "established" in the Leonard survey. It also occurs in written English of an informal nature, as in ". . . while auto sales are *way* down . . ." (*Newsweek,* May 5, 1958, 27) and ". . . (even though it was stuck *way* back on the last page)" (*The New Yorker,* Apr. 5, 1958, 125). One study (Hotchner) showed *way* occurring 50% of the time in writing, and another (Kaufman) encountered examples of it in dialogue.

Other evidence: Barnhart, Files; Bryant, *CE,* 17 (May, 1956), 489; Marckwardt and Walcott, 31, 117.

WAY, WAYS

Summary: Evidence shows a clear case of divided usage between these terms, with ways *preferred in standard speech; in formal written English, however,* way *is the strongly preferred form.*

Data: Both *way* and *ways* occur in sentences like "He walked a long *way(s)* before he stopped" and "He lives a little *way(s)* down the road." A written example is "A speaker can be heard only a short *ways* and only for an instant or two" (Leonard Bloomfield, *Language,* 1933, p. 40). The form *ways* is, no doubt, an adverbial genitive (See ADVERBIAL GENITIVE). The use of *way* is illustrated in "He has had a career that reaches a long *way* back" (*Look,* May 13, 1958, 72) and in ". . . we could go a long *way* toward solving our crime problem" (*The Atlantic Monthly,* Mar., 1958, 74).

The Linguistic Atlas records, according to one study (Malmstrom), reveal that in contexts like "a little *way* over" and "a long *way* to go," *ways* predominates in the speech of all types of informants in New England and the Middle Atlantic, the South Atlantic, the North Central and the Upper Midwest States. *Ways* is used between three and four times as often as *way* in New England and the Upper Midwest States; between four and five times as often in the Middle Atlantic and North Central States; and about seven times as often in the South Atlantic States. Many informants use both forms. According to two studies made of written English

(Hotchner, Kaufman), only *way* occurred. No examples of *ways* were found in formal writing.

Other evidence: Bryant, *CE*, 17 (May, 1956), 489; Kurath, *LANE*, Vol. I, Pt. I, Map 50-51; Malmstrom, *SVTS*, 66-68, 281-86.

WE, INDEFINITE. See THEY, INDEFINITE; YOU, INDEFINITE.

WE WAS (WERE). See WE WERE, YOU WERE, THEY WERE.

WE WERE, YOU WERE, THEY WERE

Summary: The use of was *instead of* were *in the preterit of the verb* to be *with* we, you, *and* they *is nonstandard everywhere.*

Data: The Linguistic Atlas records for New England and the Middle Atlantic and the South Atlantic States recorded the second-person preterit form in the context *"You were* talking to him." In New England the first-person plural preterit form is recorded in the context *"We were* talking to him," and in the Middle Atlantic and the South Atlantic States this form is recorded in the context *"We were* going to do it." In the North Central and the Upper Midwest States, all three preterit forms are recorded in the context *"We/you, they/were* going to do it."

According to one study (Malmstrom), the evidence shows that the use of *was* instead of *were* with *we, you,* or *they* is everywhere characteristic of uneducated usage (Type I). Although it is also used widely by informants with at least some secondary school education (Type II), it is so rare in cultivated (Type III) speech that it is probably the closest approach to a true shibboleth revealed by the Atlas investigations. One study (Freedman) of current newspapers and magazines found five instances of *they was,* all in short-story dialogue.

Other evidence: Atwood, 28-29; Kurath, *LANE*, Vol. III, Pt. 2, Map 679-80; Malmstrom, *SVTS*, 208-9; V.G. McDavid, 54.

WEAR, v.

Summary: The preterit wore *and the past participle* worn *are standard English;* wore *as a past participle is nonstandard.*

Data: According to one study (Malmstrom) of the Linguistic Atlas records for New England and the Middle Atlantic, the South Atlantic, the North Central, and the Upper Midwest States, in the context "He is *worn* out," *worn* is almost universal as the past participle in Type III (cultivated) speech in all areas and predominates in Type II (informants with at least some secondary school education) in all areas except Maryland and West Virginia, where *wore* occurs in the speech of about 55% of the Type II informants. In other areas *wore* is chiefly characteristic of Type I (uneducated) speech. Two studies (Horwitz, Klaperman) of current newspapers and periodicals found only *worn* as the past participle.

Other evidence: Atwood, 26; Malmstrom, *SVTS*, 195; V.G. McDavid, 50-51.

WEAVE, v.

Summary: The preterit wove *and the past participle* woven *or* wove *occur in standard English, meaning* "to interlace" *or* "to introduce a detail into a connected whole"; *the preterit* weaved, *meaning* "to follow a winding course," *is also standard usage.*

Data: From a recent study (J. Jacobson) comes an example of the preterit using the first meaning: "With flying fingers he *wove* a rough carpet of weeds and brambles" (Richard Connell, "The Most Dangerous Game," in *Exploring Life,* 1956, p. 181). The past participle is illustrated in "She has *woven* the material" and the use of the second preterit meaning in "The drunken man *weaved* his way along the street."

WELL. See GOOD, WELL.

WORE. See WEAR, v.

WORN. See WEAR, v.

WOVE. See WEAVE, v.

WOVEN. See WEAVE, v.

WHAT ALL

Summary: *This expression is heard in colloquial speech, particularly in the South; in formal English,* what *alone generally occurs in such sentences.*

Data: The *all* has an intensifying effect, apparently, in speech or in dialogue, as in conversational bits such as these: *"What all* do I have to do?"* (Jesse Stuart, *Beyond Dark Hills,* 1938, p. 113) and "I don't know *what all* has happened." Another colloquial use of the expression is in "and I don't know what all" added to a statement, meaning "various other unknown or unspecified things" or "and all sorts of things besides," as in "She had left for me the washing, the ironing, the cleaning, and I don't know *what all."* A variation occurs in ". . . and Lord knows *what all"* (Sinclair Lewis, *Bethel Merriday,* 1940, p. 139). However, two studies of formal and informal writings (Kane, Weber) failed to disclose a single example of this expression.

Similar to *what all* is *who all,* as in *"Who all's* coming?" or *"Who all* are coming?"* where *all* is added for an intensifying effect.

Other evidence: OED; Wentworth, 701.

WHAT-CLAUSES WITH IS (ARE). See AGREEMENT, WHAT-CLAUSES.

WHAT WITH

Summary: What with *is well established in the language and is an accepted idiom.*

Data: According to one investigator (Haase), the use of *what* in combination with a preposition to form an adverbial phrase, as in *"What with* the floods that followed, there was great hardship," goes back to the twelfth century, and has the meaning of "in consequence of, on account of, as a result of, in view of, considering (one thing or another)." A well-known example comes from Shakespeare's *Measure for Measure:* "Thus, *what with* the war, *what with* the gallows and *what with* poverty, I am custom shrunk."

More recent examples, taken from seven studies (Anderson, Bowden, Hotchner, Kane, Nanos, Speitz, Winburne), are: *"What with* working all day for Partridge and all night for yourself, you're turning into a regular hermit"* (Nina Brown Baker, *Big Catalogue,* 1956, p. 60); "Meanwhile, *what with* the housing shortage and all, the Pallisters figure that they're a good deal better off than they'd be in a small apartment . . ." (*The New Yorker,* Sept. 13, 1947, 26); "Yuletide generosity has got completely out of hand *what with* double purpose coffee grinders which also serve as bedside lamps . . ." (*The New York Times Book Review,* Dec. 1, 1957, 14).

Other evidence: Haase, *EJ,* XXXIX (Sept., 1950), 396; *OED.*

WHEN- (WHERE-) CLAUSE AFTER VERB TO BE

Summary: When- *and* where-*clauses after the verb* to be *occur in standard English writing; in explicit definitions, however, this structure is avoided by most writers, even though it is commonly heard in speech.*

Data: According to three studies (Benardete, McMillan, R. Thomas), two such constructions are common in English: (1) where indefinite *it* precedes the verb *to be,* as in ". . . it *is* only *when freedom of opinion becomes the first compulsion to debate* that the seed . . . has produced its fruit" (Walter Lippmann, *The Atlantic Monthly,* Aug., 1939, 190-91); (2) where *is* may be replaced by "occurs," "comes about," "happens," as in "The last view that we gain of the precious pair *is when they later appear before Olivia* . . ." (O. J. Campbell, *Shakespeare's Satire,* 1943, p. 83); "Experiences were many. Perhaps the most exciting *was when the* driving, sleety snowstorms came on winter nights" (Willa Cather, *The Old Beauty,* 1948, p. 108).

The above-cited studies make it clear, however, that this construction occurs very infrequently in explicit definitions, writers generally preferring "An opera is a play that is set to music" to "An opera is when a play is set to music." Nevertheless, the *when*-clause functioning as a noun after *to be* is common in colloquial definitions, and the traditional argument that "grammar" forbids such a construction cannot be supported by evidence from actual speech. "A touchdown *is when a player carries the ball across the opposing team's goal line*" is preferable to ". . . is a player's carrying the ball . . ." or ". . . is the carrying of the ball by a player . . ." The only alternative is ". . . *occurs when* . . . ," a distinction without a difference. Despite this, many educated people apparently dislike *is when* definitions and avoid them in writing.

Two studies (Hotchner, R. Thomas) found *where*-clauses used after *to be,* as in "That's *where the shoe pinches*" and "It *is where we are going.*" In writing, these instances occurred: ". . . I should think her brood would be a nervous outfit but this *is where she wants them*" (Edward Weeks, *The Atlantic Monthly,* Jan., 1952, 84); "When some years later the time for Harvard came, this field, and not that of history *was where he did his ripe study*" (Janet Whitney, *ibid.,* Apr., 1954, 30); "He wanted the tree *to be where he could enjoy it*" (*The New Yorker,* Dec. 21, 1957, 30). *Where*-clauses are also used in giving definitions, as in "Home *is where you check your hat*" (*ibid.,* Oct. 26, 1957, 34). The *is where* definitions are avoided no less in writing than the *is when* ones, but they are, nevertheless, used in colloquial speech.

Other evidence: Curme, *Syntax,* 196; Fries, *AEG,* 233; Thomas, *CE,* 10 (Apr., 1949), 406-8.

WHERE-CLAUSE AFTER VERB *TO BE.* See WHEN- (WHERE-) CLAUSE AFTER VERB *TO BE.*

WHETHER. See IF, WHETHER.

WHILE, conj.

Summary: The connective while, *meaning "whereas," occurs as frequently in standard English as* whereas *itself; it also occurs in the senses of* "during the time that" *and* "although."

Data: Although some textbooks disapprove of *while* meaning "whereas," as in "The material for the library is brick, *while* that for the dormitory is cement," this connective occurs with frequency in standard English: "Born in Godalming, Surrey, in 1894, he had for his paternal grandfather Thomas Henry Huxley . . . , *while* his maternal grandfather was Thomas Arnold . . ." (*Saturday Review*, Aug., 27, 1955, 9). One investigator (Hirsch) found forty-two examples of *while* meaning "whereas" and forty-one examples of *whereas*. Usage is divided between the two.

While as a connective has two other common meanings: (1) "during the time that," as in "She taught school *while* her husband was in the army," and (2) "although," as in *"While* the book is accurate, it is hard to read." All three meanings have been in standard use for years.

Sometimes, *while* is not clear in meaning, as in *"While* he operated a river-bottom farm he opposed flood control." Unless the context makes the meaning certain, either *during the time that* or *although* would be less ambiguous in such a sentence. In some sentence structures *while* clearly means "during the time that": "He opposed flood control *while* he operated a river-bottom farm" and "He opposed flood control, at least *while* he operated a river-bottom farm."

Other evidence: Curme, *Syntax*, 266-75; *PSA*, 79, 80; Fries, *AEG*, 236-37; *OED*.

WHO, WHOM

Summary: In speech and in dialogue, who *occurs far more frequently than* whom *as the object of the verb or preposition, most often at the beginning of a clause or sentence. In formal English,* whom *is used in these instances; in hypercorrect writing, it is sometimes mistakenly used as a subject.*

Data: In formal expository prose the function of a pronoun within its own clause determines the case of that pronoun, but in spoken English the position in the sentence is frequently decisive. For example, if the interrogative pronoun, functioning as the object of a verb or preposition, comes at the beginning of a sentence or clause, spoken English usually employs *who,* as in *"Who* do you think I met on the subway?" *"Who* are you going to invite?" "I wonder *who* I should ask" (spoken by Brooklyn College students, Dec., 1951). Written examples are: " 'It doesn't matter *who* they

lead' " (Ernest Hemingway, *Green Hills of Africa,* 1935, Permabooks, 1954, p. 17); " *'Who* does he mean . . . ?' " (*ibid.,* p. 81);
"I don't care *who* you tell this to" (F. D. Roosevelt in a letter of
1934 written to the speaker of the House of Representatives). All
of these illustrations have *who* at the beginning of the clause or sentence, but in " 'I do not care who kills *who*' " (Ernest Hemingway,
The Old Man and the Sea, 1952, p. 102), the second *who* comes
after the verb and functions as the object. Then there is the proverbial "It's not what you know; it's *who* you know." The *who*
probably is used in this way because a subject generally comes at
the beginning of a sentence or clause and the subject form is *who.*
According to one study (Wine), *who* instead of *whom* occurred
83⅓ % of the time as object of the verb or preposition in dialogue.
Of these occurrences, 80% came first in the sentence or clause;
20%, however, were placed after the verb or preposition, as in
"Found *who?"* and "Heard from *who?"*

Where relative pronouns may be used, formal English would employ *whom* as the object of a verb or preposition, but informal English would ordinarily omit the object or substitute *that,* as in "He
wrote to girls [*that*] he admired" and "He is the man [*that*] we
heard the news from." In the last example, note the change of position of the preposition to the end of the clause in informal usage.
(See PREPOSITION AT END OF CLAUSE OR SENTENCE.)

Some persons who do not really understand the grammar they
have been taught use the hypercorrect *whom* as subject, as in "His
favorite target is the Negro, *whom* he claims is constantly being
incited, . . ." ("The Bilbo Hearing," *Life,* Dec. 16, 1946, 32).
The writer, editor, and proofreaders all went astray, subconsciously
regarding *whom* as the object of the verb *claims,* not realizing that
it actually was the subject of the following verb *is.* Such confusion
often arises when a parenthetic expression like *he claims, he says,
I think, I consider* comes between the relative pronoun and the
verb it governs or selects, as in "We include those *who* [not *whom*]
we think will make good citizens." Here *who* is the subject of *will
make.* Confusion likewise arises when the pronoun is the subject
of a clause which as a whole functions as the direct object of a verb
or a preposition, as in "You must consider *who* [not *whom*] are the

judges" and "You must give it to *who* [not *whom*] comes first." The entire clause *who are the judges* is the object of *consider,* and *who comes first* is the object of the preposition *to.* *Who* in each case is the subject of the verb in its own clause.

Another illustration may be found in *Second Threshold* (Act II, Scene 1) by Philip Barry, revised by Robert E. Sherwood, where a young girl in placing her hands over someone's eyes says, "Guess *who?*—I mean *whom*" (*Theatre Arts,* Dec., 1951, 61). The first *who* is spontaneous and grammatically correct, for what the girl means is "Guess who it is," where *who* is a subjective complement in the nominative case. Having been made conscious of *who* and *whom,* she decides to take no chance on being thought illiterate and changes *who* to *whom.* She should have known that the *OED* states that *whom* is "no longer current in natural colloquial speech."

The same confusion holds for *whoever* and *whomever.* *Whoever* is established informal usage in a sentence like "Ask *whoever* you like to go with you." Here *whoever* is the object of *like,* but it is placed at the beginning of the clause and the nominative case is used. Similarly a Brooklyn College student in answering another who asked, *"Who* should we invite?" said, "I don't know. *Whoever* you want" (Dec., 1951). In formal English *whomever* would be used in each instance. Three other investigators (Benardete, Sloan, R. Thomas) contributed to this entry.

Other evidence: Fries, *AEG,* 94-96; Kenyon, *AS,* 5 (Feb., 1930), 253-55; Kurath, *LANE,* Vol. III, Pt. 2, Maps 627-28; Malone, *CE,* 10 (Oct., 1948), 37-38; Marckwardt and Walcott, 80-81; McMillan, *CE,* 7 (Nov., 1945), 104-5; Mencken, *Am. Lang.,* 201-2; Menner, *AS,* 12 (Oct., 1937), 177-78; Pooley, *TEU,* 72-77, 221; Sapir, 166-74.

WHOEVER, WHOMEVER. See WHO, WHOM.

WHOSE, OF WHICH

Summary: Although in current standard English who is used only with nouns referring to people (e.g., "the woman who was lost") and which with other nouns (e.g., "the cat which was lost" and "the pen which was lost"), its genitive whose occurs with both kinds of nouns in all varieties of English. The alternative of which is often avoided as awkward.

Data: Examples are: "Other things being equal, we should consider as best that survey . . . *whose* author shows the greatest range of adult enjoyment" (*Yale Review,* Summer, 1947, 732); "This is not merely a false assumption, but one *whose* falsity has been demonstrated . . ." (*The Atlantic Monthly,* Feb., 1950, 21); ". . . the night from *whose* depth of dark, lax satiety, provisioned in that instant . . ." (Robert Penn Warren, *Band of Angels,* 1955, p. 235). The alternative is *of which,* as in "one the falsity *of which* has been demonstrated." In one study (Howard) of fiction, poetry, magazines, general conversation, lectures, and television, *whose* was found in 60% of the cases and *of which* in 40%. Two other studies (R. Thomas, Winburne) found *whose* occurred commonly as a neuter possessive. Insistence upon the *of which* phrase often forces one to employ an awkward construction instead of a much simpler one. For example, "This is the house the roof *of which* is leaking" is more cumbersome than "This is the house *whose* roof is leaking," where *whose* is placed directly after *house* to which it refers and immediately before *roof,* which it modifies.

Whose is entirely permissible and often necessary to avoid awkward structure or a late-placed pronoun. George P. Krapp in *A Comprehensive Guide to Good English* has stated the case well: "Historically *whose* corresponds to both masculine and neuter genitive of the pronoun in Anglo-Saxon. *Whose* has always been freely used as the possessive of neuters. The use of *of which* and not *whose* is a mark of formality and theory, not natural style. The use of *of which* often leads to stiffness and pedantry" (p. 623). Some writers change the entire structure of the sentence and thereby avoid both *whose* and *of which.* For example, ". . . the place *whose* address . . ." is changed to ". . . the place *that* has an address. . . ."

Other evidence: Bryant, *CE,* 17 (Feb., 1956), 312; Curme, *Syntax,* 229-30; Fries, *AEG,* 80; Hall, 320-27; *OED;* Pooley, *TEU,* 170-72.

WILL. See SHALL, WILL.

WITHOUT, UNLESS

Summary: Without *as a variant for* unless *hardly ever occurs in standard writing, but it is heard, though rarely, in Type III (cultivated) speech in some areas.*

Data: In a context such as "I won't go *unless* he goes," *unless* predominates very strongly in New England and the Middle Atlantic, the Southern Atlantic, the North Central, and the Upper Midwest States among all types and is almost universal in Type III speech.

Without, according to one study (Malmstrom), is found, although rarely, in Type III speech only in Pennsylvania, Delaware, Georgia, and Indiana; that is, in a few Midland and Southern areas. In these areas, it has somewhat greater frequency in Type II speech (informants with at least secondary school education) than in Type III. Since it is less frequent in the cultivated speech of the western areas than in that of the comparable eastern ones, this usage does not seem to be expanding.

In formal written English *unless* generally occurs, as in *"Unless* the maximum size . . . is reduced . . . teachers cannot do an adequate job" (Benjamin Fine, *The New York Times,* Dec. 9, 1956, E9). As *unless* predominates over *without,* so it does over *except* (*if*), once common in Biblical writings (*"Except* a man be born again, he cannot see the kingdom of God"—*John* 3:3) and used by Tennyson and others at times, but now archaic. One study (Levy) showed that *unless* was used 98.2% of the time. Another (Fox) found no instance of *without* or *except* as a variant for *unless* in the reading done. *Except that,* however, may be used, meaning "with the exception (that)" or "save for the fact that," as in "I would like to see the play *except that* I must prepare for an examination."

Other evidence: Kurath, *LANE,* Vol. III, Pt. 2, Map 730; Malmstrom, *SVTS,* 45, 269-71.

WOLF, n. See HOOF, n.

WRITE, v.

Summary: The preterit wrote *and the past participle* written *are standard English;* wrote *as the past participle is nonstandard.*

Data: According to one study (Malmstrom) of the Linguistic Atlas records for New England and the Middle Atlantic, the South Atlantic, the North Central, and the Upper Midwest States in the contexts "I *have written* a note" and "I *have written* the letter," the standard form *written* as a past participle is strongly predominant in Type III (cultivated) speech in New England and the Middle Atlantic and the South Atlantic States, and practically universal in this type in the North Central and the Upper Midwest States.

In the Middle Atlantic and the South Atlantic States, *wrote* as a past participle prevails in Type II speech (informants with at least some secondary school education) and occurs with some frequency in this type in the Midland areas of the North Central States. In these areas *wrote* has the status of colloquial usage.

One investigator (Leibson) in her reading of magazines, newspapers, and fiction found fifty examples of the preterit *wrote,* as in "Once years ago, I even *wrote* a book about relations between nations" (*The New Yorker,* Sept. 26, 1959, 41), and no variant.

She also found seventy-three examples of the past participle, as in "Writers have *written* . . . tirades . . . against . . . (*The Atlantic Monthly,* July, 1958, 16) or in "Because this column is primarily concerned with the *written* word . . ." (*The New York Times Book Review,* Nov. 15, 1959, 2), and no variant.

Other evidence: Atwood, 26; Kurath, *LANE,* Vol. III, Pt. 2, Map 670; Malmstrom, *SVTS,* 197-98; V.G. McDavid, 51.

YOU ALL

Summary: You all, *often run together as one word and pronounced* [jɔl], *is a Southern expression designating the plural. It is used in speech by the educated and the uneducated throughout the South and the South Midland.*

Data: You all, pronounced as one word, may be addressed to one person, but includes the idea of others, as in "*You all* come over tonight," meaning the person and his family are invited. Two studies (Atsaves, Kafka) showed that it was used in writing to represent only regional Southern speech.

The lack of a distinctive plural second-person pronoun, caused by the obsolescence of *thou*, is compensated in various ways. Most common is adding a plural noun in close apposition, as in *you men, you girls, you people, you folks,* or colloquial *you guys.* The plural form *youse* [juz], formed by analogy to noun plurals, is substandard. It is heard principally in southeastern Pennsylvania, southern New Jersey, New York City, and northern Maryland, and occasionally in West Virginia and western North Carolina.

Other nonstandard forms are *you'ns* and *mongst-ye. You'ns* is the distinctive Midland form, occurring in the folk speech of Pennsylvania west of the Susquehanna, in large parts of West Virginia, and in the westernmost parts of Virginia and North Carolina. *Mongst-ye* occurs in the central part of Delmarva principally, but occasionally from the mouth of Chesapeake Bay to Albemarle Sound. *You'ns, mongst-ye,* and *you all* have a possessive case: *You'ns's, mongst-ye's,* and *you all's.*

You all, pronounced as two separate words, and *all of you* occur in all parts of the country. Charles Van Doren in addressing a panel on television (summer, 1958) said, *"You all* then believe. . . ."

Other Evidence: Kurath, *Word Geography,* 31, 40, 41, 67, Fig. 114; R.I. McDavid, *AED,* 519, 526; R.I. and V.G. McDavid, *AS,* 35 (Feb., 1960), 16; Shewmake, *AS,* 13 (Oct., 1938), 163-68; Vowles, *AS,* 19 (Apr., 1944), 146-47; Wentworth, 730-32.

YOU, INDEFINITE

Summary: Indefinite you *is common in Modern English and occurs both in speech and in expository writing.*

Data: Indefinite *you* is employed most frequently when one wishes to express a principle or philosophy, referring to people in general, as in *"You* can never tell what's going to happen" and *"You* never find what *you* want when *you* look for it." Written examples are: "In 'Jane,' however, he has no more conscience than *you* can find in Somerset Maugham . . ." (Brooks Atkinson, *The New York Times,* Feb. 10, 1952, Sec. 2, 1) and "And I suppose the point to be made is that, whereas *you* can have such tendencies . . . as *you* have . . . in the later Mann *you* find . . ." (*Kenyon Review,* Winter, 1952, 150).

Indefinite *you* often occurs with *if* or *as if,* as in "Differences can be nourishing if *you* don't waste time and energy fighting them" (Hannah Lees, "How to be Happy Though Incompatible," *Reader's Digest,* May, 1957, 46) and "Each pain was something all-encompassing now, as if someone were taking *you* and shaking *you* . . ." (Julie Harris, "I Was Afraid to Have a Baby," *Reader's Digest,* Apr., 1957, 44). This usage with the conjunction is more frequent in written English than in common speech. According to one study (Altman), it occurred 29% of the time in written English and 10% in spoken English, whereas the use of *you* to express a general principle occurred much more frequently in spoken English. Another investigator (R. Thomas) showed that it is often found in expository writing.

Indefinite *you* is normally found in more informal writing, the type that meets the reading taste of the general public. More direct and less formal than *one,* it is established in current usage.

We and *they,* like *you,* are also established in standard usage as indefinite pronouns in informal English, as in *"We* never can tell what will happen in the future" and *"They* don't know any history today." This means "One never can tell . . ." and "One doesn't know. . . ." French *on* and German *man* serve the same purpose and would be used in translating each one. See also AGREEMENT, INDEFINITE PRONOUNS AND THEY, INDEFINITE.

Other evidence: Marckwardt and Walcott, 72.

YOU WAS (WERE). See WE WERE, YOU WERE, THEY WERE.

YOU'NS. See YOU ALL.

YOURSELF, YOURSELVES. See MYSELF.

YOUSE. See YOU ALL.

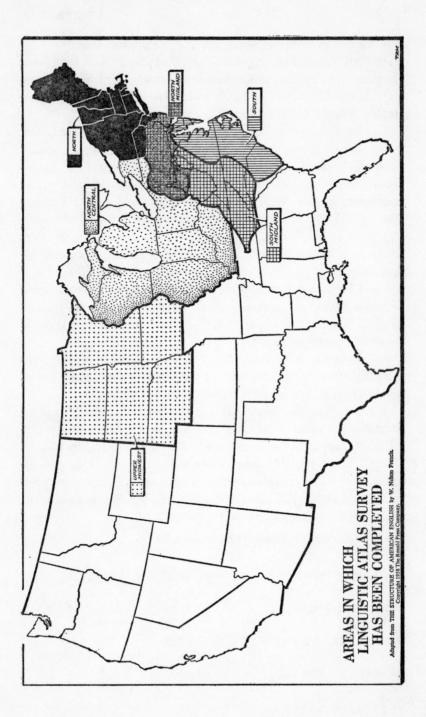

NORTH

NORTH
MIDLAND

SOUTH

NORTH
CENTRAL

SOUTH
MIDLAND

UPPER
MIDWEST

AREAS IN WHICH
LINGUISTIC ATLAS SURVEY
HAS BEEN COMPLETED

Adapted from THE STRUCTURE OF AMERICAN ENGLISH by W. Nelson Francis.
Copyright 1958 The Ronald Press Company.

APPENDIX A

Principal Regions Furnishing Data

The geographic regions that are mentioned most often are the New England, Middle Atlantic, South Atlantic, North Central, and Upper Midwest States. In these regions the Linguistic Atlas Survey has been completed and the materials have been studied. (Only the *Linguistic Atlas of New England* has been published.) The survey is continuing in other parts of the country and Canada.

For the purpose of locating contiguous areas of usage, the geographic regions have been renamed, in part, to define speech areas. These speech areas are listed below, with the states and regions included in each. A map of the United States, showing these areas, is found on page 240.

The North
New England
New York
Northern New Jersey
Northeastern Pennsylvania

The North Midland
Southern New Jersey
Southern Pennsylvania
East-Central Ohio
Northern West Virginia
Northern Delaware
North-Eastern Maryland

The North Central States
Ohio (excluding East-Central part)
Central and Western Kentucky
Indiana
Illinois
Michigan
Wisconsin

The South Midland
Western Virginia
Southern West Virginia
Western N. & S. Carolina
Eastern Kentucky
Eastern Tennessee
Western Maryland

The Upper Midwest
Minnesota
Iowa
North Dakota
South Dakota
Nebraska

The South
Delmarva
Eastern Virginia
Eastern N. & S. Carolina

APPENDIX B

A Key to Abbreviations, Pronunciations, and Symbols Used in Entries

adj. : adjective
adv. : adverb
AED : "American English Dialects" by Raven I. McDavid, Jr. (Chap. 9), W. Nelson Francis, *The Structure of American English*
AEG : *American English Grammar* (Fries)
Am. Lang. : *American Language* (Mencken)
AS : *American Speech* (periodical)
CE : *College English* (periodical)
CEA : College English Association
CEU : *Current English Usage* (Leonard)
cf. : compare
conj. : conjunction
Cur. Eng. : *Current English* (Kennedy)
DA : *Dictionary of Americanisms on Historical Principles*
Dial. Notes : *Dialect Notes* (pamphlet)
Doctrine of Correctness : *Doctrine of Correctness in English Usage, 1700-1800* (Leonard)
e.g. : for example
EJ : *English Journal* (periodical)
Eng. : English
Ess. : *Essentials of English Grammar* (Jespersen)
et al.
etc. : and the like
FEG : *A Functional English Grammar* (Bryant)
ff. : and the pages following
fig(s). : figure(s)
Files : Lexicographical Files
Gram. : Grammar
Handbk. : *A Handbook of Present-Day English* (Kruisinga)
ibid. : in the same place
i.e. : that is
LANE : *Linguistic Atlas of New England* (Kurath *et al*)
Lang. : *Language* (periodical)
MEG : *Modern English Grammar* (Jespersen)
MEU : *A Dictionary of Modern English Usage* (Fowler)
MLN : *Modern Language Notes* (periodical)
Mod. Eng. : Modern English
n. : noun
NCTE : National Council of Teachers of English
NEG : *A New English Grammar* (Sweet)
OED : *Oxford English Dictionary*

op. cit. : in the work cited

p(p). : page(s)

passim : scattered throughout

PMLA : *The Publications of the Modern Language Association* (periodical)

Prin. & Prac. : *Principles and Practices of English Grammar* (Curme)

PSA : *Parts of Speech and Accidence* (Curme)

Pt. : Part

q.v. : which see

Sec. : Section

Sup. I : *Supplement I*

Sup. II : *Supplement II*

SVTS : *A Study of the Validity of Textbook Statements About Certain Controversial Grammatical Items in the Light of Evidence from the Linguistic Atlas* (Malmstrom)

TEU : *Teaching English Usage* (Pooley)

UG : *Understanding Grammar* (Roberts)

v. : verb

Vol(s). : Volume(s)

WNID : *Webster's New International Dictionary*, 3rd ed.

The following phonetic symbols have been used in the entries:

Phonetic Symbol	Key Word	Transcription
[a]	*I*	[aɪ]
[ɑ]	*a*re	[ɑr]
[æ]	p*a*n	[pæn]
[ɛ]	m*e*t	[mɛt]
[i]	s*ee*d	[sid]
[ɪ]	f*i*t	[fɪt]
[ə]	m*e*rr*i*ly	['mɛrəlɪ]
[ɔ]	s*aw*	[sɔ]
[ʊ]	f*oo*t	[fʊt]
[ɚ]	pow*er*	['pɑʊɚ]
[j]	*y*ou	[ju]
[tʃ]	*ch*est	[tʃɛst]
[ð] *		
['] †		
[ˌ] †		

* The symbol [ð] "eth" is equivalent to *th*.

† ['] = primary stress, [ˌ] = secondary stress; both are placed before the stressed syllable.

APPENDIX C

A Glossary of Terms, Mainly Grammatical

ABSOLUTE: A construction composed of a participle with its noun or pronoun subject, object, or both, lacking connectives and being joined to the rest of the sentence only by position. When a subject is present, the construction is frequently called a nominative absolute: *"He having agreed to go,* I settled down to work."

ACTIVE VOICE: The construction of the verb that indicates that the subject is acting rather than being acted upon: "I *saw* the man."

ADJECTIVE: A word typically used as a modifier of a noun to describe, limit, or qualify, often answering the questions *Which? What? What kind of?:* "the *white* house"; "the *courageous* men"; "the men are *courageous.*"

ADVERB: A word typically used as a modifier of a verb, an adjective, another adverb, answering a great variety of questions, including *How? When? Where? Why?:* "She writes *well";* "He is coming *to-day";* "Stand *there."* Adverbs may modify prepositional phrases, clauses, and sentences: "It is rising *directly* above the treetops"; *"Just* why he went I shall never know"; *"Fortunately,* he accepted the position."

AGREEMENT: A functional or formal correspondence between two parts of speech; e.g., a subject and its verb agree in number when both of them are singular or both are plural (*he goes, they go*).

ANTECEDENT: The name given to the word or group of words to which a pronoun refers, usually placed before the pronoun: *"Everyone* is expected to show *his* paintings to Mr. Jones."

ARCHAISM: A word, expression, or construction which is still occasionally used but is recognized as belonging to an earlier period of the language (*durst,* for *dared.*)

CASE: The change of form of a noun or pronoun by means of which its relationship to other words in a sentence is indicated.

CLAUSE: A grammatical unit, a word-group, that ordinarily has a subject and a finite verb and may be all or part of a complete sentence. Clauses are classified as independent and subordinate, and as noun, adjective, and adverb.

COLLECTIVE NOUN: The name of a group or class of beings or things (*crowd, family, group, bunch*).

COLLOQUIAL: Pertaining to spoken and informal rather than to written and formal language (see Introduction, p. xxiii.

COMPARISON: The process by which adjectives or adverbs show degrees of superiority in quality, quantity, or intensity. There are generally three degrees of comparison recognized: positive, comparative, and superlative (*happy, happier, happiest*).

CONJUNCTION: A connective used to join words, phrases, clauses, or sentences. There are two main types: coordinating (*and, but, or*, etc.) and subordinating (*though, as, if, since*, etc.).

COORDINATING CONJUNCTION: A conjunction used to connect grammatical elements of equal rank—nouns with nouns, adjectives with adjectives, clauses with clauses, phrases with phrases, etc. *See* CONJUNCTION.

DEGREE: That property of adjectives and adverbs indicated by the process of comparison (*q.v.*). The three degrees are positive, comparative, and superlative (*hot, hotter, hottest*).

DEMONSTRATIVE ADJECTIVE: A term describing the word *this, that, these,* or *those* when placed before the noun it modifies (*this* table, *that* chair).

DEMONSTRATIVE PRONOUN: *This, that, these,* or *those* when used to point out and name something or someone: "*That* is my table."

DIRECT OBJECT: The person or thing affected directly by the action of a transitive verb: "He laid the *book* on the table."

GENITIVE CASE: That form of the noun generally written -'s for the singular and -*s'* for the plural, used to show a number of relationships among which possession is one of the most common (*girl's, girls'*). Other forms are the *of* genitive (the novels *of Hemingway*), the double genitive (that house *of Jack's*), and the genitive of personal and relative pronouns (*my, your, his, its, whose*, etc.).

GERUND: A verb form ending in -*ing* and acting as a noun: "*Studying* is good."

INDEFINITE PRONOUN: A class of pronouns indicating not one particular thing but any one or more of a class of things (*each, few, some, many, much*, etc.).

INDIRECT OBJECT: The person or thing indirectly affected by the action of the verb, the word that tells to or for whom something is done: "I told *him* the story."

INFINITIVE: That form of the verb usually consisting of the *present stem*, which expresses the general sense without restriction as to number, person, or time. It occurs both with and without *to*. *To go* is an infinitive, as is *go* in "can *go*." After several verbs (*can, may, must, shall, will; dare, do, need*, etc.) *to* is never or seldom used. *To* may also be omitted in a sentence like "All she does is *write*."

INFLECTION: Changes in the form of words to indicate certain grammatical relationships, as the past tense of verbs or the plural of nouns. The *s* in *boys,* the *'s* in *man's,* and the *ed* in *played* are inflections.

INTRANSITIVE VERB: A verb which, because of its meaning, does not have a direct object: "He *walks.*"

LINGUISTIC ATLAS: *The Linguistic Atlas of the United States and Canada* is composed of a number of regional research projects using similar procedures and collecting the same kinds of linguistic evidence, thus producing results that can be correlated and compared. The Atlas is under the general directorship of Hans Kurath. Along with surveys and articles derived from it, it represents a huge accumulation of data for the use of teachers and textbook writers. Using a tested sampling technique, trained fieldworkers interview native residents representing various generations, occupations, and degrees of education: those with little formal education, little reading, and restricted contacts; those with better formal education (usually high school) and/or wider reading and social contacts; and those with superior education (usually college), wide reading, and/or extensive social contacts. These groups roughly correspond to Types I, II, and III; *see* Introduction. From each person information is sought concerning about 800 language items on questions of pronunciation, grammar, or vocabulary, and each response is recorded phonetically. At present, evidence has been gathered from different areas: New England; the Middle Atlantic, the South Atlantic, the North Central, the Upper Midwest, the Rocky Mountain, and the Pacific Coast States; and parts of Canada. Preliminary work is under way in other areas. Only the *Linguistic Atlas of New England* has been completed and published.

NOMINATIVE: The name of the case denoting the subject of a sentence, a predicate noun referring to the subject, a word in apposition with either, or a word in certain absolute constructions.

NOMINATIVE ABSOLUTE: *See* ABSOLUTE.

NOUN: A part of speech, the name of a person, place, thing, quality, collection, idea, or action, answering the questions *Who? (Whom?)* or *What?* It is identifiable by position and by certain characteristics of form: "Open the *box*"; "*Trees* grow."

NOUN-ADJUNCT: A noun in the singular number followed by another noun on which there is greater stress; traditionally described as "a noun used as an adjective" (*burlap* bag, *flood* control, *floor* plan).

NUMBER: The distinction of word form that indicates the singular and plural aspects of nouns, pronouns, and verbs.

PARTICIPLE: A form of the verb ending in *ing, ed, en* (or indicated through internal change, e.g., *swum*), used in expanded constructions—the present participle (am *coming*) and the past participle (was *played,* have *written*)—or as an adjective (*closed* door).

PARTICIPIAL CONSTRUCTION: A construction introduced by a participle: *"Seeing his father,* he stopped."

PARTS OF SPEECH: The major divisions of words into which the vocabulary of a language falls, classified according to form and function.

PASSIVE VOICE: That construction of the verb which indicates what is done to the subject rather than what the subject does. All passives consist of two or more words, ending with the past participle of the verb, and all contain the auxiliary *to be* in one of its forms.

PERSON: The name for those grammatical distinctions of a pronoun or verb which indicate whether the reference is to the speaker (first person), the person spoken to (second person), or to anyone or anything else (third person), someone neither speaking nor spoken to.

PHRASE: A group of two or more words used as a grammatical unit in the sentence. It does not contain a predication (subject-verb sequence), but has the force of a single part of speech: "The boy *on the horse* is my brother."

PREDICATE: The word or words of a sentence or clause which express what is said of the subject. The predicate consists of the verb together with all the words governed by it and modifying it: "The boy *caught a glimpse of the boat."*

PRETERIT: A simple or one-word past tense of the verb (*treated, slept, wrote, had, was*).

PRINCIPAL PARTS: The forms of a verb from which the various tenses are derived. The principal parts are the present stem, the past tense, and the past participle (*wash, washed, washed; ring, rang, rung*).

PRONOUN: A word used instead of a noun to serve in one of the noun functions (subject, object, etc.).

RELATIVE CLAUSE: A clause introduced by a relative pronoun (mainly *who, whose, whom, which, that*).

SUBORDINATING CONJUNCTION: A connective used to join a dependent or subordinate clause to a main clause. *See* CONJUNCTION.

SUBSTANTIVE: A term applied to nouns and pronouns and other words or groups of words used in the functions of a noun.

SUFFIX: An addition to the end of the simple form of a word; *ment* in *amendment* and *ed* in *treated* are suffixes, added to *amend* and *treat.* A prefix is added to the beginning of a word.

SYNTAX: That part of grammar that deals with the relationship between the words or word groups in a sentence, as subjects, objects, predicates, modifiers, etc. The teacher's term "sentence construction" is a fairly close synonym.

248 APPENDIX C

TENSE: A distinctive form of the verb for expressing different time concepts, such as present, past, and future.

TRANSITIVE VERB: A verb that has a direct object.

VERB: A word, identifiable by form and position, that indicates action, state, or being.

VOICE: The form of the verb which indicates whether the subject is acting (active—David *drove*) or being acted upon (passive—David *was driven*).

APPENDIX D

Below are five linguistic studies submitted as evidence for the entries: climb, v.; contractions; it's I/me, it's we/us, it's he/him, it's she/her, it's they/them; reference, vague or indefinite: this (pronominal); and sentence modifier. They are typical examples of the kind of evidence most of the entries rest upon. For some of the entries, the greater part of the evidence was drawn from the Linguistic Atlas.

Climb, v.

Jeannette Blumengarten (Brooklyn College) in her reading found thirteen examples of the preterit *climbed*, as in "He *climbed* the steep flight of steps . . ." (Maritta Wolff, *The Big Nickelodeon*, 1956, p. 260), and one of the variant *clomb*, used by a poor, uneducated woman of the mountainous section of Virginia, c. 1856: ". . . I know Buck Keyser broke that winder an' *clomb* in an' robbed the Lord, as well as if I'd seen him do it" (Willa Cather, *Sapphira and the Slave Girl*, 1940, p. 125). She also found six examples of *climbed* as a past participle, illustrated by "John Henry had *climbed* up . . ." (Carson McCullers, *The Member of the Wedding*, 1946, p. 115) and no other variant.

Material read: (novels) Erskine Caldwell, *Place Called Estherville*, N. Y.: Duell, Sloane & Pearce, 1949 (40 pp.); Willa Cather, *Sapphira and the Slave Girl*, N. Y.: A. A. Knopf, 1940 (19 pp.); James Gould Cozzens, *By Love Possessed*, 1957 (15 pp.); *Guard of Honor*, 1948 (23 pp.), N. Y.: Harcourt, Brace; William Faulkner, *The Town*, Vol. 2, *Snopes*, N. Y.: Random House, 1957 (19 pp.); Caroline Gordon, *The Strange Children*, N. Y.: Scribner's, 1951 (29 pp.); A. B. Guthrie, Jr., *The Way West*, N. Y.: William Sloane Associates, 1949 (17 pp.); Helen Hull, *Landfall*, N. Y.: Coward-McCann, 1953 (19 pp.); Shirley Jackson, *The Bird's Nest*, N. Y.: Farrar, Straus & Young, 1954 (19 pp.); Delia Cash Jenkins, *Swamp Angel*, San Antonio: Naylor Co., 1953 (16 pp.); Mary Lasswell, *Wait for the Wagon*, Boston: Houghton Mifflin, 1951 (31 pp.); Jean Lee Latham, *Trail Blazer of the Seas*, Boston: Houghton Mifflin, 1956 (30 pp.); Sinclair Lewis, *Cass Timberlane*, N. Y.: Random House, 1945 (21 pp.); Andrew Lytle, *The Velvet Horn*, N. Y.: McDowell, Obolensky, 1957 (19 pp.); John P. Marquand, *Sincerely, Willis Wayde*, Boston: Little, Brown, 1954 (21 pp.); Carson McCullers, *The Member of the Wedding*, Boston: Houghton Mifflin, 1946 (27 pp.); Marjorie Kinnan Rawlings, *The Sojourner*, N. Y.: Scribner's, 1953 (16 pp.); John Steinbeck, *Sweet Thursday*, N. Y.;

Viking Press, 1954 (30 pp.); Philip D. Stone, *Blizzard,* Garden City, N. Y.: Doubleday, 1955 (34 pp.); Jesse Stuart, *The Good Spirit of Laurel Ridge,* N. Y.: McGraw-Hill, 1953 (32 pp.); Morton Thompson, *Not as a Stranger,* N. Y.: Scribner's, 1954 (27 pp.); James Thurber, *The White Deer,* N. Y.: Harcourt, Brace, 1945 (24 pp.); Robert Penn Warren, *Band of Angels,* N. Y.: Random House, 1955 (21 pp.); Eudora Welty, *The Ponder Heart,* N. Y.: Harcourt, Brace, 1954 (16 pp.); E. B. White, *Charlotte's Web,* N. Y.: Harper, 1952 (19 pp.); Nelia Gardner White, *The Merry Month of May,* N. Y.: Viking Press, 1952 (20 pp.); Thornton Wilder, *The Ides of March,* N. Y.: Harper, 1948 (13 pp.); William Carlos Williams, *The Build-Up,* N. Y.: Random House, 1952 (15 pp.); Sloan Wilson, *The Man in the Gray Flannel Suit,* N. Y.: Simon and Schuster, 1955 (14 pp.); Thomas Wolfe, *The Web and the Rock,* Garden City, N. Y.: Sun Dial Press, 1939 (23 pp.); Maritta Wolff, *The Big Nickelodeon,* N. Y.: Random House, 1956 (18 pp.); Richard Wright, *Native Son,* N. Y.: Grosset & Dunlap, 1940 (18 pp.); (short stories) Ray Bradbury, "The Dwarf," *The October Country,* N. Y.: Ballantine Books, 1955 (14 pp.); Truman Capote, "Children on Their Birthdays," *A Tree of Night and Other Stories,* N. Y.: Random House, 1949 (29 pp.); Martha Gellhorn, "For Better, for Worse," *Two by Two,* N. Y.: Simon and Schuster, 1958 (29 pp.); J. D. Salinger, "A Perfect Day for Bananafish," *Nine Stories,* Boston: Little, Brown, 1953 (28 pp.); Philip Wylie, "Widow Voyage," *The Best of Crunch and Des,* N. Y.: Rinehart, 1954 (20 pp.); (magazines) *American Heritage,* Oct., 1958 (11 pp.); *Art News,* Nov., 1958 (4 pp.); *The Atlantic Monthly,* Sept., 1958 (4 pp.); *Better Homes and Gardens,* Dec., 1958 (4 pp.); *Commonweal,* Dec. 19, 1958 (2 pp.); *Coronet,* Dec., 1958 (3 pp.); *Fortune,* Dec., 1958 (7 pp.); *Good Housekeeping,* Oct., 1958 (4 pp.); *Holiday,* May, 1957 (8 pp.); *Look,* Dec. 23, 1958 (3 pp.); *Mademoiselle,* Dec., 1958 (3 pp.); *New Republic,* Dec. 15, 1958 (3 pp.); *The New Yorker,* Aug. 23, 1958 (8 pp.); *Popular Photography,* Mar., 1958 (8 pp.); *Reader's Digest,* June, 1958 (6 pp.); *Saturday Evening Post,* Dec. 13, 1958 (5 pp.); *Saturday Review,* Nov. 29, 1958 (3 pp.); *School and Society,* Nov. 23, 1957 (4 pp.); *Science,* Dec. 5, 1958 (3 pp.); *Science and Society,* Summer, 1958 (12 pp.); *South Atlantic Quarterly,* Autumn, 1958 (12 pp.); *U. S. News & World Report,* Dec. 12, 1958 (8 pp.); (newspaper) *Wall Street Journal,* Nov. 10, 1958 (1 p.).

Contractions

James B. McMillan (University of Alabama) makes the following tabulation of the use of contractions in the Winter 1951-52 issue of the *American Scholar:*

Nine articles in the issue; three have contractions, six do not.

1st article (by Louis Kronenberger) has only *-n't* contractions:

Form	No.	%	Form	No.	%	Total
don't	4	80	do not	1	20	5
can't	1	50	cannot	1	50	2
shan't	2	100	shall not	0	0	2
aren't	1	50	are not	1	50	2
isn't	1	14	is not	6	86	7
won't	1	100	will not	0	0	1
couldn't	1	50	could not	1	50	2
didn't	0	0	did not	2	100	2
hasn't	0	0	has not	3	100	3
wasn't	0	0	was not	1	100	1
Total:	11	40	Total:	16	60	27

5th article (by Sidney Alexander):

Form	No.	%	Form	No.	%	Total
hasn't	1	100	has not	0	0	1
don't	1	50	do not	1	50	2
doesn't	2	66	does not	1	33	3
haven't	0	0	have not	1	100	1
isn't	0	0	is not	5	100	5
wasn't	0	0	was not	2	100	2
won't	0	0	will not	2	100	2
we're	2	50	we are	2	50	4
they're	1	50	they are	1	50	2
you're	3	60	you are	2	40	5
that's	1	50	that is	1	50	2
I'm	4	100	I am	0	0	4
I'll	2	100	I will	0	0	1
you'll	1	100	you will	0	0	1
			(others)*	21	100	21
Total:	18	30	Total:	39	70	57

* there is (2), it is (5), we have (2), I have (2), you had, he has, you have, I would, I have, what is, who are, she has, who is, he had, they had.

All of Alexander's contractions are in quotations or in paraphrases of quotations; some uncontracted forms appear in quotations. Emphasis is responsible for some of the uncontracted forms in the quotations.

7th article (by William S. Carlson):

Form	No.	%	Form	No.	%	Total
isn't	2	66	is not	1	33	3
didn't	1	33	did not	2	66	3
wasn't	3	60	was not	2	40	5
can't	1	100	cannot	0	0	1
aren't	1	100	are not	0	0	1
don't	1	100	do not	0	0	1
couldn't	3	100	could not	0	0	3
it's	3	100	it is	0	0	3
there's	2	66	there is	1	33	3
he'd	1	14	he had	6	86	7
I've	1	100	I have	0	0	1
what's	1	100	what is	0	0	1
they've	1	100	they have	0	0	1
there'd	1	100	there would	0	0	1
we've	1	100	we have	0	0	1
			(others)*	15	100	15
Total:	23	46	Total:	27	52	50

* he would (2), who will (2), would have (3), could have (2), here is, that is, he is, she is, she had, might have.

Summary: Of nine principal articles, three employ contractions. In these three articles, 134 possibilities occur; in 52 of the 134 (39%), contractions occur; in 82 (61%), uncontracted forms occur. Since six of the authors use no contractions, and the three who do use them follow clear patterns of selection, it is evident that (1) the matter is one of option (not usage level), and (2) the magazine does not forbid contractions.

Conclusion: Observing the cultural level of the authors and the intended readers, one can see that the editors of this magazine consider contractions fully appropriate standard English.

Usage note: of the 52 contractions, 27 (50%, a high proportion) are *-n't* forms, and one author uses only these contractions; there is an evident difference between *-n't* and *-'ll, -'ve, -'re, -'s,* etc.

It's I/me, it's we/us, it's he/him, it's she/her, it's they/them

The percentages shown in the following tables were tabulated by Jean Malmstrom (Western Michigan University) from information in the Linguistic Atlas records.

The Linguistic Atlas survey on usage under the general directorship of Hans Kurath is being conducted by experts in the field for the whole country. So far only the *Linguistic Atlas of New England* has been published. This significant contribution was sponsored by the American Council of Learned Societies, assisted by universities and colleges in New England, and edited by Hans Kurath, *et al.,* 1939-1943. The other regional surveys have not been published yet. To date the work for the Middle Atlantic, South Atlantic, North Central, and Upper Midwest States has been completed. (See Appendix A, p. 241 for the states and regions which comprise each area.)

Linguistic experts interview informants of different types in the various sections of the country in order to find out what is actually said in each area. The informants are classified as follows: Type I: little formal education, little reading, and restricted contacts; Type II: better formal education (usually high school) and/or wider reading and social contacts; Type III: superior education (usually college), cultured background, wide reading, and/or extensive social contacts. In New England two other types are considered: Type A: aged, and/or regarded by the field worker as old-fashioned; Type B: middle-aged or younger, and/or regarded by the field worker as more modern.

How to use the tables below: The tables should be read line by line, not as vertical columns, to find the percentage of informants who used each variant of the item indicated. Many informants used more than one variant; in such cases the combined percentages on a line add up to more than 100.

Each line shows percentages obtained for informants of different types in the state designated. The *Total* which appears at the foot of each table is the percentage obtained for each type in the entire Atlas region under consideration.

For example, in this table for the New England area, 100% of Connecticut's Type IA informants used Variant 2 ("It's me"); none used Variant 1 ("It's I"). In New Hampshire, 100% of the Type IA informants used Variant 2, but 16% of these also used Variant 1. The *Total* figures at the foot of the "Type IA" table indicate that of all the IA informants in the New England Atlas area, 96% used Variant 2 and 9% used Variant 1.

The percentages have been carried to three places and rounded off to two. Percentages which showed 5 as the third digit, by standard mathematical procedure, have been rounded off to the nearest even number. Thus 18.5% is shown as 18%, and 15.5% is shown as 16%.

Variants: 1. *It's I;*   2. *It's me.*

NEW ENGLAND

	1.	2.	1.	2.	1.	2.	1.	2.
	Type IA		*Type IB*		*Type IIA*		*Type IIB*	
Conn.	0	100	20	80	16	89	29	71
L.I.	0	0	0	0	0	0	0	0
R.I.	20	80	100	50	33	67	33	67
Mass.	10	90	17	100	35	70	30	78
Vt.	0	100	20	100	10	90	33	75
N.H.	16	100	0	100	11	100	25	75
Me.	11	100	25	100	14	100	8	100
N.B.	0	100	0	100	0	0	0	100
Total:	9	96	25	92	20	87	26	80

	Type IIIA		*Type IIIB*		*All*	
Conn.	60	40	25	75	21	81
L.I.	0	0	0	0	0	0
R.I.	100	100	100	0	48	61
Mass.	42	58	50	67	28	78
Vt.	0	100	100	100	16	90
N.H.	50	100	0	0	17	98
Me.	50	67	0	100	16	97
N.B.	0	0	0	0	0	100
Total:	50	62	53	60	23	85

Variants: 1. *It's he, she,* and *they* (all nominative case);
2. *It's him, her,* and *them* (all accusative case);
3. *It's he;*   4. *It's him;*   5. *It's she;*   6. *It's her;*
7. *It's they;*   8. *It's them.*

NEW ENGLAND

	1.	2.	3.	4.	5.	6.	7.	8.
				Type IA				
Conn.	6	94	0	0	0	0	0	0
L.I.	0	0	0	0	0	0	0	0
R.I.	0	100	0	0	0	0	0	0
Mass.	0	85	0	6	0	10	3	0
Vt.	0	100	0	0	0	0	10	0
N.H.	5	89	0	0	0	0	0	0
Me.	0	94	0	6	0	6	0	0
N.B.	0	100	0	0	0	0	0	0
Total:	2	91	0	3	0	4	2	0
				Type IB				
Conn.	17	83	0	0	0	0	0	17
L.I.	0	0	0	0	0	0	0	0

R.I.	0	0	50	0	50	0	0	50
Mass.	0	86	0	0	0	0	0	0
Vt.	0	83	0	17	17	0	0	17
N.H.	0	100	0	0	0	0	0	0
Me.	0	100	0	25	0	0	0	0
N.B.	0	100	0	0	0	0	0	10
Total:	4	82	4	7	7	0	0	11

Type IIA

Conn.	18	82	0	0	0	0	0	0
L.I.	0	0	0	0	0	0	0	0
R.I.	33	33	0	0	17	17	0	17
Mass.	16	62	0	10	0	6	3	0
Vt.	0	75	20	15	15	5	0	10
N.H.	0	89	0	5	5	5	5	0
Me.	0	78	0	4	0	4	4	0
N.B.	0	0	0	0	0	0	0	0
Total:	8	74	3	7	4	5	2	2

Type IIB

Conn.	0	100	0	0	0	0	0	0
L.I.	0	0	0	0	0	0	0	0
R.I.	17	67	0	17	0	17	17	0
Mass.	12	76	0	8	12	4	4	12
Vt.	8	83	0	0	0	8	8	8
N.H.	0	80	0	0	0	0	0	0
Me.	0	100	0	0	0	0	0	0
N.B.	0	100	0	0	0	0	0	0
Total:	7	84	0	4	4	4	4	6

Variants: 1. *It's he, she,* and *they* (all nominative case);
2. *It's him, her,* and *them* (all accusative case);
3. *It's he;* 4. *It's him;* 5. *It's she;* 6. *It's her;*
7. *It's they;* 8. *It's them.*

NEW ENGLAND (*continued*)

	1.	2.	3.	4.	5.	6.	7.	8.
			Type IIIA					
Conn.	70	30	0	0	0	0	0	0
L.I.	0	0	0	0	0	0	0	0
R.I.	100	0	0	0	0	0	0	0
Mass.	42	17	0	17	8	17	8	8
Vt.	0	0	0	0	0	0	0	0
N.H.	50	50	0	0	0	0	0	0
Me.	17	67	25	0	25	0	0	0
N.B.	0	0	0	0	0	0	0	0
Total:	49	33	3	6	6	6	3	3

Type IIIB

Conn.	60	40	0	0	0	0	0	0
L.I.	0	0	0	0	0	0	0	0
R.I.	0	0	0	0	0	0	0	0
Mass.	33	33	33	33	0	0	17	17
Vt.	100	0	0	0	0	0	0	0
N.H.	0	0	0	0	0	0	0	0
Me.	0	100	0	0	0	0	0	0
N.B.	0	0	0	0	0	0	0	0
Total:	46	38	15	15	0	0	8	8

All

Conn.	25	75	0	0	0	0	0	2
L.I.	0	0	0	0	0	0	0	0
R.I.	22	50	6	6	11	11	6	11
Mass.	13	67	2	10	3	7	4	4
Vt.	4	82	8	8	8	4	4	8
N.H.	6	85	0	2	2	2	2	0
Me.	1	87	2	4	2	3	2	0
N.B.	0	100	0	0	0	0	0	0
Total:	11	76	2	5	3	4	3	3

Variants: 1. *It's I, he, she,* and *they* (all nominative case); 2. *It's me, him, her,* and *them* (all accusative case); 3. *It's I;* 4. *It's me;* 5. *It's he;* 6. *It's him;* 7. *It's she;* 8. *It's her;* 9. *It's they;* 10. *It's them.*

MIDDLE ATLANTIC STATES

	1.	2.	3.	4.	5.	6.	7.	8.	9.	10.

Type I

	1.	2.	3.	4.	5.	6.	7.	8.	9.	10.
N.J.	0	100	0	0	0	0	0	0	0	0
N.Y.	5	60	3	19	0	21	2	5	0	6
Pa.	0	100	0	0	0	0	0	0	0	0
W. Va.	0	100	0	0	0	0	0	0	0	0
Total:	2	87	1	6	0	7	1	2	0	2

Type II

	1.	2.	3.	4.	5.	6.	7.	8.	9.	10.
N.J.	4	88	15	4	4	4	4	4	0	8
N.Y.	1	73	8	17	0	14	1	0	1	5
Pa.	1	99	0	0	0	0	0	0	0	0
W. Va.	0	100	0	0	0	0	0	0	0	0
Total:	1	89	4	6	0	5	1	0	0	3

Type III

	1.	2.	3.	4.	5.	6.	7.	8.	9.	10.
N.J.	60	40	0	0	0	0	0	0	0	0
N.Y.	32	18	41	0	4	4	9	4	4	4
Pa.	27	66	20	7	7	0	7	0	0	7

	1.	2.	3.	4.	5.	6.	7.	8.	9.	10.
W. Va.	0	100	0	0	0	0	0	0	0	0
Total:	28	48	24	2	4	2	6	2	2	4

All

	1.	2.	3.	4.	5.	6.	7.	8.	9.	10.
N.J.	8	88	8	2	2	2	2	2	0	4
N.Y.	7	60	10	15	1	15	2	2	1	6
Pa.	3	96	2	1	1	0	1	0	0	1
W. Va.	0	100	0	0	0	0	0	0	0	0
Total:	4	84	5	6	1	6	1	1	0	3

Variants: 1. *It's I, he, she,* and *they* (all nominative case);
2. *It's me, him, her,* and *them* (all accusative case);
3. *It's I;* 4. *It's me;* 5. *It's he;* 6. *It's him;*
7. *It's she;* 8. *It's her;* 9. *It's they;* 10. *It's them.*

SOUTH ATLANTIC STATES

	1.	2.	3.	4.	5.	6.	7.	8.	9.	10.
				Type I						
D.C.	0	100	0	0	0	0	0	0	0	6
Del.	0	100	0	0	0	0	0	0	0	0
Md.	0	100	0	0	0	0	0	0	0	0
Va.	0	100	0	0	0	0	0	0	0	0
N.C.	0	100	0	0	0	0	0	0	0	0
S.C.	0	100	0	0	0	0	0	0	0	0
Ga.	0	100	0	0	0	0	0	0	0	0
Total:	0	100	0	0	0	0	0	0	0	0
				Type II						
D.C.	0	0	0	0	0	0	0	0	0	0
Del.	0	100	0	0	0	0	0	0	0	0
Md.	0	100	0	0	0	0	0	0	0	0
Va.	8	88	10	2	0	6	0	4	2	0
N.C.	0	100	0	0	0	0	0	0	0	0
S.C.	0	100	2	2	0	0	0	0	0	0
Ga.	3	97	0	0	0	0	0	0	0	0
Total:	2	96	3	1	0	1	0	1	1	0
				Type III						
D.C.	0	100	0	0	0	0	0	0	0	0
Del.	50	50	0	0	0	0	0	0	0	0
Md.	29	72	0	0	0	0	0	0	0	0
Va.	29	86	29	0	7	7	14	0	0	14
N.C.	8	83	17	8	8	0	8	0	8	0
S.C.	14	97	3	3	0	0	0	0	0	0
Ga.	13	80	7	7	0	7	7	0	0	0
Total:	18	81	10	4	2	2	5	0	1	2

All

D.C.	0	100	0	0	0	0	0	0	0	0
Del.	8	92	0	0	0	0	0	0	0	0
Md.	3	97	0	0	0	0	0	0	0	0
Va.	6	92	6	1	1	3	1	1	1	1
N.C.	1	99	1	1	1	0	1	0	1	0
S.C.	3	99	2	2	0	0	0	0	0	0
Ga.	4	95	1	1	0	1	1	0	0	0
Total:	3	96	3	1	0	1	1	0	0	0

Variants: 1. *It wasn't I;* 2. *It wasn't me.*

NEW ENGLAND

	1.	2.	1.	2.	1.	2.	1.	2.
	Type IA		*Type IB*		*Type IIA*		*Type IIB*	
Conn.	0	100	0	100	0	100	0	100
L.I.	0	100	0	100	0	100	0	100
R.I.	0	100	0	100	17	83	0	100
Mass.	0	100	0	100	9	91	4	96
Vt.	0	100	0	100	0	100	0	100
N.H.	0	100	0	100	0	100	0	100
Me.	0	100	0	100	0	100	0	100
N.B.	0	100	0	100	0	100	0	100
Total:	0	100	0	100	4	96	1	99

	Type IIIA		*Type IIIB*		*All*	
Conn.	20	80	20	80	4	96
L.I.	0	0	0	0	0	100
R.I.	100	0	100	0	21	79
Mass.	42	58	14	86	82	92
Vt.	0	100	100	0	2	98
N.H.	25	75	0	0	2	98
Me.	17	83	0	100	1	99
N.B.	0	0	0	0	0	100
Total:	29	71	35	65	5	95

NORTH CENTRAL STATES

	1.	2.	1.	2.	1.	2.	1.	2.
	Type I		*Type II*		*Type III*		*All*	
Wis.	30	85	13	93	0	0	23	89
Mich.	0	100	33	67	100	0	25	75
Ont.	0	100	0	100	100	50	15	92
Ill.	0	100	5	100	33	100	4	100
Ind.	0	100	0	100	0	100	4	100
Ky.	0	100	0	100	0	100	0	100
Ohio	3	97	7	96	33	83	8	95
Total:	5	97	6	97	35	80	8	96

UPPER MIDWEST

	1.	2.	1.	2.	1.	2.	1.	2.
	Type I		*Type II*		*Type III*		*All*	
Minn.	4	96	17	83	20	80	10	90
Iowa	0	100	18	82	67	33	12	88
N.D.	0	100	10	90	0	100	4	96
S.D.	9	91	18	82	100	0	21	79
Neb.	0	100	11	90	50	50	8	92
Total:	2	98	14	86	43	57	11	89

Reference, vague or indefinite: this (*pronominal*)

C. M. Statham (University of Florida) in his reading found the following:

		No.	*%*
This	without summarizing noun referring to preceding clause, sentence, or sentences: "The cabinet agreed it would be desirable to ask Arthur to take over, but couldn't agree whether *this* would oust Garfield for the rest of the term . . ." (*Reader's Digest,* Nov., 1947, 53)	441	72
This	with definite reference: "*This* was my home . . ." (*ibid.,* 83)	171	28
		612	100

He found *this* used in the following structures:

	No.	*%*
Subject of verb *to be* + noun	215	100
Without definite reference: "Clan by clan, as long as they feel they have won a good bargain, they are satisfied and loyal, and only when *this is* not the *case* is there trouble" (*Reporter,* Dec. 12, 1957, 32)	147	68.4
With definite reference: "*This was* the *poem* that aroused the San Francisco Police Department . . ." (*ibid.,* 37)	68	31.6
Subject of verb *to be* + adjective	50	100
Without definite reference: "A close friend with large enough living quarters (*this was vital* in jam-packed Budapest) promised to take the children in . . ." (*Better Homes and Gardens,* Dec., 1957, 120)	48	96

	No.	%

With definite reference: *"This has been* very *popular* in the week it has been on display" (*Gainesville Daily Sun,* Nov. 17, 1957, 2) — 2 — 4

Subject of verb *to be* + prepositional phrase — 6 — 100

Without definite reference: "In the long run *this is like Heifetz playing the Bach 'Double Concerto' with himself . . ."* (*Southwest Review,* Autumn, 1957, 336) — 2 — 33⅓

With definite reference: "I've got news for you, Bwana. *This is for the Kiwana"* (*Saturday Evening Post,* Nov. 23, 1957, 46) — 4 — 66⅔

Subject of verb *to be* + clause — 19 — 100

Without definite reference: ". . . and *this is where differences in societies and in governmental behavior do begin to be manifest"* (*Southwest Review,* Autumn, 1957, 291) — 16 — 84

With definite reference: "and *this is where the best buys are as well"* (*Better Homes and Gardens,* Dec., 1957, 135) — 3 — 16

Subject of verb *to be* + infinitive + noun clause — 3 — 100

Without definite reference: *"This is* not *to suggest that anything in the story is either salacious or sensational"* (*Harper's,* Sept., 1957, 20) — 3 — 100

Subject of verbs other than *to be* — 164 — 100

Without definite reference: "Under the law, if a hunter has a high-powered flashlight and a rifle in his car at the same time, *this serves* as a prima-facie evidence of guilt" (*Saturday Evening Post,* Nov. 23, 1957, 53) — 114 — 69.5

With definite reference: *"This is driven* into the top of the frame . . ." (*Popular Mechanics,* Nov., 1957, 171) — 50 — 30.5

Subjective complement — 8 — 100

Without definite reference: " 'It's *this,'* said Little. 'Don't fool around with established spellbinders in big churches' " (*Saturday Evening Post,* Nov. 23, 1957, 120) — 7 — 87.5

With definite reference: " 'What I meant by specifics *is this,'* he said . . ." (*ibid.,* 114) — 1 — 12.5

	No.	%
Object of verb	69	100
Without definite reference: "But the Army says that its Nikes can search out and outrun any invading bomber or group of bombers. Can the Bomarc *do this?*" (*Reporter*, Dec. 12, 1957, 24)	50	72.5
With definite reference: "If you *produce this,* you should have your head examined" (*Theatre Arts,* Nov., 1957, 85)	19	27.5
Object of preposition	74	100
Without definite reference: "The chorus work was outstanding, noteworthy particularly for its balanced voices, incisive attacks and precise diction. *For this,* Gordon Page as director deserves high praise" (*Musical America,* Sept., 1947, 3)	53	71.6
With definite reference: "He wished his daddy would buy him a gate *like this*" (*Southwest Review,* Autumn, 1957, 306)	21	28.4
Absolute use	3	100
Without definite reference: ". . . an unexpected anouncement came . . . that Szell had signed a three-year contract with the Amsterdam Concertgebouw—*this* despite the fact that he had just extended his Cleveland tenure for the same period . . ." (*Musical America,* Sept., 1957, 19)	2	66⅔
With definite reference: "*This* and a hen, which only she could see" (*Southwest Review,* Autumn, 1957, 268)	1	33⅓
Nominative absolute	1	100
With definite reference: "Bringing the festival to a colorful close were two nights termed 'Festival of Lebanese Folklore,' which were stagings of ceremonials and dancing. Excitement ran at high pitch for days beforehand, *this being* the first affair of the kind ever given here" (*Musical America,* Sept., 1957, 15)		

Material read: Robert Penn Warren, *World Enough and Time,* N. Y.: Random House, 1950 (15 pp.); Shirley Jackson, "The Lottery" (8 pp.), Carson McCullers, "The Jockey" (5 pp.), J. D. Salinger, "A Perfect

Day for Bananafish" (11 pp.), James Thurber, "The Catbird Seat" (8 pp.), E. B. White, "The Second Tree from the Corner" (5 pp.), *55 Short Stories from the New Yorker*, N. Y.: Simon and Schuster, 1949; *Better Homes and Gardens*, Dec., 1957 (150 pp.); *Coronet*, Nov., 1957 (178 pp.); *Harper's*, Sept., 1957 (104 pp.); *Musical America*, Sept., 1957; *National Geographic Magazine*, Nov., 1957 (49 pp.); *The New Yorker*, July 27, 1957 (76 pp.); *Popular Mechanics*, Nov., 1957 (275 pp.); *Reader's Digest*, Nov., 1957 (252 pp.); *Reporter*, Dec. 12, 1957 (48 pp.); *Saturday Evening Post*, Nov. 23, 1957 (150 pp.); *Saturday Review*, Nov. 23, 1957 (46 pp.); *Science News Letter*, July 20, 1957 (15 pp.); *Southwest Review*, Autumn, 1957 (115 pp.); *Theatre Arts*, Nov., 1957 (96 pp.); *Gainesville Daily Sun*, Nov. 17-22 (106 pp.).

Sentence modifier

Micaela Hickey (Brooklyn College) in her reading found 600 sentence modifiers. Of this number 236 were clauses introduced by such conjunctions as *so, when, after, since, because, although,* and *if,* which influenced the main statement as a whole, as in (1) *"If Aunt Mary never married,* it was not because of absence of opportunity" (*Atlantic Monthly*, Nov., 1957, 88); (2) "The family legend has it that he took it over as a debt, *although this seems to be belied by facts"* (*ibid.,* 87); (3) *"When blight or improvement spreads,* it comes along the street" (*Fortune*, Apr., 1958, 139); (4) *"Because teachers' standards vary in the same measure as teachers' personalities,* there are as many standards in a traditional school as there are teachers" (*Better Homes and Gardens*, Oct., 1956, 176); (5) "In such conferences, the parent is cautioned against comparing Bill with a neighbor child or another member of the family, *since no two children are alike* (*ibid.,* 178); (6) "But by 1963, *if the U. S. population continues to grow at its present pace and the proportion of young men and women going to college keeps on increasing at its current rate,* U. S. college enrollment will hit 5.3 million" (*Popular Science*, Apr., 1957, 94). Of these clauses 187 (79%) were at the beginning of the sentence, as in Sentences (1), (3), (4); 42 (18%) at the end, as in Sentences (2) and (5); and 7 (3%) were within the sentence, as in Sentence (6).

She also found 13 present participial constructions, as in (1) *"Considering the importance of their mission,* their implements looked surprisingly crude" (*Coronet*, May, 1958, 52) and (2) "Therefore they should exert more pull on a satellite than either flat land or mountains, thus *bringing the satellite closer to the earth and . . ."* (*National Geographic Magazine*, Dec., 1957, 797); 3 past participial constructions, as in (1) *"Given these several considerations,* the situation of the American intellectual (real or self-styled) appears less horrendous"

(*Southwest Review*, Winter, 1958, 68) and (2) "What proportion of our wealth and energy should be put into defense, *given the present international political context?*" (*Current History*, Oct., 1957, 212); 5 nominative absolute constructions, as in (1) *"The very future of science and the national defense being so closely entwined*, there must be the closest harmony of effect between the two spheres" (*Bulletin of the Atomic Scientists*, May, 1958, 170), and (2) *"That done*, he gave the downbeat for a resounding triad and . . ." (*Musical America*, Apr., 1958, 14); 6 infinitival constructions, as in *"To do that*, we must maintain a balance among all our needs . . ." ("Editorial," *Wall Street Journal*, May 21, 1958, 12); 18 prepositional phrases, as in *"In this dependence on maps as some sort of higher reality*, project planners and urban designers assume they can create a promenade simply by mapping one in where they want it" (*Fortune*, Apr., 1958, 140); and 319 conjunctive adverbs (words and word groups), such as *however, nevertheless, likewise, indeed, perhaps, therefore, consequently, in the meantime, in the first place, in fact, on the other hand, in turn, on the whole, of course*, as in (1) *"Of course*, I might have chosen a more representative case" (*Commonweal*, Mar. 7, 1957, 583); (2) *"Perhaps* these few examples furnish some general notion of the literary-political picture" (*ibid.*, 583); (3) *"Conversely*, the absence of a sustaining emotion . . . may owe much to the neo-classicism now very much in vogue" (*ibid.*, 584); (4) "The so called 'scientific mind,' *on the other hand*, belongs to the longhair, the dreamer . . ." (*Bulletin of the Atomic Scientists*, May, 1958, 169); (5) "He was still busy with revisions until the second week, *in fact*" ("Editorial," *Theatre Arts*, May, 1958, 10).

All these constructions functioned as sentence modifiers—some at the beginning of the sentence, some at the end, and some embedded in the sentence, as illustrated in the preceding examples.

FREQUENCY AND POSITION OF SENTENCE MODIFIERS

	Number	First	Last	Internal
Clauses introduced by conjunctions	236 (39.3%)	187 (79%)	42 (18%)	7 (3%)
Present participial constructions	13 (2.2%)	9 (69.2%)	2 (15.4%)	2 (15.4%)
Past participial constructions	3 (.5%)	3 (100%)	0	0
Nominative absolute constructions	5 (.8%)	4 (80%)	1 (20%)	0
Infinitival constructions	6 (1%)	6 (100%)	0	0
Prepositional phrases	18 (3%)	14 (77.8%)	1 (5.5%)	3 (16.7%)
Conjunctive adverbs (words and word groups)	319 (53.2%)	245 (77.%)	10 (3%)	64 (20%)
	600 (100%)	468 (78%)	56 (9.33%)	76 (12.67%)

SENTENCE

	Clauses introduced by conjunctions				Present participial constructions				Past participial constructions			
	Position				*Position*				*Position*			
	Number	First	Last	Internal	Number	First	Last	Internal	Number	First	Last	Internal
Atlantic Monthly	15	8	5	2	2	1	1	0	0	0	0	0
Better Homes and Gardens	11	10	1	0	0	0	0	0	0	0	0	0
Bulletin of the Atomic Scientists	2	2	0	0	0	0	0	0	0	0	0	0
Commonweal	2	1	0	1	0	0	0	0	0	0	0	0
Coronet	8	6	2	0	1	1	0	0	0	0	0	0
Cosmopolitan	11	10	1	0	0	0	0	0	0	0	0	0
Current History	10	10	0	0	1	1	0	0	1	1	0	0
Fortune	7	5	2	0	1	1	0	0	0	0	0	0
Good Housekeeping	11	11	0	0	0	0	0	0	0	0	0	0
Look	8	6	2	0	1	1	0	0	0	0	0	0
Musical America	6	5	1	0	0	0	0	0	1	1	0	0
National Geographic Magazine	10	9	1	0	1	0	0	1	0	0	0	0
New York Times, Mar. 9, 1958	9	9	0	0	0	0	0	0	0	0	0	0
New York Times, Mar. 23, 1958	5	3	2	0	1	0	0	1	0	0	0	0
New York Times, Apr. 5, 1958	3	1	2	0	0	0	0	0	0	0	0	0
New York Times, Book Review, Mar. 16, 1958	8	7	0	1	0	0	0	0	0	0	0	0
New Yorker	10	6	4	0	0	0	0	0	0	0	0	0
Popular Science	15	13	1	1	0	0	0	0	0	0	0	0
Reader's Digest	15	12	1	2	0	0	0	0	0	0	0	0
Reporter	5	3	2	0	3	3	0	0	0	0	0	0
Saturday Evening Post	12	10	2	0					0	0	0	0
Saturday Review	6	3	3	0	0	0	0	0	0	0	0	0
Sewanee Review	15	12	3	0	0	0	0	0	0	0	0	0
Southwest Review	3	3	0	0	0	0	0	0	1	1	0	0
Theatre Arts	6	5	1	0	0	0	0	0	0	0	0	0
U.S. News & World Report	6	3	3	0	2	1	1	0	0	0	0	0
Wall Street Journal	4	2	2	0	0	0	0	0	0	0	0	0
Cozzens, J. G., By Love Possessed	9	9	0	0	0	0	0	0	0	0	0	0
Welty, Eudora, Delta Wedding	4	3	1	0	0	0	0	0	0	0	0	0
Totals:	236	187	42	7	13	9	2	2	3	3	0	0

MODIFIERS

Nominative absolute constructions				Infinitival constructions				Prepositional phrases				Conjunctive adverbs (words and word groups)			
Position				*Position*				*Position*				*Position*			
Number	First	Last	Internal	Number	First	Last	Internal	Number	First	Last	Internal	Number	First	Last	Internal
0	0	0	0	0	0	0	0	1	1	0	0	8	8	0	0
0	0	0	0	0	0	0	0	0	0	0	0	8	7	1	0
1	1	0	0	0	0	0	0	1	1	0	0	9	6	0	3
0	0	0	0	0	0	0	0	1	1	0	0	9	9	0	0
0	0	0	0	1	1	0	0	0	0	0	0	15	13	0	2
0	0	0	0	0	0	0	0	0	0	0	0	12	10	1	1
1	1	0	0	0	0	0	0	0	0	0	0	17	9	0	8
0	0	0	0	0	0	0	0	1	1	0	0	8	4	0	4
0	0	0	0	0	0	0	0	0	0	0	0	5	3	2	0
0	0	0	0	0	0	0	0	0	0	0	0	18	16	0	2
1	1	0	0	0	0	0	0	0	0	0	0	11	7	2	2
0	0	0	0	1	1	0	0	0	0	0	0	22	19	1	2
0	0	0	0	0	0	0	0	0	0	0	0	11	10	0	1
0	0	0	0	0	0	0	0	4	3	0	1	13	11	0	2
0	0	0	0	0	0	0	0	0	0	0	0	10	6	0	4
0	0	0	0	0	0	0	0	0	0	0	0	11	8	0	3
0	0	0	0	0	0	0	0	0	0	0	0	11	11	0	0
0	0	0	0	0	0	0	0	0	0	0	0	9	6	1	2
0	0	0	0	1	1	0	0	0	0	0	0	9	6	0	3
1	0	1	0	0	0	0	0	3	2	0	1	13	11	0	2
0	0	0	0	1	1	0	0	1	1	0	0	6	6	0	0
0	0	0	0	0	0	0	0	3	3	0	0	5	4	0	1
0	0	0	0	0	0	0	0	4	2	1	1	10	4	1	5
0	0	0	0	0	0	0	0	2	2	0	0	4	2	0	2
0	0	0	0	0	0	0	0	0	0	0	0	9	5	1	3
0	0	0	0	0	0	0	0	1	1	0	0	13	7	0	6
0	0	0	0	2	2	0	0	0	0	0	0	15	10	0	5
1	1	0	0	0	0	0	0	0	0	0	0	10	10	0	0
0	0	0	0	0	0	0	0	0	0	0	0	18	17	0	1
5	4	1	0	6	6	0	0	18	14	1	3	319	245	10	64

Material read: (fiction) James Gould Cozzens, *By Love Possessed,* New York: Harcourt, Brace and Company, 1957 (14 pp.); Eudora Welty, *Delta Wedding,* New York: Harcourt, Brace and Company, 1946 (12 pp.); (magazines and newspapers) *The Atlantic Monthly,* November, 1957 (6 pp.); *Better Homes and Gardens,* October, 1956 (9 pp.); *Bulletin of the Atomic Scientists,* May, 1958 (4 pp.); *Commonweal,* March 7, 1958 (4 pp.); *Coronet,* May, 1958 (14 pp.); *Cosmopolitan,* March, 1958 (6 pp.); *Current History,* October, 1957 (8 pp.); *Fortune,* April, 1958 (7 pp.); *Good Housekeeping,* February, 1958 (7 pp.); *Look,* April 1, 1958 (11 pp.); *Musical America,* April, 1958 (4 pp.); *National Geographic Magazine,* December, 1957 (14 pp.); *The New York Times,* March 9, 23, April 5, 1958 (5 pp.); *The New York Times Book Review,* March 16, 1958 (4 pp.); *The New Yorker,* March 8, 1958 (12 pp.); *Popular Science,* April, 1957 (16 pp.); *Reader's Digest,* March, 1958 (14 pp.); *The Reporter,* April 17, 1958 (5 pp.); *Saturday Evening Post,* April 26, 1958 (10 pp.); *Saturday Review,* March 29, 1958 (4 pp.); *Sewanee Review,* Winter, 1958 (15 pp.); *Southwest Review,* Winter, 1958 (4 pp.); *Theatre Arts,* May, 1958 (4 pp.); *U.S. News & World Report,* November 1, 1957 (12 pp.); *Wall Street Journal,* May 21, 1958 (2 pp.).

APPENDIX E
Contributors of Studies

Below are the names of the investigators who contributed one or more studies to this book. Following each name is the institution with which the investigator was affiliated while conducting the investigation, and the contribution made.

Abbot, Mildred E., Western Reserve University: if, whether; prove, *v.*
Abelack, Alvin, Brooklyn College: but what; ring, *v.*
Abowitz, Libby, Brooklyn College: bring, *v.;* lot(s), heap(s).
Adams, Klara, Western Reserve University: agreement, collective nouns; agreement, indefinite pronouns; each other, one another; one in (of, out of) four (eight, twenty, etc.).
Agress, Shirley, Brooklyn College: eat, *v.*
Algeo, John, University of Florida: get, *v.;* of in *could of, couldn't of, should of, shouldn't of, would of,* etc.
Allen, Harold B., University of Minnesota: agreement, here is (are), was (were); begin, *v.;* blow, *v.;* dive, *v.;* fit, *v.;* kind (sort) of (a, an); kneel, *v.;* like, *conj.;* off, off of, offen, from, off from; ride, *v.;* stomp, *v.;* take sick.
Alloco, Salvatore, Brooklyn College: on (the) stage.
Alter, Doris, Brooklyn College: toward, towards.

Altman, Harriet, Brooklyn College: you, indefinite.
Altman, Ileane, Brooklyn College: agreement, indefinite pronouns.
Amster, Jane, Brooklyn College: they, indefinite.
Anderson, Frances, University of Chicago: agenda, *n.;* less, fewer; let's, let us, let's us; like for; off, off of, offen, from, off from; so, *conj.;* what with.
Asman, Janet Goldberg, Brooklyn College: get, *v.*
Atsaves, Ann, Brooklyn College: you all.
Atwood, E. Bagby, University of Texas: home.
Augustine, Angela, Western Reserve University: agreement, indefinite pronouns.
Aviles, José, Brooklyn College: leave, let; let's, let us, let's us; let's not, let's don't.

Baker, William Francis, III, Brooklyn College: so, *conj.*
Banker, Brash, Western Reserve University: agreement, indefinite pronouns.
Banschick, Phyllis, Brooklyn College: nowhere near.
Baron, Alvin, Brooklyn College: case, genitive of nouns that name inanimate things; genitive case.
Basner, Charlotte, Brooklyn College: equally, equally as, just as.
Basse, Earle, Brooklyn College: awful, *adj., adv.,* awfully, *adv.*
Bauer, Heinz C., Brooklyn College: on, upon.
Baus, Charlotte, Western Reserve University: agreement, indefinite pronouns.
Beauchamp, Emerson, Jr., University of Kentucky: it.
Berg, Alan, Brooklyn College: if, whether.
Berkowitz, Edward, Brooklyn College: phenomenon.
Berkowitz, Elroy, Brooklyn College: bad, badly.
Berkowitz, Ethel, Brooklyn College: awful, *adj., adv.,* awfully, *adv.*
Berman, Donna, Brooklyn College: can't seem to.
Bernadete, Doris, Western State College of Colorado: anyplace, *adv.; between* with more than two; blame . . . for (on); different from, than, to; get, *v.;* if, whether; kind (sort) of (a, an); try and; *when-* (*where-*) clauses after verb *to be;* who, whom.
Bernstein, Ruth T., Brooklyn College: *of* in *could of, couldn't of, should of, shouldn't of, would of,* etc.
Billias, Matina, Brooklyn College: get, *v.;* I haven't.
Black, Marjorie, Western Reserve University: agreement, indefinite pronouns.
Blomquist, Helen, University of Wisconsin: as (so) long as, *conj.;* equally, equally as, just as; like, *conj.*
Blumengarten, Jeannette, Brooklyn College: climb, *v.*
Bodoh, John, University of Wisconsin: like, *conj.*
Bonander, Alice, Brooklyn College: rise, *v.*
Bongiorno, Dominick, Brooklyn College: (in) back of, behind; pretty.
Bowden, Muriel, Hunter College: agreement, number of verb after *one of* *those who* (*which, that*); any more, *adv.;* at about; (a)wake, (a)waken; bad, badly; but what; get, *v.;* less, fewer; lie, lay, *v.;* more than one; most, almost; nowhere near phenomenon; what with.
Bowman, F. E., Duke University: contractions.
Brachfeld, Harriet, Brooklyn College: like, *conj.*

Brant, Mary, Brooklyn College: at about.
Brazeau, Paula, University of Wisconsin: in regard(s) to; like, *conj.*
Breiter, Lila, Brooklyn College: folk(s).
Bring, Gloria, Brooklyn College: run, *v.*
Broth, Marilyn, Western Reserve University: agreement, indefinite pronouns.
Brown, Leon, Brooklyn College: freeze, *v.*
Bruno, Alfred, Brooklyn College: if, whether.
Bryant, Margaret M., Brooklyn College: agreement, indefinite pronouns; fix, *n. v.;* want to (should).
Buchbinder, Gwen, Brooklyn College: type, type of.
Burke, Martin, Brooklyn College: fine.

Cahill, Carol, Brooklyn College: each other, one another; see, *v.*
Cahn, Robert, Brooklyn College: had better (best); had (would) rather.
Carswell, Alice, University of Wisconsin: as (so) long as, *conj.;* like, *conj.*
Carter, Edna, Western Reserve University: agreement, indefinite pronouns.
Chapnitsky, Esther, University of Wisconsin: as (so) long as, *conj.;* as to; like, *conj.*
Cherney, Iris, Brooklyn College: myself.
Chovan, Anne, Western Reserve University: drive, *v.;* prove, *v.*
Christensen, Francis, University of Southern California: agreement, *what-*clauses; *and (but, or, nor)* at the beginning of a sentence; less, fewer; like, *conj.;* nominative absolute.
Church, Meredith, University of Wisconsin: equally, equally as, just as; like, *conj.*
Class, Marilyn, University of Wisconsin: like, *conj.*
Cohen, Arlene, Brooklyn College: rarely ever.
Cohen, Joel, University of Chicago: but what.
Cohen, Leon B., Brooklyn College: just, *adv.*
Cohen, Rhoda, Brooklyn College: just, *adv.*
Cohen, Seymour, Brooklyn College: comparative, incomplete.
Coles, Bernice, Brooklyn College: above, *adj., n.*
Collins, Ann, Brooklyn College: can't seem to; shrink, *v.*
Collins, Eileen T., Brooklyn College: shrink, *v.*
Conciglia, Philip, Brooklyn College: agreement, (n)either . . . (n)or; bad, badly.
Concool, Marilyn, Brooklyn College: different from, than, to.
Cook, A. B., III, Western Reserve University: prove, *v.;* show, *v.*
Cooper, Robert, Brooklyn College: human, *n.*
Cooperman, Sylvia, Brooklyn College: take, *v.*
Coxe, Malcolm S., Brooklyn College: agreement, collective nouns; agreement, there is (are), was (were); get, *v.;* like, *conj.*
Cutler, Gordon M., Brooklyn College: no good, worthless.

Dalles, Trudy, University of Wisconsin: like, *conj.*
Daly, Ann M., Brooklyn College: can, may, *v.*
Daly, Marie, Brooklyn College: each other, one another.
D'Ambrosio, Vinnie Marie, Brooklyn College: teach, learn.

Daughton, Eileen M., Brooklyn College: tear, v.
Desberg, Dan, Western Reserve University: prove, v.
Dickson, Arthur, City College of New York: fit, v.
Di Natale, Marian, Brooklyn College: throw, v.
Donkle, Elizabeth, University of Wisconsin: equally, equally as, just as; get, v.; like, conj.; like to, almost.
Downing, Vincent, Brooklyn College: give, v.
Drdek, Richard E.: case, of noun or pronoun subject of a gerund.
Dunlap, A. R., University of Delaware: preposition at end of clause or sentence.

Edelman, Adele, Brooklyn College: come, v.
Edelstein, Shirley, Brooklyn College: reference, vague or indefinite: this, that (pronominal).
Edgerton, Sue, University of Wisconsin: as (so) long as, conj.; as to; equally, equally as, just as; like, conj.
Eldin, S. M. Gamal, University of Texas: comparative, absolute; comparative, incomplete; superlative with two objects.
Emblen, D. L., San Diego State College: case, genitive of nouns that name inanimate things.
Erickson, Roger, University of Wisconsin: like, conj.
Etkin, Stanley, Brooklyn College: farther, further.
Everson, Ida, Wagner College: can't (cannot), couldn't (could not) help but; different from, than, to; like, conj.; reason . . . is because (reason is that).
Ezagui, Camille, Brooklyn College: wait on, wait for.

Fagen, Jane, Brooklyn College: kind (sort) of (a, an); those (these) kind (sort) of.
Fagen, Nancy, Brooklyn College: do, v.; home.
Faust, George P., University of Kentucky: it; relative pronouns and clauses; that, sub. conj.
Feeney, Kathleen, Hunter College: get, v.
Fein, Robert, Brooklyn College: dare, v.; toward, towards; type, type of.
Felberbaum, Stanley, Brooklyn College: dare, v.
Fetouh, Hilmi M., University of Texas: comparative, absolute; comparative, incomplete; comparison, illogical; superlative with two objects.
Fink, Marjorie, University of Wisconsin: equally, equally as, just as; like, conj.
Fisch, Adele, Brooklyn College: between with more than two; due to, because of, owing to.
Fischler, Norma, Brooklyn College: fine; good, well.
Flannery, Joan M., Brooklyn College: ain't, am not, is not, are not; am I not? ain't I? aren't I?; graduate (from).
Fleming, Dennis, Brooklyn College: ring, v.; sing, v.; sink, v.
Flick, Josephine, Brooklyn College: farther, further.
Fox, John J., Brooklyn College: without, unless.
Frankel, Arnold, Brooklyn College: due to, because of, owing to.

Freedman, Georgette Helen, Brooklyn College: we were, you were, they were.

Friedman, Frances, Brooklyn College: passive construction.

Fries, Suzanne, University of Wisconsin: as (so) long as, *conj.;* equally, equally as, just as; like, *conj.*

Frigand, Sidney J., Brooklyn College: agreement, collective nouns.

Frost, Mary Ann, Brooklyn College: preposition at end of clause or sentence.

Fuhr, Morton, Brooklyn College: nowhere near.

Gabel, Irving, Brooklyn College: ain't, am not, is not, are not; bust, *v., n.;* in regard(s) to.

Garey, Ann, Brooklyn College: know, *v.;* spell, *v.*

Garron, David C., Brooklyn College: don't, *v.*

Gay, Thomas, Western Reserve University: agreement, indefinite pronouns.

Geekie, William F., Brooklyn College: teach, learn.

Geensburg, Joan A., Duke University: contractions.

Geist, Robert J., Michigan State University: agreement, there is (are), was (were); as, *causal.*

Gellman, Doreen, Brooklyn College: if, whether.

Gentry, Anne, University of Alabama: agreement, indefinite pronouns.

Gerdy, Celia V., Brooklyn College: genitive case.

Gershowitz, Daniel, Brooklyn College: more than one.

Gitter, Daniel, Brooklyn College: invite, *n.;* show up, *v.*

Goetz, Ruth, Brooklyn College: not, illogically placed.

Gold, Herbert M., Brooklyn College: taxi, *n., v.*

Gold, Leonard, Brooklyn College: kind (sort) of (a, an); those (these) kind (sort) of.

Gold, Rahla, Brooklyn College: type, type of.

Goldberg, Rhoda, Brooklyn College: fix, *n., v.*

Goldfarb, Ilse, Brooklyn College: agreement, indefinite pronouns.

Goldman, Myra, Brooklyn College: lot(s), heap(s).

Goldstein, Arthur D., Brooklyn College: just, *adv.;* only, *adv.*

Golub, Rose S., Brooklyn College: comparison, dual.

Goodman, Judith, Western Reserve University: indefinite pronouns.

Greenberg, Jacob, Brooklyn College: though, although.

Greene, Ruth M., Brooklyn College: reason . . . is because (reason is that).

Gross, E. P., University of Chicago: didn't use to; get, *v.;* (in) back of, behind; less, fewer; so, *conj.*

Guskin, Allen S., Brooklyn College: lot(s), heap(s).

Hahn, S. T., Columbia University: can't (cannot), couldn't (could not) help but.

Haase, Gladys D., Brooklyn College: agreement, indefinite pronouns; *between* with more than two; broadcast, *v.;* can, may, *v.;* contact, *v.;* different from, than, to; like for; only, *adv.;* type, type of; what with.

Haggerty, Helen, Hunter College: bad, badly.

Hagopian, Jo, Western Reserve University: agreement, collective nouns.

Halbrecht, Goldie, Brooklyn College: don't, *v.*

Hansen, Ronn, University of Wisconsin: am I not? ain't I? aren't I?; like, *conj.*

Hanson, H. L., Western Reserve University: agreement, collective nouns; agreement, indefinite pronouns.

Harris, Jean, Brooklyn College: for to.

Harrison, James, University of Alabama: didn't use to.

Hartdegen, Joseph, Brooklyn College: drag, *v.;* take sick.

Hartman, Myrna, Brooklyn College: dream, *v.*

Hartman, Paul, Arizona State College: real, really.

Hartz, Renée, Brooklyn College: all the farther (further), as far as; jell, *v.*

Hearden, Jeanette, University of Wisconsin: equally, equally as, just as; like, *conj.*

Heisler, Helen, Brooklyn College: reason . . . is because (reason is that).

Henderson, P., University of Kentucky: shall, will.

Henry, Hazel, Brooklyn College: slow, slowly.

Henry, Helen, Brooklyn College: genitive case.

Herold, George A., Arizona State College: can, may, *v.*

Hessel, Frieda, Brooklyn College: preposition at end of clause or sentence.

Hewitt, Helen, Brooklyn College: every, *adv.*

Hickey, Micaela, Brooklyn College: any more, *adv.;* dangling modifier (misrelated); human, *n.;* nominative absolute; sentence modifier.

Hider, Marilyn: due to, because of, owing to.

Hirsch, Ruth, Brooklyn College: contractions; while, *conj.*

Hochberg, Shirley, Brooklyn College: anyhow, anyway, *adv.;* price.

Holihan, Brian, Brooklyn College: any more, *adv.;* date, *n., v.*

Holster, Joan B., Brooklyn College: date, *n., v.*

Hook, J. N., University of Illinois: blame . . . for (on); get, *v.;* kind (sort) of (a, an); myself; prove, *v.;* those (these) kind (sort) of.

Horn, Larry, Brooklyn College: blame . . . for (on).

Horwitz, Barbara, Brooklyn College: wear, *v.*

Hosig, Carol, University of Wisconsin: equally, equally as, just as; like, *conj.*

Hotchner, Cecilia A., Hunter College: above, *adj., n.;* agreement, number of verb after *one of those who* (*which, that*); arithmetical formulas; as (so) long as, *conj.;* as to; at about; (a)wake, (a)waken; begin, *v.;* boil, *v.;* bought(en); break, *v.;* burst, *v.;* bust, *v., n.;* but what; can, may, *v.;* can't (cannot), couldn't (could not) help but; comparative, absolute; comparative, incomplete; comparison, dual; comparison, illogical; dare, *v.;* date, *n.,v.;* dive, *v.;* drag, *v.;* dream, *v.;* drink, *v.;* drown, *v.;* due to, because of, owing to; each other, one another; every, *adv.;* feel, *v.;* freeze, *v.;* get, *v.;* good, well; graduate (from); hang, *v.;* hardly; if, whether; (in) back of, behind; it; kill, *v.;* kneel, *v.;* leave, let; less, fewer; let's, let us, let's us; lie, lay, *v.;* loan, *v.;* most, almost; no good, worthless; nominative absolute; not . . . but; not, illogically placed; nowhere near; off, off of, offen, from, off from; outside, outside of; pair(s); phenomenon; reason . . . is because (reason is that); reference, vague or indefinite: this (pronominal); ride, *v.;* ring, *v.;* sink, *v.;* sit, set, *v.;* slow, slowly; so, *adv.;* so, *conj.;* spill, *v.;* split infinitive; spoil, *v.;* stink, *v.;* strike, *v.;* the way, just as, as, *sub. conj.;* try and; *very* with past participle; want to (should);

way, away, *adv.;* way, ways; what with; *when-(where-)* clause after verb *to be.*

Howard, Barbara, Brooklyn College: whose, of which.

Isseks, Edward, Brooklyn College: different from, than, to.

Jacobson, Jack, Brooklyn College: (a)wake, (a)waken; calf, *n.;* dive, *v.;* heave, *v.;* hoof, *n.;* knife, *n.;* ox, *n.;* plead, *v.;* speed, *v.;* weave, *v.;* wolf, *n.*

Jacobson, Roy, Brooklyn College: can't (cannot), couldn't (could not) help but; double genitive.

Kafka, Irwin R., Brooklyn College: you all.

Kalina, Hermine, Brooklyn College: can't (cannot), couldn't (could not) help but; double negative; hardly.

Kane, Stephen, Brooklyn College: sure, surely; what all; what with.

Kanner, Edith, Brooklyn College: provided, providing, *conj.*

Karlin, Lillian, Brooklyn College: boil, *v.;* but what; (in) back of, behind; kill, *v.;* spill, *v.;* spoil, *v.*

Kashtan, Hadassah, Brooklyn College: arithmetical formulas.

Katzman, Allen, Brooklyn College: grow, *v.*

Kaufman, Lydia J., Brooklyn College: the way, just as, as, *sub. conj.;* way, away, *adv.;* way, ways.

Kaye, Siria Karan, Brooklyn College: draw, *v.*

Kehl, Del, University of Wisconsin: (a)wake, (a)waken; begin, *v.;* blow, *v.;* burst, *v.;* catch, *v.;* draw, *v.;* feel, *v.;* kill, *v.;* kneel, *v.;* leave, let; lie, lay, *v.;* like, *conj.;* off, off of, offen, from, off from; sit, set, *v.;* so, *conj.;* spill, *v.*

Kennedy, Constance, Brooklyn College: broadcast, *v.;* mighty, *adv.*

Kerner, Everett, Brooklyn College: stomp, *v.*

Kilimnik, Gladys, Brooklyn College: as to.

Kindschi, Karen, University of Wisconsin: as (so) long, as, *conj.;* equally, equally as, just as.

Klaperman, Libby, Brooklyn College: wear, *v.*

Kleinman, Brenda, Brooklyn College: on, onto, on to.

Kleinman, Ruth, Brooklyn College: kind (sort) of (a, an).

Klinner, Joanne, University of Wisconsin: as (so) long as, *conj.;* like, *conj.*

Kovitz, Ethel, University of Chicago: agreement, number of verb after *one of those who (which, that)*; but what; get, *v.;* split infinitive; *very* with past participle.

Krause, Edmund, Brooklyn College: till, until.

Krauss, C., University of Wisconsin: like, *conj.*

Krauss, Michael E., Western Reserve University; agreement, indefinite pronouns; one . . . one.

Kravitz, Suzanne, Western Reserve University: agreement, indefinite pronouns.

Krug, Lillian, Brooklyn College: the way, just as, as, *sub. conj.*

Krupitsky, Melvin, Brooklyn College: anyplace, *adv.*
Kurtz, Hobart William, Brooklyn College: anywhere, anywheres.

Lakso, Doris, Western Reserve University: agreement, indefinite pronouns.
Lang, Ruth, Brooklyn College: data, datum, *n.*
Lederman, Gerald J., Brooklyn College: like to, almost; nowhere near.
Leibson, Sydelle, Brooklyn College: write, *v.*
Leon, Herbert, Brooklyn College: hang, *v.*
Lerdahl, Esther, University of Wisconsin: equally, equally as, just as; like, *conj.*
Lesser, Doris, Brooklyn College: toward, towards.
Levine, Barbara, Brooklyn College: folk(s).
Levine, Harold D., Brooklyn College: good and.
Levine, Helen B., Brooklyn College: bad. badly.
Levine, Minnie, Hunter College: let's not, let's don't.
Levy, Doris, Brooklyn College: buy, *n.*
Lichtman, Murray, Brooklyn College: can't seem to; different from, than, to.
Lightcap, Carmen, Brooklyn College: inside, inside of; outside, outside of.
Lindsay, Jean, Hunter College: split infinitive.
Lipschultz, Janet, Brooklyn College: do, *v.*
Loos, Marcia, Brooklyn College: stomp, *v.;* strike, *v.*
Louis, Jean, Hunter College: ain't, am not, is not, are not.
Lucke, Jessie R., North Texas State College: one . . . one.

Malanaphy, Hugh J., Brooklyn College: good, well; such, *pron.*
Maldou, Joyce, Brooklyn College: know-how, *n.*
Malmstrom, Jean, Western Michigan University: ain't, am not, is not, are not; am I not? ain't I? aren't I?; agreement, there is (are), was (were); all the farther (further), as far as; anywhere, anywheres; a-singing and a-laughing; because, on account of; begin, *v.;* bite, *v.;* blow, *v.;* bought(en); bring, *v.;* catch, *v.;* climb, *v.;* come, *v.;* did, done; dive, *v.;* draw, *v.;* drink, *v.;* drive, *v.;* drown, *v.;* eat, *v.;* for to; freeze, *v.;* give, *v.;* grow, *v.;* he don't; home; I haven't; (in) back of, behind; -ing, -in (participial endings); it's I/me, it's we/us, it's he/him, it's she/her, it's they/them; kind (sort) of (a, an); lie, lay, *v.;* like, *conj.;* off, off of, offen, from, off from; ought not; ride, *v.;* rise, *v.;* run, *v.;* see, *v.;* shall, will; shrink, *v.;* sit, set, *v.;* swim, *v.;* take, *v.;* teach, learn; tear, *v.;* the farthest, the furthest; this (these) here, that (those) there; those, them; throw, *v.;* want off; way, ways; we were, you were, they were; wear, *v.;* without, unless; write, *v.*
Martindale, Beverle, Western Reserve University: agreement, indefinite pronouns.
Matia, Jane, Western Reserve University: agreement, collective nouns.
Mauchel, Frank, Hunter College: above, *adj.. n.*
McCann, Ruth, Brooklyn College: doctor, *v.*
McDavid, Raven I., Jr., Western Reserve University: show, *v.*
McDermott, Henry F., Brooklyn College: tear, *v.*

McGill, Patricia, Hunter College: am I not? ain't I? aren't I?

McGrath, Edward P., Brooklyn College: throw, *v.*

McMillan, James B., University of Alabama: ain't, am not, is not, are not; all (of); bust, *v., n.;* can't (cannot), couldn't (could not) help but; contractions; different from, than, to; double negative; get, *v.;* if, whether; like *conj.;* so, *adv.; very* with past participle; *when- (where-)* clause after verb *to be.*

Meder, Daniel, Brooklyn College: quick, quickly; slow, slowly.

Meerdink, Richard, University of Wisconsin: like, *conj.*

Meinell, R. J., University of Wisconsin: like, *conj.*

Meyer, Jacqueline, Western Reserve University: agreement, collective nouns.

Michalski, Eleanore, Hunter College: ain't, am not, is not, are not; am I not? ain't I? aren't I?

Middleton, Charlotte, University of Wisconsin: like, *conj.*

Mindlin, Bernice: bad, badly; buy, *n.*

Minsky, Harold, Brooklyn College: date, *n., v.*

Minsky, Pearl, Brooklyn College: eat, *v.*

Mishelkevitz, Brooklyn College: data, datum, *n.*

Miskel, Mary B., Brooklyn College: off, off of, offen, from, off from.

Moore, Kathryn, Brooklyn College: date, *n., v.*

Moore, William R., University of Florida: anyplace, *adv.*

Morris, Georgia L., Western Reserve University: agreement, collective nouns.

Naddell, Sara Anne, Brooklyn College: *either (neither)* with more than two.

Nanos, Stella, University of Chicago: let's, let us, let's us; slow, slowly; so, *conj.;* what with.

Nass, Iris, Hunter College: split infinitive.

Nelson, Phyllis E., Hunter College: reference, vague or indefinite: this (pronominal).

Nemser, Cecile, Brooklyn College: drink, *v.*

Newsome, Verna L., University of Wisconsin, Milwaukee: as, *causal.*

Nusbaum, K., University of Wisconsin: equally, equally as, just as; like, *conj.*

O'Brien, Dean, University of Wisconsin: as (so) long as, *conj.;* equally, equally as, just as; like, *conj.*

Olkin, Julian, Brooklyn College: toward, towards.

O'Rourke, Catherine V., Brooklyn College: bust, *v., n.;* raise, *v., n.*

Palmer, Beatrice, Brooklyn College: prove, *v.*

Passamonti, Ida M., Brooklyn College: home.

Pérez, Erna, Brooklyn College: awful, *adj., adv.,* awfully, *adv.*

Perrin, Shirley, University of Wisconsin: like, *conj.*

Petit, Herbert H., University of Detroit: dangling modifier (misrelated).

Pfankuch, Marge, University of Wisconsin: as to; equally, equally as, just as; like. *conj.*

Plevin, Gerald M., Brooklyn College: agreement, indefinite pronouns.

Polimeros, George, Brooklyn College: contractions; do, *v.;* leave, let.

Polonsky, Marvin, Brooklyn College: drive, *v.;* wait on, wait for.

Pooley, Robert C., University of Wisconsin: myself.

Porcelli, Vincent E., Columbia University: reason . . . is because (reason is that).

Postraw, Marsha, University of Wisconsin: as (so) long as, *conj.;* equally, equally as, just as; like, *conj.*

Pound, Louise, University of Nebraska: grounds, *sing.*

Pregenzer, Jean, Hunter College: get, *v.*

Pyles, Thomas, University of Florida: anyplace, *adv.*

Ralston, Ruth, Brooklyn College: though, although.

Ramlow, Lorna, University of Wisconsin: equally, equally as, just as; like, *conj.*

Ramsey, Mary Ann, University of Wisconsin: as (so) long as, *conj.;* as to; like, *conj.; of* in *could of, couldn't of, should of, shouldn't of, would of,* etc.

Ramsted, Betty, University of Wisconsin: as (so) long as, *conj.;* like, *conj.*

Rannie, Joan, Hunter College: agreement, number of verb after *one of those who (which, that).*

Rappa, Edward, Brooklyn College: combine, *n.;* real, really.

Rashkin, Henry, Brooklyn College: each and every.

Raybin, Shirley, Brooklyn College: comparison, illogical; correlatives.

Remes, Carol, Brooklyn College: like, *conj.*

Richardson, John, Brooklyn College: one . . . one.

Richardson, Mary Anson, University of Chicago: agreement, collective nouns; agreement, indefinite pronouns; ain't, am not, is not, are not; (a)wake, (a)waken; but what; get, *v.;* split infinitive.

Rinaldi, Irene, Brooklyn College: raise, *v., n.;* rise, *v.*

Rivituso, Paula, Brooklyn College: ought not.

Roach, Joseph J., Brooklyn College: (in) back of, behind.

Roberts, Paul, San Jose State College: reference, vague or indefinite: which.

Rollnick, Eloise B., Western Reserve University: case, of noun or pronoun subject of a gerund.

Rose, Cromwell A., University of Chicago: less, fewer.

Rosenbaum, Marilyn, Brooklyn College: different from, than, to.

Rosenblum, Marilyn, Brooklyn College: don't, *v.*

Rosenfeld, Stanley, Brooklyn College: dare, *v.*

Rosenfield, Carole, Brooklyn College: no good, worthless.

Rosenthal, Lois, Brooklyn College: bite, *v.;* good and; good, well; kill, *v.*

Rosenzweig, Charlotte, Brooklyn College: it's I/me, it's we/us, it's he/him, it's she/her, it's they/them.

Roslin, Marvin, Brooklyn College: hardly.

Rothberg, Belle, Brooklyn College: see, *v.*

Rothman, Grace, Brooklyn College: blow, *v.;* less, fewer; *of* in *could of, couldn't of, should of, shouldn't of, would of,* etc.

Rucks, Frances, University of Alabama: as . . . as, so . . . as.

Russell, I. Willis, University of Alabama: agreement, collective nouns; *and* (*but, or, nor*) at the beginning of a sentence; can't (cannot), couldn't (could not) help but; comparison, dual; data, datum, *n.;* one in (of, out of) four (eight, twenty, etc.); preposition at end of clause or sentence; reference, vague or indefinite: it, that, this, which (pronominal).

Salwen, Dorothy E., Brooklyn College: different from, than, to.

Salzberg, Albert, Brooklyn College: quite a (an).

Samkoff, Claire, Brooklyn College: adverbial genitive; had better (best); had (would) rather.

Sandler, Marilyn, Brooklyn College: off, off of, offen, from, off from; out, out of, outen.

Sapienza, Philip, Brooklyn College: let's, let us, let's us.

Sawyer, Richard, Brooklyn College: lot(s), heap(s).

Schaller, Joanne L., Columbia University: shall, will.

Schauer, Jacob, Brooklyn College: but, what; drag, *v.*

Schecter, Martin, Brooklyn College: agenda; phenomenon.

Schuchat, Sonia, Brooklyn College: arithmetical formulas.

Schwab, Eleanor, Western Reserve University: agreement, collective nouns.

Schwartz, Joseph, Brooklyn College: adverbial genitive.

Schwartz, Judith G., Brooklyn College: like, *conj.*

Schwartz, Stanley, Brooklyn College: hardly; rarely ever.

Scribner, Karen, University of Wisconsin: equally, equally as, just as; like, *conj.*

Searles, Patricia, University of Wisconsin: like, *conj.*

Sforza, Maria, Brooklyn College: bought(en).

Shafer, Barbara, Brooklyn College: ain't, am not, is not, are not.

Sheil, Marion, Western Reserve University: dive, *v.;* prove, *v.;* show, *v.;* strike, *v.;* strive, *v.*

Sheppard, Nadine, Western Reserve University: dive, *v.;* prove, *v.;* show, *v.*

Sheridan, Beatrice, Hunter College: above, *adj., n.*

Shinn, Helen, University of Wisconsin: equally, equally as, just as; like, *conj.*

Siegel, Beverly, Brooklyn College: awful, *adj., adv.;* awfully, *adv.*

Silberg, Jack Brooklyn College: can, may, *v.*

Silverstein, Philip, Brooklyn College: *very* with past participle.

Silverstein, Selma, Brooklyn College: bad, badly.

Silverton, Michael, Brooklyn College: *either* (*neither*) with more than two.

Simon, Elaine, Brooklyn College: farther, further.

Skeris, Barbara, University of Wisconsin: like, *conj.*

Sloan, Alexander, *Newark Evening News* (New Jersey): agreement, indefinite pronouns; agreement, (n)either . . . (n)or; blame . . . for (on); dangling modifier (misrelated); data, datum, *n.;* double negative; like, *conj.;* reason . . . is because (reason is that); stomp, *v.;* who, whom.

Smith, Anne M., Brooklyn College: break, *v.;* stink, *v.*

Smith, Janet, Western Reserve University: agreement, collective nouns.

Smith, Susan, University of Wisconsin: as (so) long as, *conj.;* as to; like, *conj.*

Smith, Sylvia M., Brooklyn College: a-singing and a-laughing.

Sola, Rita, Brooklyn College: they, indefinite.

Solomon, Esther, Brooklyn College: agreement, (n)either . . . (n)or; correlatives.

Solomon, Shela, Brooklyn College: syllabus.

Spanier, Alayne, Brooklyn College: preposition at end of clause or sentence.

Speitz, Gail, University of Wisconsin: as (so) long as, *conj.;* as to; equally, equally as, just as; like, *conj.;* more than one; real, really; sure, surely; what with.

Spetalnick, Victor, Brooklyn College: considerable, considerably.

Spiegel, Norman, Brooklyn College: all (of).

Starks, Rosaline, Western Reserve University: agreement, collective nouns.

Statham, C. M., University of Florida: reference, vague or indefinite: this (pronominal).

Stearns, F. S., Arizona State College: if, whether.

Sternberg, Jay, Brooklyn College: *between* with more than two.

Stevens, William J., University of Akron: begin, *v.;* drink, *v.;* light, *v.;* prove, *v.;* sing, *v.;* sink, *v.;* speed, *v.;* swim, *v.*

Stolzberg, Florence, Brooklyn College: *and* (*but, or, nor*) at the beginning of a sentence.

Stone, Beth, Birmingham-Southern College: agenda; phenomenon.

Strong, Marie, Brooklyn College: break, *v.;* doctor, *v.;* double genitive.

Swetsky, Judith, Brooklyn College: for to.

Tanderjian, Frank, Brooklyn College: had better (best).

Tatham, Jane, University of Wisconsin: equally, equally as, just as; like, *conj.*

Taub, Ernest, Brooklyn College: jell, *v.*

Tavin, Jerry, Brooklyn College: as . . . as, so . . . as.

Teitelbaum, Harry, Brooklyn College: as, *causal.*

Thiele, Carol, University of Wisconsin: like, *conj.*

Thomas, Anne Marie, University of Wisconsin: comparative, incomplete; equally, equally as, just as; like, *conj.*

Thomas, Gloria, Brooklyn College: might could; most, almost.

Thomas, Russell, Northern Michigan State University: agenda; agreement, collective nouns; agreement, indefinite pronouns; agreement, (n)either . . . (n)or; agreement, pronoun in *one of those who* (*which, that*) clauses; all (of); *all* (adv.) plus *the* (adv.) plus a comparative; anyhow, anyway, *adv.;* bad, badly; *between* with more than two; blame . . . for (on); can't (cannot), couldn't (could not) help but; comparison, dual; dangling modifier (misrelated); data, datum, *n.;* different from, than, to; each other, one another; *either* (*neither*) with more than two; genitive case; get, *v.;* if, whether; (in) back of, behind; less, fewer; let's not, let's don't; like, *conj.;* myself; preposition at end of clause or sentence; pretty; provided, providing, *conj.;* raise, *v., n.;* reason . . . is because (reason is that); show, *v.;* sit, set, *v.;* so, *adv.;* such, such a (an), *adj., adv.;* they, indefinite; this, that, *advs.;* those (these) kind (sort) of; try and; want off; *when-*(*where-*) clause after verb *to be;* who, whom; whose, of which; you, indefinite.

Tidwell James N., San Diego State College: case, of noun or pronoun subject of a gerund.

Tilkin, Abe, Brooklyn College: it's I/me, it's we/us, it's he/him, it's she/her, it's they/them.

Toback, Alice, Brooklyn College: drown, *v.*

Tobin, Alfred, Brooklyn College: try and.

Trapp, Carole, Brooklyn College: farther, further.

Trinneer, Suzanne H., Brooklyn College: on (the) campus.

Tyson, Dale, Jr., Western Reserve University: dive, *v.;* dream, *v.;* drink, *v.;* fit, *v.;* lie, lay, *v.;* shrink, *v.*

Vilardi, Frances, Brooklyn College: *between* with more than two.

Wanek, Mary Anne, Western Reserve University: agreement, collective nouns.

Warfel, Harry, University of Florida: passive construction.

Watkins, Blondelle, University of Chicago: less, fewer; like for; so, *conj.*

Watson, Lloyd R., Brooklyn College: get, *v.*

Webb, Kay, Brooklyn College: real, really.

Weber, Martin, Brooklyn College: loan, *v.;* what all.

Weil, Grace, Western Reserve University: agreement, collective nouns; agreement, indefinite pronouns.

Wein, Stewart, Brooklyn College: drown, *v.*

Weiser, Melvin, Brooklyn College: agreement, indefinite pronouns.

Weiss, Joseph M., Brooklyn College: each and every.

Wells, Carlton, University of Michigan: can't (cannot), couldn't (could not) help but.

Wetzler, Barbara, University of Wisconsin: like, *conj.*

Whalen, Mary Jane, Hunter College: get, *v.*

Whitesell, J. Edwin, University of South Carolina: slow, slowly; *very* with past participle.

Wilson, Vanon, Brooklyn College: reference, vague or indefinite: which.

Winburne, John N., Michigan State University: all (of); anyhow, anyway, *adv.;* any more, *adv.;* as . . . as, so . . . as; as (so) long as, *conj.;* as to; at about; at all, *adv.* blame . . . for (on); burst, *v.;* bust, *v., n.;* can't (cannot), couldn't (could not) help but; different from, than, to; dive, *v.;* each other, one another; fix, *n., v.;* get, *v.;* good and; good, well; home; (in)back of, behind; in regard(s) to; inside, inside of; it's I/me, it's we/us, it's he/him, it's she/her, it's they/them; kind (sort) of (a, an); like, *conj.;* lot(s), heap(s); no good, worthless; outside, outside of; pair(s); pretty; quite a (an); show up, *v.;* syllabus; try and; what with; whose, of which.

Winderbaum, Celia, Brooklyn College: due to, because of, owing to.

Wine, Celesta, Winthrop College: who, whom.

Winters, Bernice, Brooklyn College: shrink, *v.*

Winthrop, Robert D., Brooklyn College: shall, will.

Wittman, Lillie, Brooklyn College: (a)wake, (a)waken; burst, *v.;* bust, *v.; n.*

Wolf, Muriel G., Brooklyn College: boil, *v.;* passive construction; spill, *v.;* spoil, *v.*

Wolkoff, Esther, Brooklyn College: due to, because of, owing to.
Word, Charles, University of Alabama: agreement, collective nouns.

Zarcone, Marie, Brooklyn College: lie, lay, v.
Zavin, H., Brooklyn College: preposition at end of clause or sentence.
Zemlock, Edward, Brooklyn College: inside, inside of; outside, outside of.

BIBLIOGRAPHY

Abbott, O. L. "The Preterit and Past Participle of Strong Verbs in Seventeenth-Century American English," *American Speech*, XXXII (February, 1957), 31-42.

Allen, Harold B. 'On Accepting Participial "Drank," ' "Current English Forum," *College English*, Vol. 18 (February, 1957), 283-85.

————. "The Linguistic Atlases: Our New Resource," *English Journal*, XLV (April, 1956), 188-94.

Atwood, E. Bagby. *A Survey of Verb Forms in the Eastern United States.* Ann Arbor, Mich.: University of Michigan Press, 1953.

Avis, Walter S. "The Past Participle *Drank:* Standard American English?" *American Speech*, XXVIII (May, 1953), 110-11.

Ball, Carleton R. "English or Latin Plurals for Anglicized Latin Nouns?" *American Speech*, III (April, 1928), 291-325.

Barker, Howard F. "Distribution of Colloquialisms," *American Speech*, V (August, 1930), 493-95.

Barnhart, Clarence L. Lexicographical Files, Reference Books, Bronxville, N.Y.

Bartlett, Adeline C. '*Get, Have got,* and *Have Got to*' "Current English Forum," *College English*, Vol. 10 (February, 1949), 280-82; ' "Vague" Reference of *Which, That,* and *This,*' "Current English Forum," Vol. 11 (October, 1949), 40-41; 'The Case of the Noun or Pronoun with the Gerund,' "Current English Forum," Vol. 11 (May, 1950), 456-57; '*Neither* with Plural Verb,' "Current English Forum," Vol. 13 (December, 1951), 161-62; 'Dangling Participles,' "Current English Forum," Vol. 14 (March, 1953), 353-54; '*Shall* and *Will,*' "Current English Forum," Vol. 15 (October, 1953), 55-56; ['*Data* and *Agenda*'], "Current English Forum," Vol. 15 (April, 1954), 417; ['Arithmetical Formulas'], "Current English Forum," Vol. 15 (May, 1954), 477.

Beauchamp, Emerson, Jr. "A Study of 'It': Handbook Treatment and Magazine Use," *American Speech*, XXVI (October, 1951), 173-80.

Berkeley, David S. "Agreement of Subject and Verb in Anticipatory *There* Clauses," *American Speech*, XXVIII (May, 1953), 92-96; "The Past Tense of *Fit,*" XXX (December, 1955), 311.

B[ernstein], J. C. 'Double Is Nothing,' "Current English Forum," *College English*, Vol. 7 (December, 1945), 167-68.

Bird, Donald A. 'Type-Compounds,' "Current English Forum," *College English*, Vol. 17 (December, 1955), 179.

Bolinger, Dwight L. 'Ambrose Bierce and "All of," ' "Round Table," *College English*, Vol. 2 (1940), 69-70.

————. "Analogical Correlatives of *Than,*" *American Speech*, XXI (October, 1946), 199-202.

————. 'Different,' "Round Table," *English Journal* (College Ed.), XXVIII (1939), 480.

282 BIBLIOGRAPHY

Brewster, Paul G. 'Still More Indiana Sayings,' "Miscellany," *American Speech*, XVII (April, 1942), 130.

Bryant, Margaret M. *A Functional English Grammar*. Boston: D.C. Heath & Company, 1959.

————. *Modern English and Its Heritage*. New York: The Macmillan Company, 1948; 2nd ed., 1962.

————. 'The Split Infinitive,' "Current English Forum," *College English*, Vol. 8 (October, 1946), 39-40; 'The End Preposition,' "Current English Forum," Vol. 8 (January, 1947), 204-5; ['*Do; Provided, Providing*'], "Current English Forum," Vol. 10 (November, 1948), 109; '*Person . . . Their,*' "Current English Forum," Vol. 11 (March, 1950), 345-46; '*Had Ought,*' "Current English Forum," Vol. 13 (April, 1952), 398-99; ['*Toward(s), Due to*'], "Current English Forum," Vol. 15 (May, 1954), 477-88; ['Genitive Case'], "Current English Forum," Vol. 16 (October, 1954), 55-56; ['*Till* and *Until*'], "Current English Forum," Vol. 16 (November, 1954), 131-32; ['*Just* and *Only; In Back of* and *Behind*'], "Current English," Vol. 16 (January, 1955), 246-47; ['*Awful*'], "Current English," Vol. 16 (February, 1955), 310; '*Dare* or *Dares,*' "Current English Forum," Vol. 17 (October, 1955), 52; 'Sentence Modifiers,' "Current English Forum," Vol. 17 (October, 1955), 53; '*If* or *Whether,*' "Current English Forum," Vol. 17 (November, 1955), 113-14; '*Type* as Adjective,' "Current English Forum," Vol. 17 (November, 1955), 113; '*Very* or *Very Much,*' "Current English Forum," Vol. 17 (November, 1955), 113; 'The Double Possessive,' "Current English Forum," Vol. 17 (December, 1955), 178; '*Kind of,*' "Current English Forum," Vol. 17 (December, 1955), 178; '*Try and Come,*' "Current English Forum," Vol. 17 (December, 1955), 178; '*Let's Not* or *Let's Don't,*' "Current English Forum," Vol. 17 (January, 1956), 241; '*Most* or *Almost,*' "Current English Forum," Vol. 17 (January, 1956), 241; '*This (That)* as Adverb,' "Current English Forum," Vol. 17 (January, 1956), 241; ['*As to; Begin; None; Sure, Surely; Rather; Sit, Set; So . . . as; Whose, of Which*'], "Current English Forum," Vol. 17 (February, 1956), 312-13; 'Verb Plurals,' "Current English Forum," Vol. 17 (March, 1956), 361-62; ['*Not . . . but; Can't Help but; Can't Seem to; It; Graduate (From)*'], Vol. 17 (April, 1956), 414-15; ['*Way, Ways*'], "Current English Forum," Vol. 17 (May, 1956), 489; ['*Slow, Slowly*'], "Current English Forum," Vol. 18 (October, 1956), 47; '*Wake, Awake, Waken, Awaken,*' "Current English Forum," Vol. 18 (November, 1956), 111; '*Know-How,*' "Current English Forum," Vol. 19 (October, 1957), 38; '*Combine* as a Noun,' "Current English Forum," Vol. 19 (December, 1957), 130; '*Got* or *Gotten,*' "Current English Forum," Vol. 19 (January, 1958), 171; 'The Double Negative,' "Current English Forum," Vol. 19 (February, 1958), 229; '*Folk* and *Folks,*' "Current English Forum," Vol. 21 (October, 1959), 38; 'The Passive Construction,' "Current English Forum," Vol. 21 (January, 1960), 230; '*Agenda:* Singular or Plural,' "Current English Forum," Vol. 22 (January, 1961), 284; ['Work Evenings'], "Current English Forum," Vol. 22 (February, 1961), 358; 'Collective Nouns,' "Current English Forum," Vol. 22 (February, 1961), 358-59.

———. ['*Lie, Lay*'], "Current English," *English Journal,* XLV (January, 1956), 39; ['*Struck, Stricken*'], XLV (February, 1956), 109; ['*Above*'], "Current English" XLV (April, 1956), 222; 'Considerable,' "Current English," XLV (May, 1956), 285-86; ['*Proved, Proven*'], "Current English," XLV (December, 1956), 555-56; ['*At All; Pair(s)*'], "Current English," XLVI (January, 1957), 54; ['*Leave, Let*'], "Current English," XLVI (May, 1957), 300; ['*Myself*'], "Current English," XLVI (February, 1958), 98; '*Neither . . . Nor,*' "Current English," L (March, 1961), 215.

———. "*Provided* or *Providing,*" *Word Study,* XXV (May, 1950), 4-5.

———, and Aiken, Janet R. *Psychology of English.* New York: Columbia University Press, 1940; 2nd ed., New York: Frederick Ungar Publishing Co., 1962.

Burnham, Josephine M. "The -Self Forms as Personal Pronouns," *American Speech,* XXV (December, 1950), 264-67.

Byington, Steven T. 'More Notes by Mr. Byington,' "Miscellany," *American Speech,* XIX (October, 1944), 229.

Charnley, M. Bertens. "The Syntax of Deferred Prepositions," *American Speech,* XXIV (December, 1949), 268-77.

Cherry, Fannye N. "Some Evidence in the Case of 'Is Because,' " *American Speech,* VIII (February, 1933), 55-60.

Christensen, Francis. 'In Defense of the Absolute,' "Current English Forum," *College English,* Vol. 11 (April, 1950), 401-3.

———. "Number Concord with '*What*'-Clauses," *American Speech,* XXX (February, 1955), 30-37.

———. "Number Concord with '*What*'-Clauses Again," *American Speech,* XXXIII (October, 1958), 226-29.

Craigie, Sir William A., and Hulbert, J.R. (eds.). *Dictionary of American English on Historical Principles.* 4 vols. Chicago: University of Chicago Press, 1938-44.

Crowell, Thomas L. "*Have Got,* a Pattern Preserver," *American Speech,* XXXIV (December, 1959), 280-86.

Curme, George Oliver. "Origin and Force of the Split-Infinitive," *Modern Language Notes,* XXXIX (February, 1914), 41-45.

———. *Parts of Speech and Accidence.* Boston: D.C. Heath & Company, 1935 [Vol. II of Curme and Kurath, *A Grammar of the English Language*].

———. *Principles and Practices of English Grammar.* New York: Barnes & Noble, Inc., 1947.

———. *Syntax.* Boston: D.C. Heath & Company, 1931 [Vol. III of Curme and Kurath, *A Grammar of the English Language*].

Dennis, Leah. "The Progressive Tense: Frequency of Its Use in English," *Publications of the Modern Language Association,* LV (1940), 855-65.

Dickson, Arthur. 'The Past Tense (and Past Participle) of *Fit,*' "Miscellany," *American Speech,* XXXI (October, 1956), 225-26.

Drake, James A. "How *Which* Is Used in America Today," *American Speech,* XXXV (December, 1960), 275-79.

Dunlap, A. R. "Observations on American Colloquial Idiom," *American Speech*, XX (February, 1945), 12-21.

Dykema, Karl W. "The Grammar of Spoken English: Its Relation to What Is Called English Grammar," *American Speech*, XXIV (February, 1949), 43-48.

Eliason, Norman E. *Tarheel Talk*. Chapel Hill, N.C.: University of North Carolina Press, 1956.

Feinsilver, Lillian Mermin. "How Bad(ly) Do You Feel?" *American Speech*, XXIV (October, 1949), 161-70.

Fletcher, Edward G. "Addendum to 'Know-How,'" *American Speech*, XIX (December, 1944), 265; "At About," XXII (October, 1947), 192-95.

Fowler, H. W. *A Dictionary of Modern English Usage*. Oxford: Clarendon Press, 1924.

Francis, W. Nelson. *The Structure of American English*. New York: The Ronald Press Company, 1958.

Fries, Charles C. *American English Grammar*. New York: D. Appleton-Century Company, 1940.

————. "Some Notes on the Inflected Genitive in Present-Day English," *Language*, XIV (April-June, 1938), 121-33.

————. *The Structure of English*. New York: Harcourt, Brace & Company, Inc., 1952.

Galinsky, Hans. *Die Sprache des Amerikaners*. Vol. II. Heidelberg: F. H. Kerle, 1952.

Geist, Robert J. 'There Is One and . . . ,' "Current English Forum," *College English*, Vol. 14 (November, 1952), 115-16; 'There Is Again,' "Current English Forum," Vol. 16 (December, 1954), 188-89; 'Parenthetical *Plus* and *And*,' "Current English Forum," Vol. 17 (November, 1955), 115-16; 'Conjunction *As*,' "Current English Forum," Vol. 19 (April, 1957), 321-22.

Gibbens, V. E. "Notes on Indiana Speech," *American Speech*, XIX (October, 1944), 204-6.

Haase, Gladys D. '*Than*,' "Current English Forum," *College English*, Vol. 10 (March, 1949), 345-47; '*Can* and *May*,' "Current English Forum," Vol. 11 (January, 1950), 215-16; '*Like For*,' "Current English Forum," Vol. 12 (October, 1950), 38-39; 'The Placing of *Only* in the Sentence,' "Current English Forum," Vol. 12 (April, 1951), 400-2.

————. '*What With*,' "Current English," *English Journal*, XXXIX (September, 1950), 396.

Hall, J. Lesslie. *English Usage*. Chicago: Scott, Foresman & Company, 1917.

Harlan, Paul M. 'About *At About*,' "Miscellany," *American Speech*, XXIII (February, 1948), 70-71.

Hatcher, Anna Granville. "[Don't] Buy but One," *American Speech*, XXIV (February, 1949), 49-53.

————. "The English Construction *A Friend of Mine*," *Word*, Vol. 6 (April, 1950), 1-25.

————. "To Get/Be Invited," *Modern Language Notes*, LXIV (November, 1949), 433-46.

Hench, Atcheson L. 'A Further Note on *Fix*,' "Miscellany," *American Speech*, XXX (December, 1955), 309-10.

Hill, A. A. "That Special Written Dialect—Formal Written English," *CEA Critic*, XVI (December, 1954), 3-4.

Horwill, H. W. *A Dictionary of Modern American Usage*. Oxford: Clarendon Press, 1935.

Hughes, John P. 'The Rise of *Greatest of Any*,' "Current English Forum," *College English*, Vol. 17 (March, 1956), 360-61.

Jespersen, Otto. *A Modern English Grammar*. 7 vols., Parts II, III, IV, "Syntax." Heidelberg: Carl Winter, 1914, 1927, 1931.

————. *Essentials of English Grammar*. New York: Henry Holt and Company, Inc., 1933.

————. *On Some Disputed Points in English Grammar*. Society for Pure English, Tract No. XXV. Oxford: Clarendon Press, 1926.

————. *The 'Split Infinitive' and a System of Clauses*. Society for Pure English, Tract No. LIV. Oxford: Clarendon Press, 1940.

Kadison, Alexander. "Cannot Help but," *American Speech*, XXX (February, 1955), 55-56.

Kemp, Lorena E. 'Farther or Further,' "Current English Forum," *College English*, Vol. 17 (October, 1955), 53.

Kennedy, Arthur G. *Current English*. Boston: Ginn and Company, 1935.

————. *English Usage*. New York: D. Appleton-Century Company, 1942.

Kenyon, John S. 'On *Who* and *Whom*,' "Usage Department," *American Speech*, V (February, 1930), 253-55; "The Dangling Participle *Due*," VI (October, 1930), 61-70; "One of Those Who Is . . . ," XXVI (October, 1951), 161-65.

————. 'On the Position of Only,' "Current English Forum," *College English*, Vol. 13 (November, 1951), 116-17; 'Best of Any Man,' "Current English Forum," Vol. 18 (December, 1956), 171-72.

————, and Knott, Thomas A. *A Pronouncing Dictionary of American English*. Springfield, Mass.: G. & C. Merriam Co., 1944.

Kirchner, G. "*To Want* as an Auxiliary of Modality," *English Studies*, XXII (August, 1940), 129-36.

Krapp, George Philip. *A Comprehensive Guide to Good English*. Chicago: Rand McNally & Company, 1927.

Kruisinga, E. *A Handbook of Present-Day English*. 3rd ed., Vol. II, Utrecht: Kemink & Zoon, 1922; 5th ed., Part II, 1, 2, 3, "English Accidence and Syntax," Groningen: P. Noordhoff, 1931, 1932.

Kurath, Hans (dir., ed.) *et al. Linguistic Atlas of New England*. Sponsored by the American Council of Learned Societies and assisted by universities and colleges in New England. Providence, R. I.: Brown University, 1939-43.

―――. *A Word Geography of the Eastern United States.* Ann Arbor, Mich.: University of Michigan Press, 1949.

Lamberts, J. J. 'This Is It,' "Miscellany," *American Speech,* XXX (October, 1955), 239-40.

Laubscher, G. G. "Terms from Lynchburg, Virginia." *Dialect Notes,* Vol. 4, Part IV (1916). Publication of the American Dialect Society, 302.

Lee, Donald Woodward. *Functional Change in Early English.* Menasha, Wis.: George Banta Publishing Company, 1948.

Leonard, Sterling A. *Current English Usage.* (NCTE Monograph, No. 1.) Chicago: Inland Press, 1932.

―――. *Doctrine of Correctness in English Usage, 1700-1800.* (University of Wisconsin Studies in Language and Literature, No. 25.) Madison, Wis.: University of Wisconsin Press, 1929.

―――. ['*Try and; Most, Almost*'], "Usage Department," *American Speech,* IV (February, 1929), 253-54; 'The Placement of *Only,*' "Usage Department," VI (April, 1931), 292-94.

Lyman, Dean B. "Idioms in West Virginia," *American Speech,* XI (February, 1936), 63.

Malmstrom, Jean. *A Study of the Validity of Textbook Statements About Certain Controversial Grammatical Items in the Light of Evidence from the Linguistic Atlas.* University of Minnesota Dissertation, 1958 [Mic. 58-7012].

―――. '*Ain't* Again,' "Current English Forum," *College English,* Vol. 21 (April, 1960), 416-17.

―――. '*Kind of* and Its Congeners,' "Current English," *English Journal,* XLIX (October, 1960), 498-99.

Malone, Kemp. '*Whom,*' "Current English Forum," *College English,* Vol. 10 (October, 1948), 37-38.

―――. '*Don't,*' "Current English Forum," *English Journal,* XXXIX (February, 1950), 104-5.

Marckwardt, Albert H. "*Want* with Ellipsis of Verbs of Motion," *American Speech,* XXIII (February, 1948), 3-9.

―――. '*Have Got* in Expressions of Possession and Obligation,' "Current English," *College English,* Vol. 16 (February, 1955), 309-10.

―――, and Walcott, Fred. *Facts About Current English Usage.* (English Monograph No. 7, National Council of Teachers of English.) New York: D. Appleton-Century Company, 1938.

Mathews, Mitford M. (ed.). *A Dictionary of Americanisms on Historical Principles.* 2 vols. Chicago: University of Chicago Press, 1951.

McDavid, Raven I., Jr. '*Ain't I* and *Aren't I,*' "Miscellanea," *Language,* Vol. 17 (January-March, 1941), 57-59.

―――. 'Notes on the Pronunciation of *Catch,*' "Current English Forum," *College English,* Vol. 14 (February, 1953), 290-91; '*Oughtn't* and *Hadn't Ought,*' "Current English Forum," Vol. 14 (May, 1953), 472-73.

————. "The Dialects of American English," Chap. 9 in W. Nelson Francis, *The Structure of American English.* New York: The Ronald Press Company, 1958.

————, and McDavid, Virginia G. "Grammatical Differences in the North Central States," *American Speech,* XXXV (February, 1960), 5-19.

McDavid, Virginia G. *Verb Forms of the North Central States and the Upper Midwest.* University of Minnesota Dissertation, 1956 [Publication No. 20, 525].

McMillan, J. B. ['*Sit*'], "Current English Forum," *College English,* Vol. 4 (November, 1942), 137; ['*Don't*'] "Current English Forum," Vol. 5 (November, 1943), 100-1; '*Who* and *Whom*,' "Current English Forum," Vol. 7 (November, 1945), 104-5; ['*Each and Every; It Is Me*'], "Current English Forum," Vol. 9 (April, 1948), 394.

————. ['*These Kind, Those Sort*'], "Current English Forum," *English Journal,* XXXIV (May, 1945), 284.

Mencken, H. L. *The American Language: An Inquiry into the Development of English in the United States.* 4th ed. New York: Alfred A. Knopf, Inc., 1938; *Supplement I,* 1945; *Supplement II,* 1948.

Menner, Robert J. "The Verbs of the Vulgate," *American Speech,* I (January, 1926), 230-40; "Troublesome Relatives," VI (June, 1931), 341-46; "Hypercorrect Forms in American English," XII (October, 1937), 167-78; "Affirmative 'Any More' in England," XXI (April, 1946), 151.

Mermin, Lillian. "On the Placement of Correlatives in Modern English," *American Speech,* XVIII (October, 1943), 171-91.

Moore, Arthur K. "New Light on Affirmative 'Any More,'" *American Speech,* XXI (December, 1946), 301-2.

Myers, L. M. *American English.* New York: Prentice-Hall, Inc., 1952.

Newsome, Verna L. "Correct English," *American Speech,* XIII (February, 1938), 25-29.

————. '*Because, Since, As,*' "Current English Forum," *College English,* Vol. 20 (March, 1959), 298, 303.

Oxford English Dictionary (OED) (1884-1928; reissued, with supplement, 1933). (Originally known as *A New English Dictionary on Historical Principles: NED.*)

Palmer, Francis W. "Pair of Beads," *American Speech,* XXIII (April, 1948), 116.

Perrin, Porter G. '*Like for,*' "Current English Forum," *College English,* Vol. 3 (March, 1942), 591; ['*More Than One*'], "Current English Forum," Vol. 4 (December, 1942), 196; ['Sentence Modifiers'], "Current English Forum," Vol. 5 (March, 1944), 342; ['*Every* as Adverb'], "Current English Forum," Vol. 5 (May, 1944), 451.

Piper, Edwin Ford. "A Survival," *American Speech,* I (April, 1926), 442.

Pooley, Robert C. *Grammar and Usage in Textbooks on English.* Madison, Wis.: University of Wisconsin Press, 1933.

——. *Teaching English Usage.* New York: D. Appleton-Century Company, 1946.

——. "*Myself* as a Simple Personal Pronoun," *American Speech,* VII (June, 1932), 368-70; " 'Real' and 'Sure' as Adverbs," VIII (February, 1933), 60-62; "The Case of the Noun or Pronoun with the Gerund," VIII (April, 1933), 63-66; "Subject-Verb Agreement," IX (February, 1934), 31-36.

——. 'When Does a Participle Dangle?' "Current English Forum," *College English,* Vol. 14 (December, 1952), 170-71; 'The Reason . . . Is Because,' "Current English Forum," Vol. 18 (November, 1956), 110-11.

Pound, Louise. "Plural-Singulars from Latin Neuters," *American Speech,* III (October, 1927), 26-27; 'Extensions of Usage of a Pronoun,' "Miscellany," VI (April, 1931), 313-14; 'You *Want to*,' "Miscellany," VII (August, 1932), 450-51; '*Know-How*,' "Miscellany," XIX (February, 1944), 65-66; '*It* Once More: A Supplementary Note,' "Miscellany," XXIX (December, 1954), 263-67; 'More Plural-Singulars,' "Miscellany," XXXI (May, 1956), 154-57.

Poutsma, H. *A Grammar of Late Modern English.* Part I, First Half, 2nd ed.; Part I, Second Half, 2nd ed.; Part II, Section I, A; Part II, Section I, A and B; Part II, Section II. Groningen: P. Noordhoff, 1928, 1929, 1914, 1916, 1926.

Prenner, Manuel. 'Notes on Current Usage,' "Miscellany," *American Speech,* XXIV (October, 1949), 230-33.

Randolph, Vance, and Wilson, George P. *Down in the Holler—A Gallery of Ozark Folk Speech.* Norman, Okla.: University of Oklahoma Press, 1953.

Rice, Wallace. "Go Slow—Proceed Slowly," *American Speech,* II (September, 1927), 489-91; "*Get* and *Got*," VII (April, 1932), 280-96; "Who's There?—Me," VIII (October, 1933), 58-63.

——. "Usage Counsel," *English Journal,* XXIII (November, 1934), 776-78; "Usage Counsel," XXV (January, 1936), 67-69; (March, 1936), 244-46; "Usage Counsel," XXVI (January, 1937), 66-69; "Usage Counsel," XXVI (March, 1937), 238-40; "Usage Counsel," XXVI (April, 1937), 325-27.

Roberts, Paul. "Pronominal 'This': A Quantitative Analysis," *American Speech,* XXVII (October, 1952), 171-78.

——. *Understanding Grammar.* New York: Harper and Brothers, 1954.

Robertson, Stuart. "British-American Differentiations in Syntax and Idiom," *American Speech,* XIV (December, 1939), 243-54.

Russel, I. Willis. "The *All . . . Not* Idiom," *American Speech,* IX (April, 1934), 115-19; "The Dangling Participle: Illustrations of Linguistic Change," X (April, 1935), 113-18; "Notes on American Usage," XVI (February, 1941), 17-18; '*-type*,' "Among the New Words," *American Speech,* XXIII (April, 1948), 150; '*-buster*,' "Among the New Words," XXIII (October-December, 1948), 290-95; '*-type*,' "Among the New Words," XXIV (October, 1949), 228; '*Stomp*,' "Among the New Words," XXX (December, 1955), 287.

Sackett, S. J. "An Expression I Hear Often Any More," *Word Study* (December, 1957), 4.

Sapir, Edward. *Language*. New York: Harcourt, Brace and Company, 1939 ed.

Seronsky, Cecil C. "Some Uses of *on* and *to* in Pennsylvania Speech," *American Speech*, XXXIV (May, 1959), 148-49.

Sheldon, Esther K. "The Rise of the Incomplete Comparative," *American Speech*, XX (October, 1945), 161-67; "A Very Nice-Type Girl," XXIII (October-December, 1948), 251-56.

Shewmake, Edwin F. "Shakespeare and Southern 'You All,'" *American Speech*, XIII (October, 1938), 163-68; "More About *At About*," XXIII (February, 1948), 71-72.

Simpson, Harold. 'A Harmless Crime,' "Current English Forum," *College English*, Vol. 13 (May, 1952), 463-64.

Stageberg, Norman. 'Is It Really We?' "Current English," *College English*, Vol. 16 (March, 1955), 376-78.

Steinbach, Reuben. "On Usage in English," *American Speech*, IV (February, 1929), 161-65; "The Misrelated Constructions," V (February, 1930), 181-97.

Stevens, Martin. "The Derivation of *Ain't*," *American Speech*, XXIX (October, 1954), 196-201.

Sweet, Henry. *A New English Grammar*. London: Clarendon Press, 1900.

Thomas, Russell. "Concord Based on Meaning Versus Concord Based on Form: The Indefinites," *College English*, Vol. 1 (October, 1939), 38-45; 'Cannot Help but,' "Current English Forum," *College English*, Vol. 10 (October, 1948), 38-39; 'The Reason Is Because . . . ,' "Current English Forum," Vol. 10 (December, 1948), 168-69; '*When*-Clauses After *Is* (*Was*),' "Current English Forum," Vol. 10 (April, 1949), 406-8; '*Showed* as Past Participle,' "Current English Forum," Vol. 11 (December, 1949), 157-58; 'The Use of *So* as an Intensifier,' "Current English Forum," Vol. 12 (May, 1951), 453-54; 'Concord of the Verb in Relative Clauses After *One of*,' "Current English Forum," Vol. 13 (October, 1951), 43-44; 'Notes on the Inflected Genitive in Modern American Prose,' "Current English Forum," Vol. 14 (January, 1953), 236-39; '*Such* as an Intensifier,' "Current English Forum," Vol. 15 (January, 1954), 236-38; '*Each Other* or *One Another*,' "Current English Forum," Vol. 18 (May, 1957), 422-24; 'All the Harder, All the Farther,' "Current English Forum," Vol. 20 (January, 1959), 190-91.

————. "The Use of the Superlative Degree for the Comparative," *English Journal*, XXIV (December, 1935), 821-29.

Tucker, R. Whitney. "Notes on the Philadelphia Dialect," *American Speech*, XIX (February, 1944), 37-42.

Van Krimpen, John. 'Let's Us,' "Current English Forum," *College English*, Vol. 17 (January, 1956), 241.

Vowles, Guy R. 'A Few Observations on Southern "You All," ' "Miscellany," *American Speech*, XIX (April, 1944), 146-47.

Warfel, Harry R. 'Frequency of the Passive Voice,' "Current English Forum," *College English,* Vol. 15 (November, 1953), 129.

Webster's New International Dictionary (3rd ed.). Springfield, Mass.: G. & C. Merriam Company, 1961.

Wentworth, Harold (ed.). *American Dialect Dictionary.* New York: Thomas Y. Crowell Company, 1944.

Werner, W. L. 'The Absolute Negative Comparative,' "Miscellany," *American Speech,* XXI (December, 1946), 302-3.

Whyte, John. "The Future Tense in English," *College English,* Vol. 5 (March, 1944), 333-37.

Williams, Edna R. " 'Pair of Beads' in America," *American Speech,* XXX (February, 1955), 49-52.

Wise, C. M. ' "Different(ly) Than" Becomes a Model of Style,' "Miscellany," *American Speech,* XXII (October, 1947), 237.

Word Study, 'Myself,' "Webster Records." Springfield, Mass.: G. & C. Merriam Company, 1941.

Wyllie, John C. ' "This Is It," 1942,' "Miscellany," *American Speech,* XXXI (October, 1956), 230.

Zieglschmid, A. J. Friederich. *"If for Whether,"* American Speech, V (October, 1930), 50-51.